REAL-TIME SYSTEMS AND THEIR PROGRAMMING LANGUAGES

INTERNATIONAL COMPUTER SCIENCE SERIES

Consulting editors **A D McGettrick** University of Strathclyde

J van Leeuwen University of Utrecht

SELECTED TITLES IN THE SERIES

REAL-TIME SYSTEMS
AND THEIR
PROGRAMMING
LANGUAGES

Alan Burns
University of Bradford

Andy Wellings
University of York

ADDISON-WESLEY
PUBLISHING
COMPANY

Wokingham, England · Reading, Massachusetts · Menlo Park, California
New York · Don Mills, Ontario · Amsterdam · Bonn
Sydney · Singapore · Tokyo · Madrid · San Juan

The programs in this book have been included for their instructional value. They have been tested with care but are not guaranteed for any particular purpose. The publisher does not offer any warranties or representations, nor does it accept any liabilities with respect to the programs.

Many of the designations used by manufacturers and sellers to distinguish their products are claimed as trademarks. Addison-Wesley has made every attempt to supply trademark information about manufacturers and their products mentioned in this book. A list of the trademark designations and their owners appears on p. xvi.

Cover designed by Crayon Design of Henley-on-Thames and printed by The Riverside Printing Co. (Reading) Ltd.
Typeset by CRB Typesetting Services, Ely, Cambs.
Printed and bound in Great Britain by T.J. Press, Padstow, Cornwall.

First printed 1989.

British Library Cataloguing in Publication Data
Burns, Alan
  Real-time systems and their programming languages.
  1. Real time computer systems. Programming languages
  I. Title   II. Wellings, Andrew
  005.13

  ISBN 0–201–17529–0

Library of Congress Cataloging-in-Publication Data
Burns, Alan
    Real-time systems and their programming languages / Alan Burns,
  Andrew J. Wellings.
      p.   cm.
    Includes bibliographical references.
    ISBN 0–201–17529–0
    1. Real-time data processing.   2. Real-time programming.
  3. Programming languages (Electronic computers)   I. Wellings,
  Andrew J.   II. Title.
  QA76.54.B87   1990
  004'.33--dc20

004.33
B967r

240770

89–17930
CIP

Preface

In 1981 a software error caused a stationary robot to move suddenly, with impressive speed, to the edge of its operational area. A nearby worker was crushed to death.

This is just one example of the hazards of embedded real-time systems. Unfortunately, it is not an isolated incident. Every month the newsletter *Software Engineering Notes* has pages of examples of events in which the malfunctioning of real-time systems has put the public or the environment at risk. What these sobering descriptions illustrate is that there is a need to take a system-wide view of embedded systems. Indeed, it can be argued that there is a requirement for real-time systems to be recognized as a distinct engineering discipline. This book is a contribution towards the development of this discipline. It cannot, of course, cover all the topics that are apposite to the study of real-time systems engineering; it does, however, present a comprehensive description and assessment of the programming languages used in this domain. Particular emphasis is placed on language primitives and their role in the production of reliable, safe and dependable software.

Audience

The book is aimed at Final Year and Masters students in Computer Science and related disciplines. It has also been written with the professional software engineer, and real-time systems engineer, in mind. Readers are assumed to have knowledge of a sequential programming language, such as Pascal, and to be familiar with the basic tenets of software engineering. The material presented reflects the content of courses developed over a number of years by the authors at their respective universities. These courses specifically address real-time systems and their programming languages.

Structure and content

In order to give the chapters continuity three programming languages are considered in detail: Ada, Modula-2 and occam 2. These languages have been chosen because they are actually used for software production. Other theoretical or experimental languages are discussed when they offer primitives not available within the core languages. Practitioners who are primarily interested in only one of these language should find sufficient material for their needs. The authors believe that a full appreciation of a language like Ada (say) can only be obtained through a comparative study of its facilities.

In all, the book contains 17 chapters, the first 11 of which are loosely organized into the following four groups. Chapters 1 through 4 represent an extended introduction. The characteristics and requirements of real-time systems are presented, then an overview of the design of such systems is given. Design is not the primary focus of this book; nevertheless, it is important to discuss implementation within an appropriate context – this chapter attempts to provide such a context. Also considered in this chapter are general criteria by which languages can be assessed. Chapters 3 and 4 consider basic language structures through discussions on *programming in the small* and *programming in the large*. These chapters also serve to introduce Ada, Modula-2 and occam 2. Readers familiar with these languages, and the basic properties of real-time systems, can progress quickly through these four opening chapters. For other readers the material presented will help to make the book more self contained.

Chapters 5 and 6 concern themselves with the production of reliable software components. Although consideration is given to fault prevention, attention is primarily focused on fault tolerance. Both forward and backward error recovery techniques are considered. The use of an exception handling facility is discussed in Chapter 6. Both resumption and termination models are described, as are the language primitives found in Ada, CHILL and Mesa.

Real-time systems are inherently concurrent, and, therefore, the study of this aspect of programming languages is fundamental. Chapter 7 introduces the notion of process and reviews the many different models that are used by language designers. Communication between processes is considered in the following two chapters. Shared-variable methods are described including the use of semaphores and monitors. Message-based models are, however, more popular in modern languages; combining as they do communication and synchronization. These models are covered in Chapter 9. Particular attention is given to the primitives of Ada and occam 2.

It is debatable whether issues of reliability or concurrency should have been considered first within the book. Both authors have experimented with reversing the order and have found little to choose between the two possible approaches. The book can in fact be used in either mode with only one or two topics being 'out of place'. The decision to cover reliability first, reflects the authors' belief that safety is the predominant requirement of real-time systems.

The final grouping incorporates Chapters 10 and 11. In general, the relationship between system processes can be described as either cooperating (to achieve a common goal) or competing (to acquire a shared resource). Chapter 10 extends the earlier discussions on fault tolerance by describing how reliable process cooperation can be programmed. Central to this discussion is the notion of an *atomic action*. Competing processes are considered in the following chapter. An assessment is given of different language features. One important topic here is the distinction between conditional and avoidance synchronization within the concurrency model.

The remaining chapters are, essentially, self contained. Temporal requirements constitute the distinguishing characteristic of real-time systems. Chapter 12 presents a detailed discussion of these requirements and of the language facilities and implementation strategies that are used to satisfy them. Hard real-time systems have timing constraints that must be satisfied; soft systems can occasionally fail to perform adequately. Both are considered within the context of deadline scheduling. The notion of *priority* is discussed at length.

Recent advances in hardware and communications technology have made distributed computer systems a viable alternative to uniprocessor and centralized systems in many embedded application areas. Although, in some respects, distribution can be thought of as an implementation consideration, issues which arise when applications are distributed raise fundamental questions that go beyond mere implementation details. Chapter 13 considers four areas of interest: partitioning and configuration, reliability in the presence of processor and communication failure, algorithms for distributed control, and multiprocessor and distributed deadline scheduling. This chapter is specifically designed to be self-contained and can be omitted by students on shorter courses.

One important requirement of many real-time systems is that they incorporate external devices that must be programmed (that is, controlled) as part of the application software. This low-level programming is at variance with the abstract approach to software production that characterizes software engineering. Chapter 14 considers ways in which low-level facilities can be successfully incorporated into high-level languages.

A popular misconception surrounding real-time systems is that they must be highly efficient. This is not in itself true. Real-time systems must satisfy timing constraints (and reliability requirements); efficient implementation is one means of extending the realms of possibility, but it is not an end in itself. Chapter 15 reviews some of the strategies that can be used to improve the performance of language implementations.

The final major chapter of the book is a case study programmed in Ada. An example from a mine control system is used. Inevitably, a single scaled-down study cannot illustrate all the issues covered in the previous chapters; in particular, factors such as size and complexity are not addressed. Nevertheless, the case study does cover many important aspects of real-time systems.

All chapters have summaries and further reading lists. Most also have lists of exercises. These have been chosen to help readers consolidate their understanding of the material presented in each chapter. They mostly represent exercises that have been used by the authors for assessment purposes.

Ada, Modula-2 and occam 2

Currently, Ada is under review. The examples in this book conform to the ANSI/MIL-STD 1815A standard. Modula-2 is defined informally by Wirth's textbooks, however, there is a move to produce an ISO standard. The examples in this book conform to the language defined in the second edition of *Programming in Modula-2*. The occam 2 language is still in its infancy and will no doubt mature over the coming years. The occam 2 examples presented in this book conform to the occam 2 definition given by INMOS.

To facilitate easy identification of the three languages, different presentation styles are used. Ada is presented with keywords in **lower case bold**; program identifiers are given in UPPER CASE. Both Modula-2 (and Modula-1) and occam 2 require keywords to be upper case. As these languages are easily distinguished the same style of presentation has been adopted: namely keywords in UPPER CASE (UPPER CASE for occam 2) and Mixed-Case (Mixed-Case for occam 2) identifiers. All other languages have keywords in lower case.

Braille copies

Braille copies of this book, on paper or Versabraille cassette, can be made available. Enquiries should be addressed to Dr Alan Burns, Department of Computing, University of Bradford, Bradford, West Yorkshire, BD7 1DP, UK.

Acknowledgements

The material in this book has been developed over the last five years and presented to many third year and MSc students at the Universities of Bradford and York, taking Computer Science or Electronics degrees. We would like to acknowledge their contribution to the end product, for without them this book would never have been written.

Many people have read and commented on a first draft of the book. In particular we would like to thank: Martin Atkins, Chris Hoggarth, Andy Hutcheon, Andrew Lister, and Jim Welsh. We would also like to thank our colleagues at our respective Universities for providing us with a stimulating environment and for many enlightening discussions, particularly Ljerka Beus-Dukic, Geoff Davies, John McDermid, Gary Morgan, Rick Pack, Rob Stone and Hussein Zedan.

During 1988 Alan Burns was on sabbatical at the Universities of Queensland and Houston. We would like to thank all staff at these institutions particularly Andrew Lister, Charles McKay and Pat Rogers.

This book would not have been possible without the use of electronic mail over JANET. We would like to thank the Computer Board of the United Kingdom University Grants Council and the Science and Engineering Research Council for providing this invaluable service.

Finally, we would like to give special thanks to Sylvia Holmes and Carol Burns. Sylvia for the many hours she has spent painstakingly proofreading the final manuscript and Carol for the many evenings she has tolerated our meetings and discussions.

Alan Burns
Andy Wellings

November 1989

Contents

Chapter 1
Introduction to Real-time Systems

As computers become smaller, faster, more reliable and cheaper so their range of application widens. Built initially as equation solvers their influence has extended into all walks of life, from washing machines to air traffic control. One of the fastest expanding areas of computer exploitation is that involving applications, whose prime function is *not* that of information processing, but which nevertheless require information processing in order to carry out their prime function. A microprocessor-controlled washing machine is a good example of such a system. Here the prime function is to wash clothes; however, depending on the type of clothes to be washed, different 'wash programs' must be executed. These types of computer applications are generically called **real-time** or **embedded**. They place particular requirements on the computer languages needed to program them – as they have different characteristics from the more traditional information processing systems.

This book is concerned with embedded computer systems and their programming languages. It studies the particular characteristics of these systems and discusses how some modern real-time programming languages have evolved.

1.1   Definition of a real-time system

Before proceeding further it is worth trying to define the phrase 'real-time system' more precisely. There are many interpretations of the exact nature of a real-time system; however, they all have in common the notion of response time – the time taken for the system to generate output from some associated input. The Oxford Dictionary of Computing gives the following definition of a real-time system.

> Any system in which the time at which output is produced is significant. This is usually because the input corresponds to some movement in the physical world, and the output has to relate to that same movement. The lag from input time to output time must be sufficiently small for acceptable timeliness.

Here, the word timeliness is taken in the context of the total system. For example, in a missile guidance system output is required within a few milliseconds, whereas in a computer-controlled car assembly line the response may be required only within a second.

Young (1982) defines a real-time system to be:

> any information processing activity or system which has to respond to externally-generated input stimuli within a finite and specified period.

In their most general sense both these definitions cover a very wide range of computer activities. For example, an operating system like UNIX may be considered real time in that when a user enters a command he/she will expect a response within a few seconds. Fortunately, it is usually not a disaster if the response is not forthcoming. These types of systems can be distinguished from those where *failure* to respond can be considered just as bad as a wrong response. Indeed, for some, it is this aspect that distinguishes a real-time system from others where response time is important but not crucial. Consequently, *the correctness of a real-time system depends not only on the logical result of the computation, but also on the time at which the results are produced.* Practitioners in the field of real-time computer system design often distinguish between hard and soft real-time systems. **Hard real-time systems** are those where it is absolutely imperative that responses occur within the specified deadline. **Soft real-time systems** are those where response times are important but the system will still function correctly if deadlines are occasionally missed. Soft systems can themselves be distinguished from interactive ones in which there are no explicit deadlines. For example, a flight control system of a combat aircraft is a hard real-time system because a missed deadline could lead to a catastrophe, whereas a data acquisition system for a process control application is soft as it may be defined to sample an input sensor at regular intervals but to tolerate intermittent delays. In this book the term real-time system is used to mean both soft and hard real time. Where discussion is concerned specifically with hard real-time systems the term will be used explicitly.

In a hard or soft real-time system the computer is usually interfaced directly to some physical equipment and is dedicated to monitoring or controlling the operation of that equipment. A key feature of all these applications is the role of the computer as an information processing component within a larger engineering system. It is for this reason that such applications have become known as **embedded computer systems**. The terms 'real-time' and 'embedded' will be used interchangeably in this book.

1.2   Examples of real-time systems

Having defined what is meant by embedded systems some examples of their use are now given.

1.2.1   Process control

The first use of a computer as a component in a larger engineering system occurred in the process control industry in the early 1960s. Nowadays, the use of microprocessors is the norm. Consider the simple example, shown in Figure 1.1, where the computer performs a single activity: that of ensuring an even flow of liquid in a pipe by controlling a valve. On detecting an increase in flow the computer must respond by altering the valve angle; this response must occur within a finite period if the equipment at the receiving

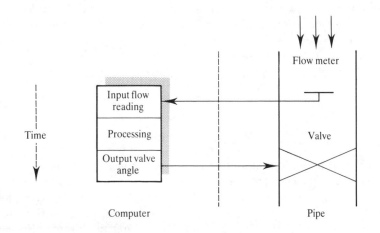

Figure 1.1   A fluid control system.

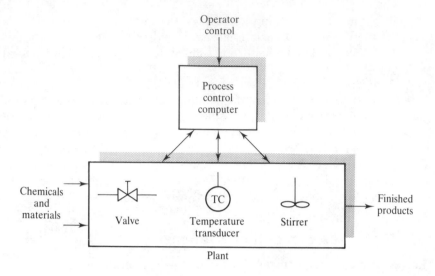

Figure 1.2   A process control system.

end of the pipe is not to become overloaded. Note that the actual response may involve quite a complex computation in order to calculate the new valve angle.

This example shows just one component of a larger control system. Figure 1.2 illustrates the role of a real-time computer embedded in a complete process-control environment. The computer interacts with the equipment using sensors and actuators. A valve is an example of an actuator and a temperature or pressure transducer is an example of a sensor. (A transducer is a device that generates an electrical signal that is proportional to the physical quantity being measured.) The computer controls the operation of the sensors and actuators to ensure that the correct plant operations are performed at the appropriate times. Where necessary, analogue to digital and digital to analogue converters must be inserted between the controlled process and the computer.

1.2.2   Manufacturing

The use of computers in manufacturing has become essential over the last few years in order that production costs can be kept low and productivity increased. Computers have enabled the integration of the entire manufacturing process from product design to fabrication. It is in the area of production control that embedded systems are best illustrated. Figure 1.3 represents, diagrammatically, the role of the production control computer

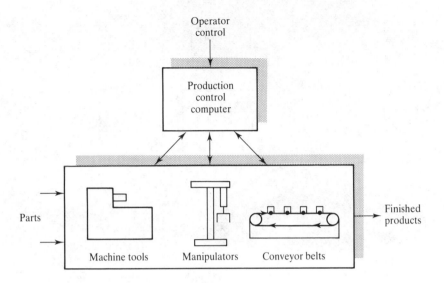

Figure 1.3 A production control system.

in the manufacturing process. The physical system consists of a variety of mechanical devices such as machine tools, manipulators and conveyor belts, all of which need to be controlled and coordinated by the computer.

1.2.3   Communication, command and control

Although **communication, command and control** is a military term there is a wide range of disparate applications which exhibit similar characteristics; for example, airline seat reservation, medical centres for automatic patient care, air traffic control and remote bank accounting. All of these systems consist of a complex set of policies, information gathering devices and administrative procedures which enable decisions to be supported, and provide the means by which they can be implemented. Often, the information gathering devices and the instruments required for implementing decisions are distributed over a wide geographical area. Figure 1.4 represents, diagrammatically, such a system.

1.2.4   Generalized embedded computer system

In each of the examples shown so far the computer is interfaced directly to physical equipment in the real world. In order to control these real-world devices the computer will need to sample the measurement devices at regular intervals, therefore, a real-time clock is required. Usually there is

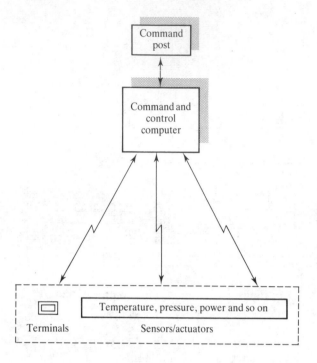

Figure 1.4   A command and control system.

also an operator's console to allow for manual intervention. The human operator is kept constantly informed of the state of the system by displays of various types including graphical ones.

Records of the system's state changes are also kept in an information base which can be interrogated by the operators at will, either for post-mortems in the case of a system crash, or to provide information for administrative purposes. Indeed, this information is increasingly being used to support decision making in the day-to-day running of systems. For example, in the chemical and process industries, plant monitoring is essential for maximizing economic advantages rather than simply maximizing production. Decisions concerning production at one plant may have serious repercussions for other plants at remote sites, particularly when the products of one process are being used as raw material for another.

A typical embedded computer system can, therefore, be represented by Figure 1.5. The software which controls the operations of the system can be written in modules which reflect the physical nature of the environment. Usually there will be a module which contains the algorithms necessary for physically controlling the devices, a module responsible for recording the system's state changes, a module to retrieve and display those changes and a module to interact with the operator.

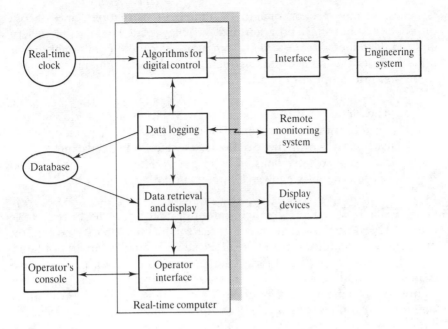

Figure 1.5   A typical embedded computer system.

1.3   Characteristics of real-time systems

A real-time system possesses many special characteristics (either inherent or imposed) which are identified in the following sections. Clearly, not all real-time systems will exhibit all these characteristics, however, any general-purpose language which is to be used for the effective program-ming of real-time systems must have facilities which support these characteristics.

1.3.1   Size and complexity

It is often said that most of the problems associated with developing software are those related to size and complexity. Writing small programs presents no significant problem as they can be designed, coded, maintained and understood by a single person. If that person leaves the company or institution that is using the software, then someone else can learn the program in a relatively short period of time. Indeed, for these programs there is an art or craft to their construction and *small is beautiful*.

Unfortunately, not all software exhibits this most desirable charac-teristic of smallness. Lehman and Belady (1985) in attempting to character-ize large systems, reject the simple and perhaps intuitive notion that largeness is simply proportional to the number of instructions, lines of code or modules comprising a program. Instead, they relate largeness to **variety**, and the degree of largeness to the amount of variety. Traditional indicators, such as the number of instructions and development effort are, therefore, just symptoms of variety.

> The variety is that of needs and activities in the real world and their reflection in a program. But the real world is continuously changing. It is evolving. So too are therefore the needs and activities of society. Thus large programs, like all complex systems, must continuously evolve (Lehman and Belady, 1985).

Embedded systems, by their definition, must respond to real-world events. The variety associated with these events must be catered for; the programs will, therefore, tend to exhibit the undesirable property of largeness. Inherent in the definition of largeness is the notion of **continuous change**. The cost of redesigning or rewriting software to respond to the continuously-changing requirements of the real world is prohibitive. Therefore, real-time systems undergo constant maintenance and enhancements during their lifetimes. They must be extensible.

Although real-time software is often complex, features provided by real-time languages and environments enable these complex systems to be broken down into smaller components which can be managed effectively. Chapters 2 and 4 will consider these features in detail.

1.3.2 Manipulation of real numbers

As was noted earlier in this chapter many real-time systems involve the control of some engineering activity. Figure 1.6 exemplifies a simple control system. The controlled entity, the plant, has a vector of output variables, y, that change over time, hence $y(t)$. These outputs are compared with the desired (or reference) signal $r(t)$ to produce an error signal, $e(t)$.

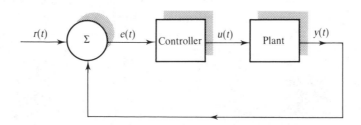

Figure 1.6 A simple controller.

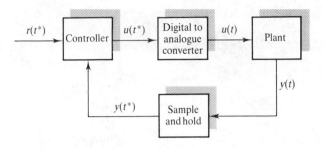

Figure 1.7   A simple computerized controller.

The controller uses this error vector to change the input variables to the plant, $u(t)$. For a very simple system the controller can be an analogue device working on a continuous signal.

Figure 1.6 illustrates a feedback controller. This is the most common form but feedforward controllers are also used. In order to calculate what changes must be made to the input variables, so that a desirable effect on the output vector takes place, it is necessary to have a mathematical model of the plant. The derivation of these models is the concern of the distinct discipline of control engineering. Often, a plant is modelled as a set of first order differential equations. These link the output of the system with the internal state of the plant and its input variables. Changing the output of the plant involves solving these equations to give required input values. Most physical systems exhibit inertia so that change is not instantaneous. A real-time requirement to move to a new set point within a fixed time-period will add to the complexity of the manipulations needed, both to the mathematical model and to the physical system. The fact that, in reality, linear first-order equations are only an approximation to the actual charac-teristics of the system also presents complications.

Because of these difficulties, the complexity of the model and the number of distinct (but not independent) inputs and outputs, most control-lers are implemented as computers. The introduction of a digital compo-nent into the system changes the nature of the control cycle. Figure 1.7 is an adaptation of the earlier model shown in Figure 1.6. Items marked with a * are now discrete values; the sample and hold operation being carried out by an analogue-to-digital converter, both converters being under the direct control of the computer.

Within the computer the differential equations can be solved by numerical techniques, although the algorithms themselves need to be adapted to take into account the fact that plant outputs are now being sampled. The design of control algorithms is a topic outside the scope of this book; the implementation of these algorithms is, however, of direct concern. They can be mathematically complex and require a high degree of precision. A fundamental requirement of a real-time programming language, therefore, is the ability to manipulate real or floating-point numbers. This is considered in Chapter 3 along with other data types.

1.3.3   Reliability and safety

The more that society relinquishes control of its vital functions to computers, the more imperative it becomes that those computers do not fail. The failure of a system involved in automatic fund transfer between banks can lead to millions of dollars being lost irretrievably; a faulty component in electricity generation could result in the failure of a vital life-support system in an intensive care unit; the premature shutdown of a chemical plant could cause expensive damage to equipment or environmental harm. These somewhat dramatic examples illustrate that computer hardware and software must be reliable and safe. Even in hostile environments, such as those found in military applications, it must be possible to design and implement systems which will fail only in a controlled way. Furthermore, where operator interaction is required, care must be taken in the design of the interface in order to minimize the possibility and effect of human error.

The sheer size and complexity of real-time systems exacerbates the reliability problem; not only must expected difficulties inherent in the application be taken into account, but also those introduced by faulty software design.

In Chapters 5 and 6 the problems of producing reliable and safe software will be considered, along with the facilities that languages have introduced in order to cope with both expected and unexpected error conditions. The issue is examined further in Chapters 10 to 13.

1.3.4   Concurrent control of separate system components

An embedded system will tend to consist of computers and several coexisting external elements with which the computer programs must simultaneously interact. It is the very nature of these external real-world elements that they exist in parallel. In our typical embedded computer example, the program has to interact with an engineering system (which will consist of many parallel activities such as robots, conveyor belts, sensors, actuators and so on) and the computer's display devices, the operator's console, the database and the real-time clock. Fortunately, the speed of a modern computer is such that usually these actions may be carried out in sequence but give the illusion of being simultaneous. In some embedded systems, however, this may not be the case, for example, where the data is to be collected and processed at various geographically distributed sites, or where the response time of the individual components cannot be met by a single computer. In these cases it is necessary to consider distributed and multiprocessor embedded systems.

A major problem associated with the production of software for systems which exhibit concurrency is how to express that concurrency in the structure of the program. One approach is to leave it all up to the programmer who must construct his/her system so that it involves cyclic execution of a program sequence to handle the various concurrent tasks. There are several reasons, however, why this is unadvisable:

- It complicates the programmer's already difficult task and involves him/her in considerations of structures which are irrelevant to the control of the tasks in hand.

- The resulting programs will be more obscure and inelegant.

- It makes proving program correctness more difficult.

- It makes decomposition of the problem more complex.

- Parallel execution of the program on more than one processor will be much more difficult to achieve.

- The placement of code to deal with faults is more problematic.

Older real-time programming languages, for example, RTL/2 and Coral 66, relied on operating system support for concurrency. However, the more modern languages, such as Ada, Mesa and occam, have direct support for concurrent programming. In Chapters 7, 8 and 9 various models of concurrent programming are considered in detail. Attention is then focused, in the following two chapters, on achieving reliable communication and synchronization between concurrent processes in the presence of design errors. In Chapter 13 issues of execution in a distributed environment are discussed, along with the problems of tolerating processor and communications failures.

1.3.5   Real-time facilities

Response time is crucial in any embedded system. Unfortunately, it is very difficult to design and implement systems which will guarantee that the appropriate output will be generated at the appropriate times under all possible conditions. To do this and make full use of all computing resources at all times is often impossible. For this reason real-time systems are usually constructed using processors with considerable spare capacity, thereby ensuring that 'worst-case behaviour' does not produce any unwelcome delays during critical periods of the system's operation.

Given adequate processing power, language and run-time support is required to enable the programmer to:

- Specify times at which actions are to be performed.
- Specify times at which actions are to be completed.
- Respond to situations where *all* the timing requirements cannot be met.
- Respond to situations where the timing requirements are changed dynamically (mode change).

These are called real-time control facilities. They enable the program to synchronize with time itself. For example, with direct digital control algorithms it is necessary to sample readings from sensors at certain periods of the day, for example, 2pm, 3pm and so on, or at regular intervals, for example, every 5 seconds (with analogue to digital converters sample rates can vary from a few hundred hertz to several hundred megahertz). As a result of these readings other actions will need to be performed. For example, in an electric power station it is necessary at 5pm on Monday to Friday each week to increase the supply of electricity to domestic consumers. This is in response to the peak in demand caused by families returning home from work, turning on lights, cooking dinner and so on. In the UK the demand for electricity reaches a peak on Christmas Day after the Queen's speech, when millions of viewers leave their living rooms, turn on lights in the kitchen and switch on the kettle in order to make a cup of tea or coffee.

An example of a mode change can be found in air flight control systems. If an aeroplane has experienced depressurization there is an immediate need for all computing resources to be given over to handling the emergency.

In order to meet response times it is necessary for a system's behaviour to be deterministic (and, moreover, predictable). This is discussed in Chapter 12, together with language facilities that assist in the programming of time-critical operations.

1.3.6   Interaction with hardware interfaces

The nature of embedded systems requires the computer components to interact with the external world. They need to monitor sensors and control actuators for a wide variety of real-world devices. These devices interface to the computer via input and output registers and their operational requirements are device and computer dependent. Devices may also generate interrupts in order to signal to the processor that certain operations have been performed or that error conditions have arisen.

In the past, the interfacing to devices has either been left under control of the operating system, or has required the application programmer to resort to assembly language inserts to control and manipulate the registers and interrupts. Nowadays, because of the variety of devices and the time-critical nature of their associated interactions, their control must be direct, and not through a layer of operating system functions. Furthermore, reliability requirements argue against the use of low-level programming techniques.

In Chapter 14 the facilities provided by real-time programming languages which enable the specification of device registers and interrupt control will be considered.

1.3.7 Efficient implementation

Since real-time systems are time-critical, efficiency of implementation will be more important than in other systems. It is interesting that one of the main benefits of using a high-level language is that it enables the programmer to abstract away from implementation details, and to concentrate on solving the problem at hand. Unfortunately, the embedded computer systems programmer cannot afford this luxury. He or she must be constantly concerned with the cost of using particular language features. For example, if a response to some input is required within a microsecond there is no point in using a language feature whose execution takes a millisecond!

In Chapter 15 the implementation of various real-time programming language primitives will be considered to see whether they really can be used in time-critical areas of operation.

SUMMARY

In this chapter a real-time system has been defined as:

> any information processing activity or system which has to respond to externally generated input stimuli within a finite and specified period.

Two classes of such systems have been identified: hard real-time systems where it is absolutely imperative that responses occur within the specified deadline; and soft real-time systems where response times are important, but the system will still function correctly if deadlines are occasionally missed.

The basic characteristics of a real-time or embedded computer system have been considered. They were:

- largeness and complexity
- manipulation of real numbers
- extreme reliability and safety
- concurrent control of separate system components
- real-time control
- interaction with hardware interfaces
- efficient implementation

Further reading

Allworth S.T. and Zobel R.N. (1987). *Introduction to Real-time System Design*. London: Macmillan

Bennett S. (1987). *Real-Time Computer Control: An Introduction*. Hemel Hempstead: Prentice-Hall

Bennett S. and Linkens D.A., eds. (1984). *Real-Time Computer Control*. London: Peter Peregrinus

Hatley D.J. and Pirbhai I.A. (1987). *Strategies for Real-Time System Specification*. New York: Dorset House

Lawrence P.D. and Mauch K. (1988). *Real-Time Microcomputers System Design: An Introduction*. Singapore: McGraw-Hill

Stankovic J.A. (1988). Misconceptions about real-time computing: a serious problem for next generation systems. *IEEE Computer*, **21**(10), 10–19

Chapter 2
Designing Real-time Systems

Clearly, the most important stage in the development of any real-time system is the generation of a consistent design that satisfies an authoritative specification of requirements. In this, real-time systems are no different from other computer applications, although their overall scale often generates quite fundamental design problems. The discipline of software engineering is now widely accepted as the focus for the development of methods and tools and techniques aimed at ensuring that the software production process is manageable, and making certain that reliable and correct programs are constructed. It is assumed here that readers are familiar with the basic tenets of software engineering and consideration is thus restricted to the particular problems and requirements furnished by real-time embedded systems. Even within this restriction it is not possible to give a comprehensive account of the many design methodologies proposed. Issues of design themselves are not the main focus of attention in this book. Rather, the investigation of language primitives, which allow designs to be realized, is the central theme. Within this context the languages Ada, Modula-2 and occam 2 will be looked at in detail. Readers should consult the further reading list at the end of this chapter for additional material on the design process.

Although almost all design approaches are top-down they are built upon an understanding of what is feasible at lower levels. In essence, all design methods involve a series of transformations from the initial statement of requirements to the executing code. This chapter gives an overview of some of the typical stages that are passed through on this route such as:

- requirements specification
- top-level design/systems design
- detailed design
- implementation
- testing

Other important activities are also discussed:

- Prototyping prior to final implementation.
- The design of the human–computer interface.
- Criteria for assessing implementation languages.

As different activities are isolated, notations are required that enable each stage to be documented. Transformations from one stage to another are, therefore, nothing more than translations from one notation to another. For example, a compiler produces executable code from source code that is expressed in a programming language. Unfortunately, other translations (further up the design hierarchy) are less well defined; usually because the notations employed are too vague and imprecise and cannot fully capture the semantics of the requirements or of the design.

2.1 Levels of notation

There are a number of ways of classifying forms of notation (or representation). For our purposes McDermid (1989) gives a useful decomposition. He names three techniques:

(1) informal
(2) structured
(3) formal

Informal methods usually make use of natural language and various forms of imprecise diagrams. It has the advantage that the notation is understood by a large group of people (that is, all those speaking the natural language). It is well known, however, that phrases in English, for example, are often open to a number of different interpretations.

Structured methods often use a graphical representation but unlike the informal diagrams these graphs are well defined. They are constructed from a small number of predefined components which are interconnected in a controlled manner. The graphical form may also have a syntactical representation in some well-defined language.

Although structured methods can be made quite rigorous they cannot, in themselves, be analysed or manipulated. It is necessary for the notation to have a mathematical basis if such operations are to be carried out. Methods that have such mathematical properties are usually known as formal. They have the clear advantage that precise descriptions can be made in these notations. Moreover, it is possible to prove that necessary properties hold; for example, that the top-level design satisfies the requirement specification. The disadvantage with formal techniques is that they cannot easily be understood by those not prepared or able to become familiar with the notation.

The high reliability requirements in real-time systems has caused a movement away from informal approaches to the structured and, increasingly, the formal. Rigorous techniques of verification are beginning to be used in the real-time industry but, at present, few software engineers have the necessary mathematical skills to exploit fully the potential of verification.

2.2 Requirements specification

Almost all computing projects start with an informal description of what is desired. This should then be followed by an extensive analysis of requirements. It is at this stage that the functionality of the system is defined. In terms of specific real-time factors, the temporal behaviour of the system should be made quite explicit as should the reliability requirements and the desired behaviour of the software in the event of component failure. The requirements phase will also define which acceptance tests should apply to the software.

In addition to the system itself, it is necessary to build a model of the environment of the application. It is a characteristic of real-time systems that they have important interactions with their environment. Hence, such issues as maximum rate of interrupts, maximum number of dynamic external objects (for example, aeroplanes in an air traffic control system) and failure modes are all important.

Some structured notations and techniques are used (such as PSL (Teichrow and Hershey, 1977) and CORE (Mullery, 1979)) in requirements analysis, for it is clearly advantageous to have an unambiguous set of requirements. Nevertheless, no structured or formal notation will enable one to capture requirements that the 'customer' has forgotten to mention. Some recent work has been carried out on formal methods for requirement analysis, notably the FOREST project (Maibaum *et al.*, 1986) which has defined a logic scheme for dealing with requirements and a method for requirement elicitation.

From the analysis phase comes an authoritative specification of requirements. It is from this that the design will emerge. There is no more critical phase in the software life cycle and yet natural language documents are still the normal notation for this specification. To give one illustration, although the syntax of computer languages can be easily stated formally (using some form of Backus-Naur Form (BNF)) the semantics are often left to wordy English prose. The language Ada is so 'defined' that it has been necessary to instigate a standing committee to pass judgement on what the defining document (which is an international standard) actually means. Compiler writers have found it necessary to forward thousands of queries to this committee. By comparison, the semantics of occam have been defined using denotation semantics (Roscoe, 1985). This opens up the possibility of formally verified compilers and rigorous program manipulation (for example, transformation) tools.

Perhaps the most popular formal method that is now beginning to be used quite widely is VDM (Jones, 1986) (for example, the international specification of the semantics of Modula-2 is in VDM). Another technique that is gaining much support is Z (Spivey, 1987). Both of these methods use set theory and predicate logic, and represent considerable improvements on informal and merely structured techniques. In their present form, however, they do not deal completely with the specification of real-time systems. This is due to the difficulty of associating time with the performance of actions.

2.3   Design activities

The design of a large, embedded system cannot be undertaken in one exercise. It must be structured in some way. To manage the development of complex real-time systems, two complementary approaches are often used: decomposition and abstraction. Together they form the basis of most software engineering methods. Decomposition, as its name suggests, involves the systematic breakdown of the complex system into smaller and smaller parts until components are isolated that can be understood and engineered by individuals or small groups. At each level of decomposition there should be an appropriate level of description and a method of documenting (expressing) this description. Abstraction enables the consideration of detail, particularly that appertaining to implementation, to be postponed. This allows a simplified view of the system and of the objects contained within it to be taken, which, nevertheless, still contains its essential properties and features. The use of abstraction and decomposition pervades the entire engineering process and has influenced the design of real-time programming languages and associated software design methods.

If a formal notation is used for the requirement specification then top-level designs may use the same notation and can thus be proven to meet the specification. Many structured notations are, however, advocated to either fill out the top-level design or to replace the formal notation altogether. Indeed, a structured top-level design may, in effect, be the authoritative specification of requirements.

2.3.1 Encapsulation

The hierarchical development of software leads to the specification and subsequent development of program subcomponents. The needs of abstraction dictate that these subcomponents should have well-defined roles, and clear and unambiguous inter-connections and interfaces. If the specification of the entire software system can be verified just in terms of the specification of the immediate subcomponents, then decomposition is said to be **compositional**. This is an important property when formally analysing programs.

Sequential programs are particularly amenable to compositional methods, and a number of techniques have been used to encapsulate and represent subcomponents. Simula introduced the significant **class** construct. Ada and Modula-2 use the less powerful, but still important, module structure. More recently, **object-oriented** languages have emerged to build upon the class construct; Chapter 4 discussed these facilities further.

Objects, whilst providing an abstract interface, cannot protect themselves against parallel (concurrent) use of this interface. Nor can they directly represent parallel objects in the application domain. The **process** abstraction is, therefore, more applicable to real-time programming. In Chapter 7 the notion of process is introduced, Chapter 8 then looks at shared variable process interaction. A more controlled and abstract interface is, however, provided by message-based process communication. This is discussed in Chapter 9.

Both object and process abstractions are important in the design and implementation of reliable embedded systems. Although the process abstraction is probably more applicable to real-time systems, the object construct is still nevertheless important. It has a role in the construction of processes themselves and, moreover, it can be used to define the interface to a process. Here the process is defined within the 'body' of the object.

2.3.2 Cohesion and coupling

The two forms of encapsulation discussed in the previous section lead to the use of modules with well-defined (and abstract) interfaces. But how should a large system be decomposed into modules? To a large extent the answer to this question lies at the heart of all software design activities. However, before discussing some of these methods it is appropriate to consider more general principles that lead to good encapsulation. Cohesion and coupling are two such metrics that describe the relationships between modules.

Cohesion is concerned with how well a module holds together – its internal strength. Allworth and Zobel (1987) give six measures of cohesion that range from the very poor to the strong:

(1)   Coincidental – elements of the module are not linked other than in a very superficial way, for example, written in the same month.

(2)   Logical – elements of the module are related in terms of the overall system but not in terms of the actual software, for example, all output device drivers.

(3)   Temporal – elements of the module are executed at similar times, for example, start-up routines.

(4)   Procedural – elements of the module are used together in the same section of the program, for example, user-interface components.

(5)   Communicational (*sic*) – elements of the module work on the same data structure, for example, algorithms used to analyse an input signal.

(6)   Functional – elements of the module work together to contribute to the performance of a single system function, for example, the provision of a distributed file system.

Coupling, by comparison, is a measure of the interdependence of program modules. If two modules pass control information between them they are said to possess high (or tight) coupling. Alternatively, the coupling is loose if only data is communicated. Another way of looking at coupling is to consider how easy it would be to remove a module (from a completed system) and replace it with an alternative one.

Within all design methods a good decomposition is one that has strong cohesion and loose coupling. This principle is equally true in sequential and concurrent programming domains.

2.3.3 Formal approaches

The use of place-transition nets (Brauer, 1980) for modelling the behaviour of concurrent systems was proposed by C.A. Petri over 20 years ago. These nets are constructed as marked directed bipartite graphs from two types of nodes; *S*-elements denoting local atomic states and *T*-elements denoting transitions. The arcs of the graph provide the relationship between the *S* and *T* elements. Markings on the graph represent tokens over the *S*-elements; the movement of a token represents a change in the state of the program. Rules are used to specify when and how a token may move from one *S*-element to another via a transition element. Petri nets are defined mathematically and are amenable to formal analysis.

Place-transition nets have the useful characteristics of being simple, abstract and graphical, and provide a general framework for analysing many kinds of concurrent and distributed systems. They have the disadvantage that they can produce very large and unwieldy representations. To allow for a more concise modelling of such systems predicate-transition nets have been introduced. With these nets an *S*-element can model several normal *S*-elements (similarly *T*-elements) and the tokens, which originally had no internal structure, can be 'coloured' by tuples of data.

Petri nets represent one way of modelling concurrent systems. Other rigorous approaches require a formal description of the proposed implementation language. Having obtained these axioms it is then possible to develop proof rules for analysing the behaviour of concurrent systems. Unfortunately, few implementation languages are developed with a formal description in mind (occam being a notable exception). The Communicating Sequential Processes (CSP) notation was developed to enable concurrent systems to be specified and analysed. In CSP a process is described in terms of external **events**, that is, the communication it has with other processes. The history of a process is represented by a **trace** which is a finite sequence of events.

A system represented in CSP can be analysed to determine its behaviour. In particular, **safety** and **liveness** properties can be examined. Owicki and Lamport (1982) characterized these two concepts as:

(1)   **safety** – 'something bad will not happen';

(2)   **liveness** – 'something good will happen'.

Although real-time systems are concurrent they also have timing requirements. Their analysis, therefore, needs an appropriate form of logic. Temporal logic is an extension to propositional and predicate calculi, with new operators being introduced in order to express properties relating to real time. Typical operators are: **always**, **sometime**, **until**, **since** and **leads-to**. For example, **sometime** ($\langle \rangle$) means that the following property will hold true at some moment in the future – for example, $\langle \rangle \; (y > N)$ implies that eventually y will take a value greater than N.

Many applications of temporal logic involve its use in verifying existing programs rather than in the hierarchical specification and rigorous development of new ones. It is possible to criticize the logic as being too global and non-modular, it usually being necessary to possess the complete program in order to analyse any part thereof. To overcome these difficulties it is possible to extend the formalism so that the transitions themselves effectively become propositions in the logic. This approach has been advocated by Lamport (1983) and Barringer and Kuiper (1983). Further refinements to the temporal logic enable deadlines to be attached to these temporal operators. So that, for example, not only will y become greater than N but that this will occur within bounded time (these schemes are known as **real-time logics**). The important issue of representing timing requirements and deadline scheduling is discussed again, in detail, in Chapter 12.

2.4   Design methods

It was noted earlier (in Section 2.3.1) that most real-time practitioners advocate a process abstraction, and that formal techniques do exist that enable concurrent time-constrained systems to be specified and analysed. Nevertheless, these techniques are not yet sufficiently mature to constitute 'tried and tested' design methods. Rather, the real-time industry uses, at best, structured methods and software engineering approaches that are applicable to all information processing systems. They do not give specific support to the real-time domain, and they lack the richness that is needed if the full power of implementation languages is to be exploited.

Typically, a structured design method uses a diagram in which annotated arrows show the flow of data through the system and designated nodes represent points at which data is transformed (that is, processes). In the following sections Jackson's System Development (JSD) and Mascot 3 are briefly outlined; both of these techniques have been used extensively in the real-time domain. An Ada-specific method, called PAMELA, is used in Chapter 16.

2.4.1   Jackson's system development

Jackson's system development method (Jackson, 1975) uses a precise notation for specification (top-level design) and implementation (detailed design). Interestingly, the implementation is not just a detailed restatement of the specification but is the result of applying transformations to the initial specification that are aimed at increasing efficiency.

A JSD graph consists of processes and a connection network. Processes are of three kinds:

(1)   input processes that detect actions in the environment and pass them on to the system;

(2)   output processes that pass system responses to the environment;

(3)   internal processes.

Processes can be linked in two distinct ways:

(1)   by asynchronous data stream connections that are buffered;

(2)   by state vector connections (or inspections).

A state vector connection allows one process to see the internal state of another process without the need to communicate with it.

The graph gives an architecture to the system. Yet to be added are the appropriate data structures for the information that is actually moving around the system, and the detail of the actions incorporated within each process. Unfortunately, JSD does not have a standard way of incorporating timing constraints and, therefore, one must add informal annotations to the diagrams.

Of course what JSD provides is a means of expressing a design, it does not do the design for you. Design inevitably incorporates human experience and creativity (as does programming). It is often said that structured and formal methods are aimed at stifling creativity; this is not true. What these techniques offer is a well-understood notation for expressing design, and techniques for checking that the creativity has been well placed, that is, that the design meets the specification and that the software implements the design.

The focus of design in JSD is the dataflow. A 'good' design is, therefore, one that incorporates this natural flow. Earlier, the factors that lead to good decomposition were discussed. These are precisely the issues that should influence a JSD design (and all other design methods). Processes themselves are categorized naturally into a few distinct types (see Section 9.9), and a top-down design approach that targets these types will result in a design that is easy to realize.

Another advantage of the dataflow focus is that timing constraints are often expressed as attributes of the data passing through the system. An interrupt generates a control signal; in essence, the control signal is a transformation of the interrupt. These transformations are undertaken within processes and they take time. An appropriate choice of processes will provide very visible deadlines that can be scheduled (although actual schedulability can not be directly checked).

Having obtained the design, its implementation must be accomplished in a systematic manner. With a message-based concurrency model within the implementation language this is much easier, as design processes and buffered dataflows can all be coded as program processes. Unfortunately, this can lead to a proliferation of processes and a very inefficient implementation. To counter this, two approaches are possible:

(1)   transform the design so that fewer processes are necessary, or;
(2)   obtain the process-excessive program and transform it to reduce the number of concurrent objects.

Most languages are not amenable to transformation techniques. (Occam 2 is again a notable exception as its semantics are formally defined.) The approach advocated within the JSD method is a transformation known as **inversion**. In this, a design process is replaced by a procedure with a single scheduler process controlling the execution of a collection of these procedures; that is, rather than a pipeline of five processes, the scheduler would call five procedures each time a data item appeared (if the five processes were identical then obviously there would only be one procedure that would be called five times). Again, time constraints do cause a problem here as they are difficult to preserve during inversion.

Although JSD was not originally used for real-time applications it has been employed with success on some recent very large systems. One submarine command system is estimated to require over 200 years of development effort. From JSD an implementation in Ada and occam 2 is derivable, much of the code being generated automatically (Lawton and France, 1988).

2.4.2   Mascot 3

Whereas JSD has only recently been used in the real-time domain, Mascot was developed specifically for the design, construction and execution of real-time software. Mascot 1 appeared in the early 1970s but was quickly superseded by Mascot 2. This version was widely used, particularly in the UK. Recently, a third version of the method has been developed to remove some of the weaknesses inherent with the earlier versions. In particular, Mascot 2 did not cope well with very large systems or multi-processor architectures; it also failed to support hierarchical design or process decomposition.

Mascot 3 is also characterized by the use of a graphical dataflow network. Modularity is the key to this method with identifiable modules being used for design, construction, implementation and testing. Importantly, a Mascot 3 design can be expressed in an equivalent textual as well as graphical form.

In addition to the dataflows a Mascot 3 description can contain:

- subsystems,
- general Intercommunication Data Areas (IDAs),
- activities (processes),

- channels (an IDA which acts as a buffer),
- pools (an IDA which acts an information repository),
- servers (a design element that communicates with external hardware devices).

Necessary synchronizations on the use of channels and pools are given. Subsystems may contain collections of other elements including further subsystems.

The Mascot 3 method normally has six stages that are iterated through. These are similar to the stages found in other methods:

(1)   requirements and constraints,

(2)   design proposal (top-level design),

(3)   network decomposition,

(4)   element decomposition,

(5)   algorithmic definition (of all interfaces and components),

(6)   integration and testing.

The implementation of a Mascot 3 design can be achieved in two quite different ways. Either an appropriate concurrent programming language is used, or a standard run-time executive. With Mascot 2 the algorithmic coding was done in a sequential language such as Coral 66 or RTL/2 (FORTRAN, Pascal, C and Algol 66 have also been used with Mascot 2) and then this software was hosted on a Mascot run-time executive. The use of a concurrent language enables the complete system to be realized in the one language, thereby significantly easing integration.

Languages such as Ada and Modula-2 that support decomposition and that have a message-based synchronization model (either predefined or programmable) clearly present a more favourable solution to the implementation activity. There is increasing support for using Ada with Mascot 3 although their basic models of action are not completely compatible (Jackson, 1986). It should be noted, however, that the problem of process proliferation is also present with Mascot.

2.5 Implementation

An important plateau between the top-level requirements specification and the executing machine code is the programming language. The development of implementation languages for real-time systems is the central theme of this book. Language design is still a very active research area. Although systems design should lead naturally into implementation, the expressive power of most modern languages is not matched by current design methodologies. Only by understanding what is possible at the implementation stage can appropriate design approaches be undertaken.

It is possible to identify three classes of programming languages which are, or have been, used in the development of real-time systems. These are assembly languages, sequential systems implementation languages and high-level concurrent languages.

2.5.1   Assembly languages

Initially, most real-time systems were programmed in the assembly language of the embedded computer. This was mainly because high-level programming languages were not well supported on most microcomputers and assembly language programming appeared to be the only way of achieving efficient implementations which could access hardware resources.

The main problem with the use of assembly languages is that they are machine-orientated rather than problem-orientated. The programmer can become encumbered with details which are unrelated to the algorithms being programmed, with the result that the algorithms themselves become obscure. This keeps development costs high and makes it very difficult to modify programs when errors are found or enhancements required.

Further difficulties arise because programs cannot be moved from one machine to another, but must be rewritten. Also, staff must be retrained if they are required to work with other machines.

2.5.2   Sequential systems implementation languages

As computers became more powerful, programming languages more mature, and compiler technology progressed, the advantages of writing real-time software in a high-level language outweighed the disadvantages. To cope with deficiencies in languages like FORTRAN, new languages were developed specifically for embedded programming. In the United States Air Force, for example, Jovial was in common use. In Great Britain the Ministry of Defence (MoD) standardized on Coral 66 and large industrial concerns like ICI standardized on RTL/2. More recently the C programming language has become popular.

All of these languages have one thing in common – they are sequential. They also tend to be weak in the facilities they provide for real-time control and reliability. As a result of these shortcomings it is often necessary to rely on operating system support and assembly code inserts.

2.5.3   High-level concurrent programming languages

In spite of the increasing use of application-tailored languages such as sequential systems implementation languages for embedded computer applications, Cobol for data processing applications and FORTRAN for scientific and engineering applications; the production of computer software became progressively more difficult during the 1970s as computer-based systems became larger and more sophisticated.

It has been common to refer to these problems as the **software crisis**. There are several symptoms of this crisis which have been recognized (Booch, 1986):

- responsiveness – production systems which have been automated often do not meet users' needs;

- reliability – software is unreliable and will often fail to perform to its specification;

- cost – software costs are seldom predictable;

- modifiability – software maintenance is complex, costly and error prone;

- timeliness – software is often delivered late;

- transportability – software in one system is seldom used in another;

- efficiency – software development efforts do not make optimal use of the resources involved.

Perhaps one of the best illustrations of the impact of the software crisis can be found in the American Department of Defense's (DoD) search for a common high-order programming language for all its applications. As hardware prices began to fall during the 1970s, the DoD's attention was focused on the rising cost of its embedded software. It estimated that, in 1973, three thousand million dollars were spent on software alone. A survey of programming languages showed that at least 450 general-purpose programming languages and incompatible dialects were used in DoD-embedded computer applications. A working group was set up to look at the possibility of standardizing on a common high-order language. There followed a series of requirement documents entitled STRAWMAN, WOODENMAN, TINMAN, IRONMAN, revised IRONMAN and finally, STEELMAN. An evaluation of existing languages occurred in 1976 against the emerging requirements. These evaluations resulted in four main conclusions (Whitaker, 1978):

(1)   no current language was suitable;

(2)   a single language was a desirable goal;

(3)   the state of the art of language design could meet the requirements;

(4)   development should start from a suitable language base; those recommended were Pascal, PL/I and Algol 68.

At this point potential contractors were invited to design a new language in accordance with the IRONMAN requirements and starting from one of the recommended bases. Four contractors were chosen to go ahead with an initial design, in competition with each other. The subsequent languages were called Green, Red, Blue and Yellow; all chose Pascal as their base. At the end of this first phase Blue and Yellow were eliminated, the requirements were updated to STEELMAN (US Department of Defense, 1978) and the Green and Red languages were revised. Green was eventually chosen and the new language was named Ada.

Although the Ada programming language effort has dominated research in embedded computer programming languages since the early 1970s other languages have emerged. For example, Modula (Wirth, 1977b), was developed by Wirth for use in programming machine devices and was intended to:

> conquer that stronghold of assembly coding, or at least to attack it vigorously.

Much of the experience gained from the implementation and use of Modula was fed into Modula-2 (Wirth, 1983) a more general-purpose systems implementation language. Other new languages of note include PEARL, used extensively in Germany for process control applications, Mesa (Xerox Corporation, 1985), used by Xerox in their office automation equipment, and CHILL (CCITT, 1980) which was developed in response to CCITT requirements for programming telecommunication applications. There is even a real-time version of BASIC which, although lacking in many features normally associated with a high-level language (such as user-defined types), does provide concurrent programming facilities and other real-time related features.

Modula, Modula-2, PEARL, Mesa, CHILL and Ada are all high-level concurrent programming languages which include features aimed at aiding the development of embedded computer systems. More recently a new language, still in its infancy, has generated much interest. Occam, by comparison with Ada, CHILL and Mesa, is a much smaller language. It provides no real support for programming large and complex systems, although the usual control structures are present and non-recursive procedures are provided. The development of occam has been closely associated with that of the **transputer** (May and Shepherd, 1984) (a processor with on-chip memory and four autonomous link controllers that allow multitransputer systems to be built easily). Occam has, therefore, an important role in the emerging field of loosely-coupled distributed embedded applications.

2.5.4 General language design criteria

Although a real-time language may be designed primarily to meet the requirements of embedded computer system programming, its use is rarely limited to that area. Most real-time languages are also used as general-purpose systems implementation languages for applications such as compilers and operating systems.

Young (1982) lists the following six (sometimes conflicting) criteria as the basis of a real-time language design: security, readability, flexibility, simplicity, portability and efficiency. A similar list also appears in the STEELMAN requirements.

Security

The security of a language design is a measure of the extent to which programming errors can be detected automatically by the compiler or language run-time support system. There is obviously a limit to the type and number of errors that can be detected by a language system; for example, errors in the programmer's logic cannot be detected automatically. A secure language must, therefore, be well structured and readable so that such errors can easily be spotted.

The benefits of security include:

- the detection of errors much earlier in the development of a program – generating an overall reduction in cost;
- compile-time checks have no overheads at run time – a program is executed much more often than it is compiled.

The disadvantage of security is that it may result in a more complicated language with an increase in compilation time and compiler complexity (and cost).

Readability

The readability of a language depends on a variety of factors including the appropriate choice of keywords, the ability to define types and the facilities for program modularization. As Young (1982) points out:

> the aim is to provide a language notation with sufficient clarity to enable the main concepts of a particular program's operation to be assimilated easily by reading the program's text only, without resort to subsidiary flowcharts and written descriptions.

The benefits of good readability include:

- reduced documentation costs,
- increased security,
- increased maintainability.

The main disadvantage is that it usually increases the length of any given program.

Flexibility

A language must be sufficiently flexible to allow the programmer to express all the required operations in a straightforward and coherent fashion. Otherwise, as with older sequential languages, the programmer will often have to resort to operating system commands or machine code inserts in order to achieve the desired result.

Simplicity

Simplicity is a worthwhile aim of any design, be it of the proposed NASA space station or a simple calculator. In programming languages, simplicity has the advantages of:

- minimizing the effort required to produce compilers;
- reducing the cost associated with programmer training;
- diminishing the possibility of making programming errors as a result of misinterpretation of the language features.

Flexibility and simplicity can also be related to the expressive power and usability (ease of use) of the language.

Portability

A program, to a certain extent, should be independent of the hardware on which it executes. For a real-time system this is difficult to achieve, as a substantial part of any program will normally involve manipulation of hardware resources. However, a language must be capable of isolating the machine dependent part of a program from the machine *independent* part.

Efficiency

In a real-time system, response times must be guaranteed; therefore, the language must be efficient. Mechanisms which lead to unpredictable run-time overheads should be avoided. Obviously, efficiency requirements must be balanced against security, flexibility and readability requirements.

2.6 Testing

With the high reliability requirements that are the essence of most real-time systems it is clear that testing must be extremely stringent. A comprehensive strategy for testing involves many techniques, most of which are applicable to all software products. Therefore, it is assumed that the reader is familiar with these techniques.

The difficulty with real-time concurrent programs is that the most intractable system errors are usually the result of subtle interactions between processes. Often, the errors are also time dependent and will only manifest themselves in rare states. Murphy's Law dictates that these rare states are also crucially important and only occur when the controlled system is, in some sense, critical. It should perhaps be emphasized here that appropriate formal design methods do not detract from the need for testing. They are complimentary strategies.

Testing is, of course, not restricted to the final assembled systems. The decomposition incorporated in the design and that is manifest within program modules (including processes) forms a natural architecture for component testing. Of particular importance (and difficulty) within real-time systems is that not only must correct behaviour in a correct environment be tested but dependable behaviour in an arbitrarily incorrect environment must be catered for. All error recovery paths must be exercised and the effects of simultaneous errors investigated.

To assist in any complex testing activity a realistic test bed presents many attractions. For software such a test environment is called a **simulator**.

2.6.1 Simulators

A simulator is a program which imitates the actions of the engineering system in which the real-time software is embedded. It simulates the generation of interrupts and performs other Input/Output (I/O) actions in real-time. Using a simulator, abnormal as well as 'normal' system behaviour can be created. Even when the final system has been completed certain error states may only be safely experimented with via a simulator. The melt-down of a nuclear reactor is an obvious example.

Simulators are able to reproduce accurately the sequence of events expected in the real system. In addition, they can repeat experiments in a way that is usually impossible in a live operation. However, in order to faithfully recreate simultaneous actions it may be necessary to have a multiprocessor simulator. Moreover, it should be noted that with very complicated applications it may not be possible to build an appropriate simulator.

Although simulators do not have high reliability requirements they are, in all other ways, real-time systems in their own right. They themselves must be thoroughly tested although occasional errors can be tolerated. One technique that is often used in real-time systems that do not have reliability requirements (another example here is flight simulators) is to remove mutual exclusion protection from shared resources. This provides greater efficiency at the cost of intermittent failure. The construction of a simulator is also eased by the process model of the embedded system itself.

Chapter 14 shows how external devices can be considered as hardware processes with interrupts being mapped onto the available synchronization primitive. If this model has been followed then the replacement of a hardware process by a software one is relatively straightforward.

Notwithstanding these points, simulators are non-trivial and expensive systems to develop. They may even require special hardware. In the NASA shuttle project the simulators cost more than the real-time software itself. This money turned out to be well spent with many system errors being found during hours of simulator 'flight'.

2.7 Prototyping

The standard 'waterfall' approach to software development, that is, requirements, specification, design, implementation, integration, testing and then delivery has the fundamental problem that faults within the initial requirements or specification phases are only recognized upon delivery of the product (or at best, during testing). To correct these faults at this late stage is time-consuming and very costly. Prototyping is an attempt to catch these faults earlier by presenting the customer with a 'mock-up' of the system.

The main purpose of a prototype is to help ensure that what the customer actually wanted has been captured in the requirements specification. This has two aspects:

(1)   Is the requirements specification correct (in terms of what the customer desires)?

(2)   Is the requirements specification complete (has the customer included everything)?

One of the benefits of running a prototype is that the customer can experience situations that were previously only vaguely understood. It is almost inevitable that changes to the requirements will be made during this activity. In particular, new error conditions and recovery paths may emerge.

Where specification techniques are not formal then prototyping can also be used to build confidence that the overall design is consistent. For example, with a large dataflow diagram a prototype may help to check that all the required connections are in place and that all pieces of data flowing through the system do actually visit the activities required.

In order to be cost effective it must be possible to build the prototype more cheaply (much more cheaply) than the actual implementation software. It is, therefore, pointless to use the same design methods to the same standards as the final system. Significantly lower costs can be accomplished by using higher-level languages. The language APL (Iverson, 1962) has been popular for prototyping; more recently, functional and logic programming languages have been used. They have the advantage that they do in fact capture the important functional behaviour of the system without requiring the detailed non-functional aspects. The clear drawback with such proto-types is that they do not exercise the real-time aspects of the application. To do this requires a simulation of the system.

It was noted in Section 1.3.5 that proving that a program will meet all time constraints under all operating conditions is very difficult. One method of examining a design to see if it is feasible is to try and simulate the behaviour of the software. By making assumptions about code structures and processor execution speed it is possible to build a model that will emulate run-time characteristics. For example, it will show the maximum rate of interrupts that can be handled whilst still meeting time constraints.

The emulation of a large real-time system is expensive; its develop-ment is costly and each emulator run may take up considerable computing resources. Normally many hundreds of such runs are needed. Nevertheless, this cost must be balanced with the economic consequences of creating a faulty real-time system.

2.8   Human–computer interaction

If one takes a wide enough context all real-time systems incorporate or affect humans. Most, in fact, involve direct communication between the executing software and one or more human operators. As human behaviour intro-duces the greatest source of variation in a running system it follows that the design of the Human–Computer Interaction (HCI) component is one of the most critical in the entire structure. There are many examples of poor HCI design and the sometimes tragic consequences that follow from this weak-ness. For example, in the nuclear incident known as Three Mile Island a number of the failures were put down to the operators being unable to cope with the sheer volume of information being generated during a series of critical events (Kemeny *et al.*, 1979).

The search for design principles on which to base HCI component construction is currently a very active one. Having spent too many years as a backwater, HCI is now appreciated to be central to the production of well-engineered software (all software). The first important issue is that of modularity; HCI activities should be isolated, and well-defined interfaces specified. These interfaces are themselves constructed in two parts, the functionality of each being quite different. Firstly, it is important to define those objects that pass between the operator and the software. Secondly (and distinctly) it is necessary to specify how these objects are to be presented to, and extracted from, the user. A rigorous definition of the first kind of interface component must include predicates about the allowable action that an operator can take in any given state of the system. For example, certain commands may need authority, or can only sensibly, or safely, be carried out when the system is so disposed. To give an illustration here, a fly-by-wire plane would ignore a command that would lead to a crash.

A Dialogue Development System for Ada (ADDS (Burns and Robinson, 1986)) has been implemented that incorporates the design predicates as Boolean functions and will only pass on an input to the application software if these Boolean functions evaluate true. A further consideration in the design of this component is the temporal behaviour of the operator. Some responses (from the operator) may be needed within a specified time period; if the human has not responded then the software must be informed so that alternative and safe procedures can be activated.

A particularly important design question in all interactive systems is: Who is in control? At one extreme the human could explicitly direct the computer to perform particular functions, at the other extreme the computer would be in full control (although it may occasionally ask the operator for information). Clearly, most real-time systems will incorporate a mixture of these extremes; they are known as **mixed initiative** (Robinson and Burns, 1985) systems. Sometimes the user is in control (for example, when giving a new command) and at other times the system is controlling the dialogue (for example, when extracting data necessary to perform a command that has been given).

The chief motivation for the design of the interface component is to capture all user-derived errors in the interface control software, not the application software of the rest of the real-time system. If this can be done then this application software can assume a **perfect user** and as a result its design and implementation are simplified (Burns, 1983). The term error in this discussion means an unintentional action. This is referred to as a **slip** by Reason (1979). He uses the term **mistake** to imply a deliberate error action. Although an interface may be able to block mistakes that would lead to hazards, it is not possible to recognize a 'sensible' change to an operating parameter as a mistake. Appropriate operator training and supervision are the only ways of eliminating these mistakes.

Although slips will inevitably occur (and, therefore, must be protected against) their frequency can be significantly reduced if the second component of the interface, the actual operator I/O module, is well defined. Within this context, however, the term 'well defined' is itself difficult to define. The specification of an I/O module is essentially in the domain of the psychologist.

One must start with a model of the end-user or operator. Unfortunately many different models exist; a useful review is given by Rouse (1981). From an understanding of these models, principles of design can be established; three important ones being:

(1)   Predictability – sufficient data should be supplied to the user so that the effect of a command is unambiguously derived from a knowledge of that command.

(2) Commutativity – the order in which the user places parameters to a command should not affect the meaning of a command.

(3) Sensitivity – if the system is subject to different modes of operation then the current mode should always be displayed.

The first two principles are reported by Dix *et al.* (1987). Real-time systems have the added difficulty that the human operators are not the only actors that are changing the state of the system. A mode change may be caused by an interrupt and the asynchronous nature of operator input could lead to a command that was valid when the operator initiated it being unavailable in a new mode.

Much of the work on HCI has been concerned with the design of screens so that the data presented is unambiguous and data entry can be accommodated with the minimum of key strokes. There are, however, other factors concerned with the ergonomics of the work-station and the wider issues of the working environment for the operators. Screen designs can be 'tested' with a prototype but job satisfaction is a metric that can only be measured over much longer time intervals than are available for experimentation with a prototype. Operators may work an eight-hour shift, five days a week for year after year. If one adds stress to the work (as in air traffic control) then job satisfaction and performance become critically dependent upon:

- the multitude of interdependent tasks that must be performed;
- the level of control the operator has;
- the degree to which the operator understands the operation of the complete system;
- the number of constructive tasks the operator is allowed to perform.

Understanding can be improved by always presenting the operator with a picture of 'what is happening'. Indeed, some process control systems can be made to illustrate the behaviour of the system in graphical, pictorial or spreadsheet form. The operator can experiment with the data to model ways in which performance can be improved. It is quite possible to incorporate such **decision support systems** into the control loop so that the operator can see the effect of minor changes to operation parameters. In this way productivity can be increased and the working environment for the operators enhanced. It may also reduce the number of mistakes made!

2.9 Managing design

This chapter has attempted to give an overview of the important issues associated with the design of real-time software. A reliable and correct product will only result if the activity of specification, design, implementation and testing are carried out to a high quality throughout. There is now a wide range of techniques that can help achieve this quality. The appropriate use of a well-defined high-level language is the primary issue in this book. Programming and design both need to be managed in order to achieve the desired result. Modern concurrent programming languages have an important role in this management process.

The key to achieving quality lies in adequate verification and valida-tion. At all stages of design and implementation there needs to be well-defined procedures for ensuring that necessary techniques and actions have been carried out correctly. Where high assurance is needed, theorem provers and checkers can be used to verify formally specified components. Many other structured activities, for example, code inspections, are used more widely. Increasingly, there is need for software tools to assist in verification and validation. One would expect such tools to be provided in an integrated project support environment. Verification and validation tools perform an important role and their use may alleviate the need for human inspection. They themselves must, therefore, be of an extremely high quality.

Such support tools are, however, not a substitute for well trained and experienced staff. The application of rigorous software engineering techniques and the use of the language features that are described in this book do make a difference to the quality and cost of real-time systems. Practitioners have a responsibility to society at large to understand and apply whatever knowledge is necessary in order to ensure that embedded systems are safe. Many deaths have already been attributed to software error. It is possible to stop a future epidemic but only if the industry moves away from arbitrary procedures, informal methods and inadequate low-level languages.

2.9.1   Other design issues

As languages have increased in sophistication there is a tendency to use their higher-level constructs as design aids. Much has been written about the use of Ada as its own Program Description Language (PDL), as it is possible to use a compiler to check the logic of a collection of specifications prior to any implementations being coded.

In this chapter, indeed in the entire book, the focus of attention has been the development of software. But normally, software development proceeds alongside hardware construction. This construction can be as simple as the bringing together of standard components or may involve the complete design and fabrication of new electronic devices. Although there would be many advantages in entirely separating the software and hard-ware activities, clearly, this is not always possible or desirable. In Chapter 13 it will be shown how a distributed processor architecture inevitably impinges upon software design. Indeed, the programming of error recovery paths may depend upon a detailed understanding of the hardware's behaviour.

The hardware may also present solutions to some of the software problems. In particular, if the real-time constraints are presenting a difficulty then the opportunity to add processor units is a useful safety net! The combination of the transputer and occam 2 is a good illustration of this flexibility. Writing occam 2 code in an inherently concurrent manner allows a relatively easy expansion path to be taken at some later date if this turns out to be necessary. The cost of extra processors (or memory) is not usually a significant factor, but the increase in size and weight may be.

SUMMARY

This chapter has outlined the major stages involved in the design and implementation of real-time systems. These include, in general, requirements specification, systems design, detailed design, coding and testing. The high reliability requirements of real-time systems dictate that, wherever possible, formal methods should be employed.

To manage the development of complex real-time systems requires the appropriate application of decomposition, encapsulation and abstraction. A hierarchical design method, therefore, isolates subcomponents, or modules, that are either object based or process based. Both forms of module should exhibit strong cohesion and loose coupling.

Implementation, which is the primary focus of attention in this book, necessitates the use of a programming language. Early real-time languages lacked the expressive power to deal adequately with this application domain. More recent languages have attempted to incorporate concurrency and error-handling facilities. A discussion of these features is contained in subsequent chapters. The following general criteria were considered a useful basis for a real-time language design:

- security
- readability
- flexibility
- simplicity
- portability
- efficiency

Irrespective of the rigour of the design process, adequate testing is clearly needed. To aid this activity prototype implementations, simulators and emulators all have an important role.

Finally in this chapter, attention was focused on the important human computer interface. For too long this subject has been viewed as containing little science, with the systematic application of engineering principles being conspicuous by its absence. This position is now changing with a realization that the interface is a significant source of potential errors, and that these can be reduced in number by the application of current research and development activities.

In many ways this chapter has been a divergent one. It has introduced more problem areas and engineering issues than can possibly be tackled in just one book. This broad sweep across the 'design process' has aimed at setting the rest of the book in context. By now focusing on language issues and programming activities the reader will be able to understand the 'end product' of design, and judge to what extent current methodologies, techniques and tools are appropriate.

Further reading

Allworth S.T. and Zobel R.N. (1987). *Introduction to Real-time System Design*. London: Macmillan

Galton A. (1988). *Temporal Logics and their Applications*. London: Academic Press

Hatley D.J. and Pirbhai I.A. (1987). *Strategies for Real-Time System Specification*. New York: Dorset House

Hayes I., ed. (1987). *Specification Case Studies*. London: Prentice-Hall

Jackson M.A. (1975). *Principles of Program Design*. London: Academic Press

Jones C.B. (1986). *Systematic Software Development Using VDM*. London: Prentice-Hall

Joseph M., ed. (1988). Formal techniques in real-time fault tolerant systems. *Lecture Notes in Computer Science*, **331**. Berlin: Springer-Verlag

Lawrence P.D. and Mauch K. (1988). *Real-Time Microcomputers System Design: An Introduction*. Singapore: McGraw-Hill

Macro A. and Buxton J. (1987). *The Craft of Software Engineering*. Wokingham: Addison-Wesley

Nielson K. and Shumate K. (1988). *Designing Large Real-Time Systems with Ada*. New York: McGraw-Hill

Sennet C.T., ed. (1989). *High Integrity Software*. London: Pitman

Woodcock J. (1988). *Software Engineering Mathematics*. London: Pitman

Young S.J. (1982). *Real Time Languages: Design and Development*. Chichester: Ellis Horwood

---

EXERCISES

2.1 To what extent should the choice of design method be influenced by:

(a) likely implementation language;

(b) support tools;

(c)   reliability requirements of the application;

(d)   training requirements of staff;

(e)   marketing considerations;

(f)   previous experiences;

(g)   cost.

2.2 In addition to the criteria given in this chapter what other factors would you use in assessing programming languages?

2.3 At what stage in the design process should the views of the end-user be obtained?

2.4 Should software engineers be liable for the consequences of faulty real-time systems?

2.5 New medicines cannot be introduced until appropriate tests and trials have been carried out. Should real-time systems be subject to similar legislation? If a proposed application is too complicated to simulate should it be constructed?

2.6 Should the Ada language be the only language used in the implementation of embedded real-time systems?

Chapter 3
Programming in the Small

In considering the features of high-level languages it is useful to distinguish between those that aid the decomposition process and those that facilitate the programming of well-defined components. These two sets of features have been described as:

- Support for programming in the large.
- Support for programming in the small.

Programming in the small is a well-understood activity and will be discussed in this chapter within the context of an overview of the languages Ada, Modula-2 and occam 2. Chapter 4 is concerned with programming in the large and will address the more problematic issue of managing complex systems.

3.1 Overview of Ada, Modula-2 and occam 2

In a book on real-time systems and their programming languages it is not possible to give a detailed description of all of the languages used in this computing domain. It has, therefore, been decided to limit detailed consideration to just three high-level concurrent programming languages. Ada is important because of the backing it obtains from major military agencies

41

(in the West), Modula-2 is favoured by those in the Pascal tradition and occam 2 is the nearest that a general-purpose language has got to embodying the formalisms of CSP (Communicating Sequential Processes). Occam 2 is also specifically designed for multicomputer execution which is of increasing application and importance in the real-time domain. Specific features of other languages will, however, be considered when appropriate.

The overview presented here will itself assume knowledge of a Pascal-like language. Sufficient detail on each language will be given to understand the example programs given later in the book. For a comprehensive description of each language the reader must refer to books that specialize on each language (Barnes, 1984; Ford and Wiener, 1985; Burns, 1988).

3.2 Lexical conventions

Programs are written once but read many times; it follows that the lexical style of the language syntax should appeal to the reader rather than the writer. One simple aid to readability is to use names that are meaningful. Languages should not, therefore, restrict the lengths of identifiers; neither Ada, Modula-2 nor occam 2 does so. The form of a name can also be improved by the use of a separator. Ada allows a '_' to be included in identifiers; occam 2 names can include a '.' (this is a somewhat unfortunate choice as '.' is often used in languages to indicate a subcomponent, for example, a field of a record). Modula-2 does not support a separator and, therefore, the technique of mixing upper and lower case characters is recommended. The following are example identifiers.

```
example_name_in_Ada
example.name.in.occam2
ExampleNameInModula2
```

A classic illustration of poor lexical convention is provided by FORTRAN. This language allows the space character to be a separator. As a consequence, a simple typing error in a program (a '.' instead of a ',') resulted in an American Viking Venus probe being lost! Rather than the intended line:

```
DO 20 I = 1,100
```

which is a loop construct (loop to label 20 with I iterating from 1 to 100), an assignment was compiled (the assignment operator is '='):

```
DO 20 I = 1.100
```

Or as spaces can be ignored in names:

```
DO20I = 1.100
```

Variables in FORTRAN need not be defined; identifiers beginning with 'D' are assumed to be reals and 1.100 is a real literal!

Not surprisingly, all modern languages require variables to be explicitly defined.

3.3 Overall style

All three languages reviewed here are, to a greater or lesser extent, block structured. A block in Ada consists of:

(1)   the declaration of objects that are local to that block (if there are no such objects then this declaration part may be omitted);

(2)   a sequence of statements, and;

(3)   a collection of exception handlers (again, this part may be omitted if empty).

A schema for such a block is:

```
declare
   ⟨declarative part⟩
begin
   ⟨sequence of statements⟩
exception
   ⟨exception handlers⟩
end;
```

Exception handlers catch errors that have occurred in the block. They are considered in detail in Chapter 6.

An Ada block may be placed in the program wherever an ordinary statement may be written. Thus, they can be used hierarchically and support decomposition within a program unit. The following simple example illustrates how a new integer variable TEMP is introduced to swap the values contained by the two integers A and B. Note that a comment in Ada starts with the double hyphen and goes on to the end of that line.

```
declare
   TEMP : INTEGER:= A;      -- initial value given to
                            -- temporary variable
begin
   A:= B;
   B:= TEMP;
end;                        -- no exception part
```

In Modula-2, blocks cannot be nested directly but form the bodies of other units, for example, procedures. The swap code would be as follows:

```
VAR
  temp : INTEGER; (* no initialization allowed *)
BEGIN
  temp:= A;
  A:= B;
  B:= temp
END
```

Before considering the occam 2 equivalent of this program some introductory remarks about this language must be made. Ada and Modula-2 are both languages in which concurrent programs can be written. However, all programs in occam 2 are concurrent. What would be a sequence of statements in Ada or Modula-2 is a sequence of processes in occam 2. This distinction is a fundamental one in comparing the nature of the concurrency models in the three languages (see Chapters 7, 8 and 9) but it does not impinge upon the understanding of the primitive elements of the language.

Occam 2, like Ada, is a fully block-structured language. Any process can be preceded by the declaration of objects to be used in that process. To swap the two integers (INTs in occam 2) requires a SEQ construct that specifies that the assignments that follow it must be executed in sequence:

```
INT temp :    -- A declaration is terminated by a colon.
SEQ
  temp:= A
  A:= B
  B:= temp
```

It is interesting to note the different ways in which the three languages separate actions. Ada uses a semicolon as a statement terminator (hence there is one at the end of B:= TEMP;). Modula-2, like Pascal, employs the semicolon as a statement separator (therefore, no semicolon after B:= temp). Occam 2 does not use the semicolon at all! It requires each action (process) to be on a separate line. Moreover, the use of indentation which merely (though importantly) improves readability in Ada and Modula-2 is syntactically significant in occam 2. The three assignments in the above code fragment have to start in the column under the Q of SEQ.

3.4   Data types

In common with all high-level languages Ada, Modula-2 and occam 2 require programs to manipulate objects that have been abstracted away from their actual hardware implementation. Programmers need not concern themselves about the representation or location of the entities that their programs manipulate. Moreover, by partitioning these entities into distinct types the compiler can check for inconsistent usage and thereby increase the security associated with using the languages.

Five classes of entities can be declared in Modula-2: constants, types, variables, procedures and modules. Procedures are considered in Section 3.6.2 and modules are described in Chapter 4. The use of constants, types and variables is similar to that of Pascal except that they may occur in any order, provided that an object is declared before it is referenced. Similarly, Ada allows constants, types and variables to be defined together. Moreover, constants can be defined of any type (including user-defined types) a facility not supported in Modula-2. By comparison with these languages occam 2's type model is more restrictive; in particular, user-defined types are not allowed.

3.4.1 Discrete types

Table 3.1 lists the predefined discrete types supported in the three languages; 'cardinal' is the non-negative integer type.

All the usual operators for these types are available. The languages are strongly typed (that is, assignments and expressions must involve objects of the same type) but explicit type conversions are supported.

In addition to these predefined types, Ada and Modula-2 allow for the definition of enumeration types. In Modula-2 the enumerated constants must be uniquely determined, however, the Ada model, by allowing names to be overloaded, is not so restrictive. Both languages provide means for manipulating objects of these enumeration types; Modula-2 by the provision of standard functions, Ada by the use of attributes. (Attributes are used throughout Ada to give information about types and objects.) The examples overpage illustrate these points.

Table 3.1 Discrete types.

Ada	Modula-2	occam 2
INTEGER	INTEGER	INT
		INT16
		INT32
		INT64
	CARDINAL	
BOOLEAN	BOOLEAN	BOOL
CHARACTER	CHAR	BYTE

```
(* Modula-2 *)
TYPE dimension = (xplane,yplane,zplane);
VAR line, force : dimension;
BEGIN
    line := xplane;
    force := INC(line)
    (* force now has the value yplane*)
END
```

```
-- Ada
type DIMENSION is (XPLANE,YPLANE,ZPLANE);
type MAP is (XPLANE,YPLANE);
LINE,FORCE : DIMENSION;
GRID : MAP;
begin
    LINE := XPLANE;
    FORCE := DIMENSION'SUCC(XPLANE);          -- force now has the
                                              -- value yplane
    -- the name 'yplane' below is unambiguous as grid is of type 'map'
    GRID := YPLANE;
    GRID := LINE;                             -- illegal – type clash
end;
```

Another facility that both Ada and Modula-2 support is the use of subranges or subtypes to restrict the values of an object (of a particular base type). This allows for a closer association between objects in the program and the values, in the application domain, that could sensibly be taken by that object.

```
(* Modula-2)
TYPE surface = [xplane .. yplane];
```

```
-- Ada
subtype SURFACE is DIMENSION range XPLANE .. YPLANE;
```

Note that the Ada equivalent to Modula-2's cardinal type is a predefined subtype called NATURAL.

Importantly, in Ada all types can be duplicated by defining a type to be a new version of a previous type:

```
type NEW_INT is new INTEGER;
type PROJECTION is new DIMENSION range XPLANE .. YPLANE;
```

Whereas objects of a type and its subtypes can be mixed (in expressions), objects of a type and a derived type cannot. The two types are distinct:

```
-- Ada
D : DIMENSION;
S : SURFACE;
P : PROJECTION;
```

```
begin
    D := S;      -- legal
    S := D;      -- legal but could cause run-time error if
                 -- D has the value 'zplane'
    P := D;      -- illegal - type clash
end;
```

This provision (and its use) significantly increases the security of Ada programs.

3.4.2 Real numbers

Many real-time applications (for example, signal processing, simulation and process control) require numerical computation facilities beyond those provided by integer arithmetic. There is a general need to be able to manipulate *real* numbers, although the sophistication of the arithmetic required varies widely between applications. In essence, there are two distinct ways of representing real values within a high-level language:

(1)   floating-point and
(2)   scaled integer.

Floating-point numbers are a finite approximation to real numbers and are applicable to computations in which exact results are not needed. A floating-point number is represented by three values: a mantissa, M, an exponent, E, and a radix, R. It has a value of the form $M*R^E$. The radix is (implicitly) implementation defined and usually has the value 2. As the mantissa is limited in length the representation has limited precision. The divergence between a floating-point number and its corresponding real value is related to the size of the number (it is said to have **relative error**).

The use of scaled integers is intended for exact numeric computation. A scaled integer is a product of an integer and a scale. With the appropriate choice of scale any value can be catered for. Scaled integers offer an alternative to floating-point numbers when non-integer calculations are required. However, the scale must be known at compile time; if the scale of a value is not available until execution then a floating-point representation must be used. Although scaled integers provide exact values not all numbers in the mathematical domain can be represented exactly. For example, 1/3 cannot be viewed as a finite scaled decimal integer. The difference between a scaled integer and its 'real' value is an **absolute error**.

Scaled integers have the advantage (over floating-point) of dealing with exact numerical values and of making use of integer arithmetic. Floating-point operations require either special hardware (a floating-point unit) or complex software that will result in numerical operations being many times slower than the integer equivalent. Scaled integers are, however, more difficult to use, especially if expressions need to be evaluated that contain values with different scales.

Traditionally, languages have supported a single floating-point type (usually known as **real**) which has an implementation-dependent precision. Use of scaled integers has normally been left to the user (that is, the programmer had to implement scaled integer arithmetic using the system-defined integer type).

Modula-2 has a 'real' type; FLOAT is the Ada term for an implementation-dependent 'real' type. There is, however, no equivalent in occam 2; here, the number of bits must be specified. The designers of occam 2 took the view that the need for an abstract 'real' type is not as great as the need for the programmer to be aware of the precision of the operations being carried out. The occam 2 'reals' are REAL16, REAL32 and REAL64.

In addition to the predefined FLOAT type, Ada provides the facilities for users to create both floating-point numbers with different precision and fixed-point numbers. Fixed point numbers are implemented as scaled integers. The following are some examples of type definitions. To define a floating-point type requires a lower and upper bound, and a statement of the necessary precision (in decimal):

type NEW_FLOAT **is digits** 10 **range** −1.0E18 .. 1.0E18;

A subtype of this type can restrict the range or the precision:

subtype CRUDE_FLOAT **is** NEW_FLOAT **digits** 2;
subtype POS_NEW_FLOAT **is** NEW_FLOAT **range** 0.0 .. 1000.0;

The statement of precision defines the minimum requirement, an implementation may give greater accuracy. If the minimum requirement cannot be accommodated then a compile-time error message is generated.

Ada's fixed-point numbers remove from the programmer the details of implementing the necessary scaled integer operators; these are pre-defined. To construct a fixed-point type requires range information and an absolute error bound called **delta**. For example, the following type defini-tion gives a delta of 0.05 or 1/20:

type SCALED_INT **is delta** 0.05 **range** −100.00 .. 100.00;

To represent all these decimal values (−100.00, −99.95, −99.90 ... 99.95, 100.00) requires a specific number of bits. This can easily be calculated. The nearest (but smaller) power of 2 to 1/20 is 1/32 which is 2^{-5}. Thus 5 bits are needed to provide the fraction part. The range

−100.00 .. 100.00 is contained within −128 .. 128 which requires 8 bits (including a sign bit). In total, therefore, 13 bits are required:

    sbbbbbbb.fffff

where s is the sign bit, b denotes an integer bit and f denotes a fractional bit. Clearly, this fixed-point type can easily be implemented on a 16-bit architecture.

Note again that although a fixed-point type represents, exactly, a range of binary fractions, not all decimal constants within the correct range will have an exact representation. For instance, decimal 5.1 will be held as 00000101.00011 (binary) or 5.09375 (decimal) in the fixed-point type defined above.

3.4.3 Structured data types

The provision for structured data types within our three languages can be stated quite easily. Occam 2 supports arrays, Ada supports arrays and records, and Modula-2 supports arrays, records and sets. Arrays first and by example:

```
-- occam2
INT Max IS 10:              -- definition of a constant in occam
[Max]REAL32 Reading:        -- Reading is an array with ten
                            -- elements Reading[0] .. Reading[9]
[Max][Max]BOOL Switches:    -- 2 dimensional array
```

All arrays in occam 2 start at element zero.

```
(* Modula-2 *)
CONST Max = 10;
TYPE Readingtype = ARRAY[0 .. Max−1] OF REAL;
CONST size = Max−1;
TYPE Switchestype = ARRAY[0 .. size],[0 .. size] OF BOOLEAN;
VAR
   Reading : Readingtype;
   Switches : Switchestype;
```

```
-- Ada
MAX : constant INTEGER:= 10;
type READINGTYPE is array(0 .. MAX−1) of FLOAT;
SIZE : constant INTEGER:= MAX−1;
type SWITCHESTYPE is array(0 .. SIZE, 0 .. SIZE) of BOOLEAN;
READING : READINGTYPE;
SWITCHES : SWITCHESTYPE;
```

Note that Ada uses round brackets for arrays whereas occam 2 and Modula-2 use the more conventional square brackets.

Although there is no fundamental reason why records have not yet been introduced into occam 2 their present omission gives some indication as to the priorities of the language's designers and implementors. The Ada and Modula-2 record types are quite straightforward:

```
(* Modula-2 *)
date= RECORD
        day : [1..31];
        month : [1..12];
        year : [1900 .. 2050]
      END;


--Ada
type DAYTYPE is new INTEGER range 1 .. 31;
type MONTHTYPE is new INTEGER range 1 .. 12;
type YEARTYPE is new INTEGER range 1900 .. 2050;
type DATE is
record
  DAY : DAYTYPE:= 1;
  MONTH : MONTHTYPE:= 1;
  YEAR : YEARTYPE;
end;
```

In the Modula-2 example, the three fields are subranged integers, whereas the Ada code has distinct new types for the components. The Ada example also shows how initial values can be given to some (but not necessarily all) fields of a record. Both languages use the dot notation to address individual components and allow record assignments. Ada also supports complete record assignments using record aggregates (array aggregates are also available):

```
-- Ada
D: DATA;
begin
  D.YEAR:= 1989;                                  -- dot notation
  -- D now has value 1-1-1989 due to initialization

  D:= (3, 1, 1953);                               -- complete
                                                  -- assignment
  D:= (YEAR ⇒ 1974, DAY ⇒ 4, MONTH ⇒ 7);
  -- complete assignment using name notation
  ...
end;
```

The use of name notation improves readability and removes the errors that could otherwise be introduced by positional faults; that is, putting (1, 3, 1953) rather than (3, 1, 1953).

Both Ada and Modula-2 provide for variant records.

As indicated earlier in this section only Modula-2 has a set type. Its structure and operations are similar to those of Pascal. Although Ada does not directly support such a construct it is possible to program a complete collection of set primitives (of any type) using a **generic package**. Generics are considered in Chapter 4.

3.4.4 Dynamic data types

There are many programming situations in which the exact size or organization of a collection of data objects cannot be predicted prior to the program's execution. Even though Ada supports variable length arrays, a flexible and dynamic data structure can only be achieved if a memory allocation facility is provided using reference, rather than direct, naming.

The implementation of dynamic data types represents a considerable overhead to the run-time support system for a language. For this reason occam 2 does not have any dynamic structures. The Modula-2 facility is similar to that of Pascal and uses a POINTER type. A linked list example is given below.

```
TYPE ptr = POINTER TO node;      (* forward referencing allowed for pointer
                                    declaration *)
        node = RECORD
                   value : integer;
                   next : ptr
               END;
VAR
  V : INTEGER;
  P1 : ptr;
BEGIN
  NEW(P1);                       (* construct first node *)
  P1 ↑ .value: = V;              (* for some appropriate value V *)
  P1 ↑ .next: = NIL;             (* nil is predefined *)
  ...
END
```

In Ada an **access type** is used rather than a pointer (though the concept is the same).

```
type NODE;                       -- incomplete declaration
type AC is access NODE;
type NODE is
record
    VALUE : INTEGER;
    NEXT : AC;
end;
```

```
V : INTEGER;
A1 : AC;
begin
    A1:= new(NODE);          -- construct first node
    A1.VALUE:= V;
    A1.NEXT:= null;          -- null is predefined
    ...
end;
```

Note that the ↑ symbol is not used in Ada.

Both of the above program fragments illustrate the use of a 'new' facility for dynamically allocating an area of memory (from the heap). In Modula-2 this takes the form of a procedure and is coupled to a DISPOSE procedure for returning storage to the heap. The **new** in Ada is an operator defined in the language; there is, however, no dispose operator. Rather, a generic procedure is provided that removes storage from designated objects. This procedure (called UNCHECKED_DEALLOCATION) does not check to see if there are outstanding references to the object.

Neither Ada nor Modula-2 requires a garbage collector to be supported. This lack of requirement is not surprising as garbage collectors usually result in heavy and unpredictable overheads in execution time. These overheads may well be unacceptable in real-time systems.

3.4.5 Files

Neither Ada, Modula-2 nor occam 2 has a file-type constructor like that of Pascal. Instead, each language allows an implementation to support files via library modules. Ada, for example, requires all implementations to provide sequential and direct-access files. Many Modula-2 systems will have similar provisions.

3.5 Control structures

Although there are some variations in the data structures supported (particularly between occam 2 and the other languages) there is much closer agreement about which control structures are required. As programming languages progressed from machine code through assembly languages to higher-level languages, control instructions evolved into control statements. There is now common agreement as to the control abstractions needed in a sequential programming language. These abstractions can be grouped together into three categories; sequences, decisions and loops. Each will be considered in turn. The necessary control structures for the concurrent parts of the language will be considered in Chapters 7, 8 and 9.

3.5.1 Sequence structures

The sequential execution of statements is the normal activity of a (non-concurrent) programming language. Most languages, including Ada and Modula-2, implicitly require sequential execution, and no specific control structure is provided. The definitions of a block in both Ada and Modula-2 indicate that between 'begin' and 'end' there is a sequence of statements. Execution is required to follow this sequence.

In occam 2 the normal execution of statements (called processes in occam 2) could quite reasonably be concurrent and it is, therefore, necessary to state explicitly that a collection of actions must follow a defined sequence. This is achieved by using the SEQ construct that was illustrated earlier in Section 3.3. For example:

```
SEQ
  action 1
  action 2
  .
  .
  .
```

If a sequence is, in a particular circumstance, empty then Ada requires the explicit use of the **null** statement:

```
-- Ada
begin
  null;
end;
```

Modula-2 allows an empty block:

```
(* Modula-2 *)
BEGIN
END
```

And occam 2 uses a SKIP process to imply no action:

```
SEQ
  SKIP    -- occam 2
```

or just:

```
SKIP
```

At the other extreme to a null action is one that causes the sequence to permanently block. Modula-2 provides a special predefined procedure named HALT that causes the entire program to terminate. The occam 2 STOP process has a similar effect. Ada does not have an equivalent primitive but an exception can be programmed to have the same result (see Chapter 6). In all three languages the severe action of prematurely terminating the program is only used to respond to the detection of an error condition that cannot be repaired. After bringing the controlled system into a safe condition the program has no further useful action to perform other than termination.

3.5.2   Decision structures

A decision structure provides a choice as to the route an execution takes from some point in a program sequence to a later point in that sequence. The decision as to which route is taken will depend upon the current values of relevant data objects. The important property of a decision control structure is that all routes eventually come back together. With such abstract control structures there is no need to use a 'goto' statement which often leads to programs that are difficult to test, read and maintain. Modula-2 and occam 2 do not possess a 'goto' statement. Ada does have a 'goto' statement but it is well hidden within the reference manual and just as the English language has forms that are now never used the Ada 'goto' will quietly drift into obscurity.

The most common form of decision structure is the 'if' statement. Although the requirements for such a structure are clear, earlier languages, such as Algol-60, suffered from a poor syntactical form which could lead to confusion. In particular, with a nested 'if' construct it was not clear to which 'if' a trailing single 'else' applied. All three of the languages under consideration in this chapter have clear unambiguous structures. To illustrate, consider a simple problem; find out if $b/a > 10$ – checking first to make sure that 'a' is not equal to zero! An Ada solution is given below; although the code has the shortcoming that the Boolean variable HIGH is not assigned a value if $a = 0$, the meaning of the program fragment is clear due to the explicit **end if** token:

```
if A /= 0 then
   if B/A > 10 then
      HIGH:= TRUE;
   else
      HIGH:= FALSE;
   end if;
end if;
```

The Modula-2 structure also has an explicit END:

```
IF a <> 0 THEN
  IF b/a > 10 THEN
    high: = TRUE
  ELSE
    high: = FALSE
  END
END
```

Note that as the semicolon is a statement separator none appear in the above Modula-2 code.

The occam 2 IF has a different style to the other two languages although the functionality is the same. Consider first the general structure. In the following let B1..Bn be Boolean expressions and A1..An be actions:

```
IF
  B1
    A1
  B2
    A2
  .

  .
  Bn
    An
```

It is important to remember that the layout of occam 2 programs is syntactically significant. The Boolean expressions are on separate lines (indented two spaces from the IF), as are the actions (indented a further two spaces). No 'then' token is used. On execution of this IF construct the Boolean expression B1 is evaluated. If it evaluates to TRUE then A1 is executed and that completes the action of the IF. However, if B1 is FALSE then B2 is evaluated. All the Boolean expressions are evaluated until one is found TRUE and then the associated action is undertaken. If no Boolean expression is TRUE then this is an error condition and the IF construct behaves like the STOP discussed in the last section.

With this form of IF statement no distinct 'else' part is required; the Boolean expression TRUE as the final test is bound to be taken if all other choices fail. The $b/a > 10$ example in occam 2, therefore, takes the form:

```
IF
  a /= 0
    IF
      b/a > 10
        high := TRUE
      TRUE
        high := FALSE
  TRUE        := FALSE    -- These last two lines are needed so that the
    SKIP                 -- IF does not become STOP when  a has the value 0
```

To give another illustration of the important 'if' construct consider a multiway branch. The following example (firstly in Ada) finds the number of digits in a positive integer variable 'number'. A maximum of five digits is assumed:

```
if NUMBER < 10 then
   NUM_DIGITS := 1;
else

   if NUMBER < 100 then
      NUM_DIGITS := 2;
   else

      if NUMBER < 1000 then
         NUM_DIGITS := 3;
      else

         if NUMBER < 10000 then
            NUM_DIGITS := 4;
         else
            NUM_DIGITS := 5;

         end if;
      end if;
   end if;
end if;
```

This form, which is quite common, involves nesting on the **else** part and results in a trail of **end if**s at the end. To remove this clumsy structure Ada and Modula-2 provide an 'elsif' statement. The above can, therefore, be written more concisely as:

```
-- Ada
                                  -- Modula-2
if NUMBER < 10 then               IF number < 10 THEN
   NUM_DIGITS := 1;                  num_digits := 1

elsif NUMBER < 100 then           ELSIF number < 100 THEN
   NUM_DIGITS := 2;                  num_digits := 2

elsif NUMBER < 1000 then          ELSIF number < 1000 THEN
   NUM_DIGITS := 3;                  num_digits := 3

elsif NUMBER < 10000 then         ELSIF number < 10000 THEN
   NUM_DIGITS := 4;                  num_digits := 4

else                              ELSE
   NUM_DIGITS := 5;                  num_digits := 5
end if;                           END
```

In occam 2 the code is quite clear:

```
IF
  number < 10
    digits := 1
  number < 100
    digits := 2
  number < 1000
    digits := 3
  number < 10000
    digits := 4
  TRUE
    digits := 5
```

The above is an example of a multiway branch constructed from a series of binary choices. In general, a multiway decision can be more explicitly stated and efficiently implemented, using a 'case' structure. All three languages have such a structure although the occam 2 version is somewhat more restricted. To illustrate consider a character (byte) value 'command' which is used to decide upon four possible actions:

```
-- Ada
case COMMAND is
  when 'A' | 'a'     ⇒ ACTION1;    -- A or a
  when 't'           ⇒ ACTION2;
  when 'e'           ⇒ ACTION3;
  when 'x' .. 'z'    ⇒ ACTION4;    -- x, y or z
  when others        ⇒ null;       -- no action
end case;
```

```
(* Modula-2 *)
CASE command OF
  'A', 'a'   : action1  |  (* A or a *)
  't'        : action2  |
  'e'        : action3  |
  'x' .. 'z' : action4  |  (* x, y or z *)
  ELSE    (* no action *)
END
```

In occam 2 alternative values and ranges are not supported; the code is, therefore, more protracted:

```
CASE command
  'A'
    action1
  'a'
    action1
```

```
't'
  action2
'e'
  action3
'x'
  action4
'y'
  action4
'z'
  action4
ELSE
  SKIP
```

3.5.3 Loop structures

A loop structure allows the programmer to specify that a statement, or collection of statements, is to be executed more than once. There are two distinct forms for constructing such loops:

(1)   Iteration

(2)   Recursion

The distinctive characteristic of iteration is that each execution of the loop is completed before the next is begun. With a recursive control structure the first loop is interrupted to begin a second loop, which may be interrupted to begin a third loop and so on. At some point loop n will be allowed to complete, this will then allow loop $n - 1$ to complete, then loop $n - 2$ and so on until the first loop has also terminated. Recursion is usually implemented via recursive procedure calls and will be mentioned again in Section 3.6. Attention here is focused on iteration.

Iteration itself comes in two forms; a loop in which the number of iterations is fixed prior to the execution of the loop construct and a loop in which a test for completion is made during each iteration. The former is known generally as the 'for' statement, the latter as the 'while' statement. Most languages' 'for' constructs also provide a counter that can be used to indicate which iteration is currently being executed.

The example code in the following illustrates the 'for' construct in our three languages; the code assigns, into the first ten elements of array 'A', the value of their position in the array. Note that all three languages have restricted the use of the loop variable. The free use of this variable in earlier languages was the cause of many errors. In addition to the above forms Ada and Modula-2 allow the loop to be executed in reverse order and Modula-2 enables an increment value other than 1 to be used.

```
-- Ada
for I in 0 .. 9 loop        -- I is defined by the loop construct
    A(I):= I;               -- I is read only in the loop
end loop;                   -- I is out of scope after the loop construct
```

```
(* Modula-2 *)
FOR i:=0 TO 9 DO           (* i must be a previously defined scalar *)
    A[i]:= i               (* i is read only in the loop *)
END;                       (* the value of i is undefined after the loop *)
```

```
-- occam 2
SEQ i:= 0 FOR 10           -- i is defined by the construct
    A[i]:= i               -- i is read only in the loop
                           -- i is out of scope after the loop
-- note that the range of i is 0 to 9,
-- as in the Ada and Modula-2 example
```

The main variation with 'while' statements concerns the point at which the test for exit from the loop is made. The most common form involves a test upon entry to the loop and subsequently before each iteration is made:

```
-- Ada
while ⟨BOOLEAN EXPRESSION⟩ loop
    ⟨STATEMENTS⟩
end loop;
```

```
(* Modula-2 *)
WHILE ⟨boolean expression⟩ DO
    ⟨statements⟩
END
```

```
-- occam 2
WHILE ⟨boolean expression⟩
    SEQ
        ⟨statements⟩
```

For situations where the loop must be executed at least once before the Boolean expression is evaluated, Modula-2 provides the 'repeat .. until' construct of Pascal. Ada goes even further with its flexibility and allows control to pass out of the loop (that is, the loop to terminate) from any point within it:

```
-- Ada
loop
   .
   .
   exit when ⟨BOOLEAN EXPRESSION⟩;
   .
   .
end loop;
```

A common programming error is a loop that either does not terminate (when it is meant to) or terminates in the wrong state. Fortunately,
formal methods of analysing loop structures are now well understood.
They involve defining the pre-and post-conditions for the loop; the termination condition and the loop invariant. The loop invariant is a statement
that is true at the end of each iteration but may not be true during the
iteration. In essence, the analysis of the loop involves showing that the pre-
condition will lead to loop termination and that upon termination the loop
invariant will lead to a proof that the post-condition is satisfied. To facilitate the use of these formal approaches, exiting from the loop during an
iteration is not advised. Where possible the standard 'while' construct is
the best to use.

The final point to make about loops is that in real-time systems it is
often required that a loop does not terminate. A control cycle will be
expected to run indefinitely (that is, until the power is turned off).
Although 'while true' would facilitate such a loop it may be inefficient and
it does not capture the essence of an infinite loop. For this reason Ada and
Modula-2 provide a simple loop structure:

```
-- Ada              (* Modula-2 *)
loop                LOOP
   ⟨statements⟩         ⟨statements⟩
end loop;           END
```

3.6 Subprograms

Even in the construction of a component or module further decomposition
is usually desirable. This is achieved by the use of procedures and functions; known collectively as **subprograms**.

Subprograms not only aid decomposition but they represent an
important form of abstraction. They allow arbitrary complex computations
to be defined and then invoked by the use of a simple identifier. This
enables such components to be reused both within a program and between
programs. The generality and, therefore, usefulness of subprograms is, of
course, increased by the use of parameters.

3.6.1 Parameter-passing modes and mechanisms

A parameter is a form of communication; it is a data object being transferred between the subprogram user and the subprogram itself. There are a number of ways of describing the mechanisms used for this transfer of data. The first of which is to consider the way that parameters are transferred. For the invoker's point of view there are three distinct modes of transfer.

(1)   Data is passed into the subprogram.
(2)   Data is passed out from the subprogram.
(3)   Data is passed into the subprogram, is changed and is then passed out of the subprogram.

These three modes are often called; **in**, **out** and **in out**.

The second mechanism of describing the transfer is to consider the binding of the formal parameter of the subprogram and the actual parameter of the call. There are two general methods of interest here: a parameter may be bound by value or by reference. A parameter that is bound by value only has the value of the parameter communicated to the subprogram (often by copying into the subprogram's memory space); no information can return to the caller via such a parameter. When a parameter is bound by reference, any updates to that parameter from within the subprogram are defined to have an affect on the memory location of the actual parameter.

A final way of considering the parameter-passing mechanism is to examine the methods used by the implementation. The compiler must satisfy the semantics of the language, be they expressed in terms of modes or binding, but is otherwise free to implement a subprogram call as efficiently as possible. For example, a large array parameter that is 'pass by value' need not be copied if no assignments are made to elements of the array in the subprogram. A single pointer to the actual array will be more efficient but behaviourally equivalent. Similarly, a call by reference parameter may be implemented by a copy in and copy out algorithm.

Ada uses parameter modes to express the meaning of data transfer to, and from, a subprogram. For example, consider a procedure which returns the real roots (if they exist) of a quadratic equation.

```
procedure QUADRATIC (A, B, C : in FLOAT;
                     R1, R2 : out FLOAT;
                     OK     : out BOOLEAN);
```

An in parameter (which is the default) acts as a local constant within the subprogram – a value is assigned to the formal parameter upon entry to the procedure or function. This is the only mode allowed for functions. Within the procedure, an out parameter acts as a write-only variable; it cannot form part of an expression. A value is assigned to the calling parameter upon termination of the procedure. An in out parameter acts as a variable in the procedure. Upon entry, a value is assigned to the formal parameter, upon termination of the procedure the value attained is passed back to the calling (actual) parameter.

Modula-2 uses the Pascal mechanism:

```
PROCEDURE quadratic (A, B, C : REAL;
                     VAR R1, R2 : REAL;
                     VAR OK : BOOLEAN);
```

The default is pass by value; the VAR tag implies pass by reference. All parameters can be updated within the procedure but only those that are reference will effect the calling parameters. (The failure to tag a changing parameter as VAR is, unfortunately, a common source of errors).

Occam 2's method is similar to Modula-2's except that the default is reference and a VAL tag is used to imply pass by value. Significantly, within the procedure (called a PROC in occam 2) a VAL parameter acts as a constant and therefore the errors that can occur in Modula-2 and Pascal by missing out the VAR tag are caught by the compiler.

```
PROC quadratic(VAL REAL32 A, B, C,
               REAL32 R1, R2, BOOL OK)
  -- note no semicolon as parameter separator
```

3.6.2 Procedures

The procedure bodies in all three languages are quite straightforward and are illustrated below by completing the 'quadratic' definitions given above. All procedures assume that a 'sqrt' function is in scope.

```
-- Ada
procedure QUADRATIC (A, B, C : in FLOAT;
                     R1, R2 : out FLOAT;
                     OK : out BOOLEAN) is
  Z : FLOAT;
begin
  Z:= B * B - 4.0 * A * C;
  if Z < 0.0 or A = 0.0 then
    OK:= FALSE;
    R1:= 0.0;                                    -- arbitrary values
    R2:= 0.0;
    -- return from a procedure before reaching logical end
    return;
  end if;
  OK:= TRUE;
  R1:= (-B + SQRT(Z)) / (2.0 * A);
  R2:= (-B - SQRT(Z)) / (2.0 * A);
end QUADRATIC;
```

```
(* Modula-2 *)
PROCEDURE quadratic (A, B, C : REAL;
                     VAR R1, R2 : REAL;
                     VAR OK : BOOLEAN);
   Z : REAL;
BEGIN
   Z:= B * B - 4.0 * A * C;
   IF Z < 0.0 OR A = 0.0 THEN
      OK:= FALSE;
      R1:= 0.0;                                 (* arbitrary values *)
      R2:= 0.0;
      RETURN                                    (* return from procedure before *)
                                                (* reaching logical end *)
   END;
   OK:= TRUE;
   R1:= (-B + SQRT(Z)) / (2.0 * A);
   R2:= (-B - SQRT(Z)) / (2.0 * A)
END quadratic;
```

```
-- occam2
PROC quadratic(VAL REAL32 A, B, C,
               REAL32 R1, R2, BOOL OK)
   REAL32 Z :
   SEQ
     Z:= (B * B) - (4.0 * (A * C))         -- brackets are needed
                                           -- to fully specify expression
     IF
       (Z < 0) OR (A = 0.0)
         SEQ
           OK:= FALSE
           R1:= 0.0                        -- arbitrary values
           R2:= 0.0
       TRUE                                -- no return statement in occam2
         SEQ
           OK:= TRUE
           R1:= (-B + SQRT(Z)) / (2.0 * A)
           R2:= (-B - SQRT(Z)) / (2.0 * A)
   :                                       -- colon needed to show
                                           -- end of PROC declaration
```

The invoking of these procedures, in all three languages, merely involves naming the procedure and giving six appropriately typed parameters in parentheses.

In addition to these basic features there are two extra facilities available in Ada that improve readability. Consider an enumeration type SETTING and an integer type that delineates ten distinct VALVES:

```
type SETTING is (OPEN, CLOSED);
type VALVE is new INTEGER range 1 .. 10;
```

The following procedure specification gives a subprogram for changing the setting of one VALVE:

```
procedure CHANGE_SETTING (VALVE_NUMBER : VALVE;
                          POSITION : SETTING := CLOSED;
                          );
```

Note that one of the parameters has been given a default value. Calls to this procedure could take a number of forms:

```
-- normal call
CHANGE_SETTING(6, OPEN);
-- default value 'closed' used
CHANGE_SETTING(3);
-- name notation
CHANGE_SETTING(POSITION ⇒ OPEN, VALVE_NUMBER ⇒ 9);
-- name notation and default value
CHANGE_SETTING (VALVE_NUMBER ⇒ 4);
```

Default values are useful if some of the parameters are nearly always given the same value. The use of name notation removes positional errors and increases readability.

Recursive (and mutually recursive) procedure calls are allowed in Ada and Modula-2. They are not supported in occam 2 because of the dynamic overhead they create at run-time.

One further distinction between the procedure mechanisms provided in the three languages is that only in Modula-2 can procedure types be defined and procedures (and functions) be passed as parameters to other procedures:

```
TYPE realproc = PROCEDURE (VAR REAL);
PROCEDURE DoSomething (X : REAL; RP : realproc);
```

The type of a procedure is defined by the number and type of its parameters. For procedures without parameters there is a predefined procedure type PROC; all procedures without parameters are considered to be objects of this type.

Procedure variables and parameters are a useful programming tool that allow certain algorithms to be expressed in a very concise form. Their omission from Ada is a direct result of the requirements specification for the language. It was felt that programs without these features would be easier to verify mechanically.

3.6.3 Functions

Both Ada and Modula-2 support functions in a manner that is similar to procedures. Consider a simple example of a function that returns the smallest of two integer values:

```
-- Ada
function MINIMUM (X, Y : in INTEGER) return INTEGER is
begin
  if X > Y then
    return Y;
  else
    return X;
  end if;
end MINIMUM;
```

```
(* Modula-2 *)
PROCEDURE minimum (X,Y : INTEGER) : INTEGER;
BEGIN
  IF X > Y THEN
    RETURN Y
  ELSE
    RETURN X
  END
END minimum;
```

As these examples show, Modula-2 does not actually use the term 'function' but considers this type of subprogram to be a procedure that returns a value. Both Ada and Modula-2 allow functions to return any valid type including structured types.

The misuse of functions is a source of many errors within programs; the golden rule about functions is that they should not have side-effects. An expression should mean what it says:

$$A := B + F(C)$$

The value of A becomes the value of B plus a value obtained from C by the application of the function F. In the execution of the above only A should have its value changed.

Side-effects can be introduced into the above expression in three ways.

(1) F could change the value of C as well as returning a value.

(2) F could change the value of B so that the expression has a different value if evaluated left to right as opposed to right to left.

(3) F could change the value of D, where D is any other variable in scope.

Ada prohibits side-effect (1) by only allowing parameters to functions to have 'in' mode. Occam 2, however, goes much further and defines the semantics of a function so that no side-effects are possible.

As with Ada, the parameters to an occam 2 function must be values. In addition, the body of a function is defined to be a VALOF. A VALOF is the sequence of statements necessary to compute the value of an object (this object will be returned from the function). The important property of the VALOF is that the only other variables that can have their values changed are those defined locally within the VALOF. This prohibits side-effects. The simple minimum function defined earlier in this section would, therefore, have the form:

```
INT FUNCTION minimum (VAL INT X, Y)
  INT Z :                            -- Z will be the value returned
  VALOF
    IF
      X <> Y
        Z:= Y
      TRUE
        Z:= X
    RESULT Z
  :
```

In concurrent languages another form of side-effect is hidden concurrency; this can have a number of unfortunate consequences. The VALOF of occam 2 is further restricted to disallow any concurrency within it.

3.6.4   Inline expansion

Although the use of subprograms is clearly beneficial in terms of decomposition, reuse and readability, for some real-time applications the overhead of implementing the actual call may be unacceptably high. One means of reducing the overhead is to substitute the code for the subprogram 'inline' whenever a call of that subprogram is made. This technique is known as **inline expansion** and has the advantage that it still allows the programmer to use subprograms but not to incur the run-time overhead.

Interestingly, occam 2, whose semantics are formally specified, uses text substitution as the method of specifying what is meant by a procedure call. All three languages, however, allow the implementor to deal with subprograms as they see fit. The only exception to this appears in Ada where the programmer can, by use of the pragma INLINE, request that inline expansion is used for the specified subprogram 'whenever possible'. Pragmas are used in Ada to give instructions to the compiler, they are not executable statements.

SUMMARY

In the title of his seminal book, Wirth (1976) expressed the now famous adage:

'Algorithms + Data Structures = Programs'

Perhaps now that the difficulties presented by very large programs are apparent the adage would be better phrased as Algorithms + Data Structures = Modules; where a module is the component program being designed and developed by an individual or a small, closely-working group of software engineers.

In this chapter the necessary language features for expressing algorithms and representing data structures in Ada, Modula-2 and occam 2 have been given. Although these languages differ, they present the programmer with very similar semantic models. Indeed, for imperative languages the necessary primitives for supporting programming in the small now seem well understood.

For expressing algorithms: blocks and well-constructed loop and decision structures are needed. The 'goto' statement is now totally discredited. To give a concrete realization of the distinct logical units found in most non-trivial modules, subprograms are also required. Procedure semantics are relatively uncontroversial (although different parameter-passing models exist) but functions are still problematic because of side-effects. Occam 2 has shown the lead here by constructing a form of function that cannot have side-effects (occam 1 had a more radical solution to side-effects; it did not have functions at all!).

The provision of a rich variety of data structures and the rules of strong typing are visible in Ada, Modula-2 and occam 2, although the occam 2 facilities are not as comprehensive. Strong typing is now universally accepted as a necessary aid to the production of reliable code. The restrictions it imposes can lead to difficulties but the provision of a controlled means of doing explicit type conversions removes these problems.

The data types themselves can be classified in a number of different ways. There is a clear division between scalar and structured data types. Scalar types can then be subdivided into discrete types (integer types and enumeration types) and real types. The structured data types can be classified in terms of three attributes; homogeneity, size and access method. A structured data type is said to be homogeneous if its subcomponents are all of the same type (for example, arrays). Alternatively, if the subcomponents can be of different types (for example, records) then the data structure is known as heterogeneous. The size attribute can be either fixed or variable. Records are fixed as are arrays in some languages. Dynamic data structures such as linked lists, trees or graphs are variable in size and are usually constructed by the programmer from a pointer type and a memory allocator. Finally, there are several access methods for getting at the subcomponents of the structure. The two most important methods are direct and indirect. Direct access, as its name implies, allows the immediate referencing of a subcomponent (for example, an element of an array or a field of a record). Indirect access means that the addressing of a subcomponent may require a chain of accesses through other components. Most dynamic structures have only indirect access.

The attributes, homogeneity, size and access method, could theoretically give rise to at least eight different structures. In reality, the attributes are related (for example, a fixed size implies direct access) and only the following categories are necessary:

(1)   Arrays with arbitrary bounds and dimensions.

(2)   Records (including variant records).

(3)   Pointers for constructing arbitrary dynamic data structures with indirect addressing.

Any language that provides appropriate control structures and all of these categories (as Ada and Modula-2 do) is well able to support programming in the small. The extra facilities for programming in the large are considered in Chapter 4.

Notwithstanding the discussion above, real-time languages may have to restrict the features available to the programmer. It is difficult, if not impossible, to make estimates of the time required to access dynamic data structures. Moreover, it is desirable to be able to guarantee before execution begins that there is sufficient memory available for the program. For this reason dynamic arrays and pointers may need to be missing from the 'authorized' list of language features for real-time applications. Additionally, recursion and unbounded loop structures may need to be restricted.

Further reading

Backhouse R.C. (1986). *Program Construction and Verification*. London: Prentice-Hall

Barnes J.G.P. (1984). *Programming in Ada*. Wokingham: Addison-Wesley

Burns A. (1988). *Programming in occam 2*. Wokingham: Addison-Wesley

Ford G.A. and Weiner R.S. (1985). *Modula-2 A Software Development Approach*. New York: John Wiley & Son

Gries D. (1981). *The Science of Computer Programming*. New York: Springer-Verlag

Jones C.B. (1986). *Systematic Software Development Using VDM*. London: Prentice-Hall

Welsh J. and Elder J. (1987). *Introduction to Modula-2*. London: Prentice-Hall

Wirth N. (1976). *Algorithms + Data Structures = Programs*. Englewood Cliffs NJ: Prentice-Hall

Young S.J. (1982). *Real Time Languages: Design and Development*. Chichester: Ellis Horwood

---

EXERCISES

3.1 Ada ends each construct with **end** ⟨construct name⟩, Modula-2 uses just END. Pascal does not use an end marker. What are the pros and cons of these language designs?

3.2 Occam 2 and Modula-2 are case sensitive; Ada is not. What are the arguments for and against case sensitivity?

3.3 Occam 2 has removed the need for operator precedence rules by requiring parentheses around all sub-expressions. What is the effect of this on readability and efficiency?

3.4 Should a language always require that initial values be given to variables?

3.5 Should a real-time programming language always support garbage collection?

3.6 Do you think the use of the **exit** statement in Ada leads to readable and reliable programs?

3.7 Why is recursion not allowed in occam 2?

3.8 List the language features you feel are desirable for secure programming.

Chapter 4
Programming in the Large

In Chapter 3 it was noted that decomposition and abstraction are the two most important methods that can be used to manage the complexity characteristic of large, embedded systems. This complexity is due not just to amount of code but to the variety of activities and requirements that are commensurate with real-world interaction. As was observed in Section 1.3.1, the real world is also subject to continuous change. Furthermore, the design, implementation and maintenance of software is often poorly managed and results in unsatisfactory products. This chapter considers those language features that help to embody and support decomposition and the use of abstraction. These features are said to aid *programming in the large*.

The key structure that is missing from older languages, such as Pascal, is the module. A module can be described, informally, as a collection of logically related objects and operations. The technique of isolating a system function within a module and providing a precise specification for the interface to the module is called **encapsulation**. Consequently, with a module structure it is possible to support:

- information hiding,
- abstract data types,
- separate compilation.

71

In the following sections the major motivations for a module structure are described. These needs are illustrated by examples coded in Ada and Modula-2. Occam 2, by comparison, does not support modular decomposition. The importance of the module structure is well witnessed by the fact that Modula-2 derives its name from MODUle LAnguage.

4.1 Information hiding

In simple languages all permanent variables have to be global. If two or more procedures wish to share data then that data must be visible to all other parts of the program. Even if a single procedure wishes to update some variable each time it is called, this variable must be declared outside the procedure, and, therefore, the possibility of misuse and error exists.

A module structure allows for reduced visibility by allowing information to be hidden inside the module's 'body'. All module structures (of which there are many different models) allow the programmer to control access to module variables. To illustrate information hiding, consider the implementation of a First-In, First-Out (FIFO) dynamic queue. The interface of the queue manager (to the rest of the program) is via three procedures that allow elements to be added to or removed from the queue, and to provide a test for the queue being empty. It is not desirable that internal information about the queue (such as the queue pointer) should be visible outside the module. The following provides a module in Modula-2 for this list structure.

```
MODULE queuemod;

    IMPORT element;
    IMPORT ALLOCATE, DEALLOCATE;
    EXPORT empty, insert, remove;

    TYPE
        queueptr = POINTER TO queuenode;
        queuenode = RECORD
                        contents : element;
                        next : queueptr
                    END;
        queue = POINTER TO RECORD
                    front : queueptr;
                    back : queueptr
                END;
    VAR
        Q : queue;
```

```
PROCEDURE create;
BEGIN
  NEW(Q);
  Q ↑ .front := NIL;
  Q ↑ .back := NIL;
END create;

PROCEDURE empty() : BOOLEAN;
BEGIN
  RETURN Q ↑ .front = NIL
END empty;

PROCEDURE insert(P : element);
VAR
  newnode : queueptr;
BEGIN
  NEW(newnode);
  newnode ↑ .contents := P;
  newnode ↑ .next := NIL;
  IF empty() THEN
    Q ↑ .front := newnode
  ELSE
    Q ↑ .back ↑ .next := newnode
  END;
  Q ↑ .back := newnode
END insert;

PROCEDURE remove(VAR P : element);
VAR
  oldnode : queueptr;
BEGIN
  oldnode := Q ↑ .front;
  P := oldnode ↑ .contents;
  Q ↑ .front := Q ↑ .front ↑ .next;
  IF Q ↑ .front = NIL THEN
    Q ↑ .back := NIL
  END;
  DISPOSE(oldnode)
END remove;
BEGIN                              (* module initialization *)
  create
END queuemod;
```

Note that only objects explicitly mentioned in the EXPORT list are visible outside the module given above. It is also important to realize that a Modula-2 module also controls access to the external objects it 'sees' within other modules. Hence, element is a type that is visible at the point of declaration of the module.

Having declared this module the queue can be used (but only by means of the exported procedures). For example:

```
IF NOT empty() THEN
    remove(E)                (* E of type element *)
END
```

It is usual to construct Modula-2 (and Ada) programs as collections of library units (see Section 4.2) but, unfortunately, this could lead to ambiguity if more than one module exports an identifier of the same name. To combat this, Modula-2 allows an identifier to be exported in a QUALIFIED state:

```
EXPORT QUALIFIED empty, insert, remove;
```

If an identifier is qualified, its name must be prefixed by the module name when used, for example:

```
IF NOT queuemod.empty() THEN
    queuemod.remove(E)
END
```

The Ada implementation of the queue module has much in common with the above. Points of difference are:

- An Ada module (called **package**) is always declared in two parts; *specification* and *body*. Only objects declared in the specification are visible externally.
- Ada uses 'open scope'. All identifiers visible at the point of the package declaration can be accessed within the **package**. There is no import list.
- All exported Ada identifiers are qualified.

The queue module in Ada is as follows:

```
package QUEUEMOD is
    function EMPTY return BOOLEAN;
    procedure INSERT (E : ELEMENT);
    procedure REMOVE (E : out ELEMENT);
end QUEUEMOD;

package body QUEUEMOD is
                                -- essentially the same as
                                -- modula-2 code
end QUEUEMOD;
```

Both the specification and the body of a **package** must be placed within the same declarative part, although other objects may be defined between the two parts. In this way two **package**s can call subprograms in each other without the need of forward declarations.

Any **package** can be used if it is in scope. To reduce the need for excessive naming a **use** statement is provided:

```
declare
  use QUEUEMOD;
begin
  if not EMPTY then
     REMOVE(E);
  end if;
end;
```

The importance of the module construct to real-time programming cannot be over emphasized. The provisions of Ada and Modula-2 are well illustrated by the above example. In terms of a general module structure they are, however, both static models. Modules and packages are not first-class objects and there are, as a result, some useful algorithms that cannot be coded in the two languages because of this restriction. Advocates of the dynamic language Simula are never slow to point out that the class concept has been available within that language since the late 1960s. More recently Smalltalk-80 has shown the power of a dynamic module structure. Smalltalk-80 is not, however, a real-time programming language.

4.2 Separate compilation

If a program is constructed from modules then there are obvious advantages in having these modules compiled separately. Such a program is said to be compiled within the context of a library. Programmers can, therefore, concentrate on the current module but be able to construct, at least in part, the complete program so that their module can be tested. Once tested, and possibly authorized, the new unit can be added to the library in a precompiled form. As well as supporting project management there are clearly resource savings if the entire program does not have to be recompiled for each minor edit.

In Ada the package specification and body, as outlined in Section 4.1, can be precompiled in a straightforward manner. If a library unit wishes to have access to any other library unit then it must indicate this, explicitly, using a **with** clause:

```
package DISPATCHER is
  -- new visible objects
end DISPATCHER;
```

```
with QUEUEMOD;
package body DISPATCHER is
  -- hidden objects
end DISPATCHER;
```

In this way a hierarchy of dependencies between library units is constructed. If for some reason a library unit is changed and has to be recompiled then all other units that are dependent upon it must also be recompiled. The main program itself uses **with** clauses to gain access to the library units it requires.

An important feature of the Ada model is that the package specification and body are seen as distinct entities in the library. Obviously, both must be present for the final program compilation. (To be completely accurate some package specifications do not require a body; for example, if they only define types or variables.) During program development, however, a library may contain only specifications. These can be used to check the logical consistency of the program prior to the detailed implementation work. Within the context of project management, specifications may well be done by more senior staff. This is because the specification represents an interface between software components. An error in such code is more serious than one within a package body.

The Modula-2 equivalent of Ada's library packages is to split a normal module structure into two parts: a definition module and an implementation module. For example, the queuemod module could be made a library unit by changing it to the following (which is very similar to the Ada structure).

```
DEFINITION MODULE queuemod;

  FROM TypeDefnModule IMPORT element;

  PROCEDURE empty() : BOOLEAN;
  PROCEDURE insert(P : element);
  PROCEDURE remove(VAR P : element)

END queuemod.

IMPLEMENTATION MODULE queuemod;
  (* this module has the same structure as the original *)
END queuemod.
```

Rather than use 'with' clauses, Modula-2 gives a more controlled mechanism. The statement:

```
FROM TypeDefnModule IMPORT element;
```

ensures that only element is imported. To gain access to ELEMENT in Ada requires all of TYPE_DEFN_MODULE to be visible:

```
with TYPE_DEFN_MODULE;
package QUEUEMOD is ...
```

Both of these separate compilation models support bottom-up programming. Library units are built up from other units until the final program can be coded. Bottom-up programming within the context of top-down design is quite acceptable; especially as it is bottom-up in terms of specifications (definitions) not implementations (bodies). Nevertheless, Ada has included a further feature of separate compilation that supports, more directly, top-down design. Within a program unit a 'stub' can be left for inclusion later by using the **is separate** keywords. For example, the following schema shows how the procedure CONVERT can be left unimplemented until after the main program has been defined:

```
with IO_MODULE; use IO_MODULE;
procedure MAIN is
   type READING is ...
   type CONTROL_VALUE is ...
   procedure CONVERT (R : READING; CV :
               out CONTROL_VALUE) is separate;
begin
   loop
     INPUT (RD);
     CONVERT(RD, CV);
     OUTPUT (CV);
   end loop;
end;
```

Later the procedure bodies are added:

```
separate (MAIN)
procedure CONVERT (R : READING; CV : out CONTROL_VALUE) is
   -- actual required code
end CONVERT;
```

In both Ada and Modula-2 separate compilation is integrated into the language specification. Most importantly, the strong typing rules that would apply if the program was constructed as a single unit apply equally across library units. This is a much more reliable mechanism than the linking together of precompiled units (as supported in some implementations of FORTRAN and Pascal). With this latter approach comprehensive type-checking is not possible. However, some languages have a specific support tool available to check consistency across compilation units, for example LINT, used with C.

4.3   Abstract data types

In Chapter 3 it was noted that one of the major advantages of high-level languages is that programmers do not have to concern themselves with the physical representation of the data in the computer. From this separation comes the idea of data types. Abstract Data Types (ADT) are a further extension of this concept. To define an ADT, a module will name a new type and then give all the operations that can be applied to that type. The structure of the ADT is hidden within the module.

Although a number of languages (that are not real time) give very powerful facilities for ADT (notably CLU (Liskov *et al.*, 1977)), adequate mechanisms for ADT are supported in both Modula-2 and Ada. These features will be described here, starting first with Modula-2 and the queue module example. The major criticisms of the module, as it has so far been given, is that only one queue has been defined. To improve the usefulness of this module a type for queue is required. This type is best given as an ADT as the structure of objects of type queue is of no concern to users of the queues. The definition module, therefore, becomes:

```
DEFINITION MODULE queuemod;

    FROM TypeDefnModule IMPORT element;

    TYPE queue;

    PROCEDURE create(VAR Q : queue);
    PROCEDURE empty(Q : queue) : BOOLEAN;
    PROCEDURE insert(VAR Q : queue; P : element);
    PROCEDURE remove(VAR Q : queue; VAR P : element);

END queuemod.
```

Note that the procedure, create, has to be incorporated into the definition module, as all objects of type queue must be initialized, not just the one that the module previously defined.

With this module a program can define arbitrary numbers of queues and operate upon them using the specified subprograms. For example:

```
VAR q1, q2 : queue;
    collection : ARRAY [1..n] OF queue;
    ...
BEGIN
  create(q1);
  ...
  insert(q1, E);
  (* and so on *)
END
```

The advantage of abstract data types is that they give a clear and complete definition of all the operations that are applicable to that type. The type is truly an abstraction. Users of this module are concerned with queues not linked lists or whatever other means are used to implement the type. Another important benefit of ADT (and other information-hiding structures) is that the hidden parts can be changed without ramifications for the rest of the program as long as the semantics of the specification are not altered.

The actual implementation of type queue, in this example, is given in the implementation module:

```
IMPLEMENTATION MODULE queuemod;


    FROM TypeDefnModule IMPORT element;
    FROM Storage IMPORT ALLOCATE,DEALLOCATE;


    TYPE
        queueptr = POINTER TO queuenode;
        queuenode = RECORD
                        contents : processid;
                        next : queueptr
                    END;
        queue = POINTER TO RECORD
                    front : queueptr;
                    back : queueptr
                END;


    PROCEDURE create(VAR Q : queue);                    (* essentially as before *)
    PROCEDURE empty(Q : queue) : BOOLEAN;               (* as before *)
    PROCEDURE insert(VAR Q : queue; P : processid);     (* as before *)
    PROCEDURE remove(VAR Q : queue; VAR P : processid); (* as before *)


END queuemod.
```

The Ada facility for ADT is complicated by the requirement for the separate compilation of a package specification from its body. As the structure of an ADT is meant to be hidden, the logical place for it to be defined is in the body. But then the compiler will not know the size of the type when it is compiling code which is using the specification. One way of getting around this problem is to use a level of indirection. Although this is quite an acceptable approach (and is, in essence, what is done in Modula-2) it is inefficient and for this reason Ada uses a different model: it allows part of the implementation to appear in the specification but to be accessible only from the package body. This is called the **private** part of the specification.

Keeping with the queue example, for comparison, the Ada definition of an ADT for QUEUE is as follows:

```
package QUEUEMOD is
  type QUEUE is limited private;
  procedure CREATE (Q : in out QUEUE);
  function EMPTY (Q : QUEUE) return BOOLEAN;
  procedure INSERT (Q : in out QUEUE; E : ELEMENT);
  procedure REMOVE (Q : in out QUEUE; E : out ELEMENT);
private
  -- none of the following declarations are externally visible
  type QUEUEMOD;
  type QUEUEPTR is access QUEUENODE;
  type QUEUENODE is
    record
      CONTENTS : ELEMENT;
      NEXT : QUEUEPTR;
    end record;
  type QUEUE is
    record
      FRONT : QUEUEPTR;
      BACK : QUEUEPTR;
    end record;
end QUEUEMOD;

package body QUEUEMOD is
  -- essentially the same as the Module-2 code
end QUEUEMOD;
```

The term **limited private** means that only those subprograms defined in this package can be applied to the type. A limited private type is, therefore, a true abstract data **type**. However, Ada recognizes that many ADTs need the assignment operator and tests for equality. Therefore, rather than have these be defined on all occasions that they are needed, a type can be declared as just **private**. If this is the case then in addition to the defined subprograms, assignment and the equality test are available to the user. The following gives a common example of an ADT in Ada. It provides a package for complex arithmetic. Note that the subprograms defined with the type COMPLEX take the form of overloaded operations and so allow 'normal' arithmetic expressions to be written:

```
package COMPLEX_ARITHMETIC is
  type COMPLEX is private;
  function " + " (X,Y : COMPLEX) return COMPLEX;
  function " - " (X,Y : COMPLEX) return COMPLEX;
  function " * " (X,Y : COMPLEX) return COMPLEX;
  function "/" (X,Y : COMPLEX) return COMPLEX;
  function COMP (A,B : FLOAT) return COMPLEX;
  function REAL_PART (X : COMPLEX) return FLOAT;
```

```
    function IMAG_PART (X : COMPLEX) return FLOAT;
private
    type COMPLEX is
        record
            REAL_PART : FLOAT;
            IMAG_PART : FLOAT;
        end record;
end COMPLEX_ARITHMETIC;
```

4.3.1   Object-oriented programming

It has become fashionable to call variables of an ADT **objects** and to designate the programming paradigm that leads to their use **Object-Oriented Design** (OOD). As Ada and Modula-2 both support a form of ADT, they can be used with OOD. Indeed, the use of Ada and OOD together has become popular (Booch, 1986).

There is, however, a stricter definition of an object abstraction (Wegner, 1987) that draws a useful distinction between objects and ADTs. In general, ADTs lack four properties that would make them suitable for object-oriented programming:

(1)   type extensibility (inheritance);

(2)   automatic object initialization (constructors);

(3)   automatic object finalization (destructors);

(4)   polymorphism.

In the queue example given earlier in Section 4.3, it was necessary to declare a queue variable and then call a create procedure to initialize it. With a language that supports OOD this initialization (using a constructor routine) would be done automatically on each queue object as it was declared. Similarly, as an object goes out of scope a destructor procedure is executed.

Properties (2) and (3) are useful but the significant concept in an object abstraction is extensibility. This enables a type to be defined as an extension of a previously defined type. The new type inherits the 'base' type but may include new fields and new operations (Wirth, 1988a).

Although a kind of inheritance can be programmed in Ada using nested generics (see the next section) this is not very satisfactory. It is not an easy technique to apply and it leads to poor readability. Other languages give much more explicit support to extensibility.

The class structure in Simula 67 (Birtwistle *et al.*, 1973) is the earliest example of extensibility. It has since been adopted in a number of derivations, notably Smalltalk-80 (Goldberg and Robson, 1983), Object Pascal (Tesler, 1986), Eiffel (Meyer, 1987) and C++ (Stroustrup, 1986, 1988).

More recently, the language Oberon (Wirth, 1988b, 1988c), which has evolved from Modula-2, has been defined. The principal new feature incorporated into Oberon is a model for type extension (a number of Modula-2 features have, however, been omitted). Modula-3 (Cardelli *et al.*, 1988) has also built upon its namesake and is perhaps a more object-oriented language than Oberon. Multiple inheritance (inheriting the attributes of more than one base type) is supported in some dialects of Lisp (Moon, 1986).

None of these examples are real-time languages. Although inheritance does appear to be a useful concept in software engineering, it is still not clear that its implementation does not have the penalty of a significant run-time overhead. Experience of the language Oberon may clarify this issue in the future.

4.4   Reusability

Software production is an expensive business with costs rising inexorably every year. One reason for the high costs is that software always seems to be constructed 'from scratch'. By comparison, the hardware engineer has a rich choice of well-tried and tested components from which systems can be built. It has been a long-held quest of software engineers to have a similar supply of software components. Unfortunately, apart from some specific areas (for example, numerical analysis) this quest has been largely unfulfilled. And yet reusable code would clearly have a beneficial effect on both the reliability and productivity of software construction.

One drawback to reusability is the strong typing model that was commended in Chapter 3. With such a model a component for sorting integers, for example, cannot be used for sorting reals or records even though the basic algorithms are identical. This type of restriction, although necessary for other reasons, severely restricts reusability. The designers of Ada have addressed this issue and have provided a facility that aids reuse without undermining the typing model. This facility allows **generic** modules to be defined. As was noted above, however, Ada does not go as far as providing full type extensibility.

A **generic** is a template from which actual components can be **instantiated**. In essence, a generic will manipulate objects without regard to their type. An instantiation specifies an actual type. The language model ensures that any assumptions made about the type within the generic are checked against the type named in the instantiation. For example, a generic may assume that a *generic parameter* is of a discrete type. When an instantiation is made the compiler will check that the specified type is discrete.

A measure of a generic's 'reusability' can be derived from the restrictions placed on the generic parameters. At one extreme if the instantiated type has to be, for example, a one dimensional array of an integer type, then the generic is not particularly reusable. Alternatively, if any type can be used at instantiation then a high level of reuse has been obtained.

The parameter model for Ada generics is comprehensive and will not be described in detail here; rather, a couple of examples will be given that have high reusability.

Generic parameters are defined in a way that specifies what operations are applied to them within the generic body. If no operations at all are applied then the parameters are said to be **limited private**. If only assignments and equality tests are performed then the parameters are **private**. Components with high reuse have limited private or private parameters. For a first example consider the QUEUEMOD package. As so far given, although an abstract data type for QUEUE is provided, all such queues must only hold objects of type ELEMENT. There is clearly a need for a generic in which the type of the object being manipulated is a parameter. Within the package body for QUEUEMOD, objects of type ELEMENT were only assigned in and out of queues. The parameter can, therefore, be private:

```
generic
   type ELEMENT is private;
package QUEUEMOD_TEMPLATE is
   type QUEUE is limited private;
   procedure CREATE (Q : in out QUEUE);
   function EMPTY (Q : QUEUE) return BOOLEAN;
   procedure INSERT (Q : in out QUEUE; E : ELEMENT);
   procedure REMOVE (Q : in out QUEUE; E : out ELEMENT);
private
   type QUEUEPTR is access QUEUENODE;
   type QUEUENODE is
      record
         CONTENTS : PROCESSID;
         NEXT : QUEUEPTR;
      end record;
   type QUEUE is
      record
         FRONT : QUEUEPTR;
         BACK : QUEUEPTR;
      end record;
end QUEUEMOD_TEMPLATE;


package body QUEUEMOD_TEMPLATE is
   -- the same as before
end QUEUEMOD_TEMPLATE;
```

An instantiation of this generic creates an actual package:

```
declare
  package INTEGER_QUEUES
          is new QUEUEMOD_TEMPLATE(INTEGER);
  type PROCESSID is
    record
      ...
    end record;
  package PROCESS_QUEUES
          is new QUEUEMOD_TEMPLATE(PROCESSID);
  Q1, Q2 : INTEGER_QUEUES.QUEUE;
  PID : PROCESS_QUEUES.QUEUE;
  P : PROCESSID;
  use INTEGER_QUEUES;
  use PROCESS_QUEUES;
begin
  CREATE(Q1);
  CREATE(PID);
  ...
  INSERT(PID,P);
  ...
end;
```

Each of these packages defines an abstract data type for QUEUE. But they are different as the element types are distinct.

The discussion so far has concentrated upon generic parameters as types. Two other forms are available: constants and subprograms. BUFFERs are often an important construct within real-time programs. They differ from QUEUEs in that they have a fixed size. The following shows the specification of a generic package for an abstract data type for BUFFERs. Again, the ELEMENT type is a generic parameter. In addition, the size of the BUFFER is a generic constant parameter; it has a default value of 32:

```
generic
  SIZE : NATURAL := 32;
  type ELEMENT is private;
package BUFFER_TEMPLATE is
  type BUFFER is limited private;
  procedure CREATE(B : in out BUFFER);
  function EMPTY(B : BUFFER) return BOOLEAN;
  procedure PLACE(B : in out BUFFER; E : ELEMENT);
  procedure TAKE(B : in out BUFFER; E : out ELEMENT);
```

```
private
    subtype BUFFER_RANGE is NATURAL range 0..SIZE-1;
    type BUFF is array(BUFFER_RANGE) of ELEMENT;
    type BUFFER is
      record
        BF : BUFF;
        TOP : BUFFER_RANGE := 0;
        BASE: BUFFER_RANGE := 0;
      end record;
end BUFFER_TEMPLATE;
```

An integer BUFFER of size 32 is instantiated as follows:

```
package INTEGER_BUFFERS is new BUFFER_TEMPLATE(INTEGER);
```

A BUFFER with 64 elements of some record type REC is constructed with a similar instantiation:

```
package REC_BUFFERS is new BUFFER_TEMPLATE(64,REC);
```

As with subprogram parameters, greater readability is furnished by using name association:

```
package REC_BUFFERS
            is new BUFFER_TEMPLATE(SIZE ⇒ 64,ELEMENT ⇒ REC);
```

An example of a generic subprogram parameter is now given. The generic package defines two procedures which both act upon an array of ELEMENTs. One procedure finds the largest ELEMENT; the other sorts the array. To implement these procedures it is necessary to compare any two ELEMENTs to see which is the greater. For scalar types the '>' operator is available; for general private types it is not. It follows that the generic package must import a GREATER_THAN function.

```
generic
    SIZE : NATURAL;
    type ELEMENT is private;
    with function GREATER_THAN(E1, E2 : ELEMENT) return BOOLEAN;
package ARRAY_SORT is
    type VECTOR is array(1..SIZE) of ELEMENT;
    procedure SORT(V : in out VECTOR);
    function LARGEST(V : VECTOR) return ELEMENT;
end ARRAY_SORT;
```

The implementation of this generic package is left as an exercise (Exercise 4.7) for the reader.

Modula-2 does not provide a generic facility that is at all comparable with Ada's. Rather, it defines a primitive facility, from which generic components can be built. With every Modula-2 implementation a module called SYSTEM is included. This module exports several data types and procedures that are machine dependent. Some of these are used to create processes and are discussed later in Chapter 7. The details of SYSTEM necessarily vary from one implementation to another but there would typically be a type WORD, and a type ADDRESS defined.

Strict type-checking can be bypassed in Modula-2 by accessing data in terms of the underlying machine representation. In particular, if a formal parameter to a procedure is given the type ARRAY OF WORD then the corresponding actual parameter may be any type, static, dynamic or structured. Within the procedure the parameter can only be accessed as an array of words. However, if only assignments and tests for equality are made on such objects then the internal structure of the calling parameter is not corrupted. It follows that a facility very similar to the private generic parameter of Ada is available in Modula-2. The only distinction between the languages is that with queue and buffer type modules the maximum size of the incoming object must be pre-set in Modula-2.

The next example shows how a module is constructed that stores a single message for some other component. No assumption is made about the type of the message other than that its size is less than 16 words. Note that the predefined function HIGH gives the actual number of words associated with the type of the calling parameter.

```
MODULE MessageStore;

  FROM SYSTEM IMPORT WORD;
  EXPORT place,take;

  VAR store : ARRAY[0..15] OF WORD;

  PROCEDURE place(A : ARRAY OF WORD);
  VAR P : CARDINAL;
  BEGIN
    FOR P : = 0 TO HIGH(A) DO
      store[P] : = A[P]
    END
  END place;

  PROCEDURE take(VAR A : ARRAY OF WORD);
  VAR P : CARDINAL;
  BEGIN
    FOR P : = 0 TO HIGH(A) DO
      A[P] : = store[P]
    END
   END take;
END MessageStore;
```

4.5   Integrated project support environments

The introduction of the module construct into modern real-time programming languages has greatly enhanced the expressive power of those languages. However, it is important to realize that there is more to software development than simply using a programming language (even when the language is well constructed). To manage effectively the development of large-scale software requires support at all stages of the life cycle, from initial requirements specification, through design and implementation, to maintenance. The bringing together, or integration, of methods and tools, can provide the basis for significant improvements in the quality of software and the productivity and predictability of software development (Hall, 1987). A computer-based environment which attempts to provide such support is called an Integrated Project Support Environment or IPSE (another term used is Software Engineering Environment – SEE).

One of the key roles for an IPSE is to provide an infrastructure for tool interaction. An IPSE has facilities (accessible through a well-defined interface) to control all data which is developed during a project's life cycle. Tools are made available to support the structuring and storing of information (for example, documents and program modules), the configuration and version control of data items, and the sharing of data among project managers, systems designers and programmers. In order to allow an IPSE to be flexible its interface is designed to be extensible so that it can support new methods and tools, and reconfigurable, so that a project can impose a particular method of working, if desired (Brown, 1988).

Initially, IPSEs were designed to support project development in a single programming language. For example, early in the design of Ada it was recognized that there was a need for an Ada Programming Support Environment (APSE) (US Department of Defense, 1980). This led to the definition of a set of requirements which outlined the basic architectural components of an APSE. A similar design is found in most IPSEs. At the heart of an APSE is a database which records data items and their relationships in a structured and accessible form. The database provides the meta-information needed for tool communication. Together with the run-time system necessary to support the execution of Ada programs (on the development system rather than the embedded target) this database facility constitutes the Kernel Ada Programming Support Environment (KAPSE). The addition of a minimal set of tools to support the creation and maintenance of Ada programs (such as compilers, editors and debuggers) forms a Minimal Ada Programming Support Environment (MAPSE). Finally, a full APSE is constructed by extending the MAPSE to provide support for different programming methodologies and techniques. An important feature of the architecture is, therefore, the interface between the KAPSE and MAPSE.

Current research focuses on integrating tools written in a variety of programming languages. Two standardization programmes have been initiated to aid the portability of tools; these concentrate on the interface between the IPSE and the tools. In the United States the DoD have proposed a military standard Common APSE Interface Set (CAIS). In Europe the ESPRIT programme has provided funds for the definition of a Portable Common Tool Environment (PCTE) to be used throughout the ESPRIT community. Although there are a number of important differences between CAIS and PCTE, there are also significant similarities. It is to be hoped that both models will evolve towards a single standard.

SUMMARY

In the evolution of programming languages one of the most important constructs to have emerged is the module. This structure enables the complexity inherent in large real-time systems to be contained and managed. In particular it supports:

(1)   information hiding,

(2)   separate compilation,

(3)   abstract data types.

Both Ada and Modula-2 have a static module structure. Ada uses 'open scope' so that all objects in scope at the declaration of a module are visible within it. Modula-2's rule gives more control; only those objects explicitly mentioned in an IMPORT list can be accessed inside the module's body. Both modules in Modula-2 and packages in Ada have well-defined specifications which act as the interface between the module and the rest of the program.

Separate compilation enables libraries of precompiled components to be constructed. This encourages reusability and provides a repository for project software. This repository must, however, be subject to appropriate project management so that issues such as version control do not become a source of unreliability. The use of an Integrated Project Support Environment (IPSE) can significantly improve the control that can be administered over the software production process.

The decomposition of a large program into modules is the essence of programming in the large. It is, however, important that this decomposition process does lead to well-defined modules.

The use of Abstract Data Types (ADTs), or object-oriented programming, provides one of the main tools that programmers can use in order to manage large software systems. Again, it is the module construct in both Ada and Module-2 that enable ADTs to be built and used. In Ada, for example, objects of a type defined to be limited private can only be manipulated via subprograms defined with the type. If assignment and tests for equality are needed with the abstract type then it should be defined to be merely private.

Languages that are strongly typed suffer from the restriction that modules cannot easily be reused as their behaviour is tied to the types of their parameters and subcomponents. This dependency is often more than is required. Ada's provision of a generic primitive is an attempt to improve the reusability of software. Generic packages and procedures can be defined which act as templates from which real code can be instantiated. Their appropriate use should reduce the cost, whilst improving the reliability, of real-time programs. Modula-2 has a form of generic facility but it is much more low level.

Further reading

Booch G. (1987). *Software Engineering with Ada*. Menlo Park CA: Benjamin Cummings

Hall J.A. (1987). Integrated project support environments. *Computer Standards and Interfaces*, **6**(1), 89–96

Hitchcock P., ed. (1990). *ASPECT: An Integrated Project Support Environment*. Cambridge MA: MIT Press

Sommerville I. (1985). *Software Engineering* 2nd edn. Wokingham: Addison-Wesley

Stroustrup B. (1986). *The C++ Programming Language*. Reading MA: Addison-Wesley

EXERCISES

4.1 Why is the procedure not sufficient as a program module?

4.2 Distinguish between separate compilation, independent compilation and multiprogramming.

4.3 What advantages and disadvantages would there be to having Ada packages and Modula-2 modules as first-class language objects?

4.4 Should a language allow procedures to be passed as parameters to procedures? How does Ada achieve this effect?

4.5 Ada uses static binding. In object-oriented languages binding is dynamic. Should a real-time programming language only use static binding?

4.6 Define an abstract data type for time. What operations are applicable on time values?

4.7 Implement the Ada generic package, ARRAY_SORT, given in Section 4.4. Illustrate its use by showing how to sort any array of buffers (assume that one buffer is 'greater than' another if it has more elements in it).

Chapter 5
Reliability and Fault Tolerance

Reliability and safety requirements are usually much more stringent for embedded systems than for other computer systems. For example, if an application which computes the solution to some scientific problem fails then it may be reasonable to abort the program as only computer time has been lost. However, in the case of a real-time system this may not be an acceptable action. A process-control computer for instance, responsible for the operation of a large gas furnace, cannot afford to close down the furnace as soon as a fault occurs. Instead it must try to provide a degraded service and prevent a costly shut-down operation. More importantly, real-time computer systems may endanger human lives if they abandon control of their application. An embedded computer controlling a nuclear reactor must not let the reactor run out of control, as this may result in a core melt-down and an emission of radiation. An avionics system should at least allow the pilot to eject before permitting the plane to crash!

Nowadays, more and more control functions previously performed by human operators or proven analogue methods, are being administered by digital computers. In 1955 only 10% of the United States weapons systems required computer software; by the early 1980s this figure had risen to 80% (Leveson, 1986). There are many examples where faults in software have resulted in mission failures. In the early 1970s, the software in a French meteorological satellite responsible for controlling high-altitude weather balloons issued an 'emergency self-destruct' request instead of a 'read data' request. The outcome was that 72 out of 141 balloons were destroyed (Leveson, 1986). Many similarly alarming examples have been documented, and it is reasonable to assume that far more have not. In 1986 Hecht and Hecht (Hecht, 1986a) studied large software systems and concluded that, typically, for every million lines of code 20 000 bugs entered the software; normally 90% of these were found by testing. A further 200 faults would surface during the first year of operation leaving 1800 bugs undetected. Routine maintenance would usually result in 200 bug fixes and 200 new faults!

The more that society relinquishes control of its vital functions to computer systems the more imperative it becomes that those systems do not fail. Without wishing to define precisely what is meant by a system failure or a fault (at the moment) there are, in general, four sources of faults which can result in an embedded system failure.

(1)   Inadequate specification. It has been suggested that the great majority of software faults stem from inadequate specification (Leveson, 1986).

(2)   Faults introduced from design errors in software components.

(3)   Faults introduced by failure of one or more processor components of the embedded systems.

(4)   Faults introduced by transient or permanent interference in the supporting communication subsystem.

It is these last three types of faults which impinge on the programming language used in the implementation of an embedded system. The errors introduced by design faults are, in general, unanticipated (in terms of their consequences), whereas those from processor and network failure are, in some senses, predictable. One of the main requirements, therefore, for any real-time programming language is that it must facilitate the construction of highly-dependable systems. In this chapter some of the general design techniques that can be used to improve the overall reliability of embedded computer systems are considered. In Chapter 6 it will be seen how **exception handling** facilities can be used to help implement some of these design philosophies, particularly those based on **fault tolerance**. Issues concerning processor and communication failure are deferred until Chapter 13.

5.1 Reliability, failure and faults

Before proceeding, more precise definitions of reliability, failures and faults are necessary. Randell *et al.* (1978b) define the **reliability** of a system to be:

> a measure of the success with which the system conforms to some authoritative specification of its behaviour.

Ideally, this specification should be complete, consistent, comprehensible and unambiguous. It should also be noted that the **response times** of the system are an important part of the specification, although discussion of the meeting of deadlines will be postponed until Chapter 12. The definition of reliability can now be used to define a system **failure**. Again quoting from Randell *et al.* (1978b).

> When the behaviour of a system deviates from that which is specified for it, this is called a failure.

Section 5.8 will deal with the metrics of reliability; for the time being *highly reliable* will be considered synonymous with a *low failure rate*.

The alert reader will have noticed that our definitions so far have been concerned with the *behaviour* of a system; that is, its *external* appearance. Failures result from unexpected problems internal to the system which eventually manifest themselves in the system's external behaviour. These problems are called **errors** and their mechanical or algorithmic cause are termed **faults**. A faulty component of a system is, therefore, a component which, under a particular set of circumstances during the lifetime of the system, will result in an error. Viewed in terms of state transitions, a system can be considered as a number of *external* and *internal* states. An external state which is not specified in the behaviour of the system is regarded as a failure of the system. The system itself consists of a number of components, each with their own states, all of which contribute to the system's external behaviour. The combined state of these components is termed the internal state of the system. An internal state which is not specified is called an error and the component which produced the illegal state transition is said to be faulty.

Three types of faults can be distinguished.

(1)   **Transient faults**. A transient fault starts at a particular time, remains in the system for some period and then disappears. Examples of such faults are hardware components which have an adverse reaction to some external interference, such as electrical fields or radioactivity. After the disturbance disappears so does the fault (although not necessarily the induced error). Many faults in communication systems are transient.

(2)   **Permanent faults**. Permanent faults start at a particular time and remain in the system until they are repaired; for example, a broken wire or a software design error.

(3)   **Intermittent faults**. These are transient faults that occur from time to time. An example is a hardware component that is heat sensitive, it works for a time, stops working, cools down and then starts to work again.

To create reliable systems all these types of faults must be prevented from causing erroneous system behaviour (that is, failure). The difficulty this presents is compounded by the indirect use of computers in the *construction* of safety critical systems. For example, in 1979 an error was discovered in a program used to design nuclear reactors and their supporting cooling systems. The fault that this caused in the reactor design had not been found during installation tests as it concerned the strength and structural support of pipes and valves. The program had supposedly guaranteed the attainment of earthquake safety standards in operating reactors. The discovery of the bug led to the shutting down of five nuclear power plants (Leveson, 1986).

5.2   Fault prevention and fault tolerance

Two approaches that can help designers improve the reliability of their systems can be distinguished (Anderson and Lee, 1981). The first is known as **fault prevention**; this attempts to eliminate any possibility of faults creeping into a system before it goes operational. The second is **fault tolerance**; this enables a system to continue functioning even in the presence of faults.

5.2.1   Fault prevention

There are two stages to fault prevention: **fault avoidance** and **fault removal**.

Fault avoidance attempts to limit the introduction of potentially faulty components during the construction of the system. For hardware this may entail (Randell *et al.*, 1978b):

- the use of the most reliable components within the given cost and performance constraints;
- the use of thoroughly-refined techniques for the interconnection of components and the assembly of subsystems;
- packaging the hardware to screen out expected forms of interference.

The software components of large, embedded systems are nowadays much more complex than their hardware counterparts. Although software does not deteriorate with use, it is virtually impossible in all cases to write fault-free programs. It was noted in Chapters 2 and 4, however, that the quality of software can be improved by:

- rigorous, if not formal, specification of requirements;
- the use of proven design methodologies;
- the use of languages with facilities for data abstraction and modularity;
- the use of project support environments to help manipulate software components and thereby manage complexity.

In spite of fault avoidance techniques, faults will inevitably be present in the system after its construction. In particular, there may be design errors in both hardware and software components. The second stage of fault prevention, therefore, is *fault removal*. This normally consists of procedures for finding and then removing the causes of errors. Although techniques such as design reviews, program verification, and code inspections may be used, emphasis is usually placed on system testing. Unfortunately, system testing can never be exhaustive and remove all potential faults. In particular, the following problems exist.

- A test can only ever be used to show the presence of faults, not their absence.
- It is sometimes impossible to test under realistic conditions – one of the major causes for concern over the American Strategic Defense Initiative is the impossibility of testing the system realistically except under battle conditions. Most tests are done with the system in simulation mode and it is difficult to guarantee that the simulation is comprehensive.

- Errors that have been introduced at the requirements stage of the system's development may not manifest themselves until the system goes operational. For example, in the design of the F18 aircraft an erroneous assumption was made concerning the length of time taken to release a wing-mounted missile. The problem was discovered when the missile failed to separate from the launcher after ignition, causing the aircraft to go violently out of control (Leveson, 1986).

In spite of all the testing and verification techniques, hardware components will fail; the fault prevention approach will, therefore, be unsuccessful when either the frequency or duration of repair times are unacceptable, or the system is inaccessible for maintenance and repair activities. An extreme example of the latter is the crewless spacecraft Voyager.

5.2.2   Fault tolerance

Because of the inevitable limitations of the fault prevention approach, designers of embedded systems must consider the use of fault tolerance. Of course this does not mean that attempts at preventing faulty systems from becoming operational should be abandoned. However, this book will focus on fault tolerance rather than fault prevention.

Several different levels of fault tolerance can be provided by a system.

- *Full fault tolerance* (or fail operational) – the system continues to operate in the presence of faults, albeit for a limited period, with no significant loss of functionality or performance.
- *Graceful degradation* (or failsoft) – the system continues to operate in the presence of errors, accepting a partial degradation of functionality or performance during recovery or repair.
- *Failsafe* – the system maintains its integrity while accepting a temporary halt in its operation.

The level of fault tolerance required will depend on the application. Although in theory most safety critical systems require full fault tolerance, in practice many settle for graceful degradation. In particular, those systems which can suffer physical damage, such as combat aircraft, may provide several degrees of graceful degradation. Also with highly complex applications which have to operate on a continuous basis (they have *high availability* requirements) graceful degradation is a necessity as full fault tolerance is not achievable for indefinite periods. For example, the new Federal Aviation Administration's Advanced Automation System, which

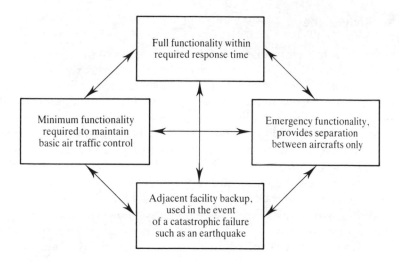

Figure 5.1   Graceful degradation and recovery in an air traffic control system.

will provide automated services to both *enroute* and terminal air traffic controllers throughout the United States, has three levels of graceful degradation for its area control computer couplers (Avizienis and Ball, 1987). This is illustrated in Figure 5.1.

In some situations it may simply be necessary to shut down the system in a safe state. These failsafe systems attempt to limit the amount of damage caused by a failure. For example, the A310 Airbus's slat and flap control computers, on detecting an error on landing, restore the system to a safe state and then shut down. In this situation a safe state is having both wings with the same settings; only asymmetric settings are hazardous in landing (Martin, 1982).

Early approaches to the design of fault-tolerant systems made three assumptions:

(1)   the algorithms of the system have been correctly designed;

(2)   all possible failure modes of the components are known;

(3)   all possible interactions between the system and the environment have been foreseen.

However, the increasing complexity of computer software and the introduction of VLSI hardware components mean that it is no longer possible to make these assumptions (if it ever was). Consequently, both anticipated and unanticipated faults must be catered for. The latter includes both hardware and software design faults.

5.2.3 Redundancy

All techniques for achieving fault tolerance rely on extra elements being introduced into the system in order to detect and recover from faults. These components are redundant in the sense that they are not required for the system's normal mode of operation. This is often called **protective redundancy**. The aim of fault tolerance is to minimize redundancy while maximizing the reliability provided, subject to the cost and size constraints of the system. Care must be taken in structuring fault-tolerant systems because the added components inevitably increase the complexity of the overall system. This itself can lead to *less* reliable systems. For example, the first launch of the space shuttle was aborted because of a synchronization difficulty with the replicated computer systems (Garman, 1981). To help reduce problems associated with the interaction between redundant components it is, therefore, advisable to separate out the fault-tolerant components from the rest of the system.

There are several different classifications of redundancy depending on which system components are under consideration and which terminology is being used. Software fault tolerance is the main focus of this chapter and, therefore, only passing reference will be made to hardware redundancy techniques. For hardware, Anderson and Lee (1981) distinguish between *static* (or masking) and *dynamic* redundancy. With static redundancy, redundant components are used inside a system (or subsystem) to hide the effects of faults. An example of static redundancy is **Triple Modular Redundancy** (TMR). TMR consists of three identical subcomponents and majority-voting circuits. The circuits compare the output of all the components, and if one differs from the other two that output is masked out. The assumption here is that the fault is not due to a common aspect of the subcomponents (such as a design error) but is either transient or due to component deterioration. Clearly, to mask faults from more than one component requires more redundancy. The general term *N* **Modular Redundancy** (NMR) is, therefore, used to characterize this approach.

Dynamic redundancy is the redundancy supplied inside a component which indicates explicitly or implicitly that the output is in error. It therefore provides an *error detection* facility rather than an error-masking facility; recovery must be provided by another component. Examples of dynamic redundancy are checksums on communication transmissions, and parity bits on memories.

For software fault tolerance two general approaches can be identified. The first is analogous to hardware-masking redundancy and is called *N*-version programming. The second is based on error detection and recovery; it is analogous to dynamic redundancy in the sense that the recovery procedures are brought into action after an error has been detected.

5.3   *N*-version programming

The success of hardware TMR and NMR have motivated a similar approach to software fault tolerance. However, software does not deteriorate with use, so the approach is used to focus on detecting design faults. *N*-version programming is defined as the independent generation of *N* (where $N \geqslant 2$) functionally equivalent programs from the same initial specification (Chen and Avizienis, 1978). The independent generation of *N* programs means that *N* individuals or groups produce the required *N* versions of the software *without interaction* (for this reason *N*-version programming is often called **design diversity**.) Once designed and written, the programs execute concurrently with the same inputs and their results are compared by a **driver process**. In principle, the results should be identical but in practice there may be some difference, in which case the consensus result, assuming there is one, is taken to be correct.

N-version programming is based on the assumptions that a program can be completely, consistently and unambiguously specified, and that programs which have been developed independently will fail independently. That is, there is no relationship between the faults in one version and the faults in another. This assumption may be invalidated if each version is written in the same programming language because errors associated with the implementation of the language may be common between versions. Consequently, different programming languages and different development environments should be used. Alternatively, if the same language is used then compilers and support environments from different manufacturers should be employed. Furthermore, in either case, to protect against physical faults, the *N*-versions must be distributed to separate machines which have fault-tolerant communication lines.

The *N*-version program is controlled by a driver process which is responsible for: *240770*

- invoking each of the versions,
- waiting for the versions to complete,
- comparing and acting on the results.

This assumes that the programs or processes run to completion before the results are compared, but for embedded systems this often will not be the case; such processes may never complete. The driver and *N* versions must, therefore, communicate during the course of their executions.

It follows that these versions, although independent, must interact with the driver program. This interaction is specified in the requirements

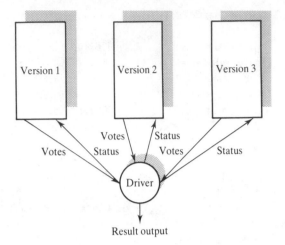

Figure 5.2   *N*-version programming.

for the versions. It consists of three components (Chen and Avizienis, 1978):

(1)   comparison vectors,

(2)   comparison status indicators

(3)   comparison points.

How the versions communicate and synchronize with the driver will depend on the programming language used and its model of concurrency (see Chapters 7,8 and 9). If different languages are used for different versions, then a real-time operating system will usually provide the means of communication and synchronization. The relationship between the *N*-versions and the driver for an $N = 3$ version system is shown diagrammatically in Figure 5.2.

Comparison vectors are the data structures which represent the outputs, or votes, produced by the versions plus any attributes associated with their calculation; these must be compared by the driver. For example, in an air traffic control system, if the values being compared are the positions of aircraft then an attribute may indicate whether the values were the result of a recent radar reading or calculated on the basis of old readings.

The comparison status indicators are communicated from the driver to the versions; they indicate the actions that each version must perform as a result of the driver's comparison. Such actions will depend on the outcome of the comparison: whether the votes agreed and whether they were delivered on time. Possible outcomes include:

- continuation,
- termination of one or more versions,
- continuation after changing one or more votes to the majority value.

The comparison points are the points in the versions where they must communicate their votes to the driver process. As Hecht and Hecht (1986b) point out, an important design decision is the frequency with which the comparisons are made. This is the **granularity** of the fault tolerance provision. Fault tolerance of large granularity, that is, infrequent comparisons, will minimize the performance penalties inherent in the comparison strategies and permit a large measure of independence in the version design. However, a large granularity will probably produce a wide divergence in the results obtained because of the greater number of steps carried out between comparisons. The problems of vote comparison or voting (as it is often called) are considered in the next section. Fault tolerance of a fine granularity requires commonality of program structures at a detailed level and therefore reduces the degree of independence between versions. A frequent number of comparisons also increases the overheads associated with this technique.

5.3.1 Vote comparison

Crucial to N-version programming is the efficiency and the ease with which the driver program can compare votes and decide whether there is any disagreement. For applications which manipulate text or perform integer arithmetic there will normally be a single correct result; the driver can easily compare votes from different versions and choose the majority decision.

Unfortunately, not all results are of an exact nature. In particular, where votes require the calculation of real numbers, it will be unlikely that different versions will produce exactly the same result. This might be due to the inexact hardware representation of real numbers or the data sensitivity of a particular algorithm. The techniques used for comparing these types of results are called **inexact voting**. One simple technique is to conduct a range check using a previous estimation or a median value taken from all N results. However, it can be difficult to find a general inexact voting approach.

Another difficulty associated with finite-precision arithmetic is the so-called **consistent comparison problem** (Brilliant *et al.*, 1987). The trouble occurs when an application has to perform a comparison based on a finite value given in the specification; the result of the comparison then

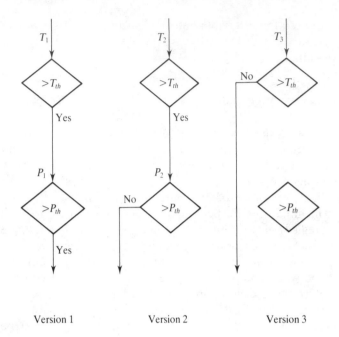

Figure 5.3   Consistent comparison problem with three versions.

determines the course of action to be taken. As an example, consider a process control system which monitors temperature and pressure sensors and then takes appropriate actions according to their values to ensure the integrity of the system. Suppose that when either of these readings passes a threshold value then some corrective course of action must be taken. Now consider a 3-version software system (V_1, V_2, V_3) each of which must read both sensors, decide on some action and then vote on the outcome (there is no communication between the versions until they vote). As a result of finite-precision arithmetic each version will calculate different values (say, T_1, T_2, T_3 for the temperature sensor and P_1, P_2, P_3 for the pressure sensor). Assuming that the threshold value for temperature is T_{th} and for pressure P_{th} then the consistent comparison problem occurs when both readings are around their threshold values.

The situation might occur where T_1 and T_2 are just below T_{th}, and T_3 just above, consequently V_1 and V_2 will follow their normal execution path and V_3 will take some corrective action. Now if versions V_1 and V_2 proceed to another comparison point, this time with the pressure sensor, then it is possible that P_1 could be just below and P_2 just above P_{th}. The overall result will be that all three versions will have followed different execution paths and, therefore, produce different results, each of which is valid. This process is represented diagrammatically in Figure 5.3.

At first sight it might seem appropriate to use inexact comparison techniques and assume that the values are equal if they differ by a tolerance δ but as Brilliant *et al.* (1987) point out, the problem reappears when the values are close to the threshold value $\pm\delta$.

Still further problems exist with vote comparison when multiple solutions to the same problem naturally exist. For example, a quadratic equation may have more than one solution. Once again it is possible for disagreement even though no fault has occurred (Anderson and Lee, 1981).

5.3.2   Principle issues in *N*-version programming

It has been shown that the success of *N*-version programming depends on several issues, which are now briefly reviewed.

(1)   *Initial specification.* It has been suggested that the great majority of software faults stem from inadequate specification (Leveson, 1986). Current techniques are a long way from producing complete, consistent, comprehensible and unambiguous specifications, although formal specification methods are proving fruitful. Clearly, a specification error will manifest itself in all *N* versions of the implementation.

(2)   *Independence of design effort.* Little work has been done to test the hypothesis that independently-produced software will display distinct failures. Some experiments have been undertaken but produce conflicting results. Knight *et al.* (1985) have shown that for a particular problem with a thoroughly refined specification, the hypothesis had to be rejected at the far from adequate 99% confidence level. In contrast, Avizienis *et al.* (1988) found that it was very rare for identical faults to be found in two versions of a six-version system. In comparing their results and those produced by Knight *et al.* they concluded that the problem addressed by Knight *et al.* had limited potential for diversity, the programming process was rather informally formulated, testing was limited, and the acceptance test was totally inadequate according to common industrial standards. Avizienis *et al.* claim that the rigorous application of the *N*-Version programming paradigm would have led to the elimination of all of the errors reported by Knight *et al.* before the acceptance of the system.

(3)   *Adequate budget.* With most embedded systems the predominate cost is software. A 3-version system will, therefore, almost triple the budget requirement. In a competitive environment it is unlikely that a potential contractor will propose a *N*-version technique unless it is mandatory.

It has also been shown that in some instances it is difficult to find inexact voting algorithms, and that unless care is taken with the consistent comparison problem then votes will differ even in the absence of faults.

Although *N*-version programming may have a role in producing reliable software it should be used with care and in conjunction with other techniques; for example, those discussed below.

5.4 Software dynamic redundancy

N-version programming is the software equivalent of static or masking redundancy, where faults inside a component are hidden from the outside. It is static because each version of the software has a fixed relationship with every other version as well as the driver; and because it operates whether or not faults have occurred. With **dynamic** redundancy, the redundant components only come into operation *when* an error has been detected.

This technique of fault tolerance has four constituent phases (Anderson and Lee, 1981).

(1)   *Error detection*. Most faults will eventually manifest themselves in the form of an error; no fault tolerance scheme can be utilized until that error is detected.

(2)   *Damage confinement and assessment*. When an error has been detected it must be decided to what extent the system has been corrupted; the delay between a fault occurring and the manifestation of the associated error means that erroneous information could have spread throughout the system.

(3)   *Error recovery*. This is one of the most important aspects of fault tolerance. Error recovery techniques should aim to transform the corrupted system into a state from which it can continue its normal operation (perhaps with degraded functionality).

(4)   *Fault treatment and continued service*. An error is a symptom of a fault; although the damage may have been repaired the fault may still exist and, therefore, may recur.

Although these four phases of fault tolerance are discussed under software dynamic redundancy techniques, they clearly can be applied to *N*-version programming. As Anderson and Lee (1981) have noted: error detection is provided by the driver which does the vote checking; damage assessment is not required because the versions are independent; error recovery involves discarding the results in error, and fault treatment is simply ignoring the version that was determined to have produced the erroneous value. However, if all versions have produced differing votes then error detection takes place but there are *no* recovery facilities.

The next sections briefly cover the above phases of fault tolerance. For a fuller discussion the reader is referred to Anderson and Lee
(1981).

5.4.1 Error detection

The effectiveness of any fault-tolerant system depends on the effectiveness
of its error detection techniques. Two classes of error detection techniques
can be identified.

(1) *Environmental detection*. These are the errors which are detected in
     the environment in which the program executes. They include those
     that are detected by the hardware such as 'illegal instruction
     executed', 'arithmetic overflow', and 'protection violation'. They
     also include errors detected by the run-time support system for the
     real-time programming language; for example, 'array bounds error',
     'null pointer referenced', and 'value out of range'. These type of
     errors will be considered in the context of the Ada programming
     language in Chapter 6.

(2) *Application detection*. These are the errors that are detected by the
     application itself. The majority of techniques that can be used by the
     application fall into the following broad categories.

     (a) *Replication checks*. It has been shown that N-version pro-
          gramming can be used to tolcrate software faults and that the
          technique can be used to provide error detection (by using
          2-version redundancy).

     (b) *Timing checks*. Two types of timing checks can be identified.
          The first involves a **watchdog timer**, a process that, if not reset
          within a certain period by a component, assumes that the
          component is in error. The software component must con-
          tinually reset the timer to indicate that it is functioning
          correctly.
              In embedded systems, where timely responses are
          important, a second type of check is required. These enable
          the detection of faults associated with missed deadlines.
          Where deadline scheduling is performed by the underlying
          run-time support system the detection of missed deadlines can
          be considered to be part of the environment. (Some of the
          problems associated with deadline scheduling will be covered
          in Chapter 12.)
              Of course, timing checks do *not* ensure that a compo-
          nent is functioning correctly, only that it is functioning on
          time! Time checks should, therefore, be used in conjunction
          with other error detection techniques.

(c)   *Reversal checks*. These are feasible in components where there is a one-to-one (isomorphic) relationship between the input and the output. Such a check takes the output, calculates what the input should be, and then compares the value with the actual input. For example, for a component which finds the square root of a number the reversal check is simply to square the output and compare it with the input. (Note that inexact comparison techniques may have to be used when dealing with real numbers.)

(d)   *Coding checks*. Coding checks are used to test for the corruption of data. They are based on redundant information contained within the data. For example, a value (checksum) may be calculated and sent with the actual data to be transmitted over a communication network. When the data is received the value can be recalculated and compared with the checksum.

(e)   *Reasonableness checks*. These are based on knowledge of the internal design and construction of the system. They check that the state of data or value of an object is reasonable, based on its intended use. Typically with modern real-time languages, much of the information necessary to perform these checks can be supplied by programmers, as type information associated with data objects. For example, integer objects which are constrained to be within certain values can be represented by subtypes of integers which have explicit ranges. Range violation can then be detected by the run-time support system.

Sometimes, explicit reasonableness checks are included in software components; these are commonly called **assertions** and take a logical expression which evaluates at run-time to true, if no error is detected.

(f)   *Structural checks*. Structural checks are used to check the integrity of data objects such as list or queues. They might consist of counts of the number of elements in the object, redundant pointers, or extra status information.

Note that many of these techniques may be applied also at the hardware level and, therefore, may result in 'environmental errors'.

5.4.2   Damage confinement and assessment

As there can be some delay between a fault occurring and an error being detected it is necessary to assess any damage that may have occurred. While the type of error that was detected will give the error handling routine some idea of the damage, erroneous information could have spread throughout the system and into its environment. Thus, damage assessment will be closely related to the damage confinement precautions that were taken by the system's designers. Damage confinement is concerned with structuring the system so as to minimize the damage caused by a faulty component. It is also known as **firewalling**.

There are two techniques that can be used for structuring systems which will aid damage confinement: **modular decomposition** and **atomic actions**. The merits of modular decomposition were discussed in Chapter 4. Here, the emphasis is simply that the system should be broken down into components where each component is represented by one or more modules. Interaction between components then occurs through well-defined interfaces and the internal details of the modules are hidden and not directly accessible from the outside. This makes it more difficult for an error in one component to be indiscriminately passed to another.

Modular decomposition provides a *static* structure to the software system in that most of that structure is lost at run-time. Equally important to damage confinement is the *dynamic* structure of the system as it facilitates reasoning about the run-time behaviour of the software. One important dynamic structuring technique is based on the use of atomic actions.

> The activity of a component is said to be atomic if there are *no* interactions between the activity and the system for the duration of the action.

That is, to the rest of the system an atomic action appears to be *indivisible* and takes place *instantaneously*. No information can be passed from within the atomic action to the rest of the system and vice versa. Atomic actions are often called **transactions** or **atomic transactions**. They are used to move the system from one consistent state to another and constrain the flow of information between components. Where two or more components share a resource then damage confinement will involve constraining access to that resource. The implementation of this aspect of atomic actions using the communication and synchronization primitives found in modern real-time languages will be considered in Chapter 10.

Other techniques which attempt to restrict access to resources are based on **protection mechanisms**, some of which may be supported by hardware. For example, each resource may have one or more modes of operation each with an associated access list (such as, read, write and execute). An activity of a component, or process, will also have an associated mode. Every time a process accesses a resource the intended operation can be compared against its **access permissions** and if necessary access is denied.

5.4.3 Error recovery

Once an error situation has been detected and the damage assessed, then error recovery procedures must be initiated. This is probably the most important phase of any fault-tolerance technique. It must transform an erroneous system state into one which can continue its normal operation, although perhaps with a degraded service. Two approaches to error recovery have been proposed: **forward** and **backward** recovery.

Forward error recovery attempts to continue from an erroneous state by making selective corrections to the system state. For embedded systems this may involve making safe any aspect of the controlled environment which may be hazardous or damaged because of the fault. Although forward error recovery can be efficient, it is system specific and depends on accurate predictions of the location and cause of errors (that is, damage assessment). Examples of forward recovery techniques include redundant pointers in data structures and the use of self-correcting codes such as Hamming Codes. An abort facility may also be required during the recovery process.

Backward error recovery relies on restoring the system to a safe state previous to that in which the error occurred. An alternative section of the program is then executed. This has the same functionality as the fault-producing section, but uses a different algorithm. As with N-version programming, it is hoped that this alternative approach will *not* result in the same fault recurring. The point to which a process is restored is called a **recovery point** and the act of establishing it is usually termed **checkpointing**. To establish a recovery point it is necessary to save appropriate system-state information at run time.

State restoration has the advantage that the erroneous state has been cleared and that it does not rely on finding the location or cause of the fault. Backward error recovery can, therefore, be used to recover from unanticipated faults including design errors. However, its disadvantage is that it cannot undo any effects that the fault may have had in the environment of the embedded system; it is difficult to undo a missile launch for example. Furthermore, backward error recovery can be time-consuming in execution, which may preclude its use in real-time applications. For instance, operations involving sensor information may be time-dependent, therefore, costly state restoration techniques may simply not be feasible. Consequently, to improve performance **incremental checkpointing** approaches have been considered. The **recovery cache** is an example of such a system (Anderson and Lee, 1981). Other approaches include audit trails or logs; in these cases the underlying support system must undo the effects of the process by reversing the actions indicated in the log.

With concurrent processes that interact with each other, state restoration is not as simple as so far portrayed. Consider two processes depicted in Figure 5.4. (The abbreviation IPC is used to indicate

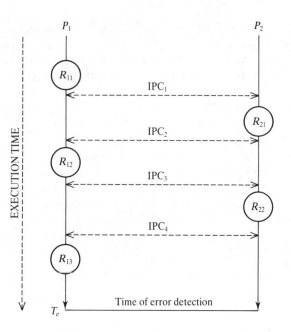

Figure 5.4   The domino effect.

Inter-Process Communication). Process P_1 establishes recovery points R_{11}, R_{12} and R_{13}. Process P_2 establishes recovery points R_{21} and R_{22}. Also, the two processes communicate and synchronize their actions via IPC_1, IPC_2, IPC_3 and IPC_4.

If P_1 detects an error at T_e then it is simply rolled back to recovery point R_{13}. However, consider the case where P_2 detects an error at T_e. If P_2 is rolled back to R_{22} then it must undo the communication IPC_4 with P_1; this requires P_1 to be rolled back to R_{12}. But if this is done, P_2 must be rolled back to R_{21} to undo communication IPC_3, and so on. The result will be that both processes will be rolled back to the beginning of their interaction with each other. In many cases this may be equivalent to aborting both processes! This phenomenon is known as the **domino effect**.

Obviously, if the two processes do not interact with each other then there will be no domino effect. When more than two processes interact, the possibility of the effect occurring increases. In this case, consistent recovery points must be designed into the system so that an error detected in one process will not result in a total rollback of all the processes with which it interacts; instead, the processes can be restarted from a consistent set of recovery points. These **recovery lines**, as they are often called, are closely linked with the notion of atomic actions, introduced earlier in this section. The issue of error recovery in concurrent processes will be revisited in

Chapter 10. For the remainder of this chapter sequential systems only will be considered.

The concepts of forward and backward error recovery have been introduced; each has its advantages and disadvantages. Not only do embedded systems have to be able to recover from unanticipated errors but they also must be able to respond in finite time; they, therefore, may require *both* forward and backward error recovery techniques. The expression of backward error recovery in sequential experimental programming languages will be considered in the next section. Because it is difficult to provide application-independent mechanisms for forward error recovery it will not be considered further in this chapter. However, in Chapter 6 the implementation of both forms of error recovery is considered within the common framework of exception handling.

5.4.4   Fault treatment and continued service

An error is a manifestation of a fault and although the error recovery phase may have returned the system to an error-free state, the fault may recur. Therefore, the final phase of fault tolerance is to eradicate the fault from the system so that normal service can be continued.

The automatic treatment of faults is difficult to implement and tends to be system-specific. Consequently, some systems make no provision for fault treatment assuming that all faults are transient; others assume that error recovery techniques are sufficiently powerful enough to cope with recurring faults.

Fault treatment can be divided into two stages (Anderson and Lee, 1981): fault location and system repair. Error detection techniques can help to trace the fault to a component. For a hardware component this may be accurate enough and it can simply be replaced. A software fault can be removed in a new version of the code. However, in most non-stop applications it will be necessary to modify the program while it is executing. This presents a significant technical problem, but will not be considered further.

5.5   The recovery block approach to software fault tolerance

Recovery blocks are **blocks** in the normal programming language sense except that, at the entrance to the block is an automatic **recovery point** and at the exit an **acceptance test**. The acceptance test is used to test that the system is in an acceptable state after the execution of the block, or **primary module** as it is often called. The failure of the acceptance test results in the program being restored to the recovery point at the beginning of the block and an **alternative module** being executed. If the alternative module also

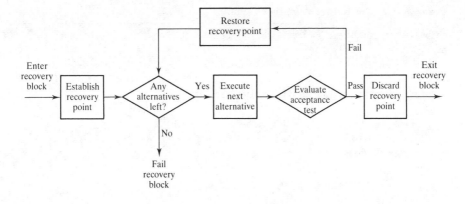

Figure 5.5   Recovery block mechanism.

fails the acceptance test then again the program is restored to the recovery point and yet another module is executed, and so on. If all modules fail then the block fails and recovery must take place at a higher level. The execution of a recovery block is illustrated in Figure 5.5.

In terms of the four phases of software fault-tolerance: error detection is achieved by the acceptance test, damage assessment is not needed as backward error recovery is assumed to clear all erroneous states, and fault treatment is achieved by use of a stand-by spare.

Although no commercially available real-time programming language has language features for exploiting recovery blocks, some experimental versions of a Pascal-like language have been developed (Shrivastava, 1978). The syntax illustrated in Program 5.1 is typically used:

Program 5.1   Recovery block syntax.

```
            ensure ⟨acceptance test⟩
            by
              ⟨primary module⟩
            else by
              ⟨alternative module⟩
            else by
              ⟨alternative module⟩
              ...
            else by
              ⟨alternative module⟩
            else error
```

Program 5.2   Nested recovery block syntax.

```
ensure ⟨acceptance test for outer recover block⟩
by
  ⟨primary module⟩
  ...
  ensure ⟨acceptance test for first inner recovery block⟩
  by
    ⟨primary module⟩
    ...
    ensure ⟨acceptance test for further nested inner recovery block⟩
    by
      ⟨primary module⟩
    else by
      ⟨alternative module⟩
      ...
    else by
      ⟨alternative module⟩
    else error
  else by
    ⟨alternative module⟩
  else error
else by
  ⟨alternative module⟩
  ...
  ensure  ⟨acceptance test for second inner recovery block⟩
  by
    ⟨primary module⟩
  else by
    ⟨alternative module⟩
  else by
    ⟨alternative module⟩
    ...
  else error
else by
  ⟨alternative module⟩
else error
```

Like ordinary blocks, recovery blocks can be nested, as Program 5.2 shows.

If a block in a nested recovery block fails its acceptance test and all its alternatives also fail, then the outer level recovery point will be restored and an alternative module to that block executed.

To show the use of recovery blocks various methods used to find the numerical solution of a system of differential equations are considered. As such methods do not give exact solutions, but are subject to various errors, it may be found that some approaches will perform better for certain classes of equations than for others. Unfortunately, methods which

Program 5.3   Outline of recovery block to solve differential equations.

```
ensure rounding_error_within_acceptable_tolerance
by
  Explicit Kutta Method
else by
  Implicit Kutta Method
else error
```

give accurate results across a wide range of equations are expensive to implement. For example, an **explicit Kutta** method will be more efficient than an **implicit Kutta** method. However, it will only give an acceptable error tolerance for particular problems. For example, there is a class of equations called **stiff** equations whose solution using an explicit Kutta leads to an accumulation of rounding errors; the more expensive implicit Kutta method can more adequately deal with this problem. Program 5.3 illustrates an approach using recovery blocks which enables the cheaper method to be employed for non-stiff equations but which does not fail when stiff equations are given.

In Program 5.3, the cheaper explicit method is usually used, however, when it fails the more expensive implicit method is employed. Although this error is anticipated, this approach also gives tolerance to an error in the design of the explicit algorithm. If the algorithm itself is in error and the acceptance test is general enough to detect both types of error result, the implicit algorithm will be used. When the acceptance test cannot be made general enough, nested recovery blocks can be used. In Program 5.4 full design redundancy is provided; at the same time the cheaper algorithm is always used if possible.

Program 5.4   Outline of nested recovery blocks to solve differential equations.

```
ensure rounding_error_within_acceptable_tolerance
by
  ensure sensible_value
  by
    Explicit Kutta Method
  else by
    Predictor-Corrector K-step Method
  else error
else by
  ensure sensible_value
  by
    Implicit Kutta Method
  else by
    Variable Order K-Step Method
  else error
else error
```

Program 5.5   Outline of nested recovery block to solve differential equations.

```
ensure sensible_value
by
  ensure rounding_error_within_acceptable_margin
  by
    Explicit Kutta Method
  else by
    Implicit Kutta Method
  else error
else by
  ensure rounding_error_within_acceptable_margin
  by
    Predictor-Corrector K-step Method
  else by
    Variable Order K-Step Method
  else error
else error
```

In Program 5.4 two explicit methods are given; when both methods fail to produce a sensible result, the Kutta implicit method is executed. The Kutta implicit method will, of course, also be executed if the value produced by the explicit methods is sensible but not within the required tolerance. Only if all four methods fail will the equations remain unsolved.

The recovery block could have been nested the other way around, as shown in Program 5.5. In this case, different behaviour will occur when a non-sensible result is also not within acceptable tolerance. In the first case, after executing the explicit Kutta algorithm, the predictor corrector method would be attempted. In the second, the implicit Kutta algorithm would be executed.

5.5.1   The acceptance test

The acceptance test provides the error detection mechanism which then enables the redundancy in the system to be exploited. The design of the acceptance test is crucial to the efficacy of the recovery block scheme. As with all error detection mechanisms there is a trade-off between providing comprehensive acceptance tests and keeping the overhead this entails to a minimum, so that normal fault-free execution is affected as little as possible. Note that the term used is **acceptance** not **correctness**; this allows a component to provide a degraded service.

All of the error detection techniques discussed in Section 5.4.1 can be used to form the acceptance tests. However, care must be taken in their design as a faulty acceptance test may lead to residual errors going undetected.

5.6   A comparison between *N*-version programming and recovery blocks

Two approaches to providing fault-tolerant software have been described: *N*-version programming and recovery blocks. They clearly share some aspects of their basic philosophy, and yet at the same time they are quite different. This section briefly reviews and compares the two.

- *Static versus dynamic redundancy.* *N*-version programming is based on static redundancy; all versions run in parallel irrespective of whether or not a fault occurs. In contrast, recovery blocks are dynamic in that alternative modules only execute when an error has been detected.

- *Associated overheads.* Both *N*-version programming and recovery blocks incur extra development cost, as both require alternative algorithms to be developed. In addition, for *N*-version programming, the driver process must be designed and recovery blocks require the design of the acceptance test.

  At run time, *N*-version programming, in general, requires *N*-times the resources of one version. Although recovery blocks only require a single set of resources at any one time, the establishment of recovery points and the process of state restoration is expensive. However, it is possible to provide hardware support for the establishment of recovery points, (Lee *et al.*, 1980), and the state restoration is only required when a fault occurs.

- *Diversity of design.* Both approaches exploit diversity in design in order to achieve tolerance of unanticipated errors. Therefore, both are susceptible to errors that originate from the requirements specification.

- *Error Detection.* *N*-version programming uses vote comparison to detect errors whereas recovery blocks use an acceptance test. Where exact or inexact voting is possible there is probably less associated overhead than with acceptance tests. However, where it is difficult to find an inexact voting technique, where multiple solutions exist or where there is a consistent comparison problem, acceptance tests may provide more flexibility.

- *Atomicity.* Backward error recovery is criticized because it cannot undo any damage which may have occurred in the environment. *N*-version programming avoids this problem because all versions are assumed not to interfere with each other: they are atomic. This requires each version to communicate with the driver process rather than directly with the environment. However, it is entirely possible to structure a program such that unrecoverable operations do not appear in a recovery block.

It should perhaps be stressed that although *N*-version programming and recovery blocks have been described as competing approaches, they also can be considered as complementary ones. For example, there is nothing to stop a designer using recovery blocks within each version of an *N*-version system.

5.7 Dynamic redundancy and exceptions

In this section a framework for implementing software fault tolerance is introduced which is based on dynamic redundancy and the notion of exceptions and exception handlers.

So far in this chapter the term 'error' has been used to indicate the manifestation of a fault, where a fault is a deviation from the specification of a component. These errors can be either anticipated, as in the case of an out of range sensor reading, due to hardware malfunction; or unanticipated, as in the case of a design error in the component. An **exception** can be defined as the occurrence of an error. Bringing an exception condition to the attention of the invoker of the operation which caused the exception, is called **raising the exception** and the invoker's response is called **handling the exception**. Exception handling can be considered a *forward error recovery* mechanism, as when an exception has been raised the system is not rolled back to a previous state; instead, control is passed to the handler so that recovery procedures can be initiated. However, as will be shown in Section 6.5, an exception handling facility can be used to provide backward error recovery.

Although an exception has been defined as the occurrence of an error, there is some controversy as to the true nature of exceptions and when they should be used. For example, consider a software component or module, which maintains a compiler symbol table. One of the operations it provides is to look up a symbol. This has two possible outcomes: **symbol present** and **symbol absent**. Either outcome is an anticipated response *and* may or may not represent an error condition. If the **lookup** operation is used to determine the interpretation of a symbol in a program body, *symbol absent* corresponds to 'undeclared identifier' which is an error condition. If, however, the *lookup* operation is used during the declaration process, the outcome *symbol absent* is probably the normal case and *symbol present*, that is, 'duplicate definition', the exception. What constitutes an error, therefore, depends on the context in which the event occurs. However, in either of these cases it could be argued that the error is not an error of the symbol table component or of the compiler in that either outcome is an anticipated result and forms part of the functionality of the symbol table module. Therefore, neither outcome should be represented as an exception.

Exception handling facilities were *not* incorporated into programming languages to cater for programmer design errors; however, it will be shown in Section 6.5 how they can be used to do just that. The original motivation for exceptions came from the requirement to handle abnormal conditions arising in the environment in which a program executes. These exceptions could be termed rare events in the functioning of the environment, and it may or may not be possible to recover from them within the program. A faulty valve or a temperature alarm might cause an exception. These are rare events which, given enough time, might well occur and must be tolerated.

Despite this, exceptions and their handlers will inevitably be used as a general purpose error handling mechanism. To conclude, exception and exception handling can be used to:

- cope with abnormal conditions arising in the environment;
- enable program design faults to be tolerated;
- provide a general purpose error detection and recovery facility.

Exceptions are considered in more detail in Chapter 6.

5.7.1   Ideal fault-tolerant system components

Figure 5.6 shows the ideal component from which to build fault-tolerant systems (Anderson and Lee, 1981). The component accepts service requests and if necessary calls upon the services of other components before yielding a response. This may be a normal response or an exception response. Two types of faults can occur in the ideal component: those due

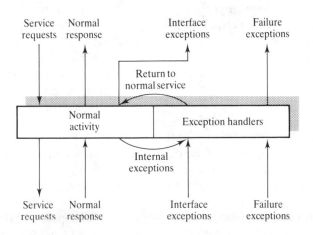

Figure 5.6   An ideal fault tolerant component.

to an illegal service request, called **interface exceptions**, and those due to a malfunction in the component itself, or in the components required to service the original request. Where the component cannot tolerate these faults, either by forward or backward error recovery, it raises **failure exceptions** in the calling component. Before raising any exceptions the component must return itself to a consistent state, if possible, in order that it may service any future request.

5.8   Measuring and predicting the reliability of software

Reliability metrics for hardware components have long been established. Traditionally, each component is regarded as a representative of a population of identical members whose reliability is estimated from the proportion of a sample that fail during testing. For example, it has been observed that, following an initial settling period, electronic components fail at a constant rate and their reliability at a time t can be modelled by:

$$R(t) = e^{-\lambda t}$$

where λ is the sum of the failure rates of all constituent components. A commonly used metric is Mean Time Between Failures (MTBF) which for a system without redundancy is equal to $1/\lambda$.

Software reliability prediction and measurement is not yet a well-established discipline. It was ignored for many years by those industries requiring extremely reliable systems because software does not deteriorate with use; it was regarded as either reliable or not. Also, in the past, particular software components were used once only, in the systems for which they were originally intended; consequently, although any errors found during testing were removed, this did not lead to the development of more reliable components which could be used elsewhere. This can be contrasted with hardware components which are mass produced; any errors found in the design can be corrected, making the next batch more reliable. However, it is now recognized that software reliability can be improved and software costs reduced by reuse of components. Unfortunately our understanding of how to build reusable software components is far from comprehensive. (See Section 4.4.)

The view that software is either correct or it is not is commonly held. If it is not, program testing or program proving will indicate the location of faults which can then be corrected. This chapter has tried to illustrate that the traditional approach of software testing, although indispensable, can never ensure that programs are fault free, especially with very large and complicated systems where there may be residual specification or design errors. Furthermore, in spite of the rapid advances made in the field of proof of correctness, the application of these techniques to non-trivial systems, particularly those involving the concept of time, is still beyond the *state of the art*. It is for all these reasons that methods of improving reliability through the use of redundancy have been advocated. Unfortunately, even with this approach, it cannot be guaranteed that systems containing software will not fail. It is, therefore, essential that techniques for predicting or measuring their reliability are developed.

Software reliability can be considered as *the probability that a given program will operate correctly in a specified environment for a specified length of time*. Several models have been proposed which attempt to estimate software reliability. These can be broadly classified as (Goel and Bastini, 1985)

- software reliability growth models,
- statistical models.

Growth models attempt to predict the reliability of a program on the basis of its error history. Statistical models attempt to estimate the reliability of a program by determining its success or failure response to a random sample of test cases, without correcting any errors found. Both these techniques are important but further research must be undertaken before their use becomes widespread.

5.9 Safety and reliability

The term safety which was defined informally in Chapter 2 can have its meaning extended to incorporate the issues raised in this chapter. Safety can thus be defined as:

> freedom from those conditions that can cause death, injury, occupational illness, damage to (or loss of) equipment (or property), or environmental harm (Leveson, 1986).

However, as this definition would consider most systems which have an element of risk associated with their use as unsafe, software safety is often considered in terms of **mishaps** (Leveson, 1986). A mishap is an **unplanned event** or **series of events** that can result in death, injury, occupational illness, damage to (or loss of) equipment (or property), or environmental harm.

Although reliability and safety are often considered as synonymous, there is a difference in their emphasis. Reliability has been defined as a measure of the success with which a system conforms to some authoritative specification of its behaviour. This is usually expressed in terms of probability. Safety, however, is the probability that conditions that can lead to mishaps do not occur *whether or not the intended function is performed.* These two definitions can conflict with each other. For example, measures which increase the likelihood of a weapon firing when required may well increase the possibility of its accidental detonation.

As with reliability, to ensure the safety requirements of an embedded system, system safety analysis must be performed throughout all stages of its life cycle development. It is beyond the scope of this book to enter into details of safety analysis; for a general discussion of software fault tree analysis – a technique used to analyse the safety of software design – the reader is referred to Leveson and Harvey (1983).

5.10 Dependability

Over the last few years much research has been carried out under the general name of reliable and fault-tolerant computing. Consequently, the terms have become overloaded and researchers have looked for new words and phrases to express the particular aspect they wish to emphasize. The terms 'safety' and 'security' are examples of this new terminology. More recently an attempt has been made to produce clear and widely-acceptable definitions of the basic concepts found within this field. To this end the notion of **dependability** has been introduced (Laprie, 1985):

> The dependability of a system is that property of the system which allows reliance to be justifiably placed on the service it delivers.

Dependability, therefore, includes as special cases the notions of reliability, safety and security. Figure 5.7, based on that given by Laprie (1985), illustrates these aspects of dependability.

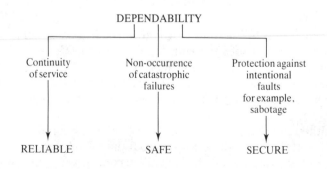

Figure 5.7 Aspects of dependability.

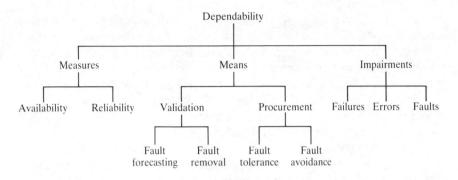

Figure 5.8 Dependability terminology.

Dependability itself can be described in terms of three attributes (Laprie, 1985).

- *impairments* – circumstances causing or resulting from non-dependability;
- *means* – the methods, tools and solutions required to deliver a dependable service with the required confidence;
- *measures* – the way in which the quality of a dependable service can be appraised.

Figure 5.8 summarizes the concept of dependability in terms of these three attributes.

In Figure 5.8 the term reliability is used as a measure of the continuous delivery of a proper service; availability is a measure of the frequency of periods of improper service.

Although there is some agreement on dependability terminology, this is far from unanimous. This book, therefore, shall continue with the established names used for the main part of this chapter.

SUMMARY

This chapter has identified reliability as a major requirement for any real-time system. The *reliability* of a system has been defined as a measure of the success with which the system conforms to some authoritative specification of its behaviour. When the behaviour of a system deviates from that which is specified for it, this is called a *failure*. Failures result from *faults*. Faults can be accidentally or intentionally introduced into a system. They can be transient, permanent or intermittent.

There are two approaches to system design which help ensure that potential faults do not cause system failure: *fault prevention* and *fault tolerance*. Fault prevention consists of *fault avoidance* (attempting to limit the introduction of faulty components into the system) and *fault removal* (the process of finding and removing faults). Fault tolerance involves the introduction of redundant components into a system so that faults can be detected and tolerated. In general, a system will provide either full fault tolerance, graceful degradation or failsafe behaviour.

Two general approaches to software fault tolerance have been discussed: *N-version programming* (static redundancy) and *dynamic redundancy* using forward and backward error recovery. N-version programming is defined as the independent generation of N (where $N \geqslant 2$) functionally equivalent programs from the same initial specification. Once designed and written, the programs execute concurrently with the same inputs and their results are compared. In principle, the results should be identical but in practice there may be some difference, in which case the consensus result, assuming there is one, is taken to be correct. N-version programming is based on the assumptions that a program can be completely, consistently and unambiguously specified, and that programs which have been developed independently will fail independently. This assumption may not always be valid and although N-version programming may have a role in producing reliable software it should be used with care and in conjunction with techniques based on dynamic redundancy.

Dynamic redundancy techniques have four constituent phases: *error detection, damage confinement and assessment, error recovery*, and *fault treatment and continued service. Atomic actions* were introduced as an important structuring technique to aid damage confinement. One of the most important phases is error recovery for which two approaches have been proposed: backward and forward. With backward error recovery it is necessary for communicating processes to reach consistent recovery points to avoid the domino effect. For sequential systems, the recovery block has been introduced as an appropriate language concept for expressing backward error recovery. Recovery blocks are blocks in the normal programming language sense except that, at the entrance to the block is an automatic *recovery point* and at the exit an *acceptance test*. The acceptance test is used to test that the system is in an acceptable state after the execution of the *primary module*. The failure of the acceptance test results in the program being restored to the recovery point at the beginning of the block and an *alternative module* being executed. If the alternative module also fails the acceptance test then the program is restored to the recovery point again and yet another module is executed, and so on. If all modules fail then the block fails. A comparison between N-version programming and recovery blocks illustrated the similarities and differences between the approaches.

Although forward error recovery is system specific, exception handling has been identified as an appropriate framework for its implementation. The concept of an ideal fault-tolerant component was introduced which used exceptions.

Finally in this chapter, the notion of software safety and dependability were introduced.

Further reading

Anderson T., ed. (1987). *Safe and Secure Computing Systems*. Oxford: Blackwell Scientific

Anderson T. and Lee P.A. (1981). *Fault Tolerance Principles and Practice*. Englewood Cliffs NJ: Prentice-Hall

Joseph M., ed. (1988). Formal techniques in real-time fault tolerant systems. *Lecture Notes in Computer Science*, **331**. Berlin: Springer-Verlag

Leveson N.G. (1986). Software safety: why, what and how. *ACM Computing Surveys*, **18**(2), 125–63

Leveson N.G. (1989). *Software Safety*. Wokingham: Addison-Wesley

Musa J., Iannino A. and Okumoto K. (1987). *Software Reliability: Measurement, Prediction and Application*. New York: McGraw-Hill

Neumann P.G. (1987). Index for computer-related risks in software engineering notes. *ACM Software Engineering Notes*, **12**(1), 22–8

Rouse W.B. (1981). Human-computer interaction in the control of dynamic systems. *Computer Surveys*, **13**(1) 77–99

Sennett C.T., ed. (1989). *High Integrity Software*. London

Shrivastava S.K., ed. (1985). *Reliable Computer Systems*. Berlin: Springer-Verlag

Also, there are two special editions of the *IEEE Transactions on Software Engineering* dedicated to software reliability: Volume SE-11, Number 12, December 1985 and Volume SE-12, Number 1, January 1986.

EXERCISES

5.1 Is a program reliable if it conforms to an erroneous specification of its behaviour?

5.2 What would the appropriate levels of degraded service be for a computer-controlled automobile?

5.3 Write a recovery block for sorting an array of integers.

5.4 To what extent is it possible to detect recovery lines at run time? (See Anderson and Lee, 1981) (Chapter 7.))

5.5 Should the end of file condition, that occurs when sequentially reading a file, be signalled to the programmer as an exception?

5.6 Data diversity is a fault-tolerance strategy that complements design diversity. Under what conditions might data diversity be more appropriate than design diversity? (See Ammann and Knight, 1988).

5.7 Should the dependability of a system be judged by an independent assessor?

Chapter 6
Exceptions and Exception Handling

Chapter 5 looked at how systems can be made more reliable and introduced exceptions as a framework for implementing software fault tolerance. In this chapter exceptions and exception handling are considered in more detail and their provision in particular real-time programming languages is discussed.

There are a number of general requirements for an exception handling facility:

(R1)   As with all language features, the facility must be simple to understand and use.

(R2)   The code for exception handling should not be so obtrusive as to obscure understanding of the program's normal error-free operation. A mechanism which intermingles code for normal processing and exceptional processing will prove difficult to understand and maintain. It may well lead to a less reliable system.

(R3)   The mechanism should be designed so that run-time overheads are incurred only when handling an exception. Although the majority of applications require that the performance of a program which uses exceptions is

125

not adversely affected under normal operating conditions, this may not always be the case. Under some
circumstances, in particular, where speed of recovery is
of prime importance, an application may be prepared to
tolerate a little overhead on the normal error-free
operation.

(R4)   The mechanism should allow the uniform treatment of
exceptions detected both by the environment and by
the program. For example, an exception such as **arithmetic overflow**, which is detected by the hardware,
should be handled in exactly the same manner as an
exception raised by the program as a result of an assertion failure.

(R5)   As already mentioned in Chapter 5, the exception
mechanism should allow recovery actions to be
programmed.

6.1   Exception handling in older real-time languages

Although the terms exception and exception handling have only recently
come into fashion, they simply express an approach to programming which
attempts to contain and handle error situations. Consequently, most
programming languages have facilities which enable at least some exceptions to be handled. This section briefly appraises these facilities in terms
of the requirements set out in the introduction.

6.1.1   Unusual return value

One of the most primitive forms of an exception handling mechanism is the
unusual return value or **error return** from a procedure or a function. Its
main advantage is that it is simple and does not require any new language
mechanism for its support. Typically it would be used as follows:

```
if function_call(parameters) = AN_ERROR then
   -- error handling code
else
   -- normal return code
end;
```

As can be seen, although this meets the simplicity requirement R1
and allows recovery actions to be programmed (R5), it fails to satisfy R2,
R3 and R4. The code is obtrusive, it entails overheads every time it is used,
and it is not clear how to handle errors detected by the environment.

6.1.2 Forced branch

In assembly languages the typical mechanism for exception handling is for subroutines to 'skip return'. In other words, the instruction immediately following the subroutine call is skipped to indicate the presence (or the absence) of an error. This is achieved by the subroutine incrementing its return address (program counter) by the length of a simple jump instruction to indicate an error-free (or error) return. In the case where more than one exceptional return is possible then the subroutine will assume that the caller has more than one jump instruction after the call, and will manipulate the program counter accordingly.

For example, assuming two possible error conditions, the following might be used to call a subroutine which outputs a character to a device.

```
jsr pc, PRINT_CHAR
jmp IO_ERROR
jmp DEVICE_NOT_ENABLED
# normal processing
```

The subroutine, for a normal return, would increment the return address by two jmp instructions.

Although this approach incurs little overhead (R3) and enables recovery actions to be programmed (R5), it can lead to obscure program structures and, therefore, violates requirements R1 and R3. R4 also cannot be satisfied.

6.1.3 Non-local goto

A high-level language version of a forced branch might require different labels to be passed as parameters to procedures or to have standard label variables (a label variable is an object to which a program address can be assigned and which can be used to transfer control). RTL/2 is an example of an early real-time language which provides the latter facility in the form of a non-local goto. RTL/2 uses **bricks** to structure its programs: a brick can be data (surrounded by the keyword data enddata), a procedure (surrounded by proc endproc) or a stack (identified by the stack keyword). A special type of data brick defined by the system is called svc (supervisor communication) data. One such brick (rrerr) provides a standard error handling facility which includes an error label variable called erl.

The following example shows how the error label may be used in RTL/2.

```
svc data rrerr
  label erl;
  ...
enddata;
```

```
proc WhereErrorIsDetected( );
  ...
  goto erl;
  ...
endproc;

proc Caller( );
  ...
  WhereErrorIsDetected( );
  ...
endproc;

proc main( );
  ...
  erl := restart;
restart:
  erl := restart;
  ...
  Caller( );
  ...
end proc;
```

Notice that when used in this way the goto is more than just a jump; it implies an abnormal return from a procedure. Consequently, the stack must be unwound, until the environment restored is that of the procedure containing the declaration of the label. The penalty of unwinding the stack is only incurred when an error has occurred so requirement R3 has been satisfied. Although the use of gotos is very flexible (satisfying R4 and R5), they can lead to very obscure programs. They, therefore, fail to satisfy the requirements R1 and R2.

6.1.4   Procedure variable

Although the RTL/2 example shows how to recover from errors using the error label, the control flow of the program has been broken. In RTL/2 the error label is generally used for unrecoverable errors and an **error procedure variable** used when control should be returned to the point where the error originated. The following example illustrates this approach.

```
svc data rrerr;
  label erl;
  proc(int) erp; % erp is a procedure variable %
enddata;
```

```
proc recover(int);
  ...
  ...
endproc;

proc WhereErrorIsDetected( );
  ...
  if recoverable then
    erp(n)
  else
    goto erl
  end;
  ...
endproc;

proc Caller( );
  ...
  WhereErrorIsDetected( );
  ...
endproc;

proc main( );
  ...
  erl := fail;
  erp := recover;
  ...
  Caller( );
  ...
fail:
  ...
end proc;
```

Again, the main criticism of this approach is that programs can become very difficult to understand and maintain.

6.2   Modern exception handling

It has been shown that the traditional approaches to exception handling often result in the handling code being intermingled with the program's normal flow of execution. The modern approach is to introduce exception handling facilities directly into the language and thereby provide a more structured exception handling mechanism. The exact nature of these facilities varies from language to language; however, there are several common threads that can be identified. These are discussed in the following sections.

6.2.1   The domain of an exception handler

Within a program there may be several handlers for a particular exception. Associated with each handler is a domain which specifies the region of computation during which, if an exception occurs, the handler will be activated. The accuracy with which a domain can be specified will determine how precisely the source of the exception can be located. In a block structured language, like Ada, the domain is normally the block. For example, consider a temperature sensor whose value should fall in the range 0 to 100°C. The following Ada block defines temperature to be an integer between 0 and 100. If the calculated value falls outside that range, the run-time support system for Ada raises a CONSTRAINT_ERROR exception. The invocation of the associated handler enables any necessary corrective action to be performed.

```
declare
    subtype TEMPERATURE is INTEGER range 0 .. 100;
begin
    -- read temperature sensor and calculate its value
exception
    -- handler for CONSTRAINT_ERROR
end;
```

The Ada details will be filled in shortly.

Where blocks form the basis of other units, such as procedures and functions, the domain of an exception handler is usually that unit.

As the domain of the exception handler specifies how precisely the error can be located, it can be argued that the granularity of the block is inadequate. For example, consider the following sequence of calculations, each of which possibly could cause CONSTRAINT_ERROR to be raised.

```
declare
    subtype TEMPERATURE is INTEGER range 0 .. 100;
    subtype PRESSURE is INTEGER range 0 .. 50;
    subtype FLOW is INTEGER range 0 .. 200;
begin
    -- read temperature sensor and calculate its value
    -- read pressure sensor and calculate its value
    -- read flow sensor and calculate its value

    -- adjust temperature, pressure and flow
    -- according to requirements
exception
    -- handler for CONSTRAINT_ERROR
end;
```

The problem for the handler is to decide which calculation caused the exception to be raised. Further difficulties arise when arithmetic overflow and underflow can occur.

With exception handler domains based on blocks the solution to this problem is to decrease the size of the block and/or nest them. Using the sensor example:

```
declare
   subtype TEMPERATURE is INTEGER range 0 .. 100;
   subtype PRESSURE is INTEGER range 0 .. 50;
   subtype FLOW is INTEGER range 0 .. 200;
begin
   begin
      -- read temperature sensor and calculate its value
   exception
      -- handler for CONSTRAINT_ERROR for temperature
   end;
   begin
      -- read pressure sensor and calculate its value
   exception
      -- handler for CONSTRAINT_ERROR for pressure
   end;
   begin
      -- read flow sensor and calculate its value
   exception
      -- handler for CONSTRAINT_ERROR for temperature
   end;
   -- adjust temperature, pressure and flow according to requirements
exception
   -- handler for other possible exceptions
end;
```

Alternatively, procedures containing handlers could be created for each of the nested blocks. However, in either case this can become long-winded and tedious. A different solution is to allow exceptions to be handled at the statement level. Using such an approach the above example would be rewritten thus:

```
-- not valid Ada
declare
   subtype TEMPERATURE is INTEGER range 0 .. 100;
   subtype PRESSURE is INTEGER range 0 .. 50;
   subtype FLOW is INTEGER range 0 .. 200;
begin
   READ_TEMPERATURE_SENSOR;
      exception      -- handler for CONSTRAINT_ERROR;
```

```
        READ_PRESSURE_SENSOR;
            exception     -- handler for CONSTRAINT_ERROR;


        READ_FLOW_SENSOR;
            exception     -- handler for CONSTRAINT_ERROR;


        -- adjust temperature, pressure and flow
        -- according to requirements

    end;
```

The CHILL programming language has such a facility. Although this enables the cause of the exception to be located more precisely, it intermingles the exception handling code with the normal flow of operation, which may result in less clear programs.

6.2.2   Exception propagation

Closely related to the concept of an exception domain is the notion of exception propagation. So far it has been implied that if a block or procedure raises an exception, then there is a handler associated with that block or procedure. However, this may not be the case, and there are two possible methods for dealing with a situation where no immediate exception handler can be found.

The first approach is to regard the absence of a handler as a programmer error which should be reported at compile time. However, it is often the case that an exception raised in a procedure can only be handled within the context from which the procedure was called. In this situation it is not possible to have the handler local to the procedure. For example, an exception raised in a procedure as a result of a failed assertion involving the parameters can only be handled in the calling context. Unfortunately, it is not always possible for the compiler to check whether the calling context includes the appropriate exception handlers, as this may require complex flow control analysis. This is particularly difficult when the procedure calls other procedures which may also raise exceptions. Consequently, languages which need compile-time error generation for such situations require that a procedure specifies which exceptions it may raise (that is, not handle locally). The compiler can then check the calling context for an appropriate handler and if necessary generate the required error message. This is the approach taken by the CHILL language.

The second approach which can be adopted when no local handler for an exception can be found is to look for handlers up the chain of invokers at run time; this is called **propagating** the exception. Ada allows exception propagation.

A potential problem with exception propagation occurs when the language requires exceptions to be declared and, thus, given scope. Under some circumstances it is possible for an exception to be propagated outside its scope, thereby making it impossible for a handler to be found. To cope with this situation most languages provide a 'catch all' exception handler. This handler is also used to save the programmer ennumerating many exception names.

An unhandled exception causes a sequential program to be aborted. If the program contains more than one process and a particular process does not handle an exception it has raised, then usually that process is aborted. However, it is not clear whether the exception should be propagated to the parent process. Exceptions in multi-process programs will be considered in detail in Chapter 10.

Another way of considering the exception propagation issue is in terms of whether the handlers are statically or dynamically associated with exceptions. Static association, as in CHILL, is done at compile time and therefore cannot allow propagation because the chain of invokers is unknown. Dynamic association is performed at run time and, therefore, can allow propagation. Although dynamic association is more flexible it does entail more run-time overhead as the handler must be searched for whereas with static association a compile-time address can be generated.

6.2.3 Resumption versus termination model

A crucial consideration in any exception handling facility is whether the invoker of the exception should continue its execution after the exception has been handled. If the invoker can continue, it may be possible for the handler to cure the problem that caused the exception to be raised and for the invoker to resume as if nothing has happened. This is referred to as the **resumption** or **notify** model. The model where control is not returned to the invoker is called **termination** or **escape**. Clearly, it is possible to have a model in which the handler can decide whether to resume the operation which caused the exception, or to terminate the operation. This is called the **signal** model.

The resumption model

To illustrate the resumption model consider three procedures P, Q and R. P invokes Q which in turn invokes R. R raises an exception r which is handled by Q, assuming there is no local handler in R. The handler for r is Hr. In the course of handling r, Hr raises exception q which is handled by Hq in procedure P (the caller of Q). Once this has been handled Hr continues its execution and when finished R continues. Figure 6.1 represents this sequence of events diagrammatically by numbered arcs 1 to 6.

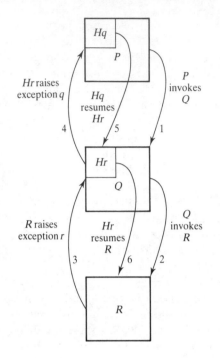

Figure 6.1   The resumption model.

The resumption model is most easily understood by viewing the handler as an implicit procedure which is called when the exception is raised.

The problem with this approach is that it is often difficult to repair errors which are raised by the run-time environment. For example, an arithmetic overflow occurring in the middle of a sequence of complex expressions may result in several registers containing partial evaluations. As a consequence of calling the handler these registers may be overwritten.

Both the languages PEARL and Mesa provide a mechanism whereby a handler can return to the context from which the exception was raised. Both languages also support the termination model.

The termination model

In the termination model when an exception has been raised and the handler has been called, control does not return to the point where the exception occurred. Instead, the block or procedure containing the handler is terminated, and control passed to the calling block or procedure. An invoked procedure, therefore, may terminate in one of a number of conditions. One of these is the **normal condition**, while the others are **exception conditions**.

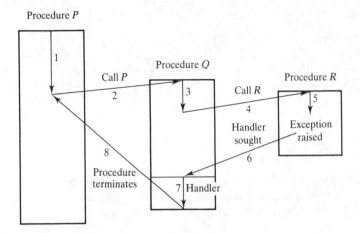

Figure 6.2   The termination model.

When the handler is inside a block, control is given to the first statement following the block after the exception has been handled; as the following example shows.

```
declare
   subtype TEMPERATURE is INTEGER range 0 .. 100;
begin
   ...
   begin
       -- read temperature sensor and calculate its value,
       -- may result in an exception being raised
   exception
       -- handler for CONSTRAINT_ERROR for temperature,
       -- once handled this block terminates
   end;

       -- code here executed when block exits normally
       -- or when an exception has been raised and handled.

exception
   -- handler for other possible exceptions
end;
```

With procedures, as opposed to blocks, the flow of control can quite dramatically change as Figure 6.2 illustrates. Again, procedure *P* has invoked procedure *Q* which has in turn called procedure *R*. An exception is raised in *R* and handled in *Q*.

Ada and CHILL have the termination model of exception handling.

The signal model

With the signal model it is up to the handler to decide if the error is recoverable. If it is, the handler can return a value and the semantics are the same as in the resumption model. If the error is not recoverable, the invoker is terminated. The signal mechanisms of Mesa and Real-time BASIC (Bull and Lewis, 1983) languages provide such a facility.

6.2.4   Parameter passing

A further consideration in the design of an exception handling facility is whether parameters may be passed to the handler with the raising of the exception. For example, an exception would normally be raised to indicate that an attempt has been made to assign a value to an object outside its permissible range of values. In this case it may be useful to pass the value to the handler. Failure to provide such a mechanism may lead to awkward global variable usage.

6.3   Exception handling in Ada, Modula-2 and occam 2

Exception handling in sequential Ada, Modula-2 and occam 2 are now considered. The three languages all have different philosophies. Exception handling in concurrent systems will be described in Chapter 10.

6.3.1   Ada

The Ada language was designed from the STEELMAN requirements. Therefore, as might be expected, the requirements for the exception handling facilities were well defined. In particular, the termination model of exception handling was specified, along with the requirement for exception propagation.

Exception declaration

Exceptions in Ada are declared in the same fashion as constants; the type of constant being defined by the key word **exception**. The following example declares an exception called STUCK_VALVE.

> STUCK_VALVE : **exception**;

An exception can be declared in the same place as any other declaration and, like every other declaration, it has scope. The language has several standard exceptions whose scopes are the whole program. These exceptions may be raised by the language's run-time support system in response to certain error conditions. They include:

- CONSTRAINT_ERROR: This is raised, for example, when an attempt is made to assign a value to an object which is outside its declared range, when an access to an array is outside the array bounds, or when access using a null pointer is attempted.

- NUMERIC_ERROR: This exception is raised by the execution of a predefined numeric operation that cannot deliver a correct result within the declared accuracy for real types. It includes the familiar divide by zero error.

- STORAGE_ERROR: This is raised when the dynamic storage allocator is unable to fulfil a demand for storage because the physical limitations of the machine have been exhausted.

Raising an exception

As well as exceptions being raised by the environment in which the program executes, they may also be raised explicitly by the program using the **raise** statement. The following example raises the exception IO_ERROR (which must have been previously declared and be in scope) if an I/O request produces device errors.

```
begin
   ...
   -- statements which request a device to perform some I/O
   if IO_DEVICE_IN_ERROR then
      raise IO_ERROR;
   end if;
   ...
end;
```

Notice that no 'else' part of the **if** statement is required because control is *not* returned to the statement following the raise.

Exception handling

As shown in Chapter 3, every block in Ada (and every subprogram or task) can contain an optional collection of exception handlers. These are declared at the end of the block (or subprogram, or task). Each handler is a sequence of statements. Preceding the sequence are: the keyword **when**, the names of the exceptions which are to be serviced by the handler, and the symbol ⇒. For example, the following block declares three exceptions and provides two handlers.

```
declare
    SENSOR_HIGH, SENSOR_LOW, SENSOR_DEAD : exception;
    -- other declarations
begin
    -- statements which may cause the above exceptions
    -- to be raised
exception
    when SENSOR_HIGH | SENSOR_LOW ⇒
        -- take some corrective action
        -- if either sensor_high or sensor_low is raised
    when SENSOR_DEAD ⇒
        -- sound an alarm if the exception
        -- sensor_dead is raised
end;
```

To avoid enumerating all possible exception names, Ada provides a **when others** handler name. This is only allowed as the last exception handling choice and stands for all exceptions not previous listed in the current collection of handlers. For example, the following block sounds an alarm when any exception except SENSOR_LOW or SENSOR_HIGH is raised (including SENSOR_DEAD).

```
declare
    SENSOR_HIGH, SENSOR_LOW, SENSOR_DEAD : exception;
    -- other declarations
begin
    -- statements which may cause the above exceptions
    -- to be raised
exception
    when SENSOR_HIGH | SENSOR_LOW ⇒
        -- take some corrective action
    when others ⇒
        -- sound an alarm
end;
```

An exception raised in an exception handler cannot be handled by that handler or other handlers in the same block (or procedure). Instead the block is terminated and a handler sought in the surrounding block or at the point of call for a subprogram.

Exception propagation

If there is no exception handler in the enclosing block or subprogram, the exception is raised again. Ada thus **propagates** exceptions. In the case of a block this results in the exception being raised in the enclosing block, or subprogram. In the case of a subprogram the exception is raised at its point of call.

A common misconception with Ada is that exception handlers can be provided in the initialization section of packages to handle exception that are raised in the execution of their nested subprograms. An exception raised and *not* handled by a subprogram is propagated to the caller of the subprogram. Therefore, such an exception will only be handled by the initialization code if it itself called the subprogram. The following example illustrates this point.

```
package TEMPERATURE_CONTROL is
   subtype TEMPERATURE is INTEGER range 0 .. 100;
   SENSOR_DEAD, ACTUATOR_DEAD : exception;

   procedure SET_TEMPERATURE(NEW_TEMP : in TEMPERATURE);
   function READ_TEMPERATURE return TEMPERATURE;
end TEMPERATURE_CONTROL;

package body TEMPERATURE_CONTROL is
   procedure SET_TEMPERATURE(NEW_TEMP : in TEMPERATURE) is
   begin
      -- inform actuator of new temperature
      if NO_RESPONSE then
         raise ACTUATOR_DEAD;
      end if;
   end SET_TEMPERATURE;

   function READ_TEMPERATURE return TEMPERATURE is
   begin
      -- read sensor
      if NO_RESPONSE then
         raise SENSOR_DEAD;
      end if;
      -- calculate temperature
      return READING;
   exception
      when CONSTRAINT_ERROR =>
         -- the temperature has gone outside
         -- its expected range;
         -- take some appropriate action
   end SET_TEMPERATURE;
begin
   -- initialization of package
   SET_TEMPERATURE(INITIAL_READING);
exception
   when ACTUATOR_DEAD =>
      -- take some corrective action
end TEMPERATURE_CONTROL;
```

In this example the procedure SET_TEMPERATURE which can be called from outside the package is also called during the initialization of the package. This procedure may raise the exception ACTUATOR_DEAD. The handler for ACTUATOR_DEAD given in the initialization section of the package *will only catch the exception when the procedure is called from the initialization code*. It will not catch the exception when the procedure is called from outside the package.

If the code which initialized a package body itself raises an exception which is not handled locally, the exception is propagated to the point where the package comes into scope.

Last wishes

An exception can also be propagated by a program reraising the exception in the local handler. The statement **raise** has the effect of reraising the last exception. This facility is useful in the programming of **last wishes**. Here it is often the case that the significance of an exception is unknown to the local handler but must be handled in order to clean up any partial resource allocation that may have occurred previous to the exception being raised. For example, consider a procedure which allocates several devices. Any exception raised during the allocation routine which is propagated to the caller may leave some devices allocated. The allocator, therefore, wishes to deallocate the associated devices if it has not been possible to allocate the full request. The following illustrates this approach.

```
subtype DEVICES is INTEGER range 1 .. MAX;

procedure ALLOCATE (NUMBER : DEVICES) is
begin
    -- request each device be allocated in turn
    -- noting which requests are granted
exception
    when others =>
        -- deallocate those devices allocated
        raise; -- reraise the exception
end ALLOCATE;
```

Used in this way the procedure can be considered to implement the failure atomicity property of an atomic action; all the resources are allocated or none are (see Chapter 10).

As a further illustration consider a procedure which sets the positions of slats and flaps on the wings of a fly-by-wire aircraft during its landing phase. These alter the amount of lift on the plane; asymmetrical wing settings on landing (or take off) will cause the plane to become unstable. Assuming that the initial settings are symmetrical, the following procedure ensures that they remain symmetrical, even if an exception is raised – either as a result of a failure of the physical system or because of a program error.[†]

```
procedure WING_SETTINGS ( -- relevant parameters) is
begin
   -- carry out the required setting
   -- of slats and flaps;
   -- exceptions may be raised
exception
   when others ⇒
      -- ensure the settings are symmetrical
      -- reraise exception to indicate
      -- a slatless and flapless landing
      raise;
end WING_SETTING;
```

Exceptions raised during elaboration of declarations

It is possible for an exception to be raised during the elaboration of a declarative part of a subprogram, block, task or package (for example, by initializing a variable to a value outside its specified range). In general, when this occurs the declarative part is abandoned and the exception is raised in the block, subprogram, task or package that caused the elaboration in the first place.

The full definition of the exception handling rules in all these cases is a little more complicated than outlined here. The reader is referred to the *Ada Language Reference Manual* (US Department of Defense, 1983), Chapter 12, for full details.

Suppressing exceptions

There is an aphorism which has become popular with programmers over the last decade; it normally takes the form: 'there is no such thing as a free lunch!'. One of the requirements for exception handling facilities (R3) was that they should not incur run-time overheads unless exceptions were raised. The facilities provided by Ada have been described and on the surface they appear to meet this requirement. However, there will always be some overhead associated with detecting possible error conditions.

For example, Ada provides a standard exception called CONSTRAINT_ ERROR which is raised when a null pointer is used, or where there is an array bound error, or where an object is assigned a value outside its permissible range. In order to catch these error conditions a compiler must generate appropriate code. For instance, when an object is being accessed

---

[†] This, of course, is a crude example used to illustrate an approach, it is not necessarily the approach that would be taken in practice.

through a pointer, a compiler will, in the absence of any global flow-control analysis (or hardware support), insert code which tests to see if the pointer is null before accessing the object. Although hidden from the programmer this code will be executed even when no exception is to be raised. If a program uses many pointers, this can result in a significant overhead both in terms of execution time and code size.

The Ada language does recognize that the standard exceptions raised by the run-time environment may be too costly for a particular application. Consequently, it provides a facility by which these checks can be suppressed. This is achieved by use of the 'suppress pragma' which eliminates a whole range of run-time checks. The pragma affects only the compilation unit in which it appears. Of course, if a run-time error check is suppressed and subsequently the error occurs, then the language considers the program to be 'erroneous' and the subsequent behaviour of the program is undefined.

A full example

The following package illustrates the use of exceptions in an abstract data type which implements a single STACK. This example was chosen as it enables the full specification and body to be given without leaving anything to the readers' imagination.

The package is generic and therefore can be instantiated for different types.

```
generic
    SIZE : NATURAL := 100;
    type ITEM is private;
package STACK is

    STACK_FULL, STACK_EMPTY : exception;

    procedure PUSH(X : in ITEM);
    procedure POP(X : out ITEM);

end STACK;

package body STACK is

    type STKIDX is new INTEGER range 0..SIZE - 1;
    type STACKARRAY is array(STKIDX) of ITEM;
    type STACK is
      record
        S : STACKARRAY;
        SP : STKIDX :=0;
      end record;
    STK : STACK;
```

```
    procedure PUSH(X : in ITEM) is
    begin
      if STK.SP = SIZE − 1 then
        raise STACK_FULL;
      end if;
      STK.SP :=STK.SP + 1;
      STK.S(STK.SP) := X;
    end PUSH;

    procedure POP(X : out ITEM) is
    begin
      if STK.SP = 0 then
        raise STACK_EMPTY;
      end if;
      X := STK.S(STK.SP);
      STK.SP := STK.SP − 1;
    end POP;

end STACK;
```

The package may be used as follows:

```
with STACK;
with TEXT_IO;
procedure USE_STACK is
  package INTEGER_STACK is new STACK(INTEGER);
  X : INTEGER;
  use INTEGER_STACK;
begin
  ...
  PUSH(X);
  POP(X);
  ...
exception
  when STACK_FULL ⇒
    TEXT_IO.PUT_LINE("stack overflow!");
  when STACK_EMPTY ⇒
    TEXT_IO.PUT_LINE("stack empty!");
end USE_STACK;
```

Difficulties with the Ada model of exceptions.   Although the Ada language provides a comprehensive set of facilities for exception handling, there are some difficulties with its ease of use.

(1)   **Exceptions and packages**. Exceptions which can be raised by the use of a package are declared in the package specification along with any subprograms that can be called. Unfortunately, it is not obvious which subprograms can raise which exceptions. If the users of the package are unaware of its implementation, they must attempt to

associate the names of exceptions with the subprogram names. In the stack example given above, the user could assume that the exception STACK_FULL is raised by the procedure POP and not PUSH! For large packages it may not be obvious which exceptions can be raised by which subprograms. The programmer in this case must resort to either enumerating all possible exceptions every time a subprogram is called, or to the use of **when others**. Writers of packages should, therefore, indicate which subprograms can raise which exceptions using comments.

(2) **Parameter passing**. Ada does not allow parameters to be passed to handlers. This can be very inconvenient. For example, where a large number of possible error conditions can arise, say in the validation of some input, it is more convenient to raise a single exception and pass a parameter which the handler can interpret. In this situation Ada forces the programmer either to enumerate all possible error conditions as distinct exceptions or to use a global variable.

(3) **Scope and propagation**. It is possible for exceptions to be propagated outside the scope of their declaration. Such exceptions can only be trapped by **when others**. However, they may go back into scope again when propagated further up the dynamic chain. This is disconcerting, although probably inevitable when using a block-structured language and exception propagation.

(4) **Using when others**. As a result of these problems, the programmer often has to resort to using the **when others** handler. Unfortunately, because parameters cannot be passed, the program cannot find out which error has been trapped. It cannot even print out the exception's name.

6.3.2   Modula-2

Modula-2, like Modula-1, does not define any exception handling facilities within the language. Such an omission clearly limits the usefulness of the language in the structured programming of reliable systems. However, the module construct of the language does permit the possibility of providing some form of exception handling mechanism. Indeed, some implementations of Modula-2 actually provide a comprehensive set of facilities; for example, the Brown, Boveri and Cie Modula-2 compiler for the PDP-11 range of computers running under the RSX-11M operating system (Brown *et al.*, 1985). To illustrate this approach the implementation of a simple Ada-like exception handling module will be considered. The handler is considered to be a parameter-less procedure whose domain is defined at run-time by calling procedures EnterDomain and ExitDomain. EnterDomain indicates that the handler for a particular exception is to be associated with the calling procedure. ExitDomain indicates that the handler should be disassociated from the exception and the calling procedure. A procedure Raise is used to signal the occurrence of the exception, and if a handler is found in the currently active procedure, this is called; after this, control is returned to the caller of the procedure which activated the exception handler. If no local handler is found, the exception is propagated down the chain of callers. Exceptions themselves are not defined.

```
DEFINITION MODULE exceptions;

  EXPORT QUALIFIED ExceptionHandler, EnterDomain, ExitDomain, Raise;

  TYPE ExceptionHandler = PROC;

  PROCEDURE EnterDomain(name: ARRAY OF CHAR; handler : ExceptionHandler);

  PROCEDURE ExitDomain(name : ARRAY OF CHAR);

  PROCEDURE Raise(name : ARRAY OF CHAR);

END exceptions.
```

The module would be used in the following way:

```
PROCEDURE ReadSensor;

  PROCEDURE SensorHighHandler;
  BEGIN
    (* Handler for the sensor high exception *)
    (* control from here is passed to the caller of ReadSensor *)
  END SensorHighHandler;

  PROCEDURE SensorLowHandler;
  BEGIN
    (* Handler for the sensor low exception *)
    (* control from here is passed to the caller of ReadSensor *)
  END SensorLowHandler;

BEGIN

  EnterDomain("SensorHigh", SensorHighHandler);
  EnterDomain("SensorLow", SensorLowHandler);

    (* statements for reading the sensor *)
    (* possibly Raise(SensorHigh) *)
    (* possibly Raise(SensorLow) *)

  ExitDomain("SensorHigh", SensorHighHandler);
  ExitDomain("SensorLow", SensorLowHandler)

END ReadSensor;
```

It is clear that the implementation of the exceptions module requires detailed knowledge of the particular Modula-2 implementation being used, and the ability to access and modify the run-time stack. Consequently, such a module will not be portable but will need to be rewritten for each implementation of the language. Even if it is assumed that such information can be obtained, say, from the SYSTEM module which provides details about the implementation, it is difficult to interface with any exceptions raised by the environment without modification to the compiler or the run-time support system.

The Modula-2 community seems to be divided as to whether exception handling would be a useful addition to the language. There are those who believe that the facility is essential and, therefore, have proposed extensions to the language (Rovner, 1986; Cardelli *et al.*, 1988). There are those who believe that exceptions are important and should be provided as an implementation supported module (Brown *et al.*, 1985). Finally, there are those who believe that exception handling is the antithesis of structured programming and therefore should not be provided or supported by the language or its implementation. This latter view is contrary to the one expressed in this book.

6.3.3   Occam 2

Occam 2 provides no exception handling facility. Furthermore, it is difficult to see how such a facility could be introduced as there is no comparable construct to the module. In general, whenever a process in occam 2 misbehaves it is defined by the language to be equivalent to the STOP process. It is up to other processes in the system to recover from such errors. In this chapter we have not considered exception handling issues for multiprocess systems, these are considered in Chapter 10.

6.4   Exception handling in other languages

In this section exception handling in CHILL, CLU and Mesa are briefly reviewed.

6.4.1   CHILL

CHILL is similar to Ada in that exceptions are part of the language definition and that the termination model of exception handling is supported. However, the other facilities that it provides are significantly different from Ada. CHILL has a slightly different syntax for its type names and object declarations than any of the other languages considered in detail in this book; an Ada-like syntax will, therefore, be used in the examples given here.

As indicated in Section 6.2.1, the domain of an exception handler in CHILL is the statement, block or process. The main difference between CHILL and Ada is therefore that exception handlers can be appended to the end of statements in CHILL. Instead of the keyword 'exception', CHILL uses on and end to surround a handler. In between, the syntax is rather like a 'case' statement. The following example illustrates a CHILL exception handler.

```
-- ada-like syntax used to illustrate concepts
-- not valid CHILL syntax
declare
  subtype temperature is integer range 0 .. 100;

  A : temperature;
  B,C : integer;
begin
  ...
  A := B + C on
            (overflow): .....;
            (rangefail): .....;
            else      .....;
          end;
  ...
end on
      -- exception handlers for the block
      (overflow): .....;
      (rangefail): .....;
      else      ....;
    end;
```

CHILL defines several standard exceptions similar to those of Ada. In the above example (arithmetic) overflow may be raised when B and C are added together; furthermore, a rangefail exception may occur if the result assigned to A is outside the range 0 to 100. The else option is equivalent to Ada's **when others**.

The association between an exception and its handler is static and, therefore, must be known at compile time. Consequently, exceptions are not predeclared. They can, however, be returned from a procedure by appropriate declarations in the procedure header. Again, using an Ada-like syntax:

```
procedure push(x : in item)  exceptions (stack_full);
procedure pop(x : out item)  exceptions (stack_empty);
```

The rule for determining a handler for an exception E which occurs during the execution of statement S is:

- it must be appended to S, or;
- it must be appended to a block directly enclosing S, or;
- it must be appended to the procedure directly enclosing S, or;
- the directly enclosing procedure must have E defined in its specification, or;
- it is appended to the process directly enclosing S.

When no exception can be found using the above rules, the program is in error. There is *no* propagation of exceptions.

6.4.2 CLU

CLU is an experimental language which although not a 'real time' language as such, does has some interesting features, one of which is its exception-handling mechanism (Liskov and Snyder, 1979). It is similar to CHILL in that a procedure declares the exceptions that it can raise. It also allows parameters to be passed to the handler.

For example, consider the function sum_stream which reads in a sequence of signed decimal integers from a character stream and returns the sum of those integers. The following exceptions are possible: overflow – the sum of the number is outside the implemented range of integers, unrepresentable_integer – a number in the stream is outside the implemented range of integers, and bad-format – the stream contains a non-integer field. With the last two exceptions the offending string is passed to the handler.

```
sum_stream = proc(s : stream) return(int)
      signals
        (overflow,
        unrepresentable_integer(string),
        bad_format(string)
        )
```

As with CHILL, there is no propagation of exceptions; an exception must be handled at the point of call.

```
x = sum_stream
      except
        when overflow:
          S1
```

```
when unrepresentable_integer(f : string):
    S2
when bad_format(f:string):
    S3
end
```

where S1, S2 and S3 are arbitrary sequences of statements.

6.4.3 Mesa

In Mesa exceptions are called **signals**. They are dynamic in that they can be propagated, and their handlers adhere to the signal model. Like Ada's exceptions, signals must be declared, but unlike Ada their declaration is analogous to a procedure type rather than a constant declaration. Consequently, they can take parameters and return values. However, they have no corresponding body but must be assigned a code which is generated by the system and used to identify the signal. The body to the signal procedure is, of course, the exception handler. Unlike procedure bodies which are *statically* bound to the procedure at compile time, exception handlers are *dynamically* bound to the signal at run time.

Handlers can be associated with blocks, as with Ada and CHILL. Like Ada, Mesa procedures and functions cannot specify which signals they will return; however, handlers can be associated with a procedure call giving a similar effect.

There are two types of signal declaration: those using the keyword 'signal' and those using 'error'. Signals which are declared as errors cannot be resumed by their corresponding handlers.

6.5 Recovery blocks and exceptions

In Chapter 5 the notion of recovery blocks was introduced as a mechanism for fault-tolerant programming. Its main advantage over forward error recovery mechanisms is that it can be used to recover from unanticipated errors, particularly from errors in the design of software components. So far in this chapter only anticipated errors have been considered, although catch-all exception handlers can be used to trap unknown exceptions. In this section the implementation of recovery blocks using exceptions and exception handlers is described.

As a reminder the structure of a recovery block is shown below:

```
ensure (acceptance test)
by
  (primary module)
else by
  (alternative module)
else by
  (alternative module)
    .
    .
    .
else by
  (alternative module)
else error
```

The error detection facility is provided by the acceptance test. This test is simply the negation of a test which would raise an exception using forward error recovery. The only problem is the implementation of state saving and state restoration. In the next example, this is shown as an Ada **package** which implements a recovery cache. The procedure SAVE stores the state of the global and local variables of the program in the recovery cache; this does not include the values of the program counter, stack pointer and so on. A call of RESTORE will reset the program variables to the states saved.

```
package RECOVERY_CACHE is
  procedure SAVE;
  procedure RESTORE;
end RECOVERY_CACHE;
```

Clearly, there is some magic going on inside the package which will require support from the run-time system and possibly even hardware support for the recovery cache. Also, this may not be the most efficient way to perform state restoration. It may be more desirable to provide more basic primitives, and to allow the program to use its knowledge of the application in order to optimize the amount of information saved.

The purpose of the next example is to show that given recovery cache implementation techniques, recovery blocks can be used in an exception handling environment. Notice also that by using exception handlers forward error recovery can be achieved before restoring the state. This overcomes a criticism of recovery blocks: that it is difficult to reset the environment.

The recovery block scheme can, therefore, be implemented using a language with exceptions plus a bit of help from the underlying run-time support system. For example, in Ada, the structure for a triple redundant recovery block would be:

```
procedure RECOVERY_BLOCK is
  PRIMARY_FAILURE, SECONDARY_FAILURE, TERTIARY_FAILURE :
    exception;
  RECOVERY_BLOCK_FAILURE : exception;
  type MODULE is (PRIMARY, SECONDARY, TERTIARY);
  function ACCEPTANCE_TEST return BOOLEAN is
  begin
    -- code for the acceptance test
  end;


procedure PRIMARY is
  begin
    -- code for primary algorithm
    if not ACCEPTANCE_TEST then
      raise PRIMARY_FAILURE;
    end if;
  exception
    when PRIMARY_FAILURE =>
      -- forward recovery to return environment to the required state
      raise;
    when others =>
      -- unexpected error
      -- forward recovery to return environment to the required state
      raise PRIMARY_FAILURE;
  end PRIMARY;


  procedure SECONDARY is
  begin
    -- code for secondary algorithm
    if not ACCEPTANCE_TEST then
      raise SECONDARY_FAILURE;
    end if;
  exception
    when SECONDARY_FAILURE =>
      -- forward recovery to return environment to the required state
      raise;
    when others =>
      -- unexpected error
      -- forward recovery to return environment to the required state
      raise SECONDARY_FAILURE;
  end SECONDARY;


  procedure TERTIARY is
  begin
    -- code for tertiary algorithm
    if not ACCEPTANCE_TEST then
      raise TERTIARY_FAILURE;
    end if;
```

```
    exception
      when TERTIARY_FAILURE ⇒
        -- forward recovery to return environment to the required state
        raise;
      when others ⇒
        -- unexpected error
        -- forward recovery to return environment to the required state
        raise TERTIARY_FAILURE;
    end TERTIARY;

begin
    RECOVERY_CACHE.SAVE;
    for TRY in MODULE loop
      begin
        case TRY is
          when PRIMARY ⇒ PRIMARY; exit;
          when SECONDARY ⇒ SECONDARY; exit;
          when TERTIARY ⇒ TERTIARY;
        end case;
      exception
        when PRIMARY_FAILURE ⇒
            RECOVERY_CACHE.RESTORE(SECONDARY);
        when SECONDARY_FAILURE ⇒
            RECOVERY_CACHE.RESTORE(TERTIARY);
        when TERTIARY_FAILURE ⇒
            raise RECOVERY_BLOCK_FAILURE;
        when others ⇒ raise RECOVERY_BLOCK_FAILURE;
      end;
    end loop;
end RECOVERY_BLOCK;
```

SUMMARY

This chapter has studied the various models of exception handling for sequential processes. Although many different models exists they all address the following issues.

- The domain of an exception handler – associated with each handler is a domain which specifies the region of computation during which, if an exception occurs, the handler will be activated. The domain is normally associated with a block or a statement.

- Exception propagation – this is closely related to the idea of an exception domain. It is possible that when an exception is raised there is no exception handler in the enclosing domain. In this case either the exception can be propagated to the next outer level enclosing domain, or it can be considered to be a programmer error (which can often be flagged at compilation time).

Table 6.1 The exception handling facilities of various languages.

Language	Domain	Propagation	Resumption/ Termination	Parameters
Ada	Block	Yes	Termination	No
CHILL	Statement	No	Termination	No
CLU	Statement	No	Termination	Yes
Mesa	Block	Yes	Signal	Yes

- Resumption or termination model – this determines the action to be taken after an exception has been handled. With the resumption model the invoker of the exception is resumed at the statement after the one at which the exception was invoked. With the termination model the block or procedure containing the handler is terminated, and control is passed to the calling block or procedure. The signal model enables the handler to choose whether to resume or to terminate.

- Parameter passing to the handler – may or may not be allowed.

The exception handling facilities of various languages are summarized in Table 6.1.

It is not unanimously accepted that exception handling facilities should be provided in a language (Black, 1982; Bull and Mitchell, 1983b). Occam 2 and Modula-2, for example, have none. To sceptics an Ada exception is a 'goto' where the destination is undeterminable and the source is unknown. They can, therefore, be considered to be the antithesis of structured programming. This, however, is not the view taken in this book.

Further reading

Bull G. and Mitchell R. (1983). Exception handling considered harmful. *IFAC/IFIP Workshop on Real-time Programming*. 93–6

Cottam I.D. (1985). Extending pascal with one-entry/multi-exit procedures. *ACM SIGPLAN Notices*, **20**(2), 21–31

Cristian F. (1982). Exception handling and software fault tolerance. *IEEE Transactions on Computing*, **c-31**(6), 531–40

Goodenough J.B. (1985). Exception handling: issues and a proposed notation. *CACM*, **18**(12), 683–96

Lee P.A. (1983). Exception handling in C programs. *Software – Practice and Experience*, **13**(5), 389–406

Yemini S. and Berry D.M. (1985). A modular verifiable exception-handling mechanism. *ACM Transactions on Programming Languages and Systems*, **7**(2), 214–43

Young S.J. (1982). *Real Time Languages: Design and Development*. Chichester: Ellis Horwood

EXERCISES

6.1 Compare and contrast the exception handling and recovery-block approaches to software fault tolerance.

6.2 The package CHARACTER_IO whose specification is given below, provides a function for reading characters from the terminal. It also provides a procedure for throwing away all the remaining characters on the current line. The package may raise the exception IO_ERROR.

```
package CHARACTER_IO is
   function GET return CHARACTER;
      -- reads a character from the terminal

   procedure FLUSH;
      -- throw away all character on the current line

   exception IO_ERROR;
end CHARACTER_IO;
```

Another package LOOK contains the function READ which scans the current input line looking for the punctuation characters comma (,) period (.) and semicolon (;). The function will return the next punctuation character found or raise the exception ILLEGAL_PUNCTUATION if a non-alphanumeric character is found. If during the process of scanning the input line, an IO_ERROR is encountered, then the exception is propagated to the caller of read. The specification of LOOK is given below.

```
package LOOK is
   type PUNCTUATION is (COMMA, PERIOD, SEMICOLON);
   function READ return PUNCTUATION;
      -- reads the next , . or ; from the terminal

   exception ILLEGAL_PUNCTUATION, IO_ERROR;
end LOOK;
```

Sketch the package body of LOOK. You should use the CHARACTER_IO package for reading characters from the terminal. On receipt of a legal punctuation character, an illegal punctuation character, or an IO_ERROR exception, the remainder of the input line should be discarded. You may assume that an input line will always have a legal or illegal punctuation character and that IO_ERRORs occur at random.

Using the LOOK package, sketch the code of a procedure GET_ PUNCTUATION which will always return the next punctuation character in spite of the exceptions that LOOK raises. You may assume an infinite input stream.

6.3 In a process-control application, gas is heated in an enclosed chamber. The chamber is surrounded by a coolant which reduces the temperature of the gas by conduction. There is also a valve which when open releases the gas into the atmosphere. The operation of the process is controlled by an Ada package whose specification is given below. For safety reasons the package recognizes several error conditions; these are brought to the notice of the user of the package by the raising of exceptions. The exception HEATER_STUCK_ON is raised by the procedure HEATER_OFF when it is unable to turn the heater off. The exception TEMPERATURE_STILL_RISING is raised by the INCREASE_COOLANT procedure if it is unable to decrease the temperature of the gas by increasing the flow of the coolant. Finally, the exception VALVE_STUCK is raised by the OPEN_VALVE procedure if it is unable to release the gas into the atmosphere.

```
package TEMPERATURE_CONTROL is
    HEATER_STUCK_ON, TEMPERATURE_STILL_RISING,
    VALVE_STUCK : exception;

    procedure HEATER_ON;
        -- turn on heater

    procedure HEATER_OFF;
        -- turn off heater
        -- raises HEATER_STUCK_ON

    procedure INCREASE_COOLANT;
        -- Causes the flow of coolant which surrounds the chamber
        -- to increase until the temperature reaches a safe level
        -- raises TEMPERATURE_STILL_RISING

    procedure OPEN_VALVE;
        -- opens a valve to release some of the gas thereby avoiding
        -- an explosion
        -- raises VALVE_STUCK

    procedure PANIC;
        -- sounds an alarm and calls the fire,
        -- hospital and police services
end TEMPERATURE_CONTROL;
```

Write an Ada procedure which when called will attempt to turn off the heater in the gas chamber. If the heater is stuck on then the flow of coolant surrounding the chamber should be increased. If the temperature still rises then the escape valve should be opened to release the gas. If this fails then the alarm must be sounded and the emergency services informed.

6.4 Write a general-purpose generic Ada package to implement nested recovery blocks. (Hint – the primary and secondary modules and so on should be passed as procedure parameters to the package, as should the acceptance test.)

6.5 To what extent could the Ada exception handling facilities be implemented outside the language by a standard package?

6.6 How would you defend the statement that an Ada exception is a goto where the destination is undeterminable and the source is unknown. Would the same argument hold for

(a)   the resumption model of exception handling and;

(b)   the CHILL termination model?

6.7 Compare the exception domains of the following apparently identical pieces of code (the variable INITIAL is of type INTEGER).

```
procedure DO_SOMETHING() is
  subtype SMALL_INT is INTEGER range -16..15;
  A : SMALL_INT := INITIAL;
begin
  ...


procedure DO_SOMETHING() is
  subtype SMALL_INT is INTEGER range -16..15;
  A : SMALL_INT;
begin
  A := INITIAL;
  ...


procedure DO_SOMETHING() is
  subtype SMALL_INT is INTEGER range -16..15;
  A : SMALL_INT;
begin
  begin
    A := INITIAL;
    ...
```

Chapter 7
Concurrent Programming

Virtually all real-time systems are inherently concurrent. Languages intended for use in this domain have greater expressive power if they provide the programmer with primitives that match the application's parallelism.

Concurrent programming is the name given to programming notation and techniques for expressing potential parallelism and solving the resulting synchronization and communication problems. Implementation of parallelism is a topic in computer systems (hardware and software) that is essentially independent of concurrent programming. Concurrent programming is important because it provides an abstract setting in which to study parallelism without getting bogged down in the implementation details (Ben-Ari, 1982).

This and the following two chapters concentrate on the issues associated with general concurrent programming. The topic of time and how it can be represented and manipulated in programs is deferred until Chapter 12.

157

7.1 The notion of process

Any language, natural or computer, has the dual property of enabling expression while at the same time limiting the framework within which that expressive power may be applied. If a language does not support a particular notion or concept then those that use the language cannot apply that notion and may even be totally unaware of its existence.

Pascal, FORTRAN and COBOL share the common property of being sequential programming languages. Programs written in these languages have a single thread of control. They start executing in some state and then proceed, by executing one statement at a time, until the program terminates. The path through the program may differ due to variations in input data but for any particular execution of the program there is only one path. This is not adequate for the programming of real-time systems.

Following the pioneering work of Dijkstra (1968a) a concurrent program is conventionally viewed as consisting of a collection of autonomous sequential processes, executing (logically) in parallel. Concurrent programming languages all incorporate, either explicitly or implicitly, the notion of process; each process itself has a single thread of control.

The actual implementation (that is, execution) of a collection of processes usually takes one of three forms. Processes can either:

(1)   multiplex their executions on a single processor;

(2)   multiplex their executions on a multiprocessor system where there is access to shared memory;

(3)   multiplex their executions on several processors which do not share memory (such systems are usually called distributed systems).

Hybrids of these three methods are also possible.

Only in cases (2) and (3) is there the possibility of true parallel execution of more than one process. The term **concurrent** indicates potential parallelism. Concurrent programming languages thus enable the programmer to express logically-parallel activities without regard to their implementation. Issues that are pertinent to true parallel execution are considered in Chapter 13.

The life of a process is illustrated, simply, in Figure 7.1. A process is created, moves into the state of initialization, proceeds to execution and termination. Note that some processes may never terminate and that others, which fail during initialization, pass directly to termination without ever executing. After termination a process goes to non-existing when it can no longer be accessed. Clearly, the most important state for a process is that of executing; however, as processors are limited not all processes can be executing at once. Consequently, the term **executable** is used to indicate that the process could execute if there is a processor available.

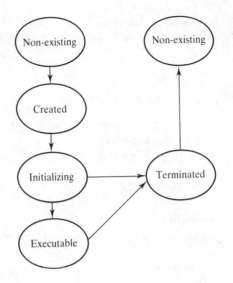

Figure 7.1 Simple state diagram for a process.

From this consideration of a process it is clear that the execution of a concurrent program is not as straightforward as the execution of a sequential program. Processes must be created and terminated, and dispatched to and from the available processors. These activities are undertaken by the Run-Time Support System (RTSS) or Run-Time Kernel (RTK). The RTSS has many of the properties of the scheduler in an operating system and sits logically between the hardware and the application software. In reality it may take one of a number of forms:

(1)   A software structure that is programmed as part of the application (in other words, as one component of the concurrent program). This is the approach adopted in Modula-2.

(2)   A standard software system generated with the program object code by the compiler. This is normally the structure with Ada programs.

(3)   A hardware structure microcoded into the processor for efficiency. An occam 2 program running on the transputer has such a run-time system.

The algorithm used for scheduling by the RTSS (that is, to decide which process to execute next if there is more than one executable) will effect the time-behaviour of the program. Although, for well-constructed programs, the logical behaviour of the program will not be dependent on the RTSS. From the program's point of view the RTSS is assumed to schedule processes non-deterministically. For real-time systems the characteristics of the scheduling are significant. They are considered further in Chapter 12.

7.1.1 Concurrent programming constructs

Although constructs for concurrent programming vary from one language to another there are three fundamental facilities that must be provided (Andrews and Schneider, 1983). These allow the following:

(1)   the expression of concurrent execution through the notion of process;
(2)   process synchronization;
(3)   inter-process communication.

In considering the interaction of processes it is useful to distinguish between three types of behaviour:

(1)   independent
(2)   cooperating
(3)   competing

Independent processes do not communicate or synchronize with each other. Cooperating processes, by comparison, regularly communicate and synchronize their activities in order to perform some common operation. For example, a component of an embedded computer system may have several processes involved in keeping the temperature and humidity of a gas in a vessel within certain defined limits. This may require frequent interactions.

A computer system has a finite number of resources which may be shared between processes; for example, peripheral devices, memory, and processor power. In order for processes to obtain their fair share of these resources they must compete with each other. The act of resource allocation inevitably requires communication and synchronization between the processes in the system. But, although these processes communicate and synchronize in order to obtain resources they are, essentially, independent.

Discussion of the facilities which support process interaction is the focus of Chapters 8–10.

7.2 Concurrent execution

Although the notion of process is common to all concurrent programming languages there are considerable variations in the models of concurrency adopted. These variations appertain to:

- structure
- level
- granularity
- initialization
- termination
- representation

The *structure* of a process may be classified as follows.

(1)   Static: the number of processes is fixed and known at compile time.
(2)   Dynamic: processes are created at any time. The number of extant processes is determined only at run time.

Another distinction between languages comes from the *level* of parallelism supported. Again two distinct cases can be identified:

(1)   Nested: processes are defined at any level of the program text; in particular, processes are allowed to be defined within other processes.
(2)   Flat: processes are defined only at the outermost level of the program text.

Table 7.1 gives the structure and level characteristics for a number of concurrent programming languages. Note that the language C is considered to incorporate the UNIX 'fork' and 'wait' primitives.

Table 7.1   The structure and level characteristics for a number of concurrent programming languages.

Language	Structure	Level
Concurrent Pascal	Static	Flat
DP	Static	Flat
occam 2 (and occam 1)	Static	Nested
Pascal-plus	Static	Nested
Modula-1	Dynamic	Flat
Modula-2	Dynamic	Flat
Ada	Dynamic	Nested
Mesa	Dynamic	Nested
C	Dynamic	Nested

Within languages that support nested constructs there is also an interesting distinction between what may be called coarse- and fine-grain parallelism. A **coarse grain** concurrent program contains relatively few processes, each with a significant life history. By comparison, programs with a **fine grain** of parallelism will have a large number of simple processes, some of which will exist for only a single action. Most concurrent programming languages, typified by Ada, display coarse-grain parallelism. Occam 2 is a good example of a concurrent language with fine-grain parallelism.

When a process is created it may need to be supplied with information pertinent to its execution (much as a procedure may need to be supplied with information when it is called). There are two ways of performing this *initialization*. The first is to pass the information in the form of parameters to the process; the second is to communicate explicitly with the process after it has commenced its execution.

Process *termination* can be accomplished in a variety of ways. The circumstances under which processes are allowed to terminate can be summarized as follows:

(1)   completion of execution of the process body;

(2)   suicide, by execution of a 'self-terminate' statement;

(3)   abortion, through the explicit action of another process;

(4)   occurrence of an untrapped error condition;

(5)   never: processes are assumed to execute non-terminating loops;

(6)   when no longer needed.

With nested levels, hierarchies of processes can be created and inter-process relationships formed. For any process it is useful to distinguish between the process (or block) that is responsible for its creation and the process (or block) which is affected by its termination. The former relationship is know as **parent/child** and has the attribute that the parent may be delayed while the child is being created and initialized. The latter relationship is termed **guardian/dependent**. A process may be dependent on the guardian process itself or on an inner block of the guardian. The guardian is not allowed to exit from a block until all dependent processes of that block have terminated (in other words, a process cannot exist outside its scope). It follows that a guardian cannot terminate until all its dependents have also terminated. This rule has the particular consequence that a program itself will not be able to terminate until all processes created within it have also terminated. However, processes within library units may or may not concur with this rule.

In some situations the parent of a process will also be its guardian. This will be the case when using languages which allow only static process

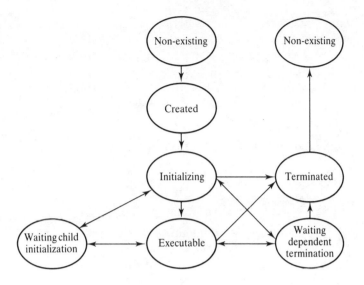

Figure 7.2   State diagram for a process.

structures (for example, occam 2). With dynamic process structures (that are also nested), the parent and guardian may or may not be identical. This will be illustrated in the discussion of Ada in Section 7.3.7.

Figure 7.2 includes the new states that have been introduced in this discussion.

One of the ways by which a process may terminate (point (3) in the last list) is by the application of an abort statement. The existence of abort in a concurrent programming language is a question of some contention and is considered in Chapter 11 within the context of resource control. For a hierarchy of processes it is usually necessary for the abort of a guardian to imply the abort of all dependents (and their dependents and so on).

The final circumstance for termination, in the last list, is considered in more detail in Section 9.5.2 when process communication methods are described. In essence, it allows a process to terminate if all other processes that could communicate with it have already terminated.

7.3   Process representation

In terms of representation there are three basic mechanisms for expressing concurrent execution: fork and join, cobegin and explicit process declaration. Coroutines are also considered.

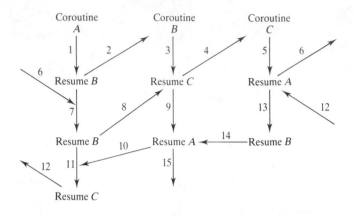

Figure 7.3   Coroutine flow of control.

7.3.1 Coroutines

Coroutines are sometimes included as a mechanism for expressing concurrent execution. They are like subroutines but they allow control to pass explicitly between them in a symmetric rather than strictly hierarchical way. Control is passed from one coroutine to another by means of the 'resume' statement which names the coroutine to be resumed. When a coroutine executes a resume it stops executing but retains local state information so that if another coroutine subsequently 'resumes' it, it can and will continue its execution. Figure 7.3 illustrates the execution of three coroutines; the numbered arrows represent the flow of control which starts in coroutine *A* and completes in coroutine *B* (having twice visited coroutine *C*).

Each coroutine may be viewed as implementing a process, however, no run-time support system is needed as the coroutines themselves sort out their order of execution. Clearly, coroutines are not adequate for true parallel processing as their semantics allow for execution of only one routine at a time. Modula-2 supports coroutines.

7.3.2 Fork and join

This simple approach does not provide a visible entity for a process but merely supports two routines. The fork statement specifies that a designated routine should start executing concurrently with the invoker of the fork. The join statement allows the invoker to synchronize with the completion of the invoked routine. For example:

```
function F return ... ;

procedure P;
  ...
  C:= fork F;

  .

  .

  .
  J:= join C;
  ...
end P;
```

Between the execution of the fork and the join, procedure P and function F will be executing in parallel. At the point of the join the procedure will wait until the function has finished (if it has not already done so).

The fork and join notation can be found in the Mesa language. A version of fork and join can also be found in Unix; here, fork is used to create a separate process image and the wait system 'call' provides the effective join.

Fork and join allow for dynamic process creation and provide a means of passing information to the child process via parameters. Usually only a single value is returned by the child on its termination. Although flexible they do not provide a structured approach to process creation and are error prone in use. For example, a guardian must explicitly 'rejoin' all dependents rather than merely wait for their completion.

7.3.3 Cobegin

The cobegin (or parbegin or par) is a structured way of denoting the concurrent execution of a collection of statements:

```
cobegin
  S1;
  S2;
  S3;
  .

  .

  .
  Sn
coend
```

This code causes the statements S1, S2 and so on, to be executed concurrently. The cobegin statement terminates when all the concurrent statements have terminated. Each of the Si statements may be any construct allowed within the language including simple assignments or procedure calls. If procedure calls are used then data can be passed to the invoked process via the parameters of the call. A cobegin statement could even include a sequence of statements that itself has a cobegin within it. In this way a hierarchy of processes can be supported.

Cobegin can be found in Edison (Brinch-Hansen, 1981a) and occam 2.

7.3.4 Explicit process declaration

Although sequential routines may be executed in parallel by means of the cobegin or fork, the structure of a concurrent program can be made much clearer if the routines themselves state whether they will be executed concurrently. Explicit process declaration provides such a facility. The following example is in Modula-1. It presents a simple structure for a robot-arm controller. A distinct process is used to control each dimension of movement. These processes loop around reading a new setting for its dimension and then calling a low level procedure move_arm to cause the arm to move.

```
MODULE main;
   TYPE dimension = (xplain, yplain, zplain);

   PROCESS control (dim : dimension);
   VAR position : integer;              (* absolute position *)
       setting : integer;              (* relative movement *)
   BEGIN
   position := 0;                      (* rest position *)
     LOOP
       new_setting (dim, setting);
       position := position + setting;
       move_arm (dim, position)
     END
   END control;

BEGIN
   control (xplain);
   control (yplain);
   control (zplain)
END main.
```

In the above, the process control is declared with a parameter to be passed on creation. The example then creates three instances of this process, passing each a distinct parameter.

Other languages that support explicit process declaration, for example Ada, also have implicit task creation. All processes declared within a block start executing, concurrently, at the end of the declarative part of that block.

The basic models for concurrent execution have now been outlined and references have been made to the languages that support particular features. To give concrete examples of actual programming languages, concurrent execution in Modula-2, occam 2 and Ada will now be considered.

7.3.5 Concurrent execution in Modula-2

Modula-2 provides a small group of primitives for process abstraction (Wirth, 1983). They are low-level features and allow for a flat process structure. As indicated in Section 7.3.1 Modula-2 uses the coroutine concept.

From the predefined module named SYSTEM, a PROCESS type and two procedures NEWPROCESS and TRANSFER are exported. These primitives can be used to build modules that support higher levels of process abstraction. Each process within a program is declared as a variable and then has a parameterless procedure associated with it that represents the body of the process. Also associated with each process is some data storage space.

```
FROM SYSTEM IMPORT
   PROCESS, NEWPROCESS, TRANSFER;

VAR P : PROCESS;

PROCEDURE pbody;
BEGIN

   ...

END pbody;

BEGIN
   NEWPROCESS(pbody, Workspace, Wsize, P);

   .
   .
   .
```

The procedure NEWPROCESS takes four parameters; the first is of type 'proc' (this is the type of all parameterless procedures), the second and third represent the start address and length of an area of storage for the stack of the process, and the final parameter is the process itself. NEW-PROCESS creates a process but it does not transfer control to it.

A process, once executing, will continue to do so until it explicitly passes control to another process, this is accomplished by the TRANSFER procedure. In the following program two processes P and Q each loop round and transfer control during each iteration.

```
VAR Main, P,Q : PROCESS;


PROCEDURE pbody;
BEGIN
  LOOP
    .

    .

    .
    TRANSFER(P,Q);                (* control moves from P to Q *)
    .

    .

    .
  END;
END pbody;


PROCEDURE qbody;
BEGIN
  LOOP
    .

    .

    .
    TRANSFER(Q,P);                (* control moves from Q to P *)
    .

    .

    .
  END;
END qbody;


BEGIN
  NEWPROCESS(pbody, ..., ..., P);
  NEWPROCESS(qbody, ..., ..., Q);
  TRANSFER(Main,P);              (* control moves from MAIN to P *)
  .

  .

  .
END.
```

A process must not 'halt' or return (even though it is a procedure) as this would cause the entire program to halt (control not being transferred).

The above point illustrates one of the major drawbacks of coroutine programs, they are not resilient to component failure. If one coroutine malfunctions then the entire program is affected. There is no run-time support system to isolate the effect of the error.

7.3.6   Concurrent execution in occam 2

Occam 2 uses a cobegin structure called PAR. For example, consider the concurrent execution of two simple assignments (A:=1 and B:=1):

```
PAR
    A := 1
    B := 1
```

This PAR structure, which can be nested, can be compared to the sequential form:

```
SEQ
    A := 1
    B := 1
```

Note that a collection of actions must be explicitly defined to be either executing in sequence or parallel; there is no default. Indeed, it can be argued that PAR is the more general form and should be the natural structure to use unless the actual code in question requires a SEQuence.

If the process designated by a PAR is an instance of a parameterized PROC (procedure) then data can be passed to the process upon creation. For example, the following code creates three processes from a single PROC and passes an element of an array to each:

```
PAR
    ExampleProcess(A[1])
    ExampleProcess(A[2])
    ExampleProcess(A[3])
```

A greater collection of processes can be created from the same PROC by the use of a 'replicator' to increase the power of the PAR:

```
PAR i = 1 FOR N
    ExampleProcess(A[i])
```

In Chapter 3 a replicator was used with a SEQ to introduce a standard 'for' loop. The only distinction between a replicated SEQ and a replicated PAR is that the number of replications (N in the above example) must be a constant in the PAR; that is, known at compile time. It follows that occam 2 has a static process structure.

The following program fragment in occam 2 is the robot-arm example given in Section 7.3.4 for Modula-1. Note that occam 2 does not support enumeration types and so the dimensions are represented by the integers 1, 2 and 3.

```
PROC control(VAL INT dim)
  INT position,                  -- absolute position
      setting:                   -- relative movement
  SEQ
    position := 0                -- rest position
    WHILE TRUE
      SEQ
        NewSetting(dim,setting)
        position := position + setting
        MoveArm(dim,position)
:
PAR
  control(1)
  control(2)
  control(3)
```

Process termination is quite straightforward in occam 2. There is no abort facility or any exceptions. A process must either terminate normally or not terminate at all (as in the above example).

In general, occam 2 has a fine grain view of concurrency. Most concurrent programming languages have the notion of process added to an essentially sequential framework. This is not the case with occam 2; the concept of process is basic to the language. All activities, including the assignment operations and procedure calls, are considered to be processes. Indeed, the notion of statement is missing from occam 2. A program is a single process that is build from a hierarchy of other processes. At the lowest level all primitive actions are considered to be processes and the constructors (IF, WHILE, CASE and so on) are themselves constructor processes.

7.3.7   Concurrent execution in Ada

The conventional unit of parallelism, the sequential process, is called a **task** in Ada. Tasks may be declared at any program level; they are created implicitly upon entry to the scope of their declaration. The following example illustrates a procedure containing two tasks (A and B)

```
procedure EXAMPLE1 is
  task A;
  task B;
```

```
task body A is
    -- local declarations for task A
begin
    -- sequence of statement for task A
end A;

task body B is
    -- local declarations for task B
begin
    -- sequence of statements for task B
end B;

begin
    -- tasks A and B start their executions before
    -- the first statement of the procedure's sequence
    -- of statements.
    .
    .
    .
end EXAMPLE1; -- the procedure does not terminate
             -- until tasks A and B have terminated.
```

Tasks like packages, consist of a specification and a body. They cannot be passed initialization data upon creation. In the above, tasks A and B (which are created when the procedure is called) are said to have an **anonymous** type as they do not have a type declared for them (compare with anonymous array types). Types could easily have been given for A and B:

```
task type A_TYPE;
task type B_TYPE;
A : A_TYPE;
B : B_TYPE;
task body A_TYPE is
    -- as before for task body A
task body B_TYPE is
    -- as before for task body B
```

With **task types** a number of instances of the same process can easily be declared using an array:

```
task type T;
A,B : T;
type LONG is array (1..100) of T;
type MIXTURE is
record
    INDEX : INTEGER;
    ACTION : T;
end record;
L : LONG; M : MIXTURE;
task body T is ...
```

A more concrete example of the use of tasks in an Ada program is the robot-arm system introduced earlier in this chapter for both Modula-1 and occam 2.

```
procedure MAIN is
    type DIMENSION is (XPLAIN, YPLAIN, ZPLAIN);
    task type CONTROL;
    SYSTEM : array (DIMENSION) of CONTROL;
    task body CONTROL is
        DIM : DIMENSION;
        -- absolute position
        POSITION : INTEGER;
        -- relative movement
        SETTING : INTEGER;
    begin
        -- obtain value for dim
        -- rest position
        POSITION := 0;
        loop
            NEW_SETTING (DIM, SETTING);
            POSITION := POSITION + SETTING;
            MOVE_ARM (DIM, POSITION);
        end loop;
    end CONTROL;
begin
    -- communicate dimension value to
    -- the three tasks
end MAIN;
```

The Ada structure clearly has the disadvantage that the three tasks generated do not know their own identity (that is, which dimension they are operating in) and it is necessary for them to have this data communicated to them after they have been created. To do this requires features of the language that have not been introduced yet; a more complete program will be given in Section 9.4.2.

By giving non-static values to the bounds of an array (of tasks) a dynamic number of tasks is created. Dynamic task creation can also be obtained explicitly using the **new** operator on an **access type** (of a task type):

```
procedure EXAMPLE2 is
    task type T;
    type A is access T;
    P : A;
    Q : A:= new T;
```

```
begin
   ...
   P:= new T;
   Q:= new T;
   ...
end EXAMPLE2;
```

Q is declared to be of type A and is given a 'value' of a new allocation of T. This creates a task that immediately starts its initialization and execution; the task is designated Q.**all** (.**all** is an Ada-naming convention used to indicate the task itself, not the access pointer). During execution of the procedure, P is allocated a task (P.**all**) followed by a further allocation to Q. There are now three tasks active within the procedure; P.**all**, Q.**all** and the task that was created first. This first task is now anonymous as Q is no longer pointing to it. In addition to these three tasks there is the task or main program executing the procedure code itself; in total, therefore, there are four distinct threads of control.

Tasks created by the operation of an allocator (**new**) have the important property that the block that acts as its guardian (or **master** as Ada calls it) is not the block in which it is created but the one that contains the declaration of the access type. To illustrate this point consider the following:

```
declare
   task type T;
   type A is access T;
begin

   .
   .

   .
   declare                     -- inner block
      X : T;
      Y : A:= new T;
   begin
      -- sequence of statements
   end;                        -- must wait for X to terminate but not Y.all

   .
                               -- Y.all could still be active although the name Y is
                               -- out of scope

   .
end;                           -- must wait for Y.all to terminate
```

Although both X and Y.**all** are created within the inner block only X has this block as its master. Y.**all** is considered to be a dependent of the outer block and therefore it does not affect the termination of the inner block.

One of the main uses of access variables is in providing another means of naming tasks. All task types in Ada are considered to be **limited**

private. Therefore, it is not possible to pass a task by assignment to another data structure or program unit. For example, if ROBOT_ARM and NEW_ARM are two variables of the same access type (the access type being obtained from a task type) then the following is illegal:

    ROBOT_ARM.**all** := NEW_ARM.**all**;   — not legal Ada

However

    ROBOT_ARM := NEW_ARM;

is quite legal and means that ROBOT_ARM is now designating the same task as NEW_ARM. Care must be exercised here as duplicated names can cause confusion and lead to programs that are difficult to understand.

If a task fails while it is being initialized (an exercise called **activation** in Ada) then the parent of that task has the exception TASKING_ERROR raised. This could occur, for example, if an inappropriate initial value is given to a variable. Once a task has started its true execution then it can catch any raised exceptions itself.

Having considered creation and representation, one is left with task termination. Ada provides a range of options; a task will terminate if:

(1)   It completes execution of its body (either normally, or as the result of an unhandled exception).

(2)   It executes a terminate alternative of a select statement (this is explained in Section 9.5.2 thereby implying that it is no longer required.

(3)   It is aborted.

If an unhandled exception has caused the task's demise then the effect of the error is isolated to just that task. Another task can enquire (by the use of an attribute) if a task has terminated:

    if T'TERMINATED **then**   — for some task T
       — error recovery action
    end if;

However, the enquiring task cannot differentiate between normal or error termination of the other task.

Any task can abort any other task whose name is in scope. When a task is aborted all of its dependents are also aborted. The abort facility allows wayward tasks to be removed. If, however, a rogue task is anonymous then it cannot be named and hence aborted. It is desirable therefore that only terminated tasks are made anonymous.

In this section the basic structure of the Ada-tasking model has been given. Unfortunately, without communication between tasks, meaningful programs cannot be presented; this will be remedied in Chapter 9. Nevertheless, it is possible to illustrate some of the differences between the occam 2 and Ada process models. In occam 2, two procedure calls are explicitly executed either sequentially or concurrently:

```
SEQ       -- sequential form
  proc1
  proc2

PAR       -- concurrent form
  proc1
  proc2
```

To achieve concurrency in Ada requires the introduction of two tasks:

```
begin                    -- sequential form
  PROC1;
  PROC2;
end;

declare                  -- concurrent form
   task ONE;
   task TWO;
   task body ONE is
   begin
     PROC1;
   end ONE;
   task body TWO is
   begin
     PROC2;
   end TWO;
begin
   null;
end;
```

Actually, it would be possible in Ada to only use one task and have the block itself make the other call.

```
declare
   task ONE;
   task body ONE is
   begin
     PROC1;
     end ONE;
begin
   PROC2;
end;
```

However, this form has lost the logical symmetry of the algorithm and is not recommended.

7.4   A simple embedded system

In order to illustrate some of the advantages and disadvantages of concurrent programming a simple embedded system will now be considered. Figure 7.4 outlines this simple system: a process *T* takes readings from a set of thermocouples (via an Analogue to Digital Converter, ADC) and makes appropriate changes to a heater (via a digitally-controlled switch). Process *P* has a similar function but for pressure (it uses a Digital to Analogue converter, DAC). Both *T* and *P* must communicate data to process *S* which presents measurements to an operator via a screen. The overall objective of this embedded system is to keep the temperature and pressure of some chemical process within defined limits. A real system of this type would clearly be more complex allowing, for example, the operator to change the limits. However, even for this simple system, implementation could take one of three forms:

(1)   *T*, *P* and *S* are written as separate programs and use operating system primitives for program/process interaction.

(2)   A single program is used which ignores the logical concurrency of *T*, *P* and *S*. No operating system support is required.

(3)   A single concurrent program is used which retains the logical structure of *T*, *P* and *S*. No operating system support is required although a run-time support system is needed.

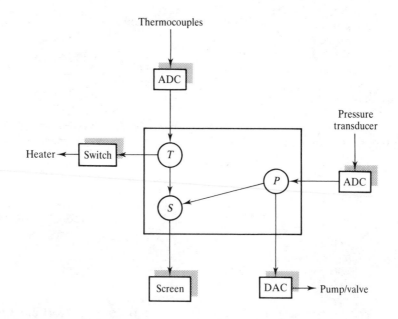

Figure 7.4   A simple embedded system.

If *T*, *P* and *S* are written as separate programs then user-defined types cannot be used for communication with *S*. Moreover, the compiler cannot be invoked to check the consistency of the complete software. It may also be the case that the processor (or processors) does not have a resident real-time operating system. For this reason solution (1) is not usually considered appropriate. Rather, the code will be targeted onto a 'bare' processor from a host computer that supports an appropriate programming environment. To illustrate solutions (2) and (3) Ada code will be given.

In order to simplify the structure of the central software the following packages will be assumed to have been implemented.

```
package DATA_TYPES is
    -- necessary type definitions
    type TEMP_READING is new INTEGER range 10 .. 500;
    type PRESSURE_READING is new INTEGER range 0 .. 750;
    type HEATER_SETTING is (ON, OFF);
    type PRESSURE_SETTING is new INTEGER range 0 .. 9;
end DATA_TYPES;
```

```
with DATA_TYPES; use DATA_TYPES;
package IO is
    -- procedures for data exchange with the environment.
    procedure READ (TR : out TEMP_READING);     -- from ADC.
    procedure READ (PR : out PRESSURE_READING);
        -- note, this is an example of overloading; two reads
        -- are defined but they have a different parameter type;
        -- this is also the case with the following WRITEs
    procedure WRITE (HS : HEATER_SETTING);      -- to switch.
    procedure WRITE (PS : PRESSURE_SETTING);    -- to DAC
    procedure WRITE (TR : TEMP_READING);     -- to screen.
    procedure WRITE (PR : PRESSURE_READING);
end IO;
```

```
with DATA_TYPES; use DATA_TYPES;
package CONTROL_PROCEDURES is
    -- procedures for converting a reading into
    -- an appropriate setting for output.
    procedure TEMP (TR : TEMP_READING;
                    HS : out HEATER_SETTING);
    procedure PRES (PR : PRESSURE_READING;
                    PS : out PRESSURE_SETTING);
end CONTROL_PROCEDURES;
```

A simple sequential control program could then have the following structure (it is known as a **cyclic executive**).

```
with DATA_TYPES; use DATA_TYPES;
with IO; use IO;
with CONTROL_PROCEDURES; use CONTROL_PROCEDURES;
procedure CONTROLLER is
   TR : TEMP_READING; PR : PRESSURE_READING;
   HS : HEATER_SETTING; PS : PRESSURE_SETTING;
begin
   loop
      -- read from ADC.
      READ(TR);
      -- convert reading to setting
      TEMP(TR,HS);
      -- write to SWITCH.
      WRITE(HS);
      -- write to screen.
      WRITE(TR);
      -- as above for pressure
      READ(PR);
      PRES(PR,PS);
      WRITE(PS);
      WRITE(PR);
      -- infinite loop, common in embedded software.
   end loop;
end CONTROLLER;
```

This code has the immediate handicap that temperature and pressure readings must be taken at the same rate which may not be in accordance with requirements. The use of counters and appropriate if statements will improve the situation, but it may still be necessary to split the computationally intensive sections (the conversion procedures TEMP and PRES) into a number of distinct actions, and interleave these actions so as to meet a required balance of work. Even if this were done there remains a serious drawback with this program structure: while waiting to READ a temperature no attention can be given to pressure (and vice versa). Moreover, if there is a system failure that results in, say, control never returning from the temperature READ, then in addition to this problem no further pressure READs would be taken.

An improvement to this sequential program can be made by including two Boolean functions in the package IO, READY_TEMP and READY_PRES, to indicate the availability of an item to read. The control program then becomes:

```
with DATA_TYPES; use DATA_TYPES;
with IO; use IO;
with CONTROL_PROCEDURES; use CONTROL_PROCEDURES;
procedure CONTROLLER is
   TR : TEMP_READING; PR : PRESSURE_READING;
   HS : HEATER_SETTING; PS : PRESSURE_SETTING;
begin
  loop
    if READY_TEMP then
       READ(TR);
       TEMP(TR,HS);
       WRITE(HS);      -- assuming write to be reliable.
       WRITE(TR);
    end if;
    if READY_PRES then
       READ(PR);
       PRES(PR,PS);
       WRITE(PS);
       WRITE(PR);
    end if;
  end loop;
end CONTROLLER;
```

This solution is more reliable; unfortunately, the program now spends a high proportion of its time in a 'busy loop' polling the input devices to see if they are ready. Busy-waits are, in general, unacceptably inefficient. They tie up the processor and make it very difficult to impose a queue discipline on waiting requests. Moreover, programs that rely on busy-waiting are difficult to design, understand or prove correct.

The major criticism that can be levelled at the sequential program is that no recognition is given to the fact that the pressure and temperature cycles are entirely independent subsystems. In a concurrent programming language this can be rectified by coding each system as a process (or in Ada terms a **task**):

```
with DATA_TYPES; use DATA_TYPES;
with IO; use IO;
with CONTROL_PROCEDURES; use CONTROL_PROCEDURES;
procedure CONTROLLER is
   task T;
   task P;
   task body T is
      TR : TEMP_READING; HS : HEATER_SETTING;
```

```
      begin
        loop
          READ(TR);
          TEMP(TR,HS);
          WRITE(HS);
          WRITE(TR);
        end loop;
      end T;
      task body P is
        PR : PRESSURE_READING; PS : PRESSURE_SETTING;
      begin
        loop
          READ(PR);
          PRES(PR,PS);
          WRITE(PS);
          WRITE(PR);
        end loop;
      end P;
    begin
      null;      -- T & P have started their executions
    end CONTROLLER;
```

Tasks T and P execute concurrently and each contains an indefinite loop within which the control cycle is defined. While one task is suspended waiting for a READ the other may be executing; if they are both suspended then a busy loop is not executed. The logic of the application is reflected in the code; the inherent parallelism of the domain is represented by concurrently executing tasks in the program.

However, one major problem remains with this two task solution. Both T and P send data to the screen, but the screen is a resource that can only sensibly be accessed by one process at a time. In Figure 7.4 control over the screen was given to a third process, S; the controller program should therefore possess three tasks. This has transposed the problem from that of concurrent access to a non-concurrent resource to one of inter-task communication. It is necessary for tasks T and P to pass data to task S. Moreover, S must ensure that it deals with only one request at a time. These requirements and difficulties are of primary importance in the design of concurrent programming languages, and are considered in the next two chapters.

SUMMARY

The application domains of most real-time systems are inherently parallel. It follows that the inclusion of the notion of process within a real-time programming language makes an enormous difference to the expressive power and ease of use of the language. These factors in turn contribute significantly to reducing the software construction costs while improving the reliability of the final system.

Without concurrency the software must be constructed as a single control loop (called a **cyclic executive**). The structure of this loop cannot retain the logical distinction between systems components. It is particularly difficult to give process-oriented timing and reliability requirements without the notion of a process being visible in the code.

However, the use of a concurrent programming language is not without its costs. In particular it becomes necessary to use a run-time support system to manage the execution of the system processes.

The behaviour of a process is best described in terms of states. In this chapter the following states were discussed:

- non-existing
- created
- initializing
- executable
- waiting dependent termination
- waiting child initialization
- terminated

Within concurrent programming languages there are a number of variations in the process model adopted. These variations can be analysed under six headings.

(1)   structure – static or dynamic process model;

(2)   level – top-level processes only (flat) or multilevel (nested);

(3)   initialization – with or without parameter passing;

(4)   granularity;

(5)   termination –

    (a)   natural
    (b)   suicide
    (c)   abortion
    (d)   untrapped error
    (e)   never
    (f)   when no longer needed

(6)   representation – coroutines, fork/join, cobegin; explicit process declarations.

Modula-2 uses a coroutine model; therefore it is not a true concurrent programming language. Occam 2 employs a cobegin (PAR) representation with nested static processes; initialization data can be given to a process although neither abortion nor 'no longer needed' termination is supported. Ada provides a dynamic model with support for nested tasks and the full range of termination options, but unfortunately initialization data cannot be given to tasks upon creation.

Further reading

Ben-Ari M. (1982). *Principles of Concurrent Programming*. Englewood Cliffs NJ: Prentice-Hall

Burns A. (1985). *Concurrent Programming in Ada*. Ada Companion Series. Cambridge: Cambridge University Press

Burns A. (1988). *Programming in Occam 2*. Wokingham: Addison-Wesley

Hoare C.A.R. (1985). *Communicating Sequential Processes*. London: Prentice-Hall

Peterson J. and Silberschatz A. (1985). *Operating System Concepts*. Reading MA: Addison-Wesley

Welsh J., Elder J. and Bustard D. (1988). *Concurrent Program Structures*. London: Prentice-Hall

Whiddett D. (1987). *Concurrent Programming for Software Engineers*. Chichester: Ellis Horwood

---

EXERCISES

7.1 Show how a cobegin can be implemented in Ada.

7.2 Can the fork and join method of process creation be implemented in Ada without using intertask communication?

7.3 Describe what happens when the following Ada function is executed.

```
task type A;

function X return A is
   A1 : A
begin
   return A1;
end;
```

What is the state of task A1 on exit from the function?

7.4 Rewrite the simple embedded system illustrated in Section 7.4 in Modula-2 and occam 2.

7.5 Show how the occam 2 process model can be implemented in Modula-2.

7.6 Show, using concurrent processes, the structure of a program to control access to a simple car park. Assume that the car park has a single entrance and a single exit barrier, and a 'full' sign.

Chapter 8
Shared Memory-based Synchronization and Communication

The major difficulties associated with concurrent programming arise from process interaction. Rarely are processes as independent of one another as they were in the simple embedded system example at the end of Chapter 7. The correct behaviour of a concurrent program is critically dependent on synchronization and communication between processes. In its widest sense, synchronization is the satisfaction of constraints on the interleaving of the actions of different processes (for example, a particular action by one process only occurring after a specific action by another process). The term is also used in the narrow sense of bringing two processes simultaneously into predefined states. Communication is the passing of information from one process to another. The two concepts are linked, since some forms of communication require synchronization, and synchronization can be considered as contentless communication.

Data communication is usually based upon either shared variables or message passing. **Shared variables** are objects to which more than one process have access; communication can therefore proceed by each process referencing these variables when appropriate. **Message passing** involves the explicit exchange of data between two processes by means of a message that passes from one process to another via some agency. Note that the choice between shared variables and message passing is one for the language designers; it does not imply that any particular implementation method should be used. Shared variables are easy to support if there is shared memory between the processes but can still be used even if the hardware incorporates a communication medium. Similarly, a message-passing primitive can be supported via shared memory or a physical message passing network. Furthermore, an application can arguably be programmed in either style and obtain the same functionality (Lauer and Needham, 1978). Message-based synchronization and communication is discussed in Chapter 9. This present chapter will concentrate on shared memory-based communication and synchronization primitives. In particular, busy waiting, semaphores, conditional critical regions and monitors are discussed.

8.1   Mutual exclusion and condition synchronization

Although shared variables appear to be a straightforward way of passing information between processes their unrestricted use is unreliable and unsafe due to multiple update problems. Consider two processes updating a shared variable, X, with the assignment:

$$X := X + 1$$

On most hardware this will not be executed as an *indivisible* (atomic) operation but will be implemented in three distinct instructions:

(1)   load the value of X into some register (or to the top of the stack);
(2)   increment the value in the register by 1; and;
(3)   store the value in the register back to X.

As the three operations are not indivisible, two processes simultaneously updating the variable could follow an interleaving that would produce an incorrect result. For example, if X was originally 5 then the two processes could each load 5 into their registers, increment and then store 6.

A sequence of statements that must appear to be executed indivisibly is called a **critical section**. The synchronization required to protect a critical section is known as **mutual exclusion**. Atomicity, although absent from the assignment operation, is assumed to be present at the memory level. Thus if one process is executing $X := 5$ simultaneously with another executing $X := 6$, the result will be either 5 or 6 (not some other value). If this were not true it would be difficult to reason about concurrent programs or implement higher levels of atomicity such as mutual exclusion synchronization. Clearly, however, if two processes are updating a structured object, this atomicity will only apply at the single word element level.

The mutual exclusion problem itself was first described by Dijkstra (1965). It lies at the heart of most concurrent process synchronization mechanisms and is of great theoretical as well as practical interest. (For a detailed discussion of a theoretical approach to the mutual exclusion problem see Lamport (1986).) Mutual exclusion is not the only synchronization of importance; indeed, if two processes do not share variables then there is no need for mutual exclusion. **Condition synchronization** is another significant requirement and is needed when a process wishes to perform an operation that can only sensibly, or safely, be performed if another process has itself taken some action or is in some defined state.

An example of condition synchronization comes with the use of buffers. Two processes that exchange data may perform better if communication is not direct but via a buffer. This has the advantage of decoupling the processes and allows for small fluctuations in the speed at which the two processes are working. For example, an input process may receive data in bursts that must be buffered for the appropriate user processes. The use of a buffer to link two processes is common in concurrent programs and is known as a **producer-consumer** system.

Two condition synchronizations are necessary if a finite bounded buffer is used. Firstly, the producer process must not attempt to deposit data onto the buffer if the buffer is full. Secondly, the consumer process cannot be allowed to extract objects from the buffer if the buffer is empty. Moreover, if simultaneous deposits or extractions are possible then mutual exclusion must be ensured so that two producers, for example, do not corrupt the next 'free slot' pointer of the buffer.

The implementation of any form of synchronization implies that processes must, at times, be held back until it is appropriate for them to proceed. In Section 8.2 mutual exclusion and condition synchronization will be programmed (in a Pascal-like language with explicit process declaration) using **busy wait** loops and **flags**. From this analysis it should be clear that further primitives are needed in order to ease the coding of algorithms that require synchronization.

8.2 Busy waiting

One way to implement synchronization is to have processes set and to check shared variables that are acting as flags. This approach works reasonably well for implementing condition synchronization but no simple method for mutual exclusion exists. In order to signal a condition a process sets the value of a flag; to wait for this condition another process checks this flag and proceeds only when the appropriate value is read:

```
process P1;              (* waiting process *)
  ...
  while flag = down do
    null
  end;
  ...
end P1;

process P2;              (* signalling process *)
  ...
  flag:= up;
  ...
end P2;
```

If the condition is not yet set (that is, flag is still down) then P1 has no choice but to loop round and recheck the flag. This is **busy waiting**; also known as **spinning** (with the flag variables called **spin locks**).

Busy wait algorithms in general are inefficient; they involve processes using up processing cycles when they cannot perform useful work. Even on a multiprocessor system they can give rise to excessive traffic on the memory bus or network (if distributed). Moreover, it is not possible to impose queuing disciplines if there is more than one process waiting on a condition (that is, checking the value of a flag).

Mutual exclusion presents even more difficulties as the algorithms required are more complex. Consider two processes (P1 and P2 again) that have mutual, critical sections. In order to protect access to these critical sections it can be assumed that each process executes an entry protocol before the critical section and executes an exit protocol afterwards. Each process can, therefore, be considered to have the following form:

```
process P;
  loop
    entry protocol
      critical section
    exit protocol
    non-critical section
  end
end P;
```

Before giving a solution that adequately provides for mutual exclusion three inappropriate approaches will be discussed. Firstly, consider a two-flag solution that is an (almost) logical extension of the busy wait condition synchronization algorithm:

```
process P1;
  loop
    flag1:= up;                (* announce intent to enter *)
    while flag2 = up do
      null                     (* busy wait if the other process *)
    end;                       (* is in its critical section *)
    <critical section>
    flag1:= down;              (* exit protocol *)
    <non-critical section>
  end
end P1;


process P2;
  loop
    flag2:= up;
    while flag1 = up do
      null
    end;
    <critical section>
    flag2:= down;
    <non-critical section>
  end
end P2;
```

Both processes announce their intention to enter their critical sections and then check to see if the other process is in its critical section. Unfortunately, this solution suffers from a not insignificant problem. Consider an interleaving that has the following progression:

```
P1 sets its flag (flag1 now up)
P2 sets its flag (flag2 now up)
P2 checks flag1 (it is up therefore P2 loops)
P2 enters its busy wait
P1 checks flag2 (it is up therefore P1 loops)
P1 enters its busy wait
```

The result is that both processes will remain in their busy wait loops. Neither can get out because the other cannot get out. This phenomenon is known as **livelock** and is a severe error condition.

The difficulty with this first approach arises because each process announces its intention to enter its critical section before checking to see if it is acceptable for it to do so. The second approach involves reversing the order of these two actions:

```
process P1;
  loop
    while flag2 = up do
      null                    (* busy wait if the other process *)
    end;                      (* is in its critical section *)
    flag1:= up;               (* announce intent to enter *)
    <critical section>
    flag1:= down;             (* exit protocol *)
    <non-critical section>
  end
end P1;


process P2;
  loop
    while flag1 = up do
      null
    end;
    flag2:= up;
    <critical section>
    flag2= down;
    <non-critical section>
  end
end P2;
```

Now an interleaving that actually fails to give mutual exclusion can be produced.

```
P1 and P2 are in their non-critical section (flag1 = flag2 = down)
P1 checks flag2 (it is down)
P2 checks flag1 (it is down)
P2 sets its flag (flag2 now up)
P2 enters critical section
P1 sets it flag (flag1 now up)
P1 enters critical section
that is, P1 and P2 are both in their critical sections.
```

The difficulty with the two structures given so far is that the setting of one's own flag and the checks on the other processes cannot be done as an indivisible action. Therefore, it might be considered that the correct approach is to use just one flag which indicates which process should next enter its critical section. As this flag decides whose turn it is to enter it will be called turn.

```
process P1;
   loop
     while turn = 2 do
        null
     end
     <critical section>
     turn:= 2
     <non-critical section>
   end
end P1;


process P2;
   loop
     while turn = 1 do
        null
     end
     <critical section>
     turn:=1;
     <non-critical section>
   end
end P2;
```

With this structure the variable turn must have either the value 1 or 2. If it is 1 then P1 cannot be indefinitely delayed and P2 cannot enter its critical section. Moreover, turn cannot become 2 while P1 is in its critical section as the only place that turn can be assigned 2 is by P1 and that is while it is in its exit protocol. A symmetric argument for turn having the value 2 implies that mutual exclusion is provided and livelock is not possible if both processes are cycling round.

Unfortunately, this latter point is significant. If P1 fails in its non-critical section then turn will eventually obtain the value 1 and will stay with that value (that is, P2 will be prohibited from entering its critical section even though P1 is no longer executing). Even when executing normally the use of a single turn variable requires the processes to cycle round at the same rate. It is not possible for P1 (say) to enter its critical section three times between visits by P2. This constraint is unacceptable for autonomous processes.

Finally, an algorithm is presented that does not give rise to the close coupling of the previous example but provides mutual exclusion and absence of livelock. The algorithm given was first presented by Peterson (Peterson and Silberschatz, 1985). Another famous algorithm, Dekker's, is discussed by Ben-Ari (1982). The approach of Peterson (and Dekker) is to have two flags (flag1 and flag2) that are manipulated by the process that owns them and a turn variable that is only used if there is contention for entry to the critical sections:

```
process P1;
  loop
    flag1:= up;                              (* announce intent to enter *)
    turn:= 2;                                (* give priority to other process *)
    while flag2 = up and turn = 2 do
      null
    end;
    <critical section>
    flag1:= down;
    <non-critical section>
  end
end P1;

process P2;
  loop
    flag2:= up;                              (* announce intent to enter *)
    turn:= 1;                                (* give priority to other process *)
    while flag1 = up and turn = 1 do
      null
    end;
    <critical section>
    flag2:= down;
    <non-critical section>
  end
end P2;
```

If only one process wishes to enter its critical section then the other process's flag will be down and entry will be immediate. However, if both flags have been raised then the value of turn becomes significant. Let us say that it has the initial value 1, then there are four possible interleavings depending on the order in which each process assigns a value to turn and then checks its value in the 'while' statement:

```
First Possibility – P1 first then P2
P1 sets turn to 2
P1 checks turn and enters busy loop
P2 sets turn to 1 (turn will now stay with that value)
P2 checks turn and enters busy loop
P1 loops around rechecks turn and enters critical section

Second Possibility – P2 first then P1
P2 sets turn to 1
P2 checks turn and enters busy loop
P1 sets turn to 2 (turn will now stay with that value)
P1 checks turn and enters busy loop
P2 loops around rechecks turn and enters critical section
```

```
Third Possibility — interleaved P1 and P2
P1 sets turn to 2
P2 sets turn to 1 (turn will stay with this value)
P2 enters busy loop;
P1 enters critical section

Fourth Possibility — interleaved P2 and P1
P2 sets turn to 1
P1 sets turn to 2 (turn will stay with this value)
P1 enters busy loop;
P2 enters critical section
```

All four possibilities lead to one process in its critical section and one process in a busy loop.

In general, although a single interleaving can illustrate the failure of a system to meet its specification, it is not possible to show that all possible interleavings lead to compliance with the specification. Normally proof methods are needed to show such compliance.

Interestingly, the above algorithm is fair in the sense that if there is contention for access (to their critical sections) and, say, P1 was successful (via either the first or third possible interleaving) then P2 is bound to enter next. When P1 exits its critical section it lowers flag1. This could let P2 into its critical section but even if it did not (because P2 was not actually executing at that time) then P1 will proceed, enter and leave its non-critical section, raise flag1, set turn to 2 and then be placed in a busy loop. There it would remain until P2 had entered and left its critical section and reset flag2 as its exit protocol.

In terms of reliability the failure of a process in its non-critical section will not affect the other process. This is not the case with failure in the protocols or critical section. Here, premature termination of a process would lead to livelock difficulties for the remaining program.

This discussion has been given at length to illustrate the difficulties of implementing synchronization between processes with only shared variables and no additional primitives other than those found in sequential languages. These difficulties can be summarized as follows:

- Protocols that use busy loops are difficult to design, understand and prove correct. (The reader might like to consider generalizing Peterson's algorithm for n processes.)

- Testing programs may not examine rare interleavings that break mutual exclusion or lead to livelock.

- Busy wait loops are inefficient and do not allow a queue discipline to be programmed.

- An unreliable (rogue) task that misuses shared variables will corrupt the entire system.

No concurrent programming language relies entirely on busy waiting and shared variables; other methods and primitives have been introduced. For shared variable systems, semaphores and monitors are the most significant constructs and are described in Sections 8.3 and 8.5.

8.3 Semaphores

Semaphores are a simple mechanism for programming mutual exclusion and condition synchronization. They were originally designed by Dijkstra (1968a) and have the two following benefits:

(1)   They simplify the protocols for synchronization.
(2)   They remove the need for busy wait loops.

A **semaphore** is a non-negative integer variable that, apart from initialization, can only be acted upon by two procedures. These procedures were called 'P' and 'V' by Dijkstra but will be referred to as 'wait' and 'signal' in this book. The semantics of wait and signal are as follows:

- wait(s) If the value of the semaphore, S, is greater than zero then decrement its value by one; otherwise, delay the process until S is greater than zero (and then decrement its value).
- signal(s) Increment the value of the semaphore, S, by one.

The additional important property of wait and signal is that their actions are atomic (indivisible). Two processes both executing wait operations on the same semaphore cannot interfere with each other. Moreover, a process cannot fail during the execution of a semaphore operation.

Condition synchronization and mutual exclusion can be programmed easily with semaphores. First consider condition synchronization:

```
(* condition synchronization *)
var consyn : semaphore;    (* initially 0 *)
process P1;                (* waiting process *)
  ...
  wait (consyn)
  ...
end P1;

process P2;                (* signalling process *)
  ...
  signal (consyn)
  ...
end P2;
```

When P1 executes the wait on a 0 semaphore it will be delayed until P2 executes the signal. This will set consyn to 1 and hence, the wait can now succeed; P1 will continue and consyn will be decremented to 0. Note that if P2 executes the signal first the semaphore will be set to 1 and so P1 will not be delayed by the action of the wait.

Mutual exclusion is similarly straightforward:

```
(* mutual exclusion *)
var mutex : semaphore        (* initially 1 *)
process P1;
  loop
    wait (mutex);
      <critical section>
    signal (mutex);
      <non-critical section>
  end
end P1;



process P2;
  loop
    wait (mutex);
      <critical section>
    signal (mutex);
      <non-critical section>
  end
end P2;
```

If P1 and P2 are in contention then they will execute their wait statements simultaneously. However, as wait is atomic then one process will complete execution of this statement before the other begins. A process will execute a wait(mutex) with mutex = 1, which will allow the process to proceed into its critical section and set mutex to 0; the other process will execute wait(mutex) with mutex = 0, and be delayed. Once the first process has exited its critical section it will signal (mutex). This will cause the semaphore to become 1 again and allow the second process to enter its critical section (and set mutex to 0 again).

With a wait/signal bracket around a section of code the initial value of the semaphore will restrict the maximum amount of concurrent execution of the code. If the initial value is zero no processes will ever enter; if it is one then a single process may enter (that is, mutual exclusion); for values greater than one that number of concurrent executions of the code are allowed.

8.3.1 Suspended processes

In the definition of wait it is clear that if the semaphore is zero then the calling process is delayed. One method of delay (busy waiting) has already been introduced and criticized. A more efficient mechanism is needed. All synchronization primitives deal with delay by removing the process from the set of executable processes. A new state of **suspended** (sometimes called *blocked* or *unrunnable*) is needed.

When a process executes a wait on a zero semaphore the Run-Time Support System (RTSS) is invoked, the process is removed from the processor, and placed in a queue of suspended processes (that is, a queue of processes suspended on that particular semaphore). The RTSS must then select another process to run. Eventually, if the program is correct, another process will execute a signal on that semaphore. As a result the RTSS will pick out one of the suspended processes awaiting a signal on that semaphore, and make it executable again. (The definition of semaphore does not usually specify the order in which processes should become executable again.)

From these considerations a slightly different definition of wait and signal can be given. This definition is closer to what an implementation would do:

```
WAIT(S) :-
if S > 0 then
  S:= S - 1
else
  number_suspended:= number_suspended + 1
  suspend calling process


SIGNALS(S) :-
if number_suspended > 0 then
  number_suspended:= number_suspended - 1
  make one suspended process executable again
else
  S:= S + 1
```

With this definition, the increment of a semaphore immediately followed by its decrement is avoided.

As indicated at the beginning of this section, all synchronization primitives lead to the possibility of a process becoming suspended. The general state diagram for a process, introduced in Figure 7.2 of Chapter 7, is therefore extended in Figure 8.1.

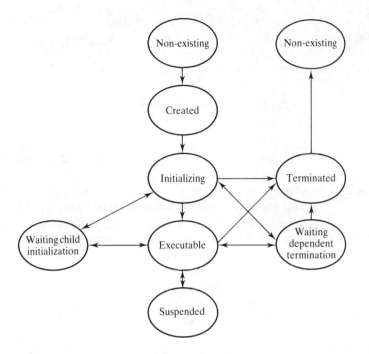

Figure 8.1 State diagram for a process.

8.3.2 Implementation

The above algorithm for implementing a semaphore is quite straight-forward, although it involves the support of a queue mechanism. Where difficulty could arise is in the requirement for indivisibility in the execution of the wait and signal operations. Indivisibility means that once a process has started to execute one of these procedures then it will continue to execute until the operation has been completed. With the aid of the RTSS this is easily achieved; the scheduler is programmed so that it does not pre-empt a process while it is executing a wait or a signal.

Unfortunately, the RTSS is not always in full control of scheduling events. Although all internal actions are under its influence, external actions happen asynchronously and could disturb the atomicity of the semaphore operations. To prohibit this the RTSS will disable interrupts for the duration of the execution of the indivisible sequence of statements. In this way no external events can interfere.

This disabling of interrupts is adequate for a single processor system but not for a multiprocessor one. With a shared memory system, two parallel processes may be executing a wait or signal (on the same sema-phore) and the RTSS is powerless to prevent it. In these circumstances a 'lock' mechanism is need to protect access to the operations. Two such mechanisms are used.

The first is a 'test and set' instruction which is provided on some processors. This allows a process to access a bit in the following way.

(1)   If the bit is zero then set it to one and return zero.

(2)   If the bit is one return one.

These actions are themselves indivisible. Two parallel processes both wishing to operate a wait (for example) will do a test and set operation on the same lock bit (which is initially zero). One process will succeed and set the bit to one; the other process will have returned a one and will therefore have to loop round and retest the lock. When the first process has completed the wait operation it will assign the bit to zero (that is, unlock the semaphore) and the other process will proceed to execute its wait operation.

If no test and set instruction is available then a similar effect can be obtained by using the second mechanism, a swap instruction. Again the lock is associated with a bit that is initially zero. A process wishing to execute a semaphore operation will swap a one with the lock bit. If it gets back a zero from the lock then it can proceed; if it gets back a one then some other process is active with the semaphore and it must retest.

As was indicated in Section 8.1 a software primitive such as a semaphore cannot conjure up mutual exclusion out of 'fresh air'. It is necessary for memory locations to exhibit the essence of mutual exclusion in order for higher-level structures to be built. Similarly, although busy wait loops are removed from the programmer's domain by the use of semaphores, it may be necessary to use busy waits (as above) to implement the wait and signal operations. It should be noted, however, that the latter use of busy waits is only *short-lived* (the time it takes to execute a wait or signal operation) whereas their use for delaying access to the program's critical sections could involve many seconds of looping.

8.3.3   Liveness provision

In Section 8.2 the error condition, livelock, was illustrated. Unfortunately (but inevitably) the use of synchronization primitives introduces other error conditions. **Deadlock** is the most serious error condition and entails a set of processes being in a state from which it is impossible for any of them to proceed. This is similar to livelock but the processes are suspended. To illustrate this condition consider two processes P1 and P2 wishing to gain access to two non-concurrent resources (that is, resources that can only be accessed by one process at a time) that are protected by two semaphores S1 and S2. If both processes access the resource in the same order then no problem arises:

```
       P1                  P2
  wait (S1);          wait (S1);
    wait (S2);          wait (S2);
      .                   .
      .                   .
      .                   .
    signal (S2);        signal (S2);
  signal (S1);        signal (S1);
```

The first process to successfully execute the wait on S1 will also successfully undertake the wait on S2 and subsequently signal the two semaphores and allow the other process in. However, if one of the processes wishes to use the resources in the reverse order, for example:

```
       P1                  P2
  wait (S1);          wait (S2);
    wait (S2);          wait (S1);
      .                   .
      .                   .
      .                   .
    signal (S2);        signal (S1);
  signal (S1);        signal (S2);
```

Then an interleaving could allow P1 and P2 to execute successfully the wait on S1 and S2, respectively, but then inevitably both processes will be suspended while waiting on the other semaphore which is now zero.

It is in the nature of an interdependent concurrent program that usually once a subset of the processes becomes deadlocked all the other processes will eventually become part of the deadlocked set.

The testing of software rarely removes other than the most obvious deadlocks; they can occur infrequently but with devastating results. This error is not isolated to the use of semaphores and is possible in all concurrent programming languages. The design of such languages so that the programming of deadlocks is impossible is a desirable, but not yet attainable goal. Issues relating to deadlock avoidance, detection and recovery will be considered in Chapters 11 and 13.

Indefinite postponement (sometimes called *lockout* or *starvation*) is a less severe error condition whereby a process that wishes to gain access to a resource, via a critical section, is never allowed to do so because there are always other processes gaining access before it. With a semaphore system a process may remain indefinitely suspended (that is, 'queued' on the semaphore) due to the way that the RTSS picks processes from this queue when a signal arrives. Even if the delay is not in fact indefinite but merely open ended (indeterminate) then this may give rise to an error in a real-time system.

If a process is free from livelocks, deadlocks and indefinite postponements then it is said to possess **liveness**. Informally, the liveness property implies that if a process wishes to perform some action then it will, eventually, be allowed to do so. In particular, if a process requests access to a critical section then it will gain access within a finite time.

8.3.4   Binary and quantity semaphores

The definition of a (general) semaphore is a non-negative integer; by implication its actual value can rise to any supported positive number. But in all the examples given so far in this chapter (that is, for condition synchronization and mutual exclusion) only the values zero and one have been used. A simple form of semaphore, known as a **binary semaphore**, can be implemented that only takes these values, that is, the signalling of a semaphore which has the value one has no effect – the semaphore retains the value one. The construction of a general semaphore from two binary semaphores and an integer can then be done if the general form is required.

Another variation on the normal definition of a semaphore is the **quantity semaphore**. With this structure the amount to be decremented by the WAIT (and incremented by the SIGNAL) is not fixed as one but is given as a parameter to the procedures:

```
WAIT (S, i) :-   if S >= i then
                     S:= S - i
                 else
                    delay
                     S:= S - i
SIGNAL (S, i) :- S:= S + i
```

An example of the use of a quantity semaphore is given later in this chapter in Section 8.5.3.

8.3.5   Example semaphore programs in Ada

Algol-68 was the first language to introduce semaphores. They formed values of type 'sema' and were manipulated by the operators 'up' and 'down'. To illustrate some simple programs that use semaphores an abstract data type for SEMAPHOREs, in Ada, will be used. The package to define the abstract data type takes the form of a generic so that the initial value of the SEMAPHORE can be given as a generic parameter (a default value of 1 is given).

```
generic
    INITIAL : NATURAL:= 1;
package SEMAPHORE_PACKAGE is
    type SEMAPHORE is limited private;
    procedure WAIT (S : SEMAPHORE);
    procedure SIGNAL (S : SEMAPHORE);
private
    type SEMAPHORE is ...
end SEMAPHORE package;
```

Ada does not directly support SEMAPHOREs, the WAIT and SIGNAL procedures can however be constructed from the Ada synchronization primitives; these have not yet been discussed and so the full definition of the type SEMAPHORE and the body of the generic package will not be given here. The essence of abstract data types is, however, that they can be used without knowledge of their implementation.

The first example is the producer/consumer system that uses a bounded BUFFER to pass integers between the two tasks:

```
procedure MAIN is
    package BUFFER is
        procedure APPEND (I : INTEGER);
        procedure TAKE (I : out INTEGER);
    end BUFFER;
    task PRODUCER;
    task CONSUMER;

    package body BUFFER is separate;        -- see next page
    use BUFFER;

    task body PRODUCER is
        ITEM : INTEGER;
    begin
        loop
            -- produce item
            APPEND (ITEM);
        end loop;
    end PRODUCER;
    task body CONSUMER is
        ITEM : INTEGER;
    begin
        loop
            TAKE (ITEM);
            -- consume item
        end loop;
    end CONSUMER;
begin
    null;
end MAIN;
```

The BUFFER itself must protect against concurrent access, the appending to a full BUFFER and the taking from an empty one. This it does by the use of three SEMAPHOREs:

```
with SEMAPHORE_PACKAGE;
separate (MAIN)
package body BUFFER is
   SIZE : constant := 32;
   type BUFFER_RANGE is new INTEGER range 0..SIZE − 1;
   BUF : array (BUFFER_RANGE) of INTEGER;
   TOP, BASE : BUFFER_RANGE := 0;

   −− default value
   package MUTUAL_EXCLUSION is new SEMAPHORE_PACKAGE;
   package CONDITION_SYNCHRONIZATION_1
              is new SEMAPHORE_PACKAGE (INITIAL ⇒ 0);
   package CONDITION_SYNCHRONIZATION_2
              is new SEMAPHORE_PACKAGE (INITIAL ⇒ SIZE);
   MUTEX : MUTUAL_EXCLUSION.SEMAPHORE;
   ITEM_AVAILABLE :
           CONDITION_SYNCHRONIZATION_1.SEMAPHORE;
   SPACE_AVAILABLE :
           CONDITION_SYNCHRONIZATION_2.SEMAPHORE;
   use MUTUAL_EXCLUSION, CONDITION_SYNCHRONIZATION_1,
                        CONDITION_SYNCHRONIZATION_2;

   procedure APPEND (I : INTEGER) is
   begin
     WAIT(SPACE_AVAILABLE);
     WAIT(MUTEX);
        BUF(TOP) := I;
        TOP := (TOP + 1) mod SIZE;
     SIGNAL(MUTEX);
     SIGNAL(ITEM_AVAILABLE);
   end APPEND;

   procedure TAKE (I : out INTEGER) is
   begin
     WAIT(ITEM_AVAILABLE);
     WAIT(MUTEX);
        I := BUF(BASE);
        BASE := (BASE + 1) mod SIZE;
     SIGNAL(MUTEX);
     SIGNAL(SPACE_AVAILABLE);
   end TAKE;
end BUFFER;
```

The initial values of the three SEMAPHOREs are different. MUTEX is an ordinary mutual exclusion semaphore and is given the default initial value of 1; ITEM_AVAILABLE protects against taking from an empty BUFFER and has the initial value 0; and SPACE_AVAILABLE (initially SIZE) is used to prevent place operations to a full BUFFER.

When the program starts any consumer task that calls TAKE will be suspended on WAIT(ITEM_AVAILABLE); only after a producer process has called APPEND, and in doing so SIGNAL(ITEM_AVAILABLE), will the consumer process continue.

The producer/consumer structure appears in many forms in real-time programs as does the second example: a resource controller. Consider a package that provides access to a particular resource:

```
package RESOURCE_CONTROLLER is
  procedure ALLOCATE;
  procedure DEALLOCATE;
end RESOURCE_CONTROLLER;
```

For simplicity, the example does not consider how the resource itself is transferred. A task wishing to use the resource would make the following calls:

```
RESOURCE_CONTROLLER.ALLOCATE

      .   -- use the resource

RESOURCE_CONTROLLER.DEALLOCATE
```

Clearly, if the resource is not available then the calling process must be suspended. Mutually exclusive access to the ALLOCATE and DEALLO-CATE operators is also needed as concurrent calls to the procedures are possible.

```
with SEMAPHORE_PACKAGE;
package body RESOURCE_CONTROLLER is
  BUSY : BOOLEAN:= FALSE;    -- state of resource
  -- number of processes presently suspended
  WAITING : NATURAL:= 0;


  package MUTUAL_EXCLUSION is new SEMAPHORE_PACKAGE;
  package CONDITION_SYNCHRONIZATION
          is new SEMAPHORE_PACKAGE (INITIAL ⇒ 0);
  MUTEX : MUTUAL_EXCLUSION.SEMAPHORE;
  AVAILABLE : CONDITION_SYNCHRONIZATION.SEMAPHORE;
  use MUTUAL_EXCLUSION, CONDITION_SYNCHRONIZATION;
```

```
procedure ALLOCATE;
begin
  WAIT(MUTEX);
  if BUSY then
    WAITING:= WAITING + 1;
    -- give up mutual exclusion
    SIGNAL(MUTEX);
    -- become suspended on a zero valued semaphore
    WAIT(AVAILABLE);
    WAITING:= WAITING - 1;
  end if;
  BUSY:= TRUE;
  SIGNAL(MUTEX);
end ALLOCATE;

procedure DEALLOCATE;
begin
  WAIT(MUTEX);
  BUSY:= FALSE;
  if WAITING > 0 then
    SIGNAL(AVAILABLE);
  else
    SIGNAL(MUTEX);
  end if;
end DEALLOCATE;
```

When the resource is deallocated a check is made to see if a process is waiting; if there is, then it is signalled and the mutual exclusive hold on the procedures is passed to this newly executing process.

8.3.6   Semaphore programming in Modula-2

It was indicated in Chapter 7 that Modula-2 provides very low-level concurrency primitives from which high-level models can be constructed. Rather than have the programmer explicitly transfer control from one coroutine to another it is possible to hide the 'TRANSFER' action inside a synchronization primitive. This section will show how to construct a general semaphore module incorporating a flat process model. The essence of this approach is that a main program will create a number of processes (coroutines) which will then execute concurrently. It will then wait for all these processes to complete their execution before continuing. Each process will itself continue to execute until it does a wait or a signal operation; transfer will then be passed on to another process. In effect, this is what many RTSS do in order to reduce the number of process switches to a minimum.

In addition to providing wait and signal procedures for semaphores the Processes module will have a procedure for starting a process. This is a higher level of abstraction for initializing a process and hides the details of NEWPROCESS and TRANSFER.

Process termination with coroutines is a difficulty. If one routine completes its execution then control is never transferred to another process and the system is blocked. However, if a process does transfer control then it never actually terminates! To get around this difficulty a terminate procedure is provided in the module. Each process must call this procedure when it wishes to terminate. The main program that has started up each process also has a termination problem. It is itself a coroutine and having started up the active processes it must wait until they have all terminated. To accommodate this the module exports an idle procedure that blocks the 'main' coroutine until all started processes have called terminate. The definition module for the new process abstraction is given below. Note that a program using this module will not reference the lower-level primitives. Only within the implementation module is their use necessary.

```
DEFINITION MODULE Processes;
    (* This module provides a semaphore-based synchronization *)
    (* scheme. It also provides a process abstraction. *)


    EXPORT QUALIFIED semaphore, initialize, wait, signal, terminate,
                     idle, startprocess;


    TYPE semaphore;


    PROCEDURE initialize (VAR S : semaphore; C : CARDINAL);
                            (* initial value to semaphore *)
    PROCEDURE wait (VAR S : semaphore);
    PROCEDURE signal (VAR S : semaphore);
    PROCEDURE terminate;
    PROCEDURE idle;
    PROCEDURE startprocess (P : PROC);


END Processes.
```

Before describing the implementation of this module an example of its use is given. Program 8.1 is a Modula-2 version of the producer/consumer example that was given in Section 8.3.5 for Ada. To show the termination facilities both processes run for a thousand iterations rather than infinitely.

Program 8.1

```
MODULE ProducerConsumer;

FROM Processes IMPORT semaphore, initialize, wait, signal,
                      terminate, idle, startprocess;

MODULE Buffer;

  IMPORT wait, signal, initialize, semaphore;

  EXPORT append, take;

  CONST size = 32;
  TYPE rng = [0 .. size − 1];
  VAR
    Buf : ARRAY[0..size − 1] OF INTEGER;
    top, base : rng;
    mutex, SpaceAvailable, ItemAvailable: semaphore;

  PROCEDURE append(I : INTEGER);
  BEGIN
    wait(SpaceAvailable);
    wait(mutex);
    Buf[top] := I;
    top := (top + 1) MOD size;
    signal(mutex);
    signal(ItemAvailable)
  END append;

  PROCEDURE take(VAR I : INTEGER);
  BEGIN
    wait(ItemAvailable);
    wait(mutex);
    I := Buf[base];
    base := (base + 1) MOD size;
    signal(mutex);
    signal(SpaceAvailable)
  END take;

  BEGIN     (* Buffer *)
    top := 0;
    base := 0;
    initialize(mutex, 1);
    initialize(SpaceAvailable, size);
    initialize(ItemAvailable, 0)
  END Buffer;
```

```
PROCEDURE producer;
  VAR I : INTEGER;
    item : INTEGER;
BEGIN
  FOR I := 1 TO 1000 DO
    (* produce item *)
    append(item)
  END;
  terminate
END producer;


PROCEDURE consumer;
  VAR I : INTEGER;
    item : INTEGER;
BEGIN
  FOR I := 1 TO 1000 DO
    take(item)
    (* consume item *)
  END;
  terminate
END consumer;


BEGIN (* main module *)
  startprocess(producer);
  startprocess(consumer);
  idle
END ProducerConsumer.
```

Note that the mutual exclusion protection on the Buffer (that is, the

```
wait(mutex);
   ...
signal(mutex);
```

structure) is not strictly needed because with coroutines a process switch can only happen when a process requests it. A switch cannot, therefore, occur during the critical section of the buffer access. Later in the book (Chapter 14) Modula-2 code is given that will deal with interrupts. This code has the effect of forcing a coroutine process to give up the processor. In doing so it is possible that mutual exclusion (based only on the correct behaviour of the coroutines) may be violated. For this reason the wait and signal operations on mutex are included.

The implementation of the process abstraction described above involves many of the activities that one would expect to find in a generated run-time support system for an Ada or occam 2-like language. In particular, it is necessary to provide the following queues of processes:

(1)   A single dispatchqueue for processes able to run but not now actually executing.

(2)   A procqueue (one per semaphore) holding processes that are suspended on a semaphore.

As PROCESS is an abstract data type, exported from the predefined SYSTEM module, it is not possible to manipulate objects of type process directly. A processid type is thus defined by a simple definition module:

```
DEFINITION MODULE PID;
   FROM SYSTEM IMPORT PROCESS;
   EXPORT QUALIFIED processid;
   TYPE processid = POINTER TO process;
END PID.
```

Queues are defined and manipulated by a module of the kind described in Chapter 4:

```
DEFINITION MODULE queuemod;

FROM PID IMPORT processid;

EXPORT QUALIFIED queue, create, empty, insert, remove;

TYPE queue;

PROCEDURE create(VAR Q : queue);
PROCEDURE empty(Q : queue) : BOOLEAN;
   (* return TRUE if Q is empty *)
PROCEDURE insert(VAR Q : queue; P : processid);
   (* add P to back of Q *)
PROCEDURE remove(VAR Q : queue; VAR P : processid);
   (* remove P from front of Q *)

END queuemod.
```

The following implements the module Processes. At all times the variable currentprocess represents the process that is actually executing.

When a process is initiated (startprocess) the count of active processes is incremented and the current process is placed at the back of the dispatch queue. A new process is created and control is transferred to it. If a process wishes to complete its execution it must call terminate; this decrements the active process counter and then attempts to find a new process to run. If the dispatchqueue is empty then a check is made to see if the main process is suspended on idle; if there are no processes to execute then the system is in deadlock and a suitable message is printed.

A call to wait will involve a reduction in the value of the semaphore (if it is greater than zero) or suspension. If it is the latter a new active process is taken from the dispatchqueue. An empty dispatchqueue is again indicative of a deadlocked system. The signal procedure is programmed to wake up a suspended process (and transfer control to it) if there is one; otherwise the semaphore is incremented and the calling process continues. The code for the implementation module is given in Program 8.2.

Program 8.2

```
IMPLEMENTATION MODULE Processes;


    FROM SYSTEM IMPORT ADDRESS, PROCESS, NEWPROCESS, TRANSFER;
    FROM Storage IMPORT ALLOCATE;
    FROM queuemod IMPORT queue, create, empty, insert, remove;
    FROM InOut IMPORT WriteString, WriteLn;
    FROM PID IMPORT processid;


    CONST ProcessSize = 10240;


    TYPE
        semaphore = POINTER TO sema;
        sema = RECORD
                    value : CARDINAL;
                    procqueue : queue
                END;


    VAR
        dispatchqueue : queue;
        NumberActiveProcesses : CARDINAL;
        currentprocess : processid;
        mainwaiting : BOOLEAN;
        idleprocess : processid;


    PROCEDURE deadlock;
    BEGIN
        WriteLn;
        WriteString('System in Deadlock');
        WriteLn;
        WriteString('Program is Aborted');
        WriteLn;
        HALT
    END deadlock;
```

Program 8.2   (cont.)

```
PROCEDURE SwitchProcess(VAR Q : queue);
(* This procedure will switch from executing currentprocess *)
(* to the one that is at the head of Q. It is assumed that      *)
(* a test for a non-empty queue has already been made          *)
VAR
   lastprocess : processid;
BEGIN
    lastprocess := currentprocess;
    remove(Q,currentprocess);                      (* get new process *)
    TRANSFER(lastprocess ↑ ,currentprocess ↑ )    (* run new process *)
END SwitchProcess;


PROCEDURE initialize (VAR S : semaphore; C : CARDINAL);
BEGIN
  NEW(S);
  S ↑ .value := C;
  create(S ↑ .Procqueue);                          (* create an empty process queue *)
END initialize;


PROCEDURE wait (VAR S : semaphore);
BEGIN
  IF S ↑ .value > 0 THEN
    S ↑ .value := S ↑ .value − 1
  ELSIF empty(dispatchqueue) THEN
    deadlock
  ELSE
    insert(S ↑ .procqueue, currentprocess);
    SwitchProcess(dispatchqueue)
  END
END wait;


PROCEDURE signal (VAR S : semaphore);
BEGIN
  IF NOT empty(S ↑ .procqueue) THEN
    insert(dispatchqueue, currentprocess);
    SwitchProcess(S ↑ .procqueue)
  ELSE
    S ↑ .value := S ↑ .value + 1
  END
END signal;


PROCEDURE terminate;
VAR
  lastprocess : processid;
```

```
BEGIN
  NumberActiveProcesses := NumberActiveProcesses − 1;
  IF NOT empty(dispatchqueue) THEN
     SwitchProcess(dispatchqueue)
  ELSIF (NumberActiveProcesses = 0) AND mainwaiting THEN
     lastprocess := currentprocess;
     currentprocess := idleprocess;
     TRANSFER(lastprocess ↑ ,currentprocess ↑ )
  ELSE
     deadlock
  END
END terminate;


PROCEDURE idle;
BEGIN
  IF NumberActiveProcesses > 0 THEN
     IF empty(dispatchqueue) THEN
        deadlock
     ELSE
        mainwaiting := TRUE;
        idleprocess := currentprocess;
        SwitchProcess(dispatchqueue)
     END
  END
END idle;


PROCEDURE startprocess (P : PROC);
VAR
  lastprocess : processid;
  workspace : ADDRESS;
BEGIN
  NumberActiveProcesses := NumberActiveProcesses + 1;
  ALLOCATE(workspace,ProcessSize);
  insert(dispatchqueue, currentprocess);
  lastprocess := currentprocess;
  NEW(currentprocess);
  NEWPROCESS(P,workspace,ProcessSize, currentprocess ↑ );
  TRANSFER(lastprocess ↑ ,currentprocess ↑ )
END startprocess;


BEGIN                                    (* module initialization *)
  create(dispatchqueue);
  NumberActiveProcesses := 0;
  mainwaiting := FALSE;
  idleprocess := NIL;
  NEW(currentprocess)
END Processes.
```

In Program 8.2 the effect of signal was to transfer control to a process that was suspended on the specified semaphore (if there was one). This was done to improve the responsiveness of the system. In terms of the semantics of signal it was unnecessary as the signal process can always continue executing. The following code implements a signal that does not cause a process switch; this form is needed in the implementation of device drivers (see Chapter 14):

```
PROCEDURE signal (VAR S : semaphore);
VAR
   waitprocess : processid;
BEGIN
   IF NOT empty(S ↑ .procqueue) THEN
      remove(S ↑ .procqueue, waitprocess);
      insert(dispatchqueue, waitprocess)
   ELSE
      S ↑ .value := S ↑ .value + 1
   END
END signal;
```

8.3.7   Criticisms of semaphores

Although the semaphore is an elegant low-level synchronization primitive, a real-time program built only upon the use of semaphores is error prone. It needs just one occurrence of a semaphore to be omitted or misplaced for the entire program to collapse. Mutual exclusion may not be assured and deadlock may appear just when the software is dealing with a rare but critical event. What is required is a more structured synchronization primitive.

What the semaphore provides is a means to program mutual exclusion over a critical section. A more structured approach would give mutual exclusion directly. This is precisely what is provided for by the constructs discussed in Sections 8.4 and 8.5.

The examples in Sections 8.3.5 and 8.3.6 showed that an abstract data type for semaphores can be constructed in Ada and Modula-2. However, no high-level concurrent programming language relies entirely on semaphores. They are important historically but are arguably not adequate for the real-time domain.

8.4   Conditional critical regions

Conditional Critical Regions (CCRs) are an attempt to overcome some of the problems associated with semaphores. A critical region is a section of code that is guaranteed to be executed in mutual exclusion. This must be compared with the concept of a critical section that should be executed under mutual exclusion (but in error may not be). Clearly, the programming of a critical section as a critical region immediately meets the requirement for mutual exclusion.

Variables that must be protected from concurrent usage are grouped together into named regions and are tagged as being resources. Processes are prohibited from entering a region in which another process is already active. Condition synchronization is provided by guards on the regions. When a process wishes to enter a critical region it evaluates the guard (under mutual exclusion); if the guard evaluates 'true' it may enter, but if it is false the process is delayed.

To illustrate the use of CCRs an outline of the bounded buffer program is given below.

```
program buffer_eg;
   type buffer_t is record
     slots      : array(1..N) of character;
     size       : integer range 0..N;
     head, tail : integer range 1..N;
   end record;


   buffer : buffer_t;


   resource buf : buffer;


   process producer;
     ...
     loop
       region buf when buffer.size < N do
         -- place char in buffer etc
       end region
       ...
     end loop;
   end;


   process consumer;
     ...
     loop
       region buf when buffer.size > 0 do
         -- take char from buffer etc
       end region
       ...
     end loop;
   end;
end;
```

One problem with CCRs is that processes must re-evaluate their guards every time a CCR naming that resource is left. A suspended process must become executable again in order to test the guard; if it is still false it must return to the suspended state.

A version of CCRs has been implemented in Edison, (Brinch-Hansen, 1981b), a language intended for embedded applications, implemented on multiprocessor systems. Each processor only executes a single process so it may continually evaluate its guards if necessary.

8.5 Monitors

The main problem with conditional regions is that they can be dispersed throughout the program. Monitors are intended to alleviate this problem by providing more structured control regions. They also use a form of condition synchronization that is more efficient to implement.

The intended critical regions are written as procedures and are encapsulated together into a single module called a **monitor**. As a module, all variables that must be accessed under mutual exclusion are hidden; additionally as a monitor, all procedure calls into the module are guaranteed to be mutually exclusive.

Monitors appeared as a refinement of conditional critical regions; initial design and analysis of the structure was undertaken by Dijkstra, (1968b), Brinch-Hansen (1973) and Hoare (1974). They are found in numerous programming languages including Modula-1, Concurrent Pascal and Mesa.

To continue, for comparison, with the bounded buffer example, a buffer monitor would have the following structure:

```
monitor buffer;
  export append, take;
  var (* declaration of necessary variables *)

  procedure append (I : integer);
    ...
  end;

  procedure take (var I : integer);
    ...
  end;
begin
  (* initialization of monitor variables *)
end
```

With languages like Modula-2 and Ada it was natural to program the buffer as a distinct module (package). This approach is also taken with a monitor. The only difference between a module and a monitor is that in the latter case concurrent calls to append and/or take (in the above example) are serialized – by definition. No mutual exclusion semaphore is needed.

Although providing for mutual exclusion there is still a need for condition synchronization within the monitor. In theory, semaphores could still be used but normally a simpler synchronization primitive is introduced. In Hoare's monitors (Hoare, 1974) this primitive is called a **condition variable** and is acted upon by two operators which, because of similarities with the semaphore structure, shall again be called wait and signal. When a process issues a wait operation it is blocked (suspended) and placed on a queue associated with that condition variable (this can be compared with a wait on a semaphore with a value of zero; however, note that a wait on a condition variable *always* blocks unlike a wait on a semaphore). A blocked process then releases its mutually exclusive hold on the monitor, allowing another process to enter. When a process executes a signal operation then it will release one blocked process. If no process is blocked on the specified variable then the *signal has no effect*. The bounded buffer example can now be given in full:

```
monitor buffer;
  export append, take;
  const size = 32;
  var BUF : array[0..size - 1] of integer;
      top, base : 0..size - 1;
      spaceavailable, itemavailable : condition;
      NumberInBuffer : integer;

  procedure append (I : integer);
  begin
    if NumberInBuffer = size then
      wait(spaceavailable);
    BUF[top] := I;
    NumberInBuffer := NumberInBuffer + 1;
    top := (top + 1) mod size
    signal(itemavailable)
  end append;

  procedure take (var I : integer);
  begin
    if NumberInBuffer = 0 then
      wait(itemavailable);
    I := BUF[base];
    base := (base + 1) mod size;
    NumberInBuffer := NumberInBuffer - 1;
    signal(spaceavailable)
  end take;
```

```
begin (* initialization *)
  NumberInBuffer := 0;
  top := 0;
  base := 0
end;
```

If a process calls (for example) take when there is nothing in the buffer then it will become suspended on itemavailable. A process appending an item will, however, signal this suspended process when an item does become available.

The semantics for wait and signal given above are not complete; as they stand two or more processes could become active within a monitor. This would occur following a signal operation in which a blocked process was freed. The freed process and the one that freed it are then both executing inside the monitor. To prohibit this clearly undesirable activity the semantics of signal must be modified. Three different approaches are used in languages:

(1)   A signal is allowed only as the last action of a process before it leaves the monitor (this is the case with the buffer example above).

(2)   A signal operation has the side-effect of executing a 'return' statement, that is, the process is forced to leave the monitor.

(3)   A signal operation which unblocks another process has the effect of blocking itself; this process will only execute again when the monitor is free.

In the latter case, which was proposed by Hoare in his original paper on monitors, the processes that are blocked because of a signal action are placed on a 'ready queue' and are chosen, when the monitor is free, in preference to processes blocked on entry.

Because of the importance of monitors, three languages that support this structure will be briefly described.

8.5.1 Modula-1

Modula-1 (as it must now be known) is the forerunner to Modula-2 but has a quite different process model. It employs explicit process declaration (not coroutines) and monitors which are termed **interface modules**. Somewhat confusingly the condition variables are called signals and are acted upon by three procedures.

(1)   The procedure wait(s, r) delays the calling process until it receives the signal s. The process when delayed is given a priority (or delay rank r) where r must be a positive valued integer expression whose default is one (the highest priority).

(2)   The procedure send(s), sends the signal s to that process with the highest priority which has been waiting for s. If several waiting processes all have the same priority then the one which has been waiting the longest receives the signal. The process executing the send is suspended. If no process is waiting the call has no effect.

(3)   The Boolean function awaited(s); this yields the value TRUE if there is at least one process blocked on s; FALSE otherwise.

The following is an example of a Modula-1 interface module. It accomplishes the resource control requirement that was programmed with semaphores in Section 8.3.5:

```
INTERFACE MODULE resource_control;

    DEFINE allocate, deallocate;    (* export list *)

    VAR busy : BOOLEAN;
      free : SIGNAL;

    PROCEDURE allocate;
    BEGIN
      IF busy THEN WAIT(free) END;
      busy := TRUE
    END;

    PROCEDURE deallocate;
    BEGIN
      busy := FALSE;
      SEND(free)
    END;

    BEGIN     (* initialization of module *)
      busy := FALSE
    END.
```

Note that in deallocate: IF AWAITED(free) THEN SEND(free); could have been inserted, but as the effect of SEND(free), when AWAITED(free) is FALSE, is null, there is nothing to be gained by doing the test.

8.5.2 Concurrent Pascal

In Concurrent Pascal (Brinch-Hansen, 1975) condition variables are replaced by queue variables; however, they differ in that only one process can be waiting on a queue variable at any one time (that is, there is not a queue!). The operators 'delay' and 'continue' are analogous to wait and signal; the definition of 'continue' causing the invoking process to return from the monitor.

8.5.3 Mesa

So far it has been assumed that when a suspended process is unblocked the condition that caused it to block no longer holds. For example, the process that is blocked waiting for the resource to be free (that is, not busy) can assume that it is free when it starts executing again. Similarly, a process delayed inside the bounded buffer monitor proceeds with its actions once executable again.

In Mesa (Lampson and Redell, 1980) a different approach is taken. There is a wait operation but processes cannot assume that, when woken, the condition that caused the block is removed. The notify operation (comparable to a signal) merely indicates that the blocked process should re-evaluate the condition. Mesa also supports a broadcast operation that notifies all processes waiting on a particular condition. (These processes are woken up one at a time to keep the monitor exclusive.)

There are three kinds of procedure allowed within a Mesa monitor: entry procedures, internal procedures and external procedures. Entry procedures operate with the monitor lock. Internal procedures can only be called from entry procedures. (In Modula-1 an internal procedure would simply be missing from the DEFINE list.) External procedures can be called without the monitor lock and are used to view the current state of the monitor. They cannot change variables, call internal procedures or use a condition variable. These restrictions are checked at compile time.

To give an example of a Mesa monitor consider a refinement of the resource allocation problem. Rather than have a single resource which is either busy or free, the monitor must control access to N instances of the resource. An allocation request passes, as a parameter, the number of instances ($<= N$) required. For simplicity this request parameter is not checked in the allocate or deallocate procedures. To obtain a secure structure it would be necessary to check that a process returning a collection of resources actually had them to return. Secure resource control is considered again in Chapter 11. The Mesa code follows; the procedure 'free_resources' is included to illustrate an external procedure. The reader should be able to understand this module without further knowledge of Mesa (note that the assignment operator is $<-$ in Mesa).

```
Resource_Control : monitor =
begin
  const N = 32;
  free : condition;
  resumes_free : positive <- N;
```

```
allocate : entry procedure[size : positive] =
  begin
    do
      if size <= resource_free then exit;     -- exit from loop
      wait free;
    endloop;
    resource_free <- resource_free - size;
end;

deallocate : entry procedure[size : positive] =
begin
  localfree[size];
  broadcast free;
end;

localfree : internal procedure[S : positive] =
begin
  resource_free <- resource_free + S;
end;

free_resources : external procedure return[p : positive] =
begin
  p <- resource_free;
end;
end;
```

As a deallocation operation could free enough resources for a number of blocked allocate processes to proceed, a broadcast is made. All blocked processes (on free) will execute, in turn, and either obtain the resources if size is now less than or equal to resource_free, or become blocked again.

If Mesa did not support a broadcast facility then it would be necessary to keep a count of the number of blocked processes and for each process to unblock the next one in the chain:

```
Resource_Control : monitor =
begin
  const N = 32;
  free : condition;
  resumes_free : positive < - N;
  number_blocked : cardinal < - 0;
  still_to_try : cardinal < - 0;

  allocate : entry procedure[size : positive] =
    begin
      do
        if size <= resource_free then exit;     -- exit from loop
        number_blocked <- number_blocked + 1;
        if still_to_try > 0 then notify free;
        wait free;
```

```
          number_blocked <- number_blocked - 1;
          still_to_try <- still_to_try - 1;
        endloop;
        resource_free <- resource_free - size;
        if still_to_try > 0 then notify free;
    end;

    deallocate : entry procedure[size : positive] =
    begin
      localfree[size];
      still_to_try <- number_blocked;
      notify free;
    end;
    ...
  end;
```

This is due to the semantics of the notify operation which does not block the execution.

This can be achieved implicitly in Modula-1 because the semantics of the SEND operation does cause a context switch to the awoken process.

```
PROCEDURE allocate(size : INTEGER);
BEGIN
  WHILE size > resource_free DO
    WAIT(free);
    SEND(free)
  END;
  resource_free := resource_free -size
END;

PROCEDURE deallocate(size : INTEGER);
BEGIN
  resource_free := resource_free + size;
  SEND(free)
END;
```

If a language supported quantity semaphores then the allocation and deallocation procedures would be very simple:

```
procedure allocate(size : integer);
begin
  wait(QS, size)
end;

procedure deallocate(size : integer);
begin
  signal(QS, size)
end;
```

where QS is a quantity semaphore initialized to the total number of resources in the system.

8.5.4   Nested monitor calls

There are many problems associated with the use of monitors but the one that has received the most attention is the semantic implications of a monitor calling a procedure within another monitor (Lister,1977).

> The controversy is over what (if anything) should be done if a process having made a nested monitor call is suspended in another monitor. The mutual exclusion in the last monitor call will be relinquished by the process, due to the semantics of the wait and equivalent operations. However, mutual exclusion will not be relinquished by processes in monitors from which the nested calls have been made. Processes that attempt to invoke procedures in these monitors will become blocked. This has performance implications, since blockage will decrease the amount of concurrency exhibited by the system (Lampson,1980).

> Various approaches to the nested monitor problem have been suggested. The most popular one, adopted by Concurrent Pascal and Mesa, is to maintain the lock. Other approaches include prohibiting nested procedure calls altogether (as in Modula-1) and providing constructs which specify that certain monitor procedures may release their mutual exclusion lock during remote calls.

8.5.5   Criticisms of monitors

The monitor gives a structured and elegant solution to mutual exclusion problems such as the bounded buffer. It does not, however, deal well with condition synchronizations outside the monitor. In Modula-1 for example, SIGNALs are a general programming feature and are not restricted to use within a monitor. A language based on monitors, therefore, presents a mixture of high-level and low-level primitives. All the criticisms surrounding the use of semaphores apply equally (if not more so) to condition variables.

Although monitors encapsulate all the entities concerned with a resource, and provide the important mutual exclusion, their internal structure may still be difficult to read due to the use of condition variables. Moreover, the monitor is a passive construct (apart from its initialization); it cannot dynamically control access to its procedures other than to ensure that they are not called concurrently.

Chapter 9 considers message-based synchronization and communication primitives. Languages that use these have, in effect, elevated the monitor to an active process in its own right. As a process can only be doing one thing at a time mutual exclusion is assured. Processes no longer communicate via shared variables but directly (or via an intermediate process). Therefore, it is possible to construct a single high-level primitive that combines communication and synchronization. This concept, although first considered by Conway (1963) has only relatively recently been employed in high-level real-time programming languages. It forms the basis of both Ada and occam 2.

SUMMARY

Process interactions require concurrent programming languages to support synchronization and data communication. Communication can be based on either shared variables or message passing. This chapter has been concerned with shared variables, the multiple update difficulties they present and the mutual exclusion synchronizations needed to counter these difficulties. In this discussion the following terms were introduced:

- critical section – code that must be executed under mutual exclusion;
- producer-consumer system – two or more processes exchanging data via a finite (bounded) buffer;
- busy waiting – a process continually checking a condition to see if it is now able to proceed;
- livelock – an error condition in which one or more processes are prohibited from progressing whilst using up processing cycles.

Examples were used to show how difficult it is to program mutual exclusion using only shared variables. Semaphores were introduced to simplify these algorithms and to remove busy waiting. A semaphore is a non-negative integer that can only be acted upon by wait and signal procedures. The executions of these procedures are atomic.

The provision of a semaphore primitive has the consequence of introducing a new state for a process; namely, suspended. It also introduces two new error conditions:

(1)   deadlock – a collection of suspended processes that cannot proceed;

(2)   indefinite postponement – a process being unable to proceed as resources are not made available for it (also called lockout or starvation).

Semaphores can be criticized as being too low level and error prone in use. Following their development two more structured primitives were introduced:

(1)   condition critical regions
(2)   monitors

Monitors are an important language feature, and are used in Modula-1, Concurrent Pascal and Mesa. They consist of a module, entry to which is assured (by definition) to be under mutual exclusion. Within the body of a monitor a process can suspend itself if the conditions are not appropriate for it to proceed. This suspension is achieved using a condition variable. When a suspended process is awoken (by a signal operation on the condition variable) it is imperative that this does not result in two processes being active in the module at the same time. To make sure this does not happen a language must prescribe one of the following:

(1)   The signal operation can only be executed as the last action of a process in a monitor.

(2)   The signal operation has the side-effect of forcing the signalling process to exit the monitor.

(3)   The signalling process is itself suspended if it results in another process becoming active in the monitor.

Although monitors provide a high-level structure for mutual exclusion, other synchronizations must be programmed using very low-level condition variables. This gives an unfortunate mix of primitives in the language design.

Further reading

Ben-Ari M. (1982). *Principles of Concurrent Programming*. Englewood Cliffs NJ: Prentice-Hall

Hoppe J. (1980). A simple nucleus written in Modula-2: a case study. *Software Practice and Experience*, **10**(9), 697–706

Peterson J. and Silberschatz A. (1985). *Operating System Concepts*. Reading MA: Addison-Wesley

Welsh J., Elder J. and Bustard D. (1988). *Concurrent Program Structures*. London: Prentice-Hall

Whiddett D. (1987). *Concurrent Programming for Software Engineers*. Chichester: Ellis Horwood

Wirth N. (1977). Modula: a language for modular multiprogramming. *Software Practice and Experience*, **7**(1), 3–84

EXERCISES

8.1   Consider a shared data structure that can be both read from and written to. Show how semaphores can be used to allow many concurrent readers or a single writer but not both.

8.2   Show how Hoare's conditional critical region can be implemented using semaphores.

8.3   Show how Hoare's (or Mesa's or Modula-1's) monitors can be implemented using semaphores.

8.4   Show how binary semaphores can be implemented using a single Modula-1 interface module. How would you modify your solution to cope with a general semaphore?

8.5   Consider the scheduling of a queue of requests to transfer data to/ from a disk. In order to minimize the disk head movement all the requests for a particular cylinder are serviced in one go. The scheduler sweeps up and down the disk servicing requests for each cylinder in turn. Write a Modula-1 interface module which provides the necessary synchronization. Assume that there are two interface procedures: one for requesting access to a particular cylinder, the other for releasing the cylinder. User processes call procedures in the following disk driver module:

```
MODULE disk_driver;

    DEFINE read, write;

    PROCEDURE read(VAR data:data_t; addr:disk_address);
    BEGIN
        (* work out cylinder address *)
        diskheadscheduler.request(cylinder);
        (* read data *)
        diskheadscheduler.release(cylinder);
    END read;

    (* similarly for write *)

END disk_driver;
```

8.6   Write a Modula-1 interface module to control the read/write access of a file in a database. In order to maintain the integrity of the file only one process may update it at once; however any number of processes may read the file as long as it is not in the process of being updated. Furthermore, requests to update the file should only be allowed when there are no current readers. However, once a request to update the file has been received all subsequent requests to read the file should be blocked until there are no more updates.

Your interface module should define four procedures startread, endread, startwrite and endwrite. You may assume the interface module will be used in the following way.

```
MODULE file_access;
  DEFINE readfile, writefile;
  USE startread, endread, startwrite, endwrite;

  PROCEDURE readfile;
  BEGIN
    startread;
    { read the file }
    endread;
  END readfile;

  PROCEDURE writefile;
  BEGIN
    startwrite;
    { write the file }
    endwrite;
  END writefile;
END file_access.
```

8.7 One of the criticisms of monitors is that condition synchronization is too low level and unstructured. Explain what is meant by this statement. A higher-level monitor synchronization primitive might take the form

```
WaitUntil boolean_expression;
```

where the process is delayed until the Boolean expression evaluates to true. For example:

```
WaitUntil x < y + 5;
```

would delay the process until $x < y + 5$.

Although this form of condition synchronization is more structured it is not found in most languages which support monitors. Explain why this in the case. Under what circumstances would the objections to the above high-level synchronisation facility be invalid? Show how the bounded buffer problem can be solved using the WaitUntil synchronization primitive inside a monitor.

8.8 Consider a system of three cigarette smoker processes and one agent process. Each smoker continuously makes a cigarette and smokes it. To make a cigarette three ingredients are needed: tobacco, paper, and matches. One of the processes has paper, another tobacco and the third has matches. The agent has an infinite supply of all three ingredients. The agent places two ingredients, chosen randomly, on a table. The smoker who has the remaining ingredient can then make and smoke a cigarette. Once it has finished smoking the smoker signals the agent who then puts another two of the three ingredients on the table, and the cycle repeats.

Sketch the structure of a monitor which will synchronize the agent and all three smokers.

8.9 Contrast the internal facilities provided by the Unix Kernel (Bach, 1986) for mutual exclusion and condition synchronization, with the corresponding facilities provided by semaphores.

8.10 Show how the internal facilities provided by Unix (Bach, 1986) can be used to control access to a shared data structure. You should assume that there will be many readers and many writers. However, although many readers should be allowed to access the data structure concurrently, only a single writer is allowed access at any one time. Furthermore, a mixture of readers and writers is not allowed. You should also give priority to readers.

8.11 Show how the operations on a semaphore can be implemented in the nucleus of an operating system for a single processor system *without* busy waiting. What hardware facility does your solution require?

8.12 Complete Exercise 7.6 using monitors for process synchronization.

Chapter 9
Message-based Synchronization and Communication

The alternative to shared-variable synchronization and communication is based on message passing. The approach is typified by the use of a single construct for both synchronization and communication. Within this broad category, however, a wide variety of language models exist. This variety in the semantics of message passing arises from, and is dominated by three issues (Gentleman, 1981):

(1)   the model of synchronization,

(2)   the method of process naming,

(3)   the message structure.

In this chapter each of these issues is considered in turn. Following this, the message passing models of various languages, including Ada and occam 2, are discussed.

9.1 Process synchronization

With all message-based systems there is the implicit synchronization that a receiver process cannot obtain a message before that message has been sent. Although this is quite obvious it must be compared with the use of a shared variable; in this case a receiver process can read a variable and not know whether it has been written to by the sender process. If a process executes an unconditional message receive operation when no message is available then it will become suspended until the message arrives.

Variations in the process synchronization model arise from the semantics of the send operation, which can be broadly classified as follows:

(1)   **Asynchronous** (or **no-wait**): the sender proceeds immediately, regardless of whether the message is received or not. The asynchronous send is found in PLITS, (Feldman, 1979), CONIC, (Kramer *et al.*, 1983), and several operating systems (Brinch-Hansen, 1970; Rashid and Robertson, 1981).

(2)   **Synchronous**: the sender proceeds only when the message has been received. The synchronous send is used in CSP (Hoare, 1978), and occam 2.

(3)   **Remote invocation**: the sender proceeds only when a reply has been returned from the receiver. The request-response paradigm of communication is modelled by remote invocation send and is found in Ada, SR, (Andrews, 1981, 1982), CONIC (Kramer *et al.*, 1983) and various operating systems (Cheriton *et al.*, 1979; Cheriton, 1984).

To appreciate the difference between these approaches consider the following analogy. The posting of a letter is an asynchronous send – once the letter has been put into the letter box the sender proceeds with his or her life; only by the return of another letter can the sender ever know that the first letter actually arrived. From the receiver's point of view a letter can only inform the reader about an out-of-date event, it says nothing about the current position of the sender. (Everyone has received sun-drenched postcards from people they know have been back at work for at least two weeks!)

A telephone is a better analogy for synchronous communication. The sender now waits until contact is made and the identity of the receiver verified before the message is sent. If the receiver can reply immediately (that is, during the same call) then the synchronization is remote invocation. Because the sender and receiver 'come together' for a synchronized communication it is often called a **rendezvous**. The remote invocation form is known as an **extended rendezvous**, as arbitrary computations can be undertaken before the reply is sent (that is, during the rendezvous).

Clearly, there is a relationship between these three forms of send. Two asynchronous events can essentially constitute a synchronous relationship if an acknowledgement message is always sent (and waited for):

```
P1                        P2
asyn_send (message)       wait (message)
wait (acknowledgement)    asyn_send (acknowledgement)
```

Moreover, two synchronous communications can be used to construct a remote invocation:

```
P1                     P2
syn_send (message)     wait (message)
wait (reply)           ...
                       construct reply
                       ...
                       syn_send (reply)
```

As an asynchronous send can be used to construct the other two it could be argued that this model gives the greatest flexibility and should, therefore, be the one that languages adopt. However, there are a number of drawbacks to using this model:

(1)   Potentially infinite buffers are needed to store messages that have not been read yet (perhaps because the receiver has terminated).

(2)   Because asynchronous communication is out of date most sends are programmed to expect an acknowledgement (that is, synchronous communication).

(3)   More communications are needed with the asynchronous model, hence programs are more complex.

(4)   It is more difficult to prove the correctness of the complete system.

Note that where asynchronous communication is desired in a synchronized message-passing language then buffer processes can easily be constructed.

9.2 Process naming

Process naming involves two distinct sub-issues: direction versus indirection, and symmetry. In a direct naming scheme, the sender of a message explicitly names the receiver:

```
send (message) to (process-name)
```

With an indirect naming scheme, the sender names some intermediate entity (known variously as a channel, mailbox, link or pipe):

```
send ⟨message⟩ to ⟨mailbox⟩
```

Note that even with a mailbox the message passing can still be synchronous (that is, the sender will wait until the message is read). Direct naming has the advantage of simplicity, while indirect naming aids the decomposition of the software; a mailbox can be seen as an interface between distinct parts of the program.

A naming scheme is symmetric if both sender and receiver name each other (directly or indirectly)

```
send ⟨message⟩ to ⟨process-name⟩
wait ⟨message⟩ from ⟨process-name⟩

send ⟨message⟩ to ⟨mailbox⟩
wait ⟨message⟩ from ⟨mailbox⟩
```

It is asymmetric if the receiver names no specific source but accepts messages from any process (or mailbox):

```
wait ⟨message⟩
```

Asymmetric naming fits the client-server paradigm in which 'server' processes provide services in response to messages from any of a number of 'client' processes. Therefore, an implementation must be able to support a queue of processes waiting for the server.

If the naming is indirect then there are further issues to consider. The intermediary could have:

- a many-to-one structure (that is, any number of processes could write to it but only one process can read from it), this again fits the client-server paradigm;
- a many-to-many structure (that is, many clients and many servers);
- a one-to-one structure (that is, one client and one server); note that with this structure no queues need to be maintained by the run-time support system.

It addition to these a one-to-many structure can be envisaged; however, this is seldom used.

9.3   Message structure

Ideally, a language should allow any data object of any defined type (predefined or user) to be transmitted in a message. Living up to this ideal is difficult, particularly if data objects have different representations at the sender and receiver, and even more so if the representation includes pointers (Herlihy and Liskov, 1982). Because of these difficulties some languages (for example, occam 1) have restricted their message content to unstructured, fixed sized objects of system-defined type. More modern languages have removed these restrictions.

9.4 Message passing semantics of Ada and occam 2

Both Ada and occam 2 allow communication and synchronization to be based on message passing. With occam 2 this is the only method available; with Ada, as seen in Chapter 8, shared-variable communication is also possible although it is not the preferred method. There are, however, important differences between the message-based schemes that the two languages incorporate. In short, Ada uses direct asymmetric remote invocation, while occam 2 incorporates indirect symmetric synchronous message passing. Both languages allow messages to have a flexible structure. The two languages will now be described; occam 2 first, as it has the simpler semantics.

9.4.1 The occam 2 model

Occam 2 processes are not named, and therefore it is necessary during communication to use indirect naming via a channel. Each channel can only be used by a single writer and a single reader process. Both processes name the channel; the syntax is somewhat terse:

```
ch ! X   -- write value of expression X
         -- onto channel ch

ch ? Y   -- read from channel ch
         -- into variable Y
```

In the above, the variable Y and the expression X will be of the same type. The communication is synchronous, therefore, whichever process accesses the channel first will be suspended. When the other process arrives, data will pass from X to Y (this can be viewed as the distributed assignment $Y := X$). The two processes will then continue their executions concurrently and independently. To illustrate this communication consider two processes that are passing 1000 integers between them:

```
CHAN OF INT ch:
PAR
  INT V:
  SEQ i = 0 FOR 1000       -- process 1
    SEQ
      -- generate value V
      ch ! V
```

```
INT C:
SEQ i = 0 FOR 1000        -- process 2
  SEQ
    ch ? C
    -- use C
```

With each iteration of the two loops a rendezvous between the two processes occurs.

Channels in occam 2 are typed and can be defined to pass objects of any valid type including structured types. Arrays of channels can also be defined.

It is important to appreciate that the input and output operations on channels are considered to be fundamental language primitives. They constitute two of the five primitive processes in occam 2. The others being SKIP, STOP and 'assignment' (see Section 3.5.1). By comparison, communication and synchronization do not have such a central role in Ada.

9.4.2   The Ada extended rendezvous model

The semantics of remote invocation have many superficial similarities with a procedure call. Data passes to a receiver, the receiver executes and then data is returned. Because of this similarity Ada supports the definition of a program's messages in a way that is compatible with the definition of procedures. In particular, the parameter-passing models are identical (that is, there is only one model that is used in both situations).

In order for a task to receive a message it must define an **entry**. As with a procedure any number of parameters, of any mode and of any type are allowed. For example:

```
task SCREEN_OUTPUT is      -- single task definition
  entry CALL (VALUE : CHARACTER, X_COORDINATE,
              Y_COORDINATE: INTEGER);
end SCREEN_OUTPUT;

task type BUFFER is        -- task type definition
  entry APPEND (I : INTEGER);
  entry TAKE ( I : out INTEGER);
end BUFFER;

task TIME_SERVER is
  entry READ_TIME (NOW : out TIME);
  entry SET_TIME (NEW_TIME : TIME);
end TIME_SERVER;
```

Ada provides a facility whereby an array of entries can, in effect, be defined – these are known as **entry families**. For instance, consider a multiplexor which has seven input channels. Rather than representing each of these as a separate entry, Ada allows them to be defined as a family:

```
type CHANNEL_NUMBER is new INTEGER range 1 .. 7;
task MULTIPLEXOR is
   entry CHANNELS(CHANNEL_NUMBER)(DATA: INPUT_DATA);
end MULTIPLEXOR;
```

The above defines seven entries, all with the same parameter specification.

To call a task (that is, send it a message) simply involves naming the receiver task and its entry (naming is direct), for example:

```
SCREEN_OUTPUT.CALL(CHAR,10,20);     -- where char is a character


B.APPEND(J);                        -- where B is of type buffer


MULTIPLEXOR.CHANNELS(3)(D);         -- where 3 indicates the index
                                    -- into the entry family and
                                    -- D is of type input_data


TIME_SERVER.READ_TIME (T);          -- where T is of type time
```

Note that in the last example the only data being transferred is passing in the opposite direction to the message itself (via an **out** parameter). This can lead to terminology confusion and hence the term message passing is not usually applied to Ada. The phrase **extended rendezvous** is less ambiguous.

If an entry call is made on a task that is no longer active then the exception TASKING_ERROR is raised at the point of the call. This allows alternative action to be taken if, unexpectedly, a task has terminated prematurely, as illustrated below.

```
begin
   OUTPUT.CALL(J);
exception
   when TASKING_ERROR =>
      -- log error and continue
end;
```

Note that this is not equivalent to checking beforehand that the task is available:

```
if OUTPUT'TERMINATED then
   -- log error and continue
else
   OUTPUT.CALL(J);
end if;
```

An interleaving could cause a task to terminate after the attribute has been evaluated but before the call is handled.

To receive a message involves accepting a call to the appropriate entry:

```
accept CALL (I : INTEGER) do
   LOCAL_VARIABLE : = I;
end CALL;

accept APPEND (I : INTEGER) do
   BUF(TOP) : = I;
end APPEND;

accept READ_TIME (NOW : out TIME) do
   NOW := CLOCK;
end READ_TIME;

accept CHANNELS(3)(DATA: INPUT_DATA) do
   -- store data from the 3rd channel
   -- in the family
end CHANNELS;
```

An **accept** statement can be placed where any other statement is valid. It can even be placed within another accept statement (though not for the same entry). All entries (and family members) should have accepts associated with them. These accepts name the entry concerned but not the task from which an entry call is sought. Naming is thus asymmetric.

To give a simple example of two tasks interacting consider, as with the occam 2 example, two tasks that loop round and pass data between them. With the Ada code the tasks will swap data. This is shown in Program 9.1.

Although the relationship between the two tasks (T1 and T2) is essentially symmetric, the asymmetric naming in Ada requires them to have quite different forms. This should be compared with the occam 2 code which retains the symmetry.

In many applications it is desirable for a task to know its own identity so that, for example, resource allocation mechanisms can be implemented reliably. Unfortunately, as indicated in Section 7.3.7, an Ada task cannot

Program 9.1

```
procedure TEST;
  task T1 is
    entry EXCHANGE (I : INTEGER; J : out INTEGER);
  end T1;

  task T2;

  task body T1 is
    A,B : INTEGER;
  begin
    for K := 1 TO 1000 loop
      -- produce A
      accept EXCHANGE (I : INTEGER; J : out INTEGER) do
        J := A;
        B := I;
      end EXCHANGE;
      -- consume B
    end loop;
  end T1;

  task body T2 is
    C,D : INTEGER;
  begin
    for K := 1 TO 1000 loop
      -- produce C
      T1.EXCHANGE(C,D);
      -- consume D
    end loop;
  end T2;

begin
  null;
end TEST;
```

---

be initialized at the time of its creation. Therefore, it is necessary to use a rendezvous to pass identification data to those tasks that require it. The robot-arm controller that was used for illustration in Chapter 7 consists of three tasks that must know the dimension for which they are responsible. To give them this information the main procedure in the program must call each of the tasks in turn, as shown in Program 9.2.

When the number of tasks to be initialized is small then the approach in Program 9.2 presents no problems, but for highly-parallel systems task initialization becomes a serious bottleneck. This has lead to criticisms of this feature of Ada (Yemini, 1982). On multiprocessor architectures Burns (1985a) has proposed an algorithm for initialization that minimize this serial bottleneck.

Program 9.2

```
procedure MAIN is
  type DIMENSION is (XPLAIN, YPLAIN, ZPLAIN);

  task type CONTROL is
    entry INITIALIZE(D : DIMENSION);
  end CONTROL;

  SYSTEM : array(DIMENSION) of CONTROL;

  task body CONTROL is
    DIM : DIMENSION;
    POSITION : INTEGER;                     -- absolute position
    SETTING : INTEGER;                      -- relative movement
  begin
    accept INITIALIZE(D : DIMENSION) do
      DIM := D;
    end INITIALIZE;
    POSITION := 0;                          -- rest position
    loop
      NEW_SETTING(DIM, SETTING);
      POSITION := POSITION + SETTING;
      MOVE_ARM(DIM, POSITION);
    end loop;
  end CONTROL;
begin
  SYSTEM(XPLAIN).INITIALIZE(XPLAIN);
  SYSTEM(YPLAIN).INITIALIZE(YPLAIN);
  SYSTEM(ZPLAIN).INITIALIZE(ZPLAIN);
end MAIN;
```

9.4.3 Exception handling and the rendezvous

As any valid Ada code can be executed during a rendezvous there is the possibility that an exception could be raised within the accept statement itself. If this occurs then either:

- there is a valid exception handler within the accept; in which case the accept will terminate normally, or;
- the raised exception is not handled within the accept and the accept is immediately terminated.

In this latter case the named exception will be raised again in both the called and calling tasks. The called task will have the exception raised immediately after the accept statement, the calling task will have it raised after the entry call. Scope problems may, however, cause the exception to be anonymous in the calling task.

Program 9.3

```
task FILE_HANDLER is
  entry OPEN(F : FILE_TYPE);
  ...
end FILE_HANDLER;


task body FILE_HANDLER is
  ...
begin
  loop
    begin
      ...
      accept OPEN(F : FILE_TYPE) do
        loop
          begin
            DEVICE_OPEN(F);
            exit;
          exception
            when DEVICE_OFF_LINE ⇒
              BOOT_DEVICE;
          end;
        end loop;
      end OPEN;
      ...
    exception
      when FILE_DOES_NOT_EXIST ⇒
        null;
    end;
  end loop;
end FILE_HANDLER;
```

To illustrate the interaction between the rendezvous and the exception models consider a task that acts as a file server, as shown in Program 9.3. One of its entries will allow a client task to open a file.

In Program 9.3 the FILE_HANDLER calls a device driver to open the specified file. This request can either succeed or lead to one of two exceptions being raised, DEVICE_OFF_LINE or FILE_DOES_NOT_EXIST. The first exception is handled within the accept; an attempt is made to 'boot' the device and then the OPEN request is repeated. As the exception handler is within the accept the client is unaware of this activity (although if the device refuses to boot it will be indefinitely suspended). The second exception is due to a faulty request by the client task. It is, therefore, not handled within the accept and will propagate out to the calling task which will need to protect itself against the exception:

```
begin
   FILE_HANDLER.OPEN(NEW_FILE);
exception
   when FILE_DOES_NOT_EXIST ⇒
      FILE_HANDLER.CREATE(NEW_FILE);
      FILE_HANDLER.OPEN(NEW_FILE);
end;
```

Note that the server task also protects itself against this exception by having a block defined within the outer loop construct.

9.5 Selective waiting

In all the forms of message passing that have so far been discussed in this chapter, the receiver of a message must wait until the specified process, or channel, delivers the communication. In general, this is too restrictive. A receiver process may actually wish to wait for any one of a number of processes to call it. Server processes receive request messages from a number of clients; the order in which the clients call being unknown to the servers. To facilitate this common program structure, receiver processes are allowed to wait selectively for a number of possible messages. But to understand selective waiting fully, Dijkstra's *guarded commands* (Dijkstra, 1975) must be explained first.

A guarded command is one which is only executed if its guard evaluates to true. For example:

$$x < y \rightarrow m := x$$

this means that if x is less than y then assign the value of x to m. A guarded command is not a statement in itself but is a component of a *guarded command set*, of which there are a number. Here, the concern is only with the choice, or alternative, construct:

```
if x <= y → m := x
☐ x >= y → m := y
fi
```

The ☐ signifies choice. In the above example the program's execution will either assign x to m or y to m. If both alternatives are possible, that is, both guards evaluate true ($x = y$ in this example), then an *arbitrary* choice is made. The programmer cannot determine which path will be taken, the construct is *non-deterministic*. A well-constructed program will be valid for all possible choices. When $x = y$, in this example, then both paths will have the same effect.

It is important to note that this non-deterministic structure is quite distinct from the deterministic form that could have been constructed using the normal 'if' statement:

> if $x <= y$ then $m := x$;
> elsif $x >= y$ then $m := y$;
> end if;

Here, the values $x = y$ would ensure that m was assigned the value x.

The general choice construct can have any number of guarded components. If more than one guard evaluates true the choice is arbitrary. But if no guard evaluates true then this is viewed to be an error condition and the statement, along with the process that executed it, is aborted.

The guarded command is a general program structure. If, however, the command being guarded is a message operator (normally the receive operator although in some languages also the send) then the statement is known as **selective waiting**. This was first introduced in CSP (Hoare, 1978) and is available in both Ada and occam 2.

9.5.1 The occam 2 ALT

Consider a process that reads integers down three channels (ch1, ch2 and ch3) and then outputs whatever integers it receives down a further channel (chout). If the integers arrived in sequence down the three channels then a simple loop construct would suffice.

```
WHILE TRUE
  SEQ
    ch1    ? I    -- for some local integer I
    chout ! I
    ch2    ? I
    chout ! I
    ch3    ? I
    chout ! I
```

However, if the order of arrival is unknown then each time the process loops, a choice must be made between the three alternatives:

```
WHILE TRUE
  ALT
    ch1    ? I
      chout    ! I
    ch2    ? I
      chout    ! I
    ch3    ? I
      chout    ! I
```

If there is an integer on ch1, ch2 or ch3, it will be read and the specified action taken; which, in this case, is always to output the newly acquired integer down the output channel chout. In a situation where more than one of the input channels is ready for communication an arbitrary choice is made as to which one is read. Before considering the behaviour of the ALT when none of the channels are ready, the general structure of an ALT will be outlined. It consists of a collection of guarded processes:

```
ALT
  G1
    P1
  G2
    P2
  G3
    P3
    :
  Gn
    Pn
```

The processes themselves are not restricted – they are any occam 2 process. The guards (which are also processes) can have one of three forms (a fourth possibility involving the specification of a time delay is considered in Chapter 12).

```
(boolean_expression) & channel_input_operation

channel_input_operation

(boolean_expression) & SKIP
```

The most general form is, therefore, a Boolean expression and a channel 'read', for example:

```
NOT BufferFull & ch ? BUFFER[TOP]
```

If the Boolean expression is simply TRUE then it can be omitted altogether (as in the earlier example). The SKIP form of guard is used to specify some alternative action to be taken when other alternatives are precluded, for example:

```
ALT
  NOT BufferFull & ch ? BUFFER[TOP]
    SEQ
      TOP := ...
  BufferFull & SKIP
    SEQ
      -- swap buffers
```

On execution of the ALT the Boolean expressions are evaluated. If none evaluate TRUE (and there are no default TRUE alternatives) then the ALT process cannot proceed and it becomes equivalent to the STOP (error) process. Assuming a correct execution of the ALT then the channels are examined to see if there are processes waiting to write to them. One of the following possibilities could then ensue :

(1)   There is only one ready alternative, that is, one Boolean expression evaluates to TRUE (with a process waiting to write or a SKIP guard) – this alternative is chosen, the rendezvous takes place (if it is not a SKIP) and the associated subprocess is executed.

(2)   There is more than one ready alternative – one is chosen arbitrarily, this could be the SKIP alternative if present and ready.

(3)   There are no ready alternatives – the ALT is suspended until some other process writes to one of the open channels of the ALT.

The ALT will, therefore, become a STOP process if all the Boolean expressions evaluate to FALSE, but will merely be suspended if there are no outstanding calls. Because of the non-shared variable model of occam 2 it is not possible for any other process to change the value of any component of the Boolean expression.

The ALT when combined with the SEQ, IF, WHILE, CASE and PAR furnishes the complete set of occam 2 program constructs. A replicator can be attached to an ALT in the same way that it has been used with other constructs. For example, consider a concentrator process that can read from 20 processes (rather than three as before); however, rather than use 20 distinct channels, the server process uses an array of channels as follows:

```
WHILE TRUE
  ALT j = 0 FOR 20
    ch[j] ? I
      chout ! I
```

Finally, it should be noted that occam 2 provides a variant of the ALT construct which is not arbitrary in its selection of ready alternatives. If the programmer wishes to give preference to a particular channel then it should be placed as the first component of a PRI ALT. The semantics of PRI ALT dictate that the textually first ready alternative is chosen. Program 9.4 gives examples of PRI ALT statements. An example of the use of PRI ALT is given in Chapter 11.

Program 9.4

```
PRI ALT
  VeryImportantChannel ? message
    -- action
  ImportantChannel ? message
    -- action
  LessImportantChannel ? message
    -- action

WHILE TRUE
  PRI ALT j = 0 FOR 20   -- ch[0] is given highest preference
    ch[j] ? I
      chout ! I
```

9.5.2 The Ada select

Ada's many-to-one message-passing relationship can deal easily with a number of clients by having them all call the same entry. However, where a server must deal with possible calls to two or more different entries an ALT type structure is again required; in Ada this is called a **select**. Consider, for illustration, a task that provides protected access to an integer variable. It does this by providing two entries READ and WRITE:

```
task PROTECTION is
  entry READ (I : out INTEGER);
  entry WRITE (I : INTEGER);
end;
```

Because the task itself can only execute one accept statement at a time there are no multiple update difficulties. In the body of the task a call to WRITE must be accepted first (to give it an initial value), after that calls to READ and WRITE must both be handled. The task body, therefore, has the form shown in Program 9.5.

Note that Program 9.5 shows how a task can have more than one accept statement for any particular entry.

As with the first occam 2 example in Section 9.5.1 this Ada program does not illustrate the use of Boolean expressions in guards. The general form of the Ada select is shown in Program 9.6. There can be any number of alternatives. Apart from accept alternatives (of which there must be one) there are three further forms:

(1)   a **terminate** alternative,

(2)   an **else** alternative,

(3)   a **delay** alternative.

Program 9.5

```
            task body PROTECTION is
              VARIABLE : INTEGER;
            begin
              accept WRITE (I : INTEGER) do
                VARIABLE := I;
              end WRITE;
              loop
                select
                  accept READ (I : out INTEGER) do
                    I := VARIABLE;
                  end READ;
                or
                  accept WRITE (I : INTEGER ) do
                    VARIABLE := I;
                  end WRITE;
                end select;
              end loop;
            end PROTECTION;
```

The **delay** alternative is considered, with the occam 2 equivalent, in Chapter 12. The **else** alternative is defined to be executed when (and only when) no other alternative is *immediately* executable. This can only occur when there are no outstanding calls on entries which have Boolean expressions that evaluate TRUE (or no Boolean expressions at all).

The **terminate** alternative has no equivalent in occam 2 but is an important primitive. It has the following properties:

(1)   If it is chosen the task that executed the select statement is terminated.

(2)   It can only be chosen if there are no longer any tasks that can call the select.

Program 9.6

```
            select
              when ⟨BOOLEAN-EXPRESSION⟩ ⇒
                accept ⟨ENTRY⟩ do
                  ..
                end ⟨ENTRY⟩;
                —— any sequence of statements
            or
              —— similar
              ...
            end select;
```

To be more precise, a task will terminate if all tasks that are dependent on the same master have already terminated or are similarly waiting on selects with terminate alternatives. The effect of this alternative is to allow server tasks to be constructed that need not concern themselves with termination but will nevertheless terminate when they are no longer needed. The lack of this provision in occam 2 leads to complex termination conditions with associated deadlock problems (Burns, 1988).

The execution of the select follows a similar sequence to that of the ALT. Firstly, the Boolean expressions are evaluated; those that produce a FALSE, lead to that alternative being closed for that execution of the select. Following this phase, a collection of possible alternatives is derived. If this collection is empty then the exception PROGRAM_ERROR is raised immediately after the select. For normal execution one alternative is chosen. The choice is arbitrary if there is more than one alternative with an outstanding call. If there are no outstanding calls on eligible alternatives then either:

- the else alternative is executed if there is one;
- the task is suspended waiting for a call to be made (or a timeout to expire – see Chapter 12);
- the task is terminated if there is a terminate option *and* there are no other tasks that could call it (as described above);

Note that shared variables can be contained in guards but this is not recommended.

9.5.3   The bounded buffer example in Ada and occam 2

To illustrate the use of the select statement and the ALT construct, the bounded-buffer problem will be programmed in both Ada and occam 2. Buffers are important components of many real-time systems and in Chapter 8 their implementation as monitors was given. A monitor buffer is a passive construct; in message-based languages the buffer becomes a process in its own right. Consider first the more straightforward Ada structure. A task is needed which exports two entries, one for TAKE and the other for APPEND:

```
task BUFFER is
  entry APPEND(I : DATA);
  entry TAKE(I : out DATA);
end BUFFER;
```

where DATA is the type of the data items that will be placed in the buffer.

The body of the task must arbitrarily select between calls to TAKE and APPEND and must implement, by the use of guards, the usual condition synchronizations as shown in Program 9.7.

Program 9.7

```
task body BUFFER is
  SIZE : constant POSITIVE := 32;
  subtype N_RANGE is INTEGER range 0 .. N − 1;
  TOP, BASE : N_RANGE := 0;
  BUFF : array (N_RANGE) of DATA;
  NUMBER_IN_BUFFER : INTEGER range 0 .. N := 0;
begin
  loop
    select
      when NUMBER_IN_BUFFER /= SIZE ⇒
        accept APPEND (I : DATA) do
          BUFF(TOP) := I;
        end APPEND;
        TOP := (TOP + 1) mod SIZE;
        NUMBER_IN_BUFFER := NUMBER_IN_BUFFER + 1;
    or
      when NUMBER_IN_BUFFER /= 0 ⇒
        accept TAKE (I : out DATA) do
          I := BUFF(BASE);
        end TAKE;
        BASE := (BASE + 1) mod SIZE;
        NUMBER_IN_BUFFER := NUMBER_IN_BUFFER − 1;
    or
        terminate;
    end select;
  end loop;
end BUFFER;
```

To implement a single reader and single writer buffer in occam 2 requires the use of two channels that link the buffer process to the client processes (to cater for more readers and writers would require arrays of channels):

```
CHAN OF DATA TAKE, APPEND:
```

Unfortunately, the natural form for this buffer would be as shown in Program 9.8.

Output operations in this context are not allowed in occam 2. Only input operations can form part of an ALT guard. The reason for this restriction is implementational efficiency on a distributed system. The essence of the problem is that the provision of symmetric guards could lead to a channel being accessed by an ALT at both ends. The arbitrary decision of one ALT would therefore be dependent on the decision of the other (and vice versa). If the ALTs are on different processors then the agreement on a collective decision would involve the passing of a number of low-level protocol messages.

Program 9.8

```
VAL INT size IS 32:
INT TOP, BASE, number_in_buffer:
[size]DATA BUFFER:
SEQ
  number_in_buffer := 0
  TOP := 0
  BASE := 0
  WHILE TRUE
    ALT
      number_in_buffer < size & APPEND ? BUFFER[TOP]
        SEQ
          number_in_buffer := number_in_buffer + 1
          TOP := (TOP + 1) REM size
      number_in_buffer > 0 & TAKE ! BUFFER[BASE]    -- not legal occam
        SEQ
          number_in_buffer := number_in_buffer - 1
          BASE := (BASE + 1) REM size
```

To circumvent the restriction on guards occam 2 forces the TAKE operation to be programmed as a double interaction. The client process must indicate that it wishes to TAKE and then it must TAKE; a third channel is thus needed:

```
CHAN OF DATA TAKE, APPEND, REQUEST:
```

The client must make the following calls

```
SEQ
  REQUEST ! Any    -- Any is an arbitrary token
  TAKE ? D         -- D is of type DATA
```

Program 9.9 shows the form of the BUFFER process itself. The correct functioning of the BUFFER is thus dependent on correct usage by the client processes. This dependence is a reflection of poor modularity. Although the Ada select is also asymmetric (that is, you cannot select between accepts and entry calls) the fact that data can pass in the opposite direction to the call removes the difficulty that manifests itself in occam 2.

Not only is the Ada BUFFER more independent of its clients it can easily be turned into an abstract data type by building the task into a package, this is shown in Program 9.10.

Program 9.9

```
VAL INT size IS 32:
INT TOP, BASE, NumberInBuffer:
[size]DATA BUFFER:
SEQ
  NumberInBuffer := 0
  TOP := 0
  BASE := 0
  DATA Any:
  WHILE TRUE
    ALT
      NumberInBuffer < size & APPEND ? BUFFER[TOP]
        SEQ
          NumberInBuffer := NumberInBuffer + 1
          TOP := (TOP + 1) REM size
      NumberInBuffer > 0 & REQUEST ? Any
        SEQ
          TAKE ! BUFFER[BASE]
          NumberInBuffer := NumberInBuffer - 1
          BASE := (BASE + 1) REM size
```

Program 9.10

```
package BUFFERS is
  type BUFFER is limited private;
  procedure PUT (I : DATA; B : in out BUFFER);
  procedure GET (I : out DATA; B : in out BUFFER);
private
  task type BUFFER is
    entry APPEND (I : DATA);
    entry TAKE(I : out DATA);
  end BUFFER;
end BUFFERS;


package body BUFFERS is
  procedure PUT (I : DATA; B : in out BUFFER) is
  begin
    B.APPEND(I);
  end PUT;


  procedure GET (I : out DATA; B : in out BUFFER) is
  begin
    B.TAKE(I);
  end GET;
```

Program 9.10   (cont.)

```
task body BUFFER is
  SIZE : constant POSITIVE := 32;
  subtype N_RANGE is INTEGER range 0 .. N – 1;
  TOP, BASE : N_RANGE := 0;
  BUFF : array (N_RANGE) of DATA;
  NUMBER_IN_BUFFER : INTEGER range 0 .. N := 0;
begin
  loop
    select
      when NUMBER_IN_BUFFER /= SIZE ⇒
        accept APPEND (I : DATA) do
          BUFF(TOP) := I;
        end APPEND;
        TOP := (TOP + 1) mod SIZE;
        NUMBER_IN_BUFFER := NUMBER_IN_BUFFER + 1;
    or
      when NUMBER_IN_BUFFER /= 0 ⇒
        accept TAKE (I : out DATA) do
          I := BUFF(BASE);
        end TAKE;
        BASE := (BASE + 1) mod SIZE;
        NUMBER_IN_BUFFER := NUMBER_IN_BUFFER – 1;
    or
        terminate;
    end select;
  end loop;
end BUFFER;
end BUFFERS;
```

Finally, the BUFFER package can be made type independent by constructing a generic:

```
generic
  SIZE : POSITIVE;
  type DATA is private;
package BUFFERS is
  type BUFFER is limited private;
  procedure PUT(I : DATA; B : in out BUFFER);
  procedure GET(I : out DATA; B : in out BUFFER);
private
  task type BUFFER is
    entry APPEND(I : DATA);
    entry TAKE(I : out DATA);
  end BUFFER;
end BUFFERS;
```

This shows the power of Ada to combine type, data and process abstraction.

To give a further example, consider the SEMAPHORE_PACKAGE outlined in Section 8.3, the complete code is given in Program 9.11. To obtain indivisibility on the WAIT and SIGNAL operations a task must be

Program 9.11

```
generic
   INITIAL : NATURAL:= 1;
package SEMAPHORE_PACKAGE is
   type SEMAPHORE is limited private;
   procedure WAIT (S : SEMAPHORE);
   procedure SIGNAL (S : SEMAPHORE);
private
   task type SEMAPHORE is
      entry WAIT;
      entry SIGNAL;
   end SEMAPHORE;
end SEMAPHORE_PACKAGE;


package body SEMAPHORE_PACKAGE is
   task body SEMAPHORE is
      S : NATURAL := INITIAL;
   begin
      loop
         select
            when S > 0 =>
            accept WAIT;
            S := S - 1;
         or
            accept SIGNAL;
            S := S + 1;
         or
            terminate;
         end select;
      end loop;
   end SEMAPHORE;
   procedure WAIT (S : SEMAPHORE) is
   begin
      S.WAIT;
   end;
   procedure SIGNAL (S : SEMAPHORE) is
   begin
      S.SIGNAL;
   end;
end SEMAPHORE_PACKAGE;
```

used. As with the BUFFER example the task is defined in the private part of the generic package and the exported procedures are mapped onto entry calls within the package body:

9.5.4 Non-determinism and selective waiting

In the discussion in Section 9.5.3 it was noted that when there is more than one ready alternative in a selective waiting construct, then the choice between them is arbitrary. The rationale behind making the select construct arbitrary is that concurrent languages usually make few assumptions about the order in which processes are executed. The scheduler is assumed to schedule processes non-deterministically. (Although individual schedulers will have deterministic behaviour.)

To illustrate this relationship consider a process P that will execute a selective wait construct upon which processes S and T could call. If the scheduler's behaviour is assumed to be non-deterministic then there are a number of possible interleavings or 'histories' for this program:

(1) P runs first; it is blocked on the select. S (or T) then runs and rendezvous with P.

(2) S (or T) runs first and blocks on the call to P; P now runs and executes the select with the result that a rendezvous takes place with S (or T).

(3) S (or T) runs first and blocks on the call to P; T (or S) now runs and is also blocked on P. Finally, P runs and executes the select on which T and S are waiting.

These three possible and legal interleavings lead to P having either none, one or two calls outstanding on the selective wait. The select is defined to be arbitrary precisely because the scheduler is assumed to be non-deterministic. If P, S and T can execute in any order then, in case (3), P should be able to choose to rendezvous with S or T – it will not affect the programs correctness.

A similar argument applies to any queue that a synchronization primitive defines. Non-deterministic scheduling implies that all such queues should release processes in a non-deterministic order. Although semaphore queues are often defined in this way, entry queues and monitor queues are specified to be FIFO. The rationale here is that FIFO queues prohibit starvation. This argument is however spurious; if the scheduler is non-deterministic then starvation can occur (a process may never be given a processor). It is inappropriate for the synchronization primitive to attempt to prevent starvation. It is arguable that entry queues should also be non-deterministic.

The scheduling of processes which have priorities assigned is considered in detail in Section 11.3.6 and Chapter 12.

9.6   Modula-2 and message passing

One of the main attractions of the low-level nature of the Modula-2 concurrency facility is that many different process abstractions can be built using the coroutine mechanism. For example, in Section 8.3.6 it was shown how Modula-2 coroutines could be used to implement a process abstraction based on semaphores.

Wirth (1984) showed how a synchronization model, similar to the channel construct available in occam 2, could be implemented in Modula-2. The definition module in Program 9.12 is an extension of this model

Program 9.12

```
DEFINITION MODULE processes;
    (* This module provides a process abstraction with a *)
    (* message-based synchronization scheme. *)
    FROM SYSTEM IMPORT WORD;
    TYPE channel;
        guardedchannel = RECORD
          chan : channel;
          guard : BOOLEAN
        END;

    PROCEDURE send(VAR C : channel; M : ARRAY OF WORD);
    PROCEDURE receive(VAR C : channel; VAR M : ARRAY OF WORD);

    PROCEDURE select(VAR gdchans : ARRAY OF guardedchannel; VAR M : ARRAY OF
            WORD; VAR alt : CARDINAL);
    PROCEDURE selectorterminate(VAR gdchans : ARRAY OF guardedchannel;
            VAR M : ARRAY OF WORD; VAR alt : CARDINAL);
    PROCEDURE selectelsecontinue(VAR gdchans : ARRAY OF guardedchannel;
            VAR M : ARRAY OF WORD; VAR alt : CARDINAL; VAR continued : BOOLEAN);

    PROCEDURE initialize(VAR C : channel);
      (* from main block *)

    PROCEDURE sendreg(VAR C : channel);
      (* form user process *)
    PROCEDURE receivereg(VAR C : channel);
      (* from user process *)

    PROCEDURE terminate;
    PROCEDURE idle;
    PROCEDURE startprocess (P : PROC);
END processes.
```

that incorporates an Ada-like select facility and more secure communication. The type channel is provided in the processes module as an abstract data type. Before any declared channel can be used it must be initialized in the main program and registered for send and receive operations in the two processes (PROCs) that will use it. The semantics of channel usage allow only a single reader and a single writer process. A channel can be used to communicate objects of any type and size; communication is synchronous. A run-time check is made to ensure that the size of object in the send and receive are identical. No other checks can be made with the low-level generic facilities of Modula-2.

Three variations of selective waiting are provided. These correspond to Ada's facilities of a normal select, select with terminate alternative, and select with else part. As the parameters to the different forms are not identical an interface of distinct procedures was preferred. The ordinary select works on an array of guarded channels, and returns not only the message 'read' but also a flag to show which channel was used. Note that in the form given here all channels used in a select must pass data of the same type. This restriction could, however, be removed by returning a variant record.

A process can select between a number of otherwise distinct channels by assigning these channels into a local array of guardedchannels. The sending process is unaware whether a select or a receive is to be used for communication with the send. For example, the following program fragment illustrates the FIFO buffer. Assume one producer process sends to channel inchan and a single consumer receives from channel outchan having first indicated the wish to consume on channel ready. The buffer process has a local array[0 .. 1] of guardedchannel choice declared; the code would be as follows:

```
choice[0].chan := inchan;
choice[1].chan := ready;
LOOP
   choice[0].guard := NOT full;
   choice[1].guard := NOT empty;
   select(choice,item,branch,dynamic);
   IF branch = 1 THEN            (* inchan *)
      put(item)                  (* in buffer *)
   ELSE                          (* ready *)
      get(item);                 (* from buffer *)
      send(outchan,item)
   END
END;
```

A full implementation of an extended version of this module is discussed in Appendix A. The module is extended to include some of the real-time control primitives that are introduced in Chapter 12.

9.7   The CHILL language

Within this book attention is primarily focused on the languages Ada, Modula-2 and occam 2. There are, of course, many other languages that are used for real-time applications but it would be impossible to cover them all comprehensively within a single volume. It is, nevertheless, one of the aims of this book to discuss particular features of other languages if they are distinctive and/or important. In this section a brief description is given of the concurrency model in CHILL. Other features of CHILL such as its exception handling model have already been discussed in Section 6.4.1.

The development of CHILL follows a similar path to that of Ada. Its intended application domain is, however, more restricted – telecommunications switching systems. Notwithstanding this restriction, such systems have all the characteristics of general real-time applications: they are large and complex, have specified time constraints and have high reliability requirements. In the early 1970s the Comite Consultatif International Telegraphique et Telephonique (CCITT) recognized the need for a single high-level language that would make telecommunication systems more independent of the hardware manufacturers. By 1973 it was decided that no existing language met their requirements and a group was set up to bring forward a preliminary language proposal. This language was used on several trial implementations and after a number of design iterations a final language proposal was agreed in the autumn of 1979. The name CHILL is derived from the international telecommunications committee (Ccitt HIgh Level Language).

CHILL's concurrency model is of interest here because of its pragmatic design. Processes can only be declared at the outermost level but they can be passed parameters when they are started. Consider the simple robot-arm controller given earlier in Section 9.4.2. A process type control has as a parameter the dimension of movement (that is, in the X, Y or Z plane). The action of the process is to read a new relative position for its plane of action and they cause the robot arm to move:

```
newmode dimension = set(xplane, yplane,
                        zplane);              /* enumeration type */


control = process(dim dimension);
   dcl position, setting int;                 /* declare variables position */
                                              /* and setting to be integers */

   position := 0;
   do for ever;
     new_setting(dim, setting);
     position := position + setting;
     move_arm(dim, position);
   od;
end control;
```

To indicate the execution of three control processes (one for each dimension) the start statement is used:

```
start control(xplane);
start control(yplane);
start control(zplane);
```

This will cause three anonymous processes to commence their executions. If it is desired to identify each instance of a process then unique names can be given as part of the start statement. (A name is a variable of type instance).

```
dcl xinst, yinst, zinst instance;
```

```
start control(xplane) set xinst;
start control(yplane) set yinst;
start control(zplane) set zinst;
```

A process instance may terminate itself by executing a stop statement.

9.7.1 Communication in CHILL

It is in its communication and synchronization mechanism that CHILL can be described as being pragmatic. Rather than having a single model it supports three distinct approaches:

(1)   regions – these provide mutual exclusion to shared variables (that is, they are monitors);

(2)   buffers – these allow for asynchronous communication between processes;

(3)   signals – these are a form of channel and can be compared with the occam mechanism.

The motivation for having three separate structures seems to be a recognition that there is no single model that is universally agreed to be the best:

One communication mechanism may not be able to function optimally in both distributed and common memory architectures (Smedema *et al.*, 1983).

A region explicitly grants access to its procedures; within the region events can be used to delay processes. Events are acted upon by delay and continue. These have similar semantics to the wait and signal operations of Modula-1. The following implements a simple resource controller:

```
resource : region
  grant allocate, deallocate;
  syn max = 10;    /* declare constant */
  decl used int := 0;
  no_resources event;

  allocate : proc;
    if used < max then
      used := used + 1;
    else
      delay(no_resource);
      used := used + 1;
    fi;
  end allocate;

  deallocate : proc
    used := used - 1;
    continue(no_resource)
  end deallocate;

end resource;
```

Buffers are predefined to have send (put) and receive (get) operators:

```
syn size = 32;
dcl buf buffer(size) int;    /* declare integer buffer */

  send buf(I);               /* I is an int */

  receive case
    (buf in J) :             /* statements */
  esac
```

The receive is placed within a case statement for, in general, a process may attempt to read from more than one buffer. If all such buffers are empty the process is delayed. It is also possible for a process reading from a buffer to know the name (instance) of the process that placed that data in the buffer. This is particularly important in telecommunication systems where links have to be made between consumer and producer processes.

Signals are defined in terms of the type of data they communicate and the destination process (type):

```
signal channel = (int) to consumer;
```

Here, consumer is a process type. To transmit data (I) via this signal again uses the send statement:

```
send channel(I) to con;
```

where con is a process instance of type consumer. The receive operation uses the case statement thereby providing selective waiting (without guards).

It is interesting to consider the naming convention applied to CHILL signals. The send operation names the signal and the process instance; the receive mentions only the signal but it can find out the identity of the associated process.

9.8   Remote procedure call

This chapter has so far concentrated on how processes can communicate and synchronize their activities. Discussions on the implications of this when processes reside on different machines connected by a network are postponed until Chapter 13. However, for completeness the concept of a **Remote Procedure Call** (RPC) is introduced here as it is a common method of transferring control in a distributed environment.

In a single-processor system processes execute procedures in order to transfer control from one section of code to another; only when they need to communicate and synchronize with another process do they require interprocess communication. Remote procedure calls extend this idea to enable a single process to execute code which resides on more than one machine. They allow a process currently executing on one processor to execute a procedure on another; whether this should be done transparently to the application programmer is arguable and will be discussed in Chapter 13. The execution of the procedure may involve communication with processes which reside on the remote machine; this is achieved either by shared memory methods (for example, monitors) or by message passing (for example, rendezvous).

It is worth noting that remote invocation message passing can be made to appear syntactically like a procedure call, with the message encoded in the input parameters and the reply encoded in the output parameters (see for example, Ada entries and accepts). However, this syntactic convenience can be misleading, since the semantics of remote invocation message passing are quite different from those of a procedure call. In particular, remote invocation relies on the active cooperation of the receiver process in executing an explicit 'receive' operation. A procedure call, on the other hand, is not a form of interprocess communication, but a transfer of control to a passive piece of code. When the procedure is local (on the same machine as the caller) its body can be executed by the calling process; in the case of a remote procedure call the body may have to be executed on behalf of the caller by an anonymous surrogate process on the remote machine. The involvement of another process in this case is a matter of implementation, not of semantics. For a remote procedure call to have the same semantics as a (re-entrant) local one, the implementation must allow an arbitrary number of calls to be handled simultaneously. This requires a process to be created for each call, or the existence of a pool of processes large enough to handle the maximum number of concurrent calls. The cost of process creation or maintenance may sometimes dictate that the degree of concurrency be limited.

9.9 Process idioms

The use of concurrency is not restricted to real-time programming. It is a general concept with wide applicability. Within the real-time domain however the use of processes can be seen to follow common lines. From these approaches it is possible to identify a number of tasking idioms, the use of which can greatly simplify the construction of real-time software.

Pyle (1985) has suggested that there are two basic kinds of processes: *active* and *passive*. Active processes are used to model coexisting objects, whereas passive processes provide synchronization agents. This is a similar view to the client-server paradigm in which server processes protect system resources from unsynchronized client usage. A more comprehensive list of process idioms is given by Buhr (1984) and Cherry (1986) in the context of Ada. For example, Cherry gives the following 13 basic building idioms for tasks. He argues that they constitute a complete software construction kit.

(1)   cyclic – a cycle of repeated and regular actions,

(2)   state machine – an arbitrary client process,

(3)   device driver,

(4)   interrupt handler,

(5)   monitor,

(6)   semaphore,

(7)   bounded buffer,

(8)   unbounded buffer,

(9)   bounded stack,

(10)   unbounded stack,

(11)   message forwarder – implements an asynchronous send,

(12)   pump – extracts message and forwards it,

(13)   hybrid – a combination of two or more idioms in the same process.

Device drivers and interrupt handlers are discussed in Chapter 14. Examples of bounded buffer and semaphore processes have already been given in this chapter in Section 9.5.3 and it is left to the reader to construct unbounded and stack structures. Chapter 11 considers cyclic resource controllers, and, therefore, it remains in this chapter to give example programs for message forwarders and pumps.

9.9.1 Asynchronous agents

Normal interprocess communication is synchronous. There are, however, instances when an asynchronous relationship between processes is desirable, for example, where a server process does not wish to block if a client is unable to receive the results of a previous request. To achieve this in a synchronous language requires the introduction of a new process that is placed, logically, between the two communicating partners. In Ada these agents can be given a general generic form. Firstly, the asynchronous message forwarder is given below. This generic package provides a task which stores a single message (for the client that created it) and passes on this message by calling the procedure DESTINATION which is provided as a generic parameter. The type of the message is also generic.

```
generic
  type MESS is private;
  with procedure DESTINATION(M : MESS);
package NO_WAIT_SEND is
  task type AGENT is
    entry FORWARD(M : MESS);
  end AGENT;
  type AGT is access AGENT;
end NO_WAIT_SEND;


package body NO_WAIT_SEND is
  task body AGENT is
    TEMP : MESS;
  begin
    accept FORWARD(M : MESS) do
      TEMP := M;
    end;
    DESTINATION(TEMP);
  end AGENT;
end NO_WAIT_SEND;
```

A simple example of the use of the above package is a main program calling (indirectly) the entry REQUEST in the task SERVER:

```
with NO_WAIT_SEND;
procedure MAIN is
   type MESSAGE is new INTEGER;
   task SERVER is
      entry REQUEST(M : MESSAGE);
   end SERVER;
   package MESSENGER is new NO_WAIT_SEND(MESS ⇒ MESSAGE,
                            DESTINATION ⇒ SERVER.REQUEST);
   use MESSENGER;
   PHIDIPPIDES : AGT := new AGENT;
   M : MESSAGE;
   task body SERVER is separate;
begin
   -- obtain value for m
   PHIDIPPIDES.FORWARD(M);
   -- continue execution
end MAIN;
```

A pump process does a double call:

```
generic
   type MESS is private;
   with procedure DESTINATION(M : out MESS);
   with procedure SOURCE(M : MESS);
package NO_WAIT_SEND is
   task type AGENT;
   type AGT is access AGENT;
end NO_WAIT_SEND;
```

```
package body NO_WAIT_SEND is
   task body AGENT is
      TEMP : MESS;
   begin
      SOURCE(TEMP);
      DESTINATION(TEMP);
   end AGENT;
end NO_WAIT_SEND;
```

Finally, although not one of the idioms described above, it is possible to define an asynchronous MAILBOX task that is, in terms of direction of 'call', the inverse of the pump:

```
generic
   type MESS is private;
package MAILBOX is
   task type AGENT is
      entry DEPOSIT(M : MESS);
      entry COLLECT(M : out MESS);
   end AGENT;
   type AGT is access AGENT;
end MAILBOX;

package body MAILBOX is
   task body AGENT is
      TEMP : MESS;
   begin
      accept DEPOSIT(M : MESS) do
         TEMP := M;
      end;
      accept COLLECT(M : out MESS) do
         M := TEMP;
      end;
   end AGENT;
end MAILBOX;
```

With this generic package a task type is provided that has two entries, one for the message to be deposited and the other to allow the client task to collect the message when it is ready to do so.

With all of these structures a task is created, it obtains a message, passes it on and then terminates. A new task is needed for the next message, if there is one. If two processes are passing data (asynchronously) on a regular basis then it may be better to set up the agent process permanently. This approach is more natural with the static occam 2 language. The message forwarder would be structured as follows; note that an infinite loop is used and the message is, in this example, of type integer (INT):

```
INT temp:
WHILE TRUE
  SEQ
    in ? temp
    out ! temp
```

The most general form that this occam 2 process can take is shown below, this is a procedure (PROC) where the two channels are specified as parameters together with a value that gives the termination condition for the loop.

```
PROC MessageForwarder(CHAN OF INT in, out, VALUE CloseDown)
  INT temp:
  SEQ
    in ? temp
    WHILE temp <> CloseDown
      SEQ
        out ! temp
        in ? temp
    out ! CloseDown    -- pass close down token on
  :
```

SUMMARY

The semantics of message-based communication are defined by three issues:

(1)   the model of synchronization;
(2)   the method of process naming, and;
(3)   the message structure.

Variations in the process synchronization model arise from the semantics of the send operation. Three broad classifications exist:

(1)   asynchronous – sender process does not wait;
(2)   synchronous – sender process waits for message to be read;
(3)   remote invocation – sender process waits for message to be read, acted upon and a reply generated.

Remote invocation can be made to appear syntactically similar to a procedure call. This can cause confusion when Remote Procedure Calls (RPCs) are used in a distributed system. RPCs are, however, an implementation strategy; remote invocation defines the semantics of a particular message-passing model. The two processes involved in this communication may be on the same processor, or they may be distributed; the semantics are the same.

Process naming involves two distinct issues; direct or indirect, and symmetry.

Both Ada and occam 2 define a message-based communication model. Ada uses remote invocation with direct asymmetric naming. Occam 2, by comparison, contains a synchronous indirect symmetric scheme. Messages can take the form of any system or user-defined type.

For two processes to communicate in occam 2 requires the definition of a channel (of appropriate type protocol) and the use of the two channel operators ? and !. Communication in Ada requires one task to define an entry and then, within its body, accept any incoming call. A rendezvous occurs when one task calls an entry in another.

In order to increase the expressive power of message-based concurrent programming languages it is necessary to allow a process to choose between alternative communications. The language primitive that supports this facility is known as selective waiting. Here, a process can choose between different alternatives; on any particular execution some of these alternatives can be closed off by using a Boolean guard. Occam 2's construct, which is known as ALT, allows a process to choose between an arbitrary number of guarded receive operations. Ada supports a similar language feature (the select statement). It has two extra facilities however:

(1)   A select statement may have an else part which is executed if there are no outstanding calls on open alternatives.

(2)   A select statement may have a terminate alternative which will cause the process executing the select to terminate if none of the other tasks that could call it are still executable.

An important feature of Ada's extended rendezvous is its interaction with the exception handling model. If an exception is raised but not handled during a rendezvous then it is propagated to both the calling and called tasks. A calling task must, therefore, protect itself against possibly anonymous exceptions being generated as a result of making a message passing call.

Buffers form an important construct within concurrent programs. Illustrations have been given in this chapter on how to program bounded buffers in both Ada and occam 2. The general solution to this problem requires a selective wait construct that can choose between sending and receiving messages. Neither Ada nor occam 2 support this feature. The problem is less acute in Ada because data can flow in the opposite direction to the message (that is, a receive operation can send information). The buffer problem was also used to illustrate how a message-based communication facility can be built upon the Modula-2 coroutine model.

In order to give a further example of a language design an overview of CHILL was given. CHILL has an unusually pragmatic design, incorporating:

- initialization data for processes
- process names
- monitors (called regions)
- buffers (allow asynchronous communication)
- signals (a synchronous channel mechanism)

The chapter concludes by looking at process idioms. In all, there are perhaps only 13 different structures for processes. Within Ada many of these can be represented as reusable generic units.

Further reading

Burns A. (1985). *Concurrent Programming in Ada*. Ada Companion Series. Cambridge: Cambridge University Press

Burns A. (1988). *Programming in Occam 2*. Wokingham: Addison-Wesley

Burns A., Lister A.M. and Wellings A.J. (1987). A review of Ada tasking. *In Lecture Notes in Computer Science*, **262**. Berlin: Springer-Verlag

Hoare C.A.R. (1985). *Communicating Sequential Processes*. London: Prentice-Hall

Peterson J. and Silberschatz A. (1985). *Operating System Concepts*. Reading MA: Addison-Wesley

Whiddett D. (1987). *Concurrent Programming for Software Engineers*. Chichester: Ellis Horwood

---

EXERCISES

9.1 If an Ada task has two entry points is it possible for it to accept the entry of the calling task which has been waiting for the longest period of time?

9.2 Show how to implement a binary semaphore using Ada tasking. How can it be initialized? What happens if a task issuing a P is aborted before it can issue a V?

9.3 Show how Ada tasking can be used to implement Hoare's monitor.

9.4 Figure 9.1 represents a process in occam 2.

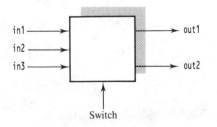

Figure 9.1   A process in occam 2.

Integers are read down channels in1, in2, in3. The process takes these integers as they arrive. Initially all input integers are output to channel out1. If there is any input down channel switch then output is moved to channel out2. Subsequent inputs down switch will change the output channel.

Write an occam 2 PROC that implements this process.

9.5 To what extent can an Ada rendezvous be considered a remote procedure call? Discuss the following code which purports to implement a particular remote procedure. Consider both the called procedure and the implications for the calling task.

```
task type RPC_IMPLEMENTATION is
    entry RPC(PARAM1:TYPE1; PARAM2:TYPE2);
end RPC_IMPLEMENTATION;

task body RPC_IMPLEMENTATION is
begin
    accept RPC(PARAM1:TYPE1; PARAM2:TYPE2) do
    -- body of procedure
    end RPC;
end RPC_IMPLEMENTATION;

-- declare an array of 1000 rpc_implementation tasks
FOR_CONCURRENT_INVOCATION :
        array(1 .. 1000) of RPC_IMPLEMENTATION;
```

9.6 Complete Exercise 7.6 using the occam 2 channel for process synchronization.

Chapter 10
Atomic Actions, Concurrent Processes and Reliability

Chapter 5 considered how reliable software could be produced in the presence of a variety of errors. Modular decomposition and atomic actions were identified as two techniques essential for damage confinement and assessment. Also, the notions of forward and backward error recovery were introduced as approaches to dynamic error recovery. It was shown that where processes communicate and synchronize their activities, backward error recovery may lead to the *domino effect*. In Chapter 6, exception handling was discussed as a mechanism for providing both forward and backward error recovery in sequential processes. Chapters 7, 8 and 9 then considered the facilities provided by real-time languages for concurrent programming. This chapter brings together exception handling and concurrency in order to show how processes can interact reliably in the presence of other processes and in the presence of faults. The notion of an atomic action is explored in more detail.

Cooperating and competing processes

In Chapter 7 the interaction of processes was described in terms of three types of behaviour:

(1)   independent
(2)   cooperating
(3)   competing.

Independent processes do not communicate or synchronize with each other. Consequently, if an error occurs within one process, then recovery procedures can be initiated by that process in isolation from the rest of the system. Recovery blocks and exception handling can be used as described in Chapters 5 and 6.

Cooperating processes, by comparison, regularly communicate and synchronize their activities in order to perform some common operation. If any error condition occurs it is necessary for all processes involved to perform error recovery. The programming of such error recovery is the topic of this chapter.

Competing processes communicate and synchronize in order to obtain resources; they are however, essentially, independent. An error in one should have no affect on the others. Unfortunately, this is not always the case, particularly if the error occurred while a process was in the act of being allocated a resource. Reliable resource allocation is considered in the next chapter.

Where cooperating processes communicate and synchronize through shared resources then recovery may involve the resource itself. This aspect of resource allocation will also be considered in the next chapter.

10.1 Atomic actions

One of the main motivations for introducing concurrent processes into a language is that they enable parallelism in the real world to be reflected in application programs. This enables such programs to be expressed in a more natural way and leads to the production of more reliable and maintainable systems. Disappointingly, however, concurrent processes create many new problems which did not exist in the purely sequential program. Consequently, Chapters 7–9 have been dedicated to discussing some of the solutions to these problems; in particular, communication and synchronization between processes using shared memory (correctly) and message

passing. This was undertaken in a fairly isolated manner and no consideration has yet been given to the way in which groups of concurrent processes
should be structured in order to coordinate their activities.

The interaction between two processes has, so far, been expressed in
terms of a single communication. In reality this is not always the case. For
example, withdrawal from a bank account may involve a ledger process
and a payment process in a sequence of communications to authenticate
the drawer, check the balance and pay the money. Furthermore, it may be
necessary for more than two processes to interact in this way to perform
the required action. In all such situations it is imperative that the processes
involved see a consistent system state. With concurrent processes it is all
too easy for groups of processes to interfere with one other.

What is required is for each group of processes to execute their joint
activity as an **indivisible** or **atomic action**. Of course, a single process may
also want to protect itself from the interference of other processes (for
example, during resource allocation). It follows that an atomic action may
involve one or more processes.

There are several, almost equivalent, ways of expressing the properties of an atomic action (Lomet, 1977; Randell et al., 1978).

(1)   An action is atomic if the processes performing it are not aware of
      the existence of any other active process, and no other active process
      is aware of the activity of the processes during the time the processes
      are performing the action.

(2)   An action is atomic if the processes performing it do not communi-
      cate with other processes while the action is being performed.

(3)   An action is atomic if the processes performing it can detect no state
      change except those performed by themselves and if they do not
      reveal their state changes until the action is complete.

(4)   Actions are atomic if they can be considered, so far as other pro-
      cesses are concerned, to be indivisible and instantaneous, such that
      the effects on the system are as if they were interleaved as opposed
      to concurrent.

These are not quite all equivalent. For example, consider the second
expression: an action is atomic if the processes performing it communicate
only amongst themselves and not with other processes in the system.
Unlike the other three this does not really define the true nature of an
atomic action. While it will guarantee that the action is indivisible, it is too
strong a constraint on the processes. Interactions between an atomic action
and the rest of the system can be allowed as long as they have no impact on
the activity of the atomic action and do not provide the rest of the system
with any information concerning the progress of the action (Anderson and
Lee, 1981). In general, in order to allow such interactions requires detailed

knowledge of the atomic action's function and its interface to the rest of the system. As this can not be supported by a general language implementation, it is tempting, following Anderson and Lee (1981), to adopt the more restrictive (second) definition. This can only be done, however, if the resources necessary to complete an atomic action are acquired by the underlying implementation, not by instructions given in the program. If resources are to be acquired and released when the programmer desires then processes within atomic actions will have to communicate with general-purpose resource managers.

Although an atomic action is viewed as being indivisible, it can have an internal structure. To allow modular decomposition of atomic actions the notion of a **nested atomic action** is introduced. The processes involved in a nested action must be a subset of those involved in the outer level of the action. If this were not the case then a nested action could smuggle information concerning the outer level action to an external process. The outer level action would then no longer be indivisible.

10.1.1 Two-phase atomic actions

Ideally, all processes involved in an atomic action should obtain the resources they require, for the duration of the action, prior to its commencement. These resources could then be released after the atomic action had terminated. If these rules were followed then there would be no need for an atomic action to interact with any external entity and the stricter definition of atomic action could be adopted.

Unfortunately, this ideal can lead to poor resource utilization and hence, a more pragmatic approach is needed. As a first step it is necessary to allow an atomic action to start without its full complement of resources. At some point a process within the action will request a resource allocation; the atomic action must then communicate with the resource manager. If a strict definition of atomic action is adhered to, then this resource manager would have to form part of the atomic action, with the effect of serializing all actions involving this resource manager. Clearly, this is undesirable and hence an atomic action is allowed to communicate externally with resource managers.

Within this context a resource manager is defined to be a custodian of non-sharable system utilities. It protects these utilities against inappropriate access but does not, itself, perform any actions upon them.

A further improvement in resource allocation can be made if a process is allowed to release a resource prior to completion of the associated atomic action. In order for this premature release to make sense, the state of the resource must be identical to that which would appertain if the resource was retained until completion of the atomic action. Its early release will, however, enhance the concurrency of the whole system.

If resources are to be obtained late and released early it could be possible for an external state change to be affected by a released resource and observed by the acquisition of a new resource. This would break the definition of atomic action. It follows that the only safe policy for resource usage is one that has two distinct phases. In the first 'growing' phase resources can be requested (only); in the second 'shrinking' phase resources can be released (but no new allocations can be made). With such a structure the integrity of the atomic action is assured. However, it should be noted that if resources are released early then it will be more difficult to provide recovery if the atomic action fails. This is because the resource has been updated and another process may have observed the new state of the resource. Any attempt to invoke recovery in the other process may lead to the domino effect.

In all the following discussions atomic actions are assumed to be two phase; recoverable actions do not release any resources until the action successfully completes.

10.1.2 Atomic transactions

Within the theories of operating systems and databases the term atomic transaction is often used. An **atomic transaction** has all the properties of an atomic action plus the added feature that its execution is allowed either to succeed or fail. By failure is meant that an error has occurred from which the transaction cannot recover, normally a processor failure. If an atomic action fails then the components of the system which are being manipulated by the action may be left in an inconsistent state. With an atomic transaction this cannot happen because the components are returned to their original state (that is, the state they were *before* the transaction commenced). Atomic transactions are sometimes called *recoverable actions* and, unfortunately, the terms *atomic action* and *atomic transaction* are often interchanged (Liskov, 1985).

The two distinctive properties of atomic transactions are:

(1)   failure atomicity; meaning that the transaction must either complete successfully or (in the case of failure) have no effect;

(2)   synchronization atomicity; meaning that the transaction is indivisible in the sense that its partial execution cannot be observed by any concurrently executing transaction.

Although atomic transactions are useful for those applications which involve the manipulation of databases, by themselves they are not suitable for programming fault-tolerant systems. This is because they imply that some form of recovery mechanism will be supplied by the system. Such a mechanism would be fixed, with the programmer having no control over its operation. Although atomic transactions provide a form of backward error recovery, they do not allow recovery procedures to be performed. Furthermore, they do not allow forward error recovery. Notwithstanding these points, atomic transactions do have a role in protecting the integrity of a real-time system database. Some recent operating systems that have been designed for real-time applications do provide kernel-level support for atomic transactions; for example the Alpha kernel (Northcutt, 1987).

Atomic transactions are considered in Chapter 13 in the context of distributed systems and processor failures.

10.1.3 Requirements for atomic actions

If a real-time programming language is to be capable of supporting atomic actions then it must be possible to express the requirements necessary for their implementation. These requirements are independent from the notion of a process and the form of interprocess communication provided by a language (Jalote, 1985). They are:

(1)   **Well-defined boundaries**: Each atomic action should have a start, end and a side boundary. The start boundary is the location in each process involved in the atomic action where the action is deemed to start. The end boundary is the location in each process involved in the atomic action where the action is deemed to end. The side boundary separates those processes involved in the atomic action from those in the rest of the system.

(2)   **Indivisibility**: An atomic action must not allow the exchange of any information between the processes active inside the action and those outside (resource managers excluded). If two atomic actions do share data then the value of that data after the atomic actions is determined by the strict sequencing of the two actions in some order.

There is no implied synchronization at the start of an atomic action. Processes can enter at different times. However, there is an implied synchronization at the end of an atomic action; processes are not allowed to leave the atomic action until all processes are willing and able to leave.

(3)   **Nesting**: Atomic actions may be nested as long as they do not overlap with other atomic actions. Consequently, in general, only strict nesting is allowed (two structures are strictly nested if one is completely contained within the other).

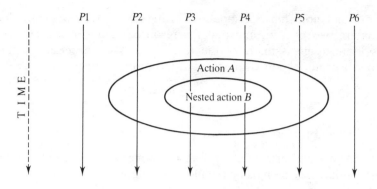

Figure 10.1   Nested atomic actions.

(4)   **Concurrency**: It should be possible to execute different atomic actions concurrently. One way to enforce indivisibility is to run atomic actions sequentially. However, this could seriously impair the performance of the overall system and therefore should be avoided. Nevertheless, the overall effect of running a collection of atomic actions concurrently must be the same as that which would be obtained from serializing their executions.

(5)   **Recovery procedures**: As it is the intention that atomic actions should form the basis of damage confinement, they must allow recovery procedures to be programmed.

Figure 10.1 represents, diagrammatically, the boundaries of a nested atomic action in a system of six processes. Action *B* involves only processes *P*3 and *P*4, whereas action *A* also includes *P*2 and *P*5. The other processes (*P*1 and *P*6) are outside the boundaries of both atomic actions.

10.2   Atomic actions in concurrent languages

Atomic actions provide structuring support for the software of large embedded systems. To get the full benefit of this aid requires the support of the real-time language. Unfortunately, such support is not provided by any of the major languages. This section considers the suitability of the various communication and synchronization primitives, discussed in Chapters 8 and 9, for programming atomic actions. Following this, a possible language framework is given and then this framework is extended to provide forward and backward error recovery.

The problem of resource allocation is postponed until the next chapter. For now it is assumed that resources have two modes of use: sharable and non-sharable; with some resources being amenable to both sharable and non-sharable modes. Furthermore, it is assumed that all actions are two phased, and that the resource manager will ensure that appropriate usage is made of the resources. Also, processes within an action synchronize their own access to the resource in order to avoid any interference.

10.2.1 Semaphores

An atomic action performed by a single process can be implemented by simple mutual exclusion using a binary semaphore.

```
wait(mutual_exclusion_semaphore)
  atomic_action
signal(mutual_exclusion_semaphore)
```

This 'semaphore' solution is, however, complicated when more then one process is involved in the atomic action. For example, consider a non-sharable resource which needs to be manipulated by two processes. Program 10.1 illustrates how processes P1 and P2 can achieve this resource manipulation while avoiding any interference from other processes. The semaphores atomic_action_begin1 and atomic_action_begin2 allow only two processes into the action. Any other process is blocked. Two further semaphores, atomic_action_end1 and atomic_action_end2, ensure that neither process can leave the action until the other is ready to leave. It should be noted that other semaphores are also needed to control access to the shared resource (and to allocate the resource in the first place).

The structure in Program 10.1 provides the necessary protection, and again illustrates that semaphores can be used to program most synchronization problems; unfortunately, there are several drawbacks with the approach. Firstly, although only two process have been allowed into the atomic action there is no guarantee that they are the correct two. Secondly, semaphores were criticized in Chapter 8 as being error prone; a single access without protection (that is, leaving out the wait-signal structure) would break the atomicity. Finally, to extend the solution to N processes becomes much more complicated and, hence, even more error prone.

10.2.2 Monitors

By encapsulating the atomic action in a monitor it is much easier to ensure that partial executions are not observed. Program 10.1 implemented as a monitor is shown in Program 10.2. The if statement at the start of each procedure ensures that only one process has access. The condition variables then provide the correct synchronizations within the action.

Program 10.1

```
atomic_action_begin1, atomic_action_begin2 : semaphore := 1;
atomic_action_end1, atomic_action_end2 : semaphore := 0;

procedure code_for_first_process is
begin
    -- start atomic action
    wait(atomic_action_begin1)
        -- get resource in non-sharable mode
        -- update resource

        -- signal second process that it is ok
        -- for it to access resource

        -- any final processing

    wait(atomic_action_end2);
    -- return resource
    signal(atomic_action_end1);
    signal(atomic_action_begin1);
end code_for_first_process;

procedure code_for_second_process is
begin
    -- start atomic action
    wait(atomic_action_begin2)
        -- initial processing

        -- wait for first process to signal
        -- that it is ok to access resource

        -- access resource

    signal(atomic_action_end2);
    wait(atomic_action_end1);
    signal(atomic_action_begin2);
end code_for_second_process;
```

There are, however, two problems with this solution. It is not possible for the two processes to be active inside the monitor simultaneously. This is often more restrictive than necessary. Furthermore, the implementation of nested actions, and resource allocation, will require nested monitor calls. The difficulties associated with nested monitor calls were discussed in Chapter 7. Maintaining the monitor lock while executing a nested monitor call could unnecessarily delay processes trying to execute within the outer action.

Program 10.2

```
monitor atomic_action
    export code_for_first_process, code_for_second_process;

    first_process_active : boolean := false;
    second_process_active : boolean := false;
    first_process_finished : boolean := false;
    second_process_finished : boolean := false;
    no_first_process, no_second_process : condition;
    atomic_action_ends1, atomic_action_ends2 : condition;

procedure code_for_first_process
begin
    if first_process_active then
      wait(no_first_process);
    first_process_active := true;
      -- get resource in non-sharable mode
      -- update resource

      -- signal second process that it is ok
      -- for it to access resource

      -- any final processing
    if not second_process_finished then
      wait(atomic_action_end2);
    first_process_finished := true;
    -- release resource
    signal(atomic_action_end1);
    first_process_active := false;
    signal(no_first_process);
end;

procedure code_for_second_process
begin
    if second_process_active then
      wait(no_second_process);
    second_process_active := true;
      -- initial processing

      -- wait for first process to signal
      -- that it is ok to access resource

      -- access resource

    signal(atomic_action_end2);
     second_process_finished := true;
    if not first_process_finished then
      wait(atomic_action_end1);
    second_process_active := false;
    signal(no_second_process);
end;
```

10.2.3   Atomic actions in Ada

With languages whose communication and synchronization primitives are based on message passing, all single process actions are atomic if there are no shared variables and the process itself does not communicate during the action. For example, the extended rendezvous in Ada is designed to enable a common form of atomic action to be programmed. This is where a task communicates with another task to request some computation; the called task undertakes this execution and then replies via the 'out' parameters of the rendezvous. The atomic action takes the form of an accept statement; it possesses synchronization atomicity as long as;

(1)   it does not update any variable that another task can access, and;

(2)   it does not rendezvous with any other task.

An atomic action in Ada for three tasks can be programmed as shown in Program 10.3.

Program 10.3

```
package ACTION_X is
  procedure CODE_FOR_FIRST_TASK(--params);
  procedure CODE_FOR_SECOND_TASK(--params);
  procedure CODE_FOR_THIRD_TASK(--params);
end ACTION_X;

package body ACTION_X is
  task ACTION_CONTROLLER is
    entry FIRST;
    entry SECOND;
    entry THIRD;
    entry FIRST_FINISHED;
    entry SECOND_FINISHED;
    entry THIRD_FINISHED;
  end ACTION_CONTROLLER;

  task body ACTION_CONTROLLER is
    FIRST_HERE : BOOLEAN;
    SECOND_HERE : BOOLEAN;
    THIRD_HERE : BOOLEAN;
  begin
    loop
      FIRST_HERE := FALSE;
      SECOND_HERE := FALSE;
      THIRD_HERE := FALSE;
      while not (FIRST_HERE and SECOND_HERE and THIRD_HERE) loop
        select
          when not FIRST_HERE =>
            accept FIRST;
            FIRST_HERE := TRUE;
```

Program 10.3   (cont.)

```
        or
          when not SECOND_HERE ⇒
            accept SECOND;
            SECOND_HERE := TRUE;
        or
          when not THIRD_HERE ⇒
            accept THIRD;
            THIRD_HERE := TRUE;
        end select;
      end loop;
      -- the order of the following nested accept is not important as
      -- they must all finish before the action completes
      accept FIRST_FINISHED do
        accept SECOND_FINISHED do
          accept THIRD_FINISHED;
        end;
      end;
    end loop;
  end ACTION_CONTROLLER;

  procedure CODE_FOR_FIRST_TASK(--params) is
  begin
    ACTION_CONTROLLER.FIRST;
    -- acquire resources
    -- the action itself, communicates with tasks executing B
    -- and C via resources
    ACTION_CONTROLLER.FIRST_FINISHED;
    -- release resources
  end CODE_FOR_FIRST_TASK;

    -- similar for second and third task
  begin
    -- any initialization of local resources
  end;
```

In Program 10.3 the ACTION is synchronized by the ACTION_CONTROLLER task. This ensures that only three tasks can be active in the ACTION at any one time and that they are synchronized on exit.

10.2.4   Atomic actions in occam 2

The occam 2 implementation of an atomic action, shown in Program 10.4, is similar in structure to that of Ada. The only difference being that, as the occam 2 rendezvous is not extended, a double interaction with the controller is required at the end of the action. Also, as occam 2 channels have only

Program 10.4

```
VAL INT max IS 20 : -- maximum number of client processes
                    -- in any of the three groups


[max]CHAN OF INT First, Second, Third:
CHAN OF INT First.Finished, Second.Finished, Third.Finished:
CHAN OF INT First.Continue, Second.Continue, Third.Continue:
-- all the above channels are used for synchronization only
-- they are defined to be of protocol INT as a default


PROC Action.Controller
  BOOL First.Here, Second.Here, Third.Here:
  INT Any:
  WHILE TRUE
    SEQ
      First.Here := FALSE
      Second.Here := FALSE
      Third.Here := FALSE
      WHILE NOT (First.Here AND Second.Here AND Third.Here)
        ALT
          ALT i = 0 FOR max
            NOT First.Here & First[i]?Any
              First.Here := TRUE
          ALT i = 0 FOR max
            NOT Second.Here & Second[i]?Any
              Second.Here := TRUE
          ALT i = 0 FOR max
            NOT Third.Here & Third[i]?Any
              Third.Here := TRUE
      First.Finished?Any
      Second.Finished?Any
      Third.Finished?Any
      PAR
        First.Continue!Any
        Second.Continue!Any
        Third.Continue!Any
:


PROC action.1(CHAN OF INT first.client)
  INT Any:
  SEQ
    first.client!Any

    -- the action itself
    First.Finished!Any
    First.Continue?Any
:
```

Program 10.4   (cont.)

```
-- similarly for action.2 and action.3

PAR
    -- all processes in the system including
    Action.Controller
```

a single reader and a single writer it is necessary for the action controller to have an array of channels for each component of the action. Potential processes are allocated a channel from this array.

10.2.5   A language framework for atomic actions

Although the various language models described so far have enabled a simple atomic action to be expressed, they all rely on programmer discipline to ensure that no interactions with external processes occur (apart from with resource allocators). Moreover, they assume that no process within an atomic action is aborted; if the real-time language supports an abort facility then a process could be asynchronously removed from the action leaving the action in an inconsistent state.

In general, it is not possible to add either forward or backward error recovery facilities to the paradigms given so far. This is because few of the languages considered in this book support recovery blocks or asynchronous exceptions. Language mechanisms have been proposed, however, which do enable forward and backward error recovery between groups of processes. In order to discuss these mechanisms a simple language framework for atomic actions is introduced. The proposed recovery mechanisms are then discussed in the context of this framework.

To simplify the framework only static processes will be considered. Also, it will be assumed that all the processes taking part in an atomic action are known at compile time. Each process involved in an action declares an action statement which specifies: the action name, the other processes taking part in the action, and the code to be executed by the declaring process on entry to the action. For example, a process P1 which wishes to enter into an atomic action A with processes P2 and P3 would declare the following action:

```
action A with (P2, P3) do
    -- acquire resources
    -- communicate with P2 and P3
    -- release resources
end A;
```

It is assumed that resource allocators are known and that communication inside the action is restricted to the three P processes (together with external calls to the resource allocators). These restrictions are checked at compile time. All other processes declare similar actions, and nested actions are allowed as long as strict nesting is observed. Note that if the processes are not known at compile time, then any communication between processes must be checked at run-time to ensure that both processes are active in the same atomic action.

The imposed synchronization on the action is as follows. Processes entering the action are not blocked. A process is only blocked inside the action if it has to wait for a resource to be allocated, or if it attempts to communicate with another process inside the action and that process is either: active in the action but not in a position to accept the communication; or is not, as yet, active in the action.

Processes may leave the action only when all processes active in the action wish to leave. This was not the case in the examples given earlier in this section for semaphores, monitors, Ada and occam 2. There it was assumed that all processes must enter the action before any could leave. Here it is possible for a subset of the named processes to enter the action and subsequently leave (without recourse to any interactions with the missing processes). This facility is deemed to be essential in a real-time system where deadlines are important. It solves the **deserter** problem where all processes are held in an action because one process has not arrived. This will be considered along with error recovery in Sections 10.3 and 10.4.

10.3   Atomic actions and backward error recovery

In Section 10.2 the notion of an atomic action was considered. Atomic actions are important because they constrain the flow of information around the system to well-defined boundaries and, therefore, can provide the basis for both damage confinement and error recovery. In this section two approaches to backward error recovery between concurrent processes are described. Discussion of backward error recovery in the context of processor failure is deferred until Chapter 13.

In Chapter 5 it was shown that when backward error recovery is applied to groups of communicating processes it is possible for all the processes to be rolled back to the start of their execution. This was the so-called *domino effect*. The problem occurred because there was no consistent set of recovery points or a recovery line. An atomic action provides that recovery line automatically. If an error occurs inside an atomic action then the processes involved can be rolled back to the start of the action and alternative algorithms executed; the atomic action ensures that processes have not passed any erroneous values through communication with processes outside the action. When atomic actions are used in this way they are called **conversations** (Randell, 1975).

10.3.1 Conversations

With conversations each action statement contains a recovery block. For example:

```
action A with (P2, P3) do
   ensure (acceptance test)
   by
      -- primary module
   else by
      -- alternative module
   else by
      -- alternative module
   else error
end A;
```

Other processes involved in the conversation declare their part in the action similarly. The basic semantics of a conversation can be summarized as follows:

- On entry to the conversation the state of a process is saved. The set of entry points forms the recovery line.
- While inside the conversation a process is only allowed to communicate with other processes active in the conversation and general resource managers. As conversations are built from atomic actions, this property is inherited.
- In order to leave the conversation, all processes active in the conversation must have passed their acceptance test. If this is the case then the conversation is finished and all recovery points are discarded.
- If any process *fails* its acceptance test, all processes have their state *restored to that saved at the start of the conversation and they execute their alternative modules*. Therefore, it is assumed that any error recovery to be performed inside a conversation *must* be performed by *all* processes taking part in the conversation.
- Conversations can be nested but only strict nesting is allowed.
- If all alternatives in the conversation fail then recovery must be performed at a higher level.

It should be noted that in conversations as defined by Randell (1975) all processes taking part in the conversation must have entered the conversation before any of the other processes can leave. This differs from the semantics described here. If a process does not enter into a conversation, either because of tardiness or because it has failed, then as long as the other processes active in the conversation do not wish to communicate with it then the conversation can complete successfully. If a process does attempt to communicate with a missing process then it can either block and wait for the process to arrive or it can continue. Adopting this approach has two benefits (Gregory and Knight, 1985):

(1)   It allows conversations to be specified where participation is not compulsory.

(2)   It allows processes with deadlines to leave the conversation, continue and, if necessary, take some alternative action.

Although conversations allow groups of processes to coordinate their recovery they have been criticized. One important point is that when a conversation fails all the processes are restored and all enter their alternative modules. This forces the same processes to communicate again to achieve the desired effect; a process cannot break out of the conversation. This may be not what is required. Gregory and Knight (1985) point out that, in practice, when one process fails to achieve its goal in a primary module through communication with one group of processes, it may wish to communicate with a completely new group of processes in its secondary module. Furthermore, the acceptance test for this secondary module may be quite different. There is no way to express these requirements using conversations.

10.3.2   Dialogs and colloquys

To overcome some of the problems associated with conversations Gregory and Knight (1985) have proposed an alternative approach to backward error recovery between concurrent processes. In their scheme, a group of processes which wish to take part in a backward recoverable atomic action, indicate their desire to do so by executing a **dialog** statement. The dialog statement has three functions: it identifies the atomic action, declares a global acceptance test for the atomic action and specifies the variables which are to be used in the action. The dialog statement takes the form:

```
DIALOG name_and_acceptance_test SHARES (variables)
```

Note that the DIALOG's name is the same name as that of the function defining the acceptance test.

Each process which wishes to participate in the action defines a **discuss** statement naming the action. The format of the discuss statement is:

```
DISCUSS dialog_name BY
  -- sequence of statements
TO ARRANGE boolean_expression;
```

The `boolean_expression` is the process's local acceptance test for the action.

The discuss statement is a component of the atomic action and therefore has all the properties defined in Section 10.1. The group of discuss statements which together form the complete action defines the recovery line. The state of every process which enters into the dialog is, therefore, saved. No process can leave the dialog unless all the active processes have successfully passed their local acceptance tests and the global acceptance test has also passed. If any of these acceptance tests fail then the dialog is deemed to have failed and the processes are restored to their state on entry to the atomic action.

This ends the operation of the discuss statement. There are no alternative modules which are executed, instead, discuss statements can be combined using another statement called a **dialog sequence**. By analogy, if the discuss statement is equivalent to an Ada accept statement then the dialog sequence is equivalent to the Ada select statement. Syntactically it can be represented as below:

```
SELECT
  dialog_1
OR
  dialog_2
OR
  dialog_3
ELSE
  -- sequence of statements
END SELECT;
```

On execution, the process first attempts `dialog_1`, if this succeeds then control is passed to the statement following the select statement. If the `dialog_1` fails then `dialog_2` is attempted and so on. It is important to note that `dialog_2` may involve a completely different set of processes to that involved in `dialog_1`. It is the combined execution of associated select statements that is called a **colloquy**.

If all attempted dialogs fail then the statements following the `ELSE` are executed. This gives the programmer a last chance to salvage the situation. If this fails then any surrounding colloquy fails. Note that a process can explicitly fail a dialog or colloquy by executing the 'fail' statement.

To enable the colloquy concept to be used in real-time systems it is possible to associate a timeout with the select. This is discussed in Section 12.5.2.

10.4   Atomic actions and forward error recovery

It was pointed out, in Chapter 5, that although backward error recovery enables recovery from unanticipated errors, it is difficult to undo any operation that may have been performed in the environment in which the embedded system operates. Consequently, forward error recovery and exception handling must be considered. In this section exception handling between the concurrent processes involved in an atomic action is discussed.

With backward error recovery, when an error occurs all processes involved in the atomic action participate in recovery. The same is true with exception handling and forward error recovery. If an exception occurs in one of the processes active in an atomic action then that exception is raised in *all* processes active in the action. The following is a possible Ada-like syntax for an atomic action supporting exception handling.

```
action A with (P2, P3) do
  -- the action
exception
  when exception_a =>
    -- sequence of statements
  when exception_b =>
    -- sequence of statements
  when others =>
    raise atomic_action_failure;
end A;
```

With the termination model of exception handling the atomic action completes normally if all processes active in the action have a handler, and if they all handle the exception without raising any further exception. If a resumption model is used, then, when the exception has been handled, the processes active in the atomic action resume their execution at the point where the exception was raised.

With either model, if there is no exception handler *in any one of the processes active in the action* or one of the handlers fails, then *the atomic action fails* with a standard exception atomic_action_failure. This exception is raised in all the involved processes.

There are two issues which must be considered when exception handling is added to atomic actions: resolution of concurrently raised exceptions and exceptions in nested actions (Campbell and Randell, 1983). These are now briefly reviewed.

10.4.1   Resolution of concurrently raised exceptions

It is possible for more than one process active in an atomic action to raise
different exceptions at the same time. As Campbell and Randell (1983)
point out this event is likely if the errors resulting from some fault cannot
be uniquely identified by the error-detection facility provided by each
component of the atomic action. If two exceptions are simultaneously
raised in an atomic action then there may be two separate exception
handlers in each process. It may be difficult to decide which one should be
chosen. Furthermore, the two exceptions in conjunction constitute a third
exception which is the exception that indicates that both the other two
exceptional conditions have occurred.

In order to resolve concurrently-raised exceptions Campbell and
Randell propose the use of an **exception tree**. If several exceptions are
raised concurrently then the exception used to identify the handler is that
at the root of the smallest subtree that contains all the exceptions. Each
atomic action component can declare its own exception tree; the different
processes involved in an atomic action may well have different exception
trees.

10.4.2   Exceptions and internal atomic actions

Where atomic actions are nested it is possible for one process active in an
action to raise an exception when other processes in the same action are
involved in a nested action. Figure 10.2 illustrates the problem.

When the exception is raised all processes involved must participate
in the recovery action. Unfortunately, the internal action, by definition, is
indivisible. To raise the exception in that action would potentially compromise that indivisibility. Furthermore, the internal action may have no
knowledge of the possible exception that can be raised.

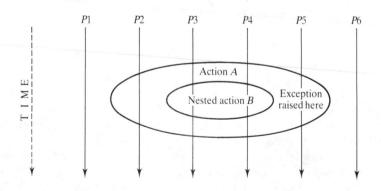

Figure 10.2   An exception in a nested atomic action.

Campbell and Randell (1983) have discussed two possible solutions to this problem. The first solution is to hold back the raising of the exception until the internal action has finished. This they reject because:

- In a real-time system the exception being raised may be associated with the missing of a deadline. To hold back the recovery procedure may place the action's timely response in serious jeopardy.

- The error condition detected may indicate that the internal action may never terminate because some deadlock condition has arisen.

For these reasons, Campbell and Randell have a second solution which is to allow internal actions to have a predefined abortion exception. This exception is raised to indicate to the action that an exception has been raised in a surrounding action and that the preconditions under which the action was invoked are no longer valid. If such an exception is raised, the internal action should invoke fault-tolerant measures to abort itself. Once the action has been aborted, the containing action can handle the original exception.

If the internal action cannot abort itself then it must signal an atomic action failure exception. This then may be combined with the outstanding exception so as to affect the choice of recovery performed by the surrounding action. If no abortion exception is defined then the surrounding action must wait for the internal action to complete. Alternatively, a default handler could be provided which would raise the atomic action failure exception.

10.5 Recovery and concurrent processes in real-time languages

Although forward and backward error recovery have been discussed separately, in reality, they may need to be combined in many real-time systems. Backward error recovery is needed to recover from unanticipated errors and forward error recovery is needed to undo any interaction with the environment. Asynchronous exception handling can be used to implement a backward error recovery scheme; this, however, is left as an exercise for the reader (see Exercise 10.8).

As discussed in Section 10.2, none of the major real-time languages directly support atomic actions. Furthermore, they also fail to support the notion of asynchronously raising an exception between processes. One research-oriented language which does support such a facility is Real-time Euclid; an example of its use is given in Section 12.5.1 in the context of missed deadlines.

Although earlier versions of the Ada language supported the asynchronous raising of exceptions, they were taken out of the final definition. The reasons for this decision were:

(1)   A task may not be in a position to handle the exception and would therefore be terminated.

(2)   The raising of an exception may leave a data structure (perhaps in a shared library unit) in an inconsistent state.

(3)   The implementational overhead may be high (particularly on distributed systems).

(4)   All server tasks in all programs would need to protect themselves against these exceptions.

(5)   There was no need for this facility and abort; abort was considered to be absolutely necessary and so the exception facility was withdrawn.

(6)   The exception may be accidentally trapped by **when others** and therefore be lost.

Point (4) can be lessened (a little) if only one predefined exception can be used for this asynchronous effect. This exception was called FAILURE in an earlier definition of Ada.

Ada does, however, allow exceptions which are raised during a rendezvous to be propagated to the calling task if it is not handled within the accept statement. Of course, the exception is still propagated to the accepting task. An exception therefore raised in a nested rendezvous can propagate to all the tasks involved in the nested rendezvous.

This chapter has shown that there is clearly a need for one task to be able to affect asynchronously the flow of control of another task. Given that asynchronous exceptions are not supported in Ada, occam 2 or Modula-2 it is impossible to extend the atomic actions presented in Section 10.2 to enable recoverable actions to be programmed in an elegant way. In Ada, for example, to achieve the desired result requires all tasks involved in the atomic action to communicate with each other periodically, thus allowing exceptions to be synchronously passed through a nested rendezvous. One way of doing this would be to extend the ACTION_ CONTROLLER task defined in Section 10.2.3 to have several further entries and defined exceptions. The tasks then taking part in the atomic action could synchronize at intervals with the controller task. Such a scheme is illustrated in Program 10.5. If any of the three tasks communicate an atomic action failure error condition, then no further synchronization takes place and each task must exit the atomic action with the appropriate exception. Error conditions (1) and (2) are deemed to be recoverable. Even if exceptions associated with these error conditions are raised then the tasks will complete the atomic action normally. Note that the example has a

Program 10.5

```
type ERRORS is (NONE, CONDITION_1, CONDITION_2, FAILURE );
COND_1, COND_2, COND_1_2 : exception;
ACTION_FAILURE : exception;
REQUIRED_NUMBER_OF_SYNCHRONIZATIONS: INTEGER;
   -- predefined value that could be set in the entry protocol


task ACTION_CONTROLLER is
   entry FIRST_HERE;
   entry SECOND_HERE;
   entry THIRD_HERE;


   entry FIRST_SYNCHRONIZE(ERROR_CODE : ERRORS);
   entry SECOND_SYNCHRONIZE(ERROR_CODE : ERRORS);
   entry THIRD_SYNCHRONIZE(ERROR_CODE : ERRORS);


   entry FIRST_FINISHED;
   entry SECOND_FINISHED;
   entry THIRD_FINISHED;
end ACTION_CONTROLLER;


task body ACTION_CONTROLLER is
   ERROR1, ERROR2, FAILURE_ERROR : BOOLEAN;
begin
   loop
     begin
       loop
         -- entry protocol
       end loop;
       -- the order of the following nested accept is not
       -- important as they must all be synchronized before
       -- the action can continue
       ERROR1 := FALSE; ERROR2 := FALSE; FAILURE_ERROR :=FALSE;
       for I in 1 .. REQUIRED_NUMBER_OF_SYNCHRONIZATIONS loop
         begin
           accept FIRST_SYNCHRONIZE(ERROR_CODE : ERRORS) do
             case ERROR_CODE is
               when CONDITION_1 ⇒
                 ERROR1 := TRUE;
               when CONDITION_2 ⇒
                 ERROR2 := TRUE;
               when FAILURE ⇒
                 FAILURE_ERROR := TRUE;
               when NONE ⇒
                 null;
             end case;
```

Program 10.5   (cont.)

```
            accept SECOND_SYNCHRONIZE(ERROR_CODE : ERRORS) do
              case ERROR_CODE is
                when CONDITION_1 ⇒
                  ERROR1 := TRUE;
                when CONDITION_2 ⇒
                  ERROR2 := TRUE;
                when FAILURE ⇒
                  FAILURE_ERROR := TRUE;
                when NONE ⇒
                  null;
              end case;
              accept THIRD_SYNCHRONIZE(ERROR_CODE : ERRORS) do
                case ERROR_CODE is
                  when CONDITION_1 ⇒
                    ERROR1 := TRUE;
                  when CONDITION_2 ⇒
                    ERROR2 := TRUE;
                  when FAILURE ⇒
                    FAILURE_ERROR := TRUE;
                  when NONE ⇒
                    null;
                end case;
                if FAILURE_ERROR then raise ACTION_FAILURE; end if;
                if ERROR1 and ERROR2 then raise COND_1_2; end if;
                if ERROR1 then raise COND_1; end if;
                if ERROR2 then raise COND_2; end if;
              end THIRD_SYNCHRONIZE;
            end SECOND_SYNCHRONIZE;
          end FIRST_SYNCHRONIZE;
        exception
          when COND_1 | COND_2 | COND_1_2 ⇒
            null;
        end;
      end loop;

      -- action termination protocol

  exception
    when ACTION_FAILURE ⇒
      null;
  end;
 end loop;
end ACTION_CONTROLLER;
```

preset number of synchronizations to check for error conditions; in practice this could be dynamically determined during the atomic action itself.

   The tasks involved in the ACTION can then program recovery procedures in the appropriate exception handlers.

Although this gives the appearance of a recoverable atomic action it does suffer from several major drawbacks.

- It relies on the tasks periodically synchronizing with the ACTION_CONTROLLER task. If the error condition is associated with the tardiness of one of the tasks involved in the ACTION then there is no way to influence that task, other than by aborting it, until it calls the ACTION_CONTROLLER.

- If one of the tasks raises an exception which it does not handle, or is aborted, then it will not be able to inform the ACTION_CONTROLLER that it will not be able to participate in the rendezvous.

- Nested recoverable actions can not be aborted without aborting the tasks involved.

- It is difficult to extend the solution for an arbitrary number of participating tasks.

SUMMARY

Reliable execution of processes is essential if real-time embedded systems are to be used in critical applications. When processes interact it is necessary to constrain their interprocess communication so that recovery procedures can be programmed, if required. Atomic actions have been discussed in this chapter as a mechanism by which programs, consisting of many tasks, can be structured to facilitate damage confinement and error recovery.

Actions are atomic if they can be considered, so far as other processes are concerned, to be indivisible and instantaneous, such that the effects on the system are as if they are interleaved as opposed to concurrent. An atomic action has well-defined boundaries and can be nested. Resources used in an atomic action are allocated during an initial *growing phase*, and released either as part of a subsequent *shrinking phase* or at the end of the action (if the action is to be recoverable).

None of the languages considered in this book directly support the notion of an atomic action, although the indivisibility effect (and therefore damage confinement) can be implemented using semaphores, monitors, message passing and so on. The other motivation for atomic actions is to enable recovery procedures to be programmed. Unfortunately, backward and forward error recovery between groups of processes *cannot* be expressed in languages like Ada, occam 2 or Modula-2. Consequently, it is necessary to look at experimental language constructs to provide the required framework. The syntax of an atomic action can be expressed by an action statement. The following statement executed within process P1 indicates that P1 wishes to enter into an atomic action with P2 and P3.

```
action A with (P2, P3) do
  -- sequence of statements
end A;
```

P2 and P3 must execute similar statements.

A *conversation* is an atomic action with backward error recovery facilities (in the form of recovery blocks).

```
action A with (P2, P3) do
  ensure (acceptance test)
  by
    -- primary module
  else by
    -- alternative module
  else error
end A;
```

On entry to the conversation, the state of the process is saved. While inside the conversation a process is only allowed to communicate with other processes active in the conversation and general resource managers. In order to leave the conversation all processes active in the conversation must have passed their acceptance test. If any process fails its acceptance test, all processes have their state restored to that saved at the start of the conversation and they execute their alternative modules. Conversations can be nested, and if all alternatives in an inner conversation fail then recovery must be performed at an outer level.

Conversations are limited because when a conversation fails all the processes are restored and all enter their alternative modules. This forces the same processes to communicate again to achieve the desired affect; a process cannot break out of the conversation. Often, when one process fails to achieve its goal in a primary module through communication with one group of processes, it may wish to communicate with a completely new group of processes in its secondary module. Dialogs and colloquys remove the limitations of conversations.

Forward error recovery via exception handlers can also be added to atomic actions. If an exception is raised by one process then all processes active in the action must handle the exception.

```
action A with (P2, P3) do
  -- the action
exception
  when exception_a =>
    -- sequence of statements
  when others =>
    raise atomic_action_failure;
end A;
```

Two issues which must be addressed when using this approach are the resolution of concurrently raised exceptions and exceptions in internal actions.

Further reading

Anderson T. and Lee P.A. (1981). *Fault Tolerance Principles and Practice.* Englewood Cliffs NJ: Prentice-Hall

Bernstein P.A., Hadzilacos V. and Goodman N. (1987). *Concurrency Control and Recovery in Database Systems.* Reading MA: Addison-Wesley

Joseph M., ed. (1988). Formal techniques in real-time fault tolerant systems. *Lecture Notes in Computer Science*, **331**. Berlin: Springer-Verlag

Northcutt J.D. (1987). *Mechanisms for Reliable Distributed Real-time Operating Systems: The Alpha Kernel.* Orlando FL: Academic Press

Sha L., Lehoczky J.P. and Jensen E.D. (1988). Modular concurrency control and failure recovery. *IEEE Transactions on Computers*, **37**(2), 146–59

Shrivastava S.K., ed. (1985). *Reliable Computer Systems.* Berlin: Springer-Verlag

Shrivastava S.K., Mancini L. and Randell B. (1987). On the duality of fault tolerant structures. *Lecture Notes in Computer Science*, **309**, 19–37. Berlin: Springer-Verlag

EXERCISES

10.1 Distinguish between an atomic *action* and an atomic *transaction*. What is the relationship between an atomic transaction and a conversation?

10.2 Extend the semaphore implementation of an atomic action, given in Section 10.2.1, from a two process interaction to a three process interaction.

10.3 Rewrite the monitor implementation of an atomic action, given in Section 10.2.2, to allow both the processes to be active in the action simultaneously.

10.4 Rewrite the ACTION_X Ada package given in Section 10.2.3 so that it becomes a general-purpose package for controlling a three task conversation. (Hint: use **generics**).

10.5 Can your solution to 10.4 be extended to cope with an arbitrary number of tasks participating in the atomic action?

10.6 What would be the implications of extending Ada to enable one task to raise an exception in another?

Program 10.6

```
x,y,z : INTEGER;

PROCESS B;

PROCESS A;
BEGIN
  ...
  ACTION conversation (B) do
    ENSURE A_acceptance_test
    BY
      -- A_primary
      -- uses x,y
    ELSE BY
      -- A_secondary
      -- uses y,z
    ELSE
      ERROR
  END conversation;
  ...
END A;

PROCESS B;
BEGIN
  ...
  ACTION conversation (A) do
    ENSURE B_acceptance_test
    BY
      -- B_primary
      -- uses x,y
    ELSE BY
      -- B_secondary
      -- uses y,z
    ELSE
      ERROR
  END conversation;
  ...
END B;
```

10.7 Program 10.6 illustrates a simple conversation between two processes. Show how this can be constructed as a colloquy.

10.8 In Section 6.5 it was shown how exceptions could be used to implement recovery blocks. Can this approach be used with asynchronous exceptions to implement conversations?

Chapter 11
Resource Control

Chapter 10 considered the problem of achieving reliable process cooperation. It was pointed out that coordination between processes is also required if they are to share access to scarce resources such as external devices, files, shared data fields, buffers and encoded algorithms. These processes were termed *competing* processes. Much of the logical (that is, non temporal) behaviour of real-time software is concerned with the allocation of resources between competing processes. Although the processes do not communicate directly with each other to pass information concerning their own activities, they may communicate to coordinate access to the shared resources. A few resources are amenable to unlimited concurrent access, however, most are restricted in their usage in some way.

This chapter discusses the problem of reliable resource control. The general allocation of resources between competing processes is considered. Although such processes are independent of each other, the act of resource allocation has implications for reliability. In particular, failure of a process could result in an allocated resource becoming unavailable to other processes. Processes may be starved of resources if other processes are allowed to monopolize them. Furthermore, processes can become deadlocked by holding resources that other processes require while at the same time requesting more resources.

11.1   Resource control and atomic actions

Although processes need to communicate and synchronize in order to perform resource allocation, this need not be in the form of an atomic action. This is because the only information exchanged is that necessary to achieve harmonious resource sharing; it is not possible to exchange arbitrary information (Shrivastava and Banatre, 1978). As a result of this, the resource controller, be it a process or a monitor, is able to ensure the global acceptability of any change to its local data. If this were *not* the case, then when a process which had been allocated a resource failed, it would be necessary to inform all processes which had recently communicated with the resource controller of its failure. However, the code necessary for a particular process to communicate with the controller should be an atomic action; thus, no other process in the system can disrupt the process when it is being allocated, or is freeing, a resource. Furthermore, a resource allocator and client process may use forward and backward error recovery to cope with any anticipated or unanticipated error conditions.

Although in Chapter 10 it was shown that, in general, no real-time language supported atomic actions, the indivisibility effect can be achieved by careful use of the available communication and synchronization primitives. Unfortunately, the presence of the abort statement in Ada makes the programming of an atomic action difficult, as is shown in the next section.

11.2   Resource management

Concerns of modularity (in particular, information hiding) dictate that resources must be encapsulated and be accessed only through a high-level procedural interface; for example, in Ada a package should be used wherever possible:

```
package RESOURCE_MANAGER is

    type RESOURCE is private;
    function ALLOCATE return RESOURCE;
    procedure FREE(THIS_RESOURCE : RESOURCE);

private
    type RESOURCE is ...

end RESOURCE_MANAGER;
```

In occam 2 the natural form of a resource manager is a process that has been instantiated from a procedure (PROC) with channel parameters:

```
PROC resource.manager([] CHAN OF Any request,
                      [] CHAN OF resource allocate,
                      [] CHAN OF resource free)
  ...
:
```

In Chapter 9 it was noted that processes can, in general, be classified into a limited number of types. One of the most useful classifications is to consider processes as either *servers* or *clients*. Server processes control access to (and encapsulate) system resources. Client processes make use of the services available. This distinction leads to the *client-server* paradigm for program construction. Where communication and synchronization is based on monitors, it is often possible to encapsulate a resource with just a monitor – no server process is required.

Bloom (1979) has suggested criteria for evaluating synchronization primitives in the context of resource management. Her criteria can be extended to cover any client-server interaction, of which resource management is a particular case. This analysis forms the basis to the next section which looks at the expressive power and ease of use of these synchronization primitives for resource control. After this discussion, Section 11.4, which is on security, will look at how a resource controller can protect itself against misuse.

11.3 Expressive power and ease of use

Bloom uses the term 'expressive power' to mean the ability of a language to express required constraints on synchronization. Ease of use of a synchronization primitive encompasses:

(1)   the ease with which it expresses each of these synchronization constraints;
(2)   the ease with which it allows the constraints to be combined in order to achieve more complex synchronization schemes.

In the context of client-server interactions and resource control, the information needed to express these constraints can be categorized (following Bloom) as follows:

- the type of service request;
- the order in which requests arrive;
- the state of the server and any objects it manages;
- the parameters of a request.

To this list should be added

- the priority of the client.

A full discussion of process priority is given in Chapter 12. For the purpose of this chapter, the priority of a process is taken to be a measure of the process's importance.

In general there are two linguistic approaches to constraining access to a service (Liskov *et al.*, 1986). The first is the **conditional wait**: all requests are accepted, but any process whose request cannot currently be met is suspended on a queue. The conventional monitor (Hoare, 1974) typifies this approach: a process whose request cannot be met is queued on a condition variable, and resumed when the request can be serviced. The second approach is **avoidance**: requests are not accepted unless they can be met. The conditions under which a request can safely be accepted are expressed as a guard on the action of acceptance. Ada (and occam 2) adopts this second approach. A study of expressive power in this context thus becomes a study of the expressive power of the selective wait.

11.3.1   Request type.

Information about the type of operation requested can be used to give preference to one type of request over another (for example, read requests over write requests to a real-time database). With monitor-based synchro-nization the read and write operations could be programmed as distinct procedures, but the semantics of a monitor usually imply that outstanding calls on these monitor procedures are handled in a First-In, First-Out (FIFO) way. It is not possible, therefore, to deal with read requests first; nor is it feasible to know how many outstanding calls there are to monitor procedures.

A similar problem arises if a low-level primitive such as a semaphore is used to control access within a module. Indeed, the semantics of the signal operation (on a semaphore) often require that the process to be woken up (if there is more than one) is chosen arbitrarily.

In Ada, different request types can readily be represented by dif-ferent entries in the server task(s). The most natural way of giving prefer-ence to particular request types is through guards which use the COUNT attribute of entries. The following shows a case in which READ requests are intended to have priority over WRITE requests:

```
task SERVER is
   entry READ(VALUE : out VALUE_TYPE);
   entry WRITE(VALUE : VALUE_TYPE);
end SERVER;
```

```
task body SERVER is
begin
  loop
    accept WRITE (VALUE : VALUE_TYPE) do
      -- initial value written
    end WRITE;
    select
      accept READ (VALUE : out VALUE_TYPE) do
        -- read operation
      end READ;
    or
      when READ'COUNT = 0 =>
        accept WRITE (VALUE : VALUE_TYPE) do
          -- write operation
        end WRITE;
    or
      terminate;
    end select;
  end loop;
end SERVER;
```

Unfortunately, a SERVER programmed in this way may not always operate correctly, since the time-out of a queued entry call (see Chapter 12) or abortion of a calling task may alter the value of the COUNT attribute after the corresponding guard has been evaluated. The result will at best be unnecessary delay, and at worst deadlock. A safer solution, given below, separates the case of dealing with the first call to any entry (when the SERVER is suspended) and acceptance of any number of outstanding READ entry calls.

```
task SERVER is
  entry READ (VALUE : out VALUE_TYPE) ;
  entry WRITE(VALUE : VALUE_TYPE);
end SERVER;

task body SERVER is
begin
  accept WRITE (VALUE : VALUE_TYPE) do
    -- initial value written
  end WRITE;
  loop
    loop
      select
        accept READ (VALUE : out VALUE_TYPE) do
          -- read operation
        end READ;
```

```
          else
             exit;
          end select;
       end loop;
       -- writer may get priority if
       -- a read request occurs at this
       -- point
       select
          accept WRITE (VALUE : VALUE_TYPE) do
             -- write operation
          end WRITE;
       or
          accept READ (VALUE : out VALUE_TYPE) do
             -- read operation
          end READ;
       or
          terminate;
       end select;
    end loop;
end SERVER;
```

This solution is acceptable in most circumstances. However, it is not strictly correct, since it is possible for a writer to be accepted when there is an outstanding reader. This may happen in the pathological case that a READ entry call occurs just after several outstanding readers have been serviced but before the SERVER has serviced a pending WRITE request. Safe solutions to this type of problem become even more intricate when there are more than two request types.

In the occam 2 language each request type is associated with a different channel group. Occam 2 has the added feature, however, that it provides a form of selective waiting that gives each alternative a different priority. The read-write server is thus easily structured, as shown below.

```
WHILE TRUE
  PRI ALT
    ALT i = 0 FOR max
      read[i] ? Any
        -- read operation incorporating an output operation
        -- such as:
        output[i] ! object
    ALT j = 0 FOR max
      write[j] ? object
        -- write operation
```

Note that the read operation has to be constructed as a double interaction because the ALT can only deal with inputs. The corresponding action associated with the read operation must, therefore, involve the client process in making a double call:

```
SEQ
  read[MyChannelToServer] ! Any
  output[MyChannelToServer] ? OBJECT
```

The use of PRI ALT gives a static deterministic select. It has been argued (Elrad and Maymir-Ducharme, 1986) (in the context of Ada) that a more dynamic form is required. In order to achieve this each arm of the select statement is given a priority (or preference) expression that is evaluated each time the select is executed. The arm with the greatest priority level and open guard is chosen (if there are outstanding calls on more than one entry).

The above examples show a simple structure for a read operation being given preference over a write. More complicated reader/writer structures are possible if the actions are assumed to have significant duration so that simultaneous reads should be permitted. Various solutions to reader/ writer problems are to be found in books on concurrent programming and operating systems. Some exercises are given at the end of this chapter.

11.3.2 Request order

Certain synchronization constraints may be formulated in terms of the order in which requests are received (to ensure fairness, for example, or to avoid starvation of a client). As has already been observed in Section 11.3.1 monitors usually deal with requests in FIFO order and therefore immediately meet this requirement. In Ada, outstanding requests of the same type (calls to the same entry) are also serviced in a FIFO manner. Outstanding requests of different types (calls to different entries within a select statement) are serviced in an arbitrary order outside the programmer's control. Thus, there is no way of servicing requests of different types according to order of arrival unless all clients first call a common REGISTER entry, that is,

```
SERVER.REGISTER;
SERVER.READ(...);
```

With occam 2's one-to-one naming structure it is impossible for outstanding requests to a single ALT construct to be dealt with in the order of their arrival. A process may have a number of input channels to choose from but cannot detect which channel has had a process waiting for the longest time. It should also be noted here that an occam 2 server process must know the number of possible clients it has; to each must be allocated a separate channel. Ada's model is much more amenable to the client-server paradigm as any number of clients can call an entry and each entry is dealt with in a FIFO order.

11.3.3 Server state

Some operations may be permissible only when the server and the objects it administers are in a particular state. For example, a resource can be allocated only if it is free, and an item can be placed in a buffer only if there is an empty slot. In a message-based model (for example, Ada or occam 2) a server is a process, therefore the state of a server is synonymous with the state of the corresponding process and the values of its local variables. Constraints based on server state are expressed by the positioning of inter-process communications and as guards to appropriate selective waiting constructs. Monitors are similarly quite adequate – with condition variables being used to implement constraints.

11.3.4 Request parameters

The order of operations of a server may also be constrained by information contained in the parameters of requests. Such information typically relates to the identity or (in the case of quantifiable resources like memory) to the size of the request. A straightforward monitor structure (in Modula-1, taken from Section 8.5.1) for a general resource controller is given below. A request for a set of resources contains a parameter that indicates the size of the set required, if not enough resources are available then the caller is suspended; when any resources are released all suspended clients are woken up (in turn) to see if their request can now be met.

```
INTERFACE MODULE resource_control;

    DEFINE allocate, deallocate;    (* export list *)

    CONST instances_of_resource = ...;

    VAR free : SIGNAL;
      resource_free : INTEGER;
```

```
PROCEDURE allocate(size : INTEGER);
BEGIN
   WHILE size > resource_free DO
      WAIT(free);
      SEND(free)
   END;
   resource_free : = resource_free − size
END;

PROCEDURE deallocate(size : INTEGER);
BEGIN
   resource_free : = resource_free + size;
   SEND(free)
END;

BEGIN     (∗ initialization of module ∗)
   resource_free : = instances_of_resource
END.
```

In message-based languages the data being carried with the message cannot be accessed until the message has been read. Therefore, it is necessary to construct a request as a double interaction. The following discusses how a resource allocator that will cater for this problem can be constructed in Ada. The associated structure for occam 2 is left as an exercise for the reader (see Exercise 11.3). This Ada example is an adaptation of one given by Burns *et al.* (1987).

Resource allocation and Ada – an example

A way of tackling the problem in Ada is to associate an entry family with each type of request. Each permissible parameter value is mapped onto a unique index of the family so that requests with different parameters are directed to different entries. Obviously, this is only appropriate if the parameter is of discrete type.

The approach is illustrated in the package in Program 11.1, which shows how lack of expressive power leads to a complex program structure (that is, poor ease of use). Again, consider an example of resource allocation in which the size of the request is given as a parameter of the request. As indicated above, the standard approach is to map the request parameters on to the indices of a family of entries, so that requests of different sizes are directed to different entries. For small ranges the technique described in Section 11.3.1 for 'request type' can be used, with the select statements enumerating the individual entries of the family. However, for larger ranges a more complicated solution is needed (Ichbiah *et al.*, 1979a).

Program 11.1

```
package RESOURCE_MANAGER is
  MAX_RESOURCES : constant INTEGER := 100;
  type RESOURCE_RANGE is new INTEGER range 1 .. MAX_RESOURCES;
  subtype INSTANCES_OF_RESOURCE is RESOURCE_RANGE range 1 .. 50;
  procedure ALLOCATE(SIZE : INSTANCES_OF_RESOURCE);
  procedure FREE(SIZE : INSTANCES_OF_RESOURCE);
end RESOURCE_MANAGER;

package body RESOURCE_MANAGER is

  task MANAGER is
    entry SIGN_IN(SIZE : INSTANCES_OF_RESOURCE);
    entry ALLOCATE(INSTANCES_OF_RESOURCE);
    entry FREE(SIZE : INSTANCES_OF_RESOURCE);
  end MANAGER;

  procedure ALLOCATE(SIZE : INSTANCES_OF_RESOURCE) is
  begin
    MANAGER.SIGN_IN(SIZE);        -- size is a parameter
    MANAGER.ALLOCATE(SIZE);       -- size is an index into a family
  end ALLOCATE;

  procedure FREE(SIZE : INSTANCES_OF_RESOURCE) is
  begin
    MANAGER.FREE(SIZE);
  end;

  task body MANAGER is
    PENDING : array(INSTANCES_OF_RESOURCE) of
      NATURAL := (others => 0);
    RESOURCE_FREE : RESOURCE_RANGE := RESOURCE_RANGE'LAST;
  begin
    loop
      select
        accept SIGN_IN(SIZE : INSTANCES_OF_RESOURCE) do
          PENDING(SIZE) := PENDING(SIZE) + 1;
        end SIGN_IN;
      or
        accept FREE(SIZE : INSTANCES_OF_RESOURCE) do
          RESOURCE_FREE := RESOURCE_FREE + SIZE;
        end FREE;
      end select;
      loop -- accept any pending sign-in or frees, do not wait
        select
          accept SIGN_IN(SIZE : INSTANCES_OF_RESOURCE) do
            PENDING(SIZE) := PENDING(SIZE) + 1;
          end SIGN_IN;
```

```
        or
            accept FREE(SIZE : INSTANCES_OF_RESOURCE) do
                RESOURCE_FREE := RESOURCE_FREE + SIZE;
            end FREE;
        else
            exit;
        end select;
    end loop;


    for REQUEST in reverse INSTANCES_OF_RESOURCE loop
        if PENDING(REQUEST) > 0
        and RESOURCE_FREE >= REQUEST then
        accept ALLOCATE(REQUEST);
        PENDING(REQUEST) := PENDING(REQUEST) − 1;
        RESOURCE_FREE := RESOURCE_FREE − REQUEST;
        exit ;        −−loop to accept new sign-ins
        end if;
    end loop;
    end loop;
    end MANAGER;
end RESOURCE_MANAGER;
```

The MANAGER gives priority to large requests. In order to acquire resources a two-stage interaction with the MANAGER is required: a SIGN_IN request and an ALLOCATE request. This double interaction is hidden from the user of the resource by encapsulating the MANAGER in a package and providing a single procedure (ALLOCATE) to handle the request.

When there are no outstanding calls, the MANAGER waits for a SIGN_IN request or a FREE request (to release RESOURCEs). When a SIGN_IN arrives, its size is noted in the array of PENDING requests. A loop is then entered to record all SIGN_IN and FREE requests that may be outstanding. This loop terminates as soon as there are no more requests.

A **for loop** is then used to scan through the PENDING array, and the request with the greatest size that can be accommodated is accepted. The main loop is then repeated in case a request with greater SIZE has attempted to SIGN_IN.

The solution is complicated by the need for the double rendezvous interaction. It is also expensive, as an entry is required for every possible size.

A much simpler system is to be found in the language SR (Andrews, 1982). Here, guards on selective construct are allowed to access (that is, refer to) 'in' parameters. A rendezvous is, therefore, only started when the task knows that it is in a state in which the request can be accommodated. The double call is not needed.

11.3.5   Double interactions and atomic actions

So far in Section 11.3 examples have been given, in both Ada and occam 2 which require the client process to make a double call on the server. One of the main factors that necessitates this double interaction is the lack of expressive power in message-based synchronizations. To program reliable resource control procedures, this structure must therefore be implemented as an atomic action. In occam 2 the double call:

```
SEQ
  read[MyChannelToServer] ! Any
  output[MyChannelToServer] ? OBJECT
```

does form an atomic action as the client is guaranteed to read the object having sent the request. Unfortunately, with Ada this guarantee cannot be made (Wellings *et al.*, 1984). Between the two calls; that is, after SIGN_IN but before ALLOCATE an intermediate state of the client is observable from outside the 'atomic action':

```
begin
  MANAGER.SIGN_IN(SIZE);
  MANAGER.ALLOCATE(SIZE);
end;
```

This state is observable in the sense that another task can abort the client between the two calls and leave the SERVER in some difficulty:

(1)   If the SERVER assumes that the client will make the second call then the abort will leave the SERVER waiting for the call (that is, deadlocked).

(2)   If the SERVER protects itself against the abort of a client (by not waiting indefinitely for the second call), it may assume the client has been aborted when in fact it is merely slow in making the call; hence the client is blocked erroneously.

In the context of real-time software three approaches have been advocated for dealing with the abort problem:

(1)   Define the abort primitive to apply to an atomic action rather than a process; forward or backward error recovery can then be used when communicating with the server.

(2)   Assume that abort is only used in extreme situations where the breaking of the atomic action is of no consequence.

(3)   Try and protect the server from the effect of client abort.

Approach (3), in Ada, involves using an AGENT task to make the calls on behalf of the client:

```
task type AGENT is
  entry DEPOSIT(SIZE : INSTANCE_OF_RESOURCE);
  entry COLLECT;
end AGENT;

type AGT is access AGENT;

task body AGENT is
  S : INSTANCE_OF_RESOURCE;
begin
  accept DEPOSIT(SIZE : INSTANCE_OF_RESOURCE) do
    S := SIZE;
  end DEPOSIT;
  MANAGER.SIGN_IN(S);
  MANAGER.ALLOCATE(S);
  accept COLLECT;
end AGENT;
```

The client first creates a new AGENT task and then has a rendezvous with it:

```
declare
  NEW_AGENT : AGT := new AGENT;
begin
  NEW_AGENT.DEPOSIT(SIZE);
  NEW_AGENT.COLLECT;
end;
```

The intermediate task is constructed by the **new** operator so that it is anonymous (and hence cannot be aborted in its own right) and is not a dependent of the client. If the client is aborted the AGENT task remains. The interaction between the AGENT and the SERVER is thus atomic.

Unfortunately, the use of dynamic allocation is often unacceptable in real-time systems. When an agent task has completed its work its memory should be freed; an activity known as **deallocation**. The use of the run-time system to periodically deallocate unwanted storage is called **garbage collection**. It is because garbage collection results in heavy and unpredictable overheads in execution time that dynamic allocation can be unacceptable.

There is no requirement in Ada for an implementation to provide garbage collection. The only solution therefore is to use a pool of reusable agents. This structure is non-trivial and has a complexity far greater then the problem to be solved. It can be concluded that Ada does not give 'ease of use' when it comes to programming reliable double interactions. Solutions that use a pool of reusable agents are to be found in Burns (1985b).

11.3.6   Requester priority

The final criteria for evaluating synchronization primitives for resource management involves the use of client priority. If a collection of processes are runnable then the dispatcher can order their executions according to priority. The dispatcher cannot, however, have any control over processes suspended waiting for resources. It is therefore necessary for the order of operations of the resource server to be also constrained by the relative priorities of the client processes.

No current real-time languages provides this functionality. For example; processes are released from primitives such as semaphores or condition variables in either an arbitrary or FIFO manner; monitors are FIFO on entry; selective waits are arbitrary and entry queues are FIFO. To cope with client priority, processes with distinct priorities are programmed to access the resource via a different interface:

```
type PRI is (HIGH, MEDIUM, LOW);

task RESOURCE_CONTROL is
   entry TAKING(PRI)(...);    -- a family definition
   entry RETURNING(...);
end RESOURCE_CONTROL;
```

Within the package body preference is given to calls to TAKING-(HIGH)(...) over the other two family members. This is an identical structure to that in Section 11.3.4 on *request parameters*.

Unfortunately, this approach of associating the priority of the client with a distinct interface is only meaningful if the priority of the client is static (see Chapter 12 for a discussion as to why priorities should be dynamic).

11.3.7   Summary so far

In Sections 11.3.1–11.3.6, the five requirements given at the beginning of Section 11.3 have been used to judge the appropriateness of current language structures for dealing with general resource control. Monitors deal well with request parameters; message-passing primitives have the edge on request type. Semaphores, and their equivalent, are poor on request order and server state. None of the common structures satisfy the requester priority requirement.

It should, however, be noted that the requirements themselves are not mutually consistent. There may well be conflict between the priority of the client and the order of arrival of the requests; or between the operation requested and the priority of the requester. For example, in occam 2 (because it has a deterministic selective wait) a read request was given priority over a write by:

```
WHILE TRUE
  PRI ALT
    read ? request
      -- read operation incorporating an output operation
      -- such as: output ! object
    write ? object
      -- write operation
```

Arguably, if a caller to write has a higher priority than a caller to read then the write operation should take place first. These objectives cannot both be satisfied and there is a need for synchronization primitives to be developed that will allow the programmer to deal, in a high-level way, with this conflict. This is discussed further in Chapter 12.

It has been shown that it is necessary to construct the client's interaction with a server, as an atomic action. The absence of language primitives to support atomic actions and the existence of an abort statement makes this difficult; processes can be asynchronously removed from monitors or terminated between two related calls to a server process. Abort is used to eliminate erroneous or redundant processes. If a monitor is constructed correctly then it can be assumed that a rogue process can do no damage whilst in a monitor (given that the knowledge that it is rogue was only available after it entered). Similarly, a rogue client can do no damage if it is just waiting to make a second synchronous call. It follows that there are well-specified situations in which a process should not be aborted (to be accurate; the effect of the abort will still occur but is postponed). If these semantics were incorporated into a language then atomic actions for all resource control events could be programmed.

11.4   Asymmetric naming and security

In languages that have direct symmetric naming a server process always knows the identity of the client process with which it is dealing. This is also the case with indirect naming schemes based on a one-to-one intermediary (such as an occam 2 channel). Asymmetric naming, however, results in the server being unaware of the identity of the client. It was noted earlier that this has the advantage that general-purpose servers can be written but it can lead to poor security on the use of resources. In particular, a server process may wish to know the identity of the calling client so that:

- a request can be refused on the grounds of deadlock prevention (see Section 11.6) or fairness (that is, to grant the request would be unfair to other clients);

- it can be guaranteed that resources are released only by the process that obtained them earlier.

In CHILL, processes can have an instance or name associated with them (see Section 9.7) which enables a resource controller (a region in CHILL) to know the identity of calling processes. Ada, by comparison, has no such naming facility. A server task must either require a name parameter to be supplied with each entry or, more securely, it must incorporate its own identity stamp. Welsh and Lister (1981) have shown how to achieve the latter by using a key that is issued when a resource is allocated (for example) and checked when it is released:

```
package SECURITY is
   type KEY is limited private;
   procedure REQUEST(K : out KEY; ... );
   procedure RELEASE(K : in out KEY; ... );
private
   type KEY is record
      VALUE : INTEGER := INTEGER'FIRST;
   end record;
end SECURITY;
```

The key is constructed as a single component record so that an initial value can be assigned. This initial value is considered to be a non-valid key. The type of the key is limited private so that it can be neither altered nor copied externally. When RELEASE is called the key is returned to its initial value (if this is appropriate, that is, all held resources have been returned). To make the client identification scheme secure an active key should never be reused. The range of integers is usually adequate for this.

11.5   Resource usage

When competing or cooperating processes require resources the normal mode of operation is for them to: *request* the resource (waiting if necessary), *use* the resource, and then *release* it. A resource can be requested for use in one of two modes of access. These are shared access or exclusive access. Shared access is where the resource can be used concurrently by more than one process; for example a read-only file. Exclusive access requires that only one process be allowed access to the resource at any one time; for example a physical resource like a line printer. Some resources can be used in either mode. In this case, if a process requests access to the resource in sharable mode whilst it is being accessed in exclusive mode, then that process must wait. If the resource was already being accessed in sharable mode then the process could continue. Similarly, if exclusive access to a resource is requested then the process making the request must wait for the processes currently accessing the resource in sharable mode to finish.

As processes may be blocked when requesting resources, it is imperative that they do not request resources until they need them. Furthermore, once allocated they should release them as soon as possible. If this is not done then the performance of the system can drop dramatically as processes continually wait for their share of a scarce resource. Unfortunately, if processes release resources too soon and then fail, they may have passed on erroneous information through the resource. For this reason, the *two-phased* resource usage, introduced in Section 10.1.1, must be modified so that resources are not released until the action is completed. Any recovery procedure within the action must either release the resources, if successful recovery is performed, or undo any affects on the resource. The latter is required if recovery cannot be achieved and the system must be restored to a safe state. With forward error recovery these operations can be performed by exception handlers. With backward error recovery, it is not possible to perform these operations without some additional language support (Shrivastava and Banatre, 1978; Shrivastava, 1979a, 1979b).

11.6 Deadlock

With many processes competing for a finite number of resources a situation may occur where one process, P_1, has sole access to a resource, R_1, while waiting for access to another resource, R_2. If process P_2, already has sole access to R_2 and is waiting for access to R_1, then *deadlock* has occurred because both processes are waiting for each other to release a resource. With deadlock all affected processes are suspended indefinitely. A similar acute condition is where a collection of processes are inhibited from proceeding but are still executing. This situation is known as *livelock*. A typical example would be a collection of interacting processes stuck in loops from which they cannot proceed, but in which they are doing no useful work.

Another possible problem occurs when several processes are continually attempting to gain sole access to the same resource; if the resource allocation policy is not fair, one process may never get its turn to access the resource. This is called *indefinite postponement* or *starvation* or *lockout* (see Section 8.3.3). In concurrent systems *liveness* means that if something is supposed to happen, it eventually will. Breaches of liveness result from deadlock, livelock or starvation. Note that liveness is not as strong a condition as fairness. It is, however, difficult to give a single precise definition of fairness.

The remainder of this section concentrates on deadlock and how it can be prevented, avoided, detected and recovered from.

11.6.1   Necessary conditions for deadlock to occur

There are four necessary conditions that must hold if deadlock is to occur:

(1)   **mutual exclusion** – only one process can use a resource at once (that is, the resource is non-sharable or at least limited in its concurrent access);

(2)   **hold and wait** – processes must exist which are holding resources while waiting for others;

(3)   **no pre-emption** – a resource can only be released voluntarily by a process, and;

(4)   **circular wait** – a circular chain of processes must exist such that each process holds resources which are being requested by the next process in the chain.

11.6.2   Methods of handling deadlock

If a real-time system is to be reliable it must address the issue of deadlock. There are three possible approaches:

(1)   deadlock prevention,

(2)   deadlock avoidance,

(3)   deadlock detection and recovery.

These are now briefly discussed. For a more comprehensive discussion the reader is referred to any book on operating systems; for example Lister, (1984), Deitel (1984) or Peterson and Silberschatz (1985).

Deadlock prevention

Deadlock can be prevented by ensuring that at least one of the four conditions required for deadlock never occurs.

Mutual exclusion: If resources are sharable they can not be involved in a deadlock. Unfortunately, although a few resources are amenable to concurrent access most are, in some way, restricted in their usage.

Hold and wait: One very simple way in which deadlock can be avoided is to require that processes either request resources before they begin their execution, or at stages in their execution when they have no resources allocated. Unfortunately, this tends to be inefficient in its use of resources and can lead to starvation.

No pre-emption: If the constraint that resources should not be pre-empted from processes is relaxed then deadlock can be prevented. There are several approaches including releasing all the resources of a process if it tries to allocate a further resource and fails; and stealing a resource if a process requests a resource which is allocated to another process which is blocked (waiting for another resource). The blocked process is now waiting for one extra resource. The disadvantage of this approach is that it requires the state of the resource to be saved and restored; in many cases this may not be possible.

Circular waits: To avoid circular waits, a linear ordering on all resource types can be imposed. Each resource type can then be allocated a number according to this ordering. Suppose R is the set of resource types thus

$$R = \{r_1, r_2, \ldots r_n\} \text{ the set of all resources}$$

and the function F takes a resource type and returns its position in the linear order. If a process has resource r_j and it requests resource r_k, the request will only be considered if

$$F(r_j) < F(r_k).$$

Alternatively, a process requesting a resource r_j must first release all resources r_i where

$$F(r_i) < F(r_j).$$

Note that the function F should be derived according to the usage of the resource.

Another approach to prevention is to analyse the program formally so that it is possible to verify that circular waits are not possible. The ease with which programs can be so analysed is very dependent upon the concurrency model employed. Low-level synchronization primitives are extremely difficult to examine in this way; message-based structures are, by comparison, much more amenable to the application of formal proof rules. Occam 2 is particularly well designed for this purpose. Its semantics have been formally specified and much of the theory of deadlock-free programs that has been developed for CSP is equally applicable to occam 2.

Deadlock avoidance

If more information on the pattern of resource usage is known then it is possible to construct an algorithm which will allow all the four conditions necessary for deadlock to occur but which will also ensure that the system never enters a deadlock state. This is known as *deadlock avoidance*. A deadlock avoidance algorithm will dynamically examine the resource allocation state and take action to ensure that the system can never enter into deadlock. However, it is not sufficient merely to ask whether the next new state is deadlock; for if it is, it may not be possible to take any alternative action that would avoid this condition. Rather, it is necessary to ask if the system remains in a *safe state*. The resource allocation state is given by:

state = number of resources available, number allocated and
maximum demand on resources of each process

The system is *safe* if the system can allocate resources to each process (up to the maximum they require) in some order and still avoid deadlock. For example, consider a data acquisition system which requires access to bulk secondary storage. Suppose it has 12 magnetic tape units and consists of three processes: P_0 which requires a maximum of 10 tape units, P_1 which requires 4, and P_2 which requires 9. Suppose at a time T_i that P_0 has 5 tape units P_1 has 2 and P_2 has 2 (3 tape units are, therefore, available) as illustrated in Table 11.1.

This is a safe state because there exists a sequence $\langle P_1, P_0, P_2 \rangle$ which will allow all the processes to terminate. If at time T_{i+1}, Process P_2 requests 1 tape unit and it is allocated then the state becomes; P_0 has 5, P_1 has 2 and P_2 has 3 and there are 2 available, as shown in Table 11.2.

This is no longer a safe state; with the available tape units only P_1 can terminate leaving: P_0 with 5, P_2 with 3 but only 4 available. Neither P_0 nor P_2 can therefore be satisfied so the system may enter a deadlock situation. The request from P_2 at T_{i+1} should be blocked by the system.

Obviously, deadlock is an unsafe state. A system which is unsafe may lead to deadlock but *it may not*. However, if the system remains safe it will *not* deadlock.

With more than one resource type the avoidance algorithm becomes more complicated. A common one in use is the *Banker's* algorithm. A discussion of this can be found in most operating systems texts.

Table 11.1   Safe state.

Process	Has	Needs
P_0	5	10
P_1	2	4
P_2	2	9
Total	9	

Tape units available = 3

Table 11.2   Unsafe state.

Process	Has	Needs
P_0	5	10
P_1	2	4
P_2	3	9
Total	10	
Tape units available = 2		

Deadlock detection and recovery

In many real-time systems the resource allocation usage is a priori unknown. Even if it is known, the cost of deadlock avoidance is often prohibitive. Consequently, many of these systems will ignore the problems of deadlock until they enter a deadlock state. They then take some corrective action. Unfortunately, if there are many processes it may be quite difficult to detect deadlock. One approach is to use *resource allocation graphs* (sometimes called *resource dependency graphs*.) The notation given in Figure 11.1 is used.

To detect whether a group of processes are deadlocked requires the resource allocation system to be aware of which resources have already been allocated to which processes, and which processes are blocked waiting for resources that have already been allocated. If it has this information

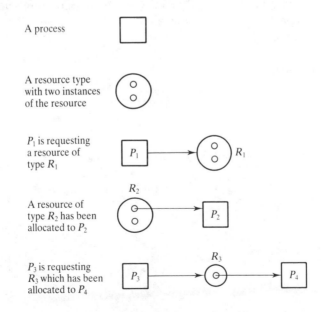

A process

A resource type
with two instances
of the resource

P_1 is requesting
a resource of
type R_1

A resource of
type R_2 has been
allocated to P_2

P_3 is requesting
R_3 which has been
allocated to P_4

Figure 11.1   Notation for resource allocation graphs.

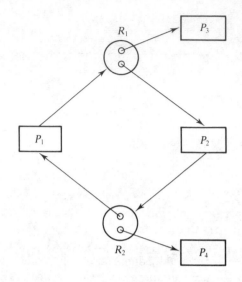

Figure 11.2   A resource allocation graph.

it can construct a resource allocation graph. Figure 11.2 shows the graph for four processes and two resource types.

Using the graph, the system can determine whether deadlock exists. It does this by first examining those processes which are not blocked. It then reduces the graph by removing those processes (in this case P_3 and P_4) and freeing up their resources (R_1 and R_2). The assumption being that if the processes continue to run they will eventually terminate. The graph is now shown in Figure 11.3.

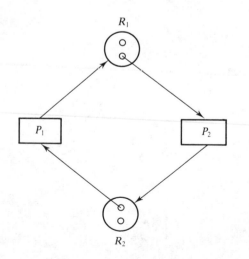

Figure 11.3   A partially reduced graph.

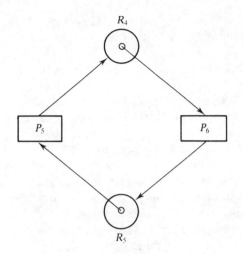

Figure 11.4   A resource allocation graph with a circular wait and deadlock.

From this it can be seen that both processes P_1 and P_2 are able to have their resource demands satisfied. The graph can be further reduced until it disappears completely.

A simple graph which cannot be completely reduced is shown in Figure 11.4.

The reason that the graph cannot be reduced is that there is a circular wait. As neither P_5 or P_6 can continue it is not possible to free up their resources. Therefore, the system is in deadlock.

In general, if no cycles appear in a resource allocation graph, no deadlock has occurred. However, if there is a cycle the system may *or may not* be in deadlock depending on other processes in the graph. Therefore, resource allocation graphs can be used to prevent deadlock. Every time a resource is requested, the graph is updated. If a cycle exists then potentially deadlock may occur, and the request must therefore be refused.

If deadlock can be detected then recovery can take place by: breaking mutual exclusion on one or more resources, aborting one or more processes, or by pre-empting some resources from one or more deadlocked processes. Breaking mutual exclusion, although easy to achieve, could leave the system in an inconsistent state; if a resource was sharable then it should be made sharable. Aborting one or more processes is a very drastic measure to take and again may leave the system in an inconsistent state. If either of these options are adopted, account must be taken of the cost of the action which may include considerations of process priority, how long a process has been executing, how many more resources it needs, and so on.

Pre-emption requires that one or more victims be selected. Selection should include consideration of the priority of the processes, whether the resources are simple to pre-empt, and how near the processes are to completion. Once selected, the course of action will depend on what form of error recovery is used. With backward error recovery the process is restarted at a recovery point prior to the allocation of the resource. With forward error recovery an appropriate exception is raised in the victim, which must then take some corrective action.

Clearly, care must be taken to ensure that the same process is not continuously rolled back and therefore starved of resources. The most common solution to this problem is to include, as part of the cost factor, the number of times a process gets pre-empted.

This section has briefly reviewed the possible approaches that a system can adopt to avoid or cope with deadlock. The majority of these are very expensive to implement and may well be prohibitive in a real-time system. This is particularly true if the system is distributed (see Chapter 13). Consequently, some systems use simple timeouts on resource allocation requests. If the timeout expires then processes can assume potential deadlock and take some alternative course of action.

SUMMARY

In every computer system there are many processes competing for a limited set of resources. Algorithms are required which both manage the resource allocation/deallocation procedures (the mechanism of resource allocation) and which guarantee that resources are allocated to processes according to predefined behaviour (the policy of resource allocation). These algorithms are also responsible for ensuring that processes cannot deadlock whilst waiting for resource allocation requests to be fulfilled.

Sharing resources between processes requires those processes to communicate and synchronize. Therefore, it is essential that the synchronization facilities provided by a real-time language have sufficient expressive power to allow a wide range of synchronization constraints to be specified. These constraints can be categorized as follows:

- the type of service request;
- the order in which requests arrive;
- the state of the server and any objects it manages;
- the parameters of a request;
- the priority of the client.

Monitors deal well with request parameters; message-passing primitives cope adequately with request types. Semaphores, and their equivalent, are poor on request order and server state. None of the common structures satisfy the requester priority requirement.

Where there is insufficient expressive power, processes are often forced into a double interaction with a resource manager. This must be performed as an atomic action, otherwise it is possible for the client process to be aborted after the first interaction but before the second. If this possibility does exist then it is very difficult to program reliable resource managers.

One of the key requirements of resource management is the provision of deadlock-free usage. There are four necessary conditions that must hold if deadlock is to occur:

(1)   mutual exclusion,

(2)   hold and wait,

(3)   no pre-emption.

(4)   circular wait.

If a real-time system is to be reliable it must address the issue of deadlock. There are three possible approaches:

(1)   Deadlock prevention – preventing deadlock by ensuring that at least one of the above four conditions give above never occurs.

(2)   Deadlock avoidance – using information on the pattern of resource usage to construct an algorithm which will allow all the four conditions to occur, but which will also ensure that the system never enters a deadlock state.

(3)   Deadlock detection and recovery – allowing deadlock to occur (and be detected) and then recovering by: breaking mutual exclusion on one or more resources, aborting one or more processes, or by pre-empting some resources from one or more deadlocked processes.

Further reading

Bloom T. (1979). Evaluating synchronisation mechanisms. In *Proceedings of the Seventh Symposium on Operating Systems Principles, ACM*

Burns A., Lister A.M. and Wellings A.J. (1987). A review of Ada tasking. *Lecture Notes in Computer Science*, **262**. Berlin: Springer-Verlag

Peterson J.L. and Silberschatz A., (1988). *Operating Systems Concepts*. Alternate edn. Reading MA: Addison-Wesley

EXERCISES

11.1 The following task purports to give priority to readers over writers of a shared variable.

```
task SHARED_VARIABLE_MANAGER is
  entry READ(VALUE: out V_TYPE);
  entry WRITE(VALUE: in V_TYPE);
end SHARED_VARIABLE_MANAGER;

task body SHARED_VARIABLE_MANAGER is
  THE_VARIABLE: V_TYPE;
begin
  loop
    select
      accept READ(VALUE: out V_TYPE) do
        VALUE := THE_VARIABLE;
      end READ;
    or
      when READ'COUNT = 0 ⇒
        accept WRITE(VALUE : in V_TYPE) do
          THE_VARIABLE := VALUE;
        end WRITE;
    or
      terminate;
    end select;
  end loop;
end SHARED_VARIABLE_MANAGER;
```

Under what conditions will this task fail to produce the desired result? How would you modify the task to give a more secure solution? What are the advantages and disadvantages of your algorithm?

11.2 The following resource controller attempts to associate priorities with REQUEST.

```
type LEVEL is (URGENT, MEDIUM, LOW);

task CONTROLLER is
  entry REQUEST(LEVEL) (D:DATA);
end CONTROLLER;

task body CONTROLLER is
  ...
begin
  loop
    ...
```

```
    select
      accept REQUEST(URGENT)(D:DATA) do
        ...
      end;
    or
      when REQUEST(URGENT)'COUNT = 0 ⇒
        accept REQUEST(MEDIUM)(D:DATA) do
          ...
        end;
    or
      when REQUEST(URGENT)'COUNT = 0 and
           REQUEST(MEDIUM)'COUNT = 0 ⇒
        accept REQUEST(LOW)(D:DATA) do
          ...
        end;
    end select
    ...
  end loop;
end CONTROLLER;
```

Explain this solution and indicate under what conditions it will fail. Why would it not be advisable to extend the above solution to cope with a numeric priority which falls in the range 0 to 1000? Sketch an alternative solution which will cope with larger-priority ranges. You may assume that the calling tasks issue simple entry calls and are not aborted.

11.3 Show how the Ada resource manager given in Section 11.3.4 can be programmed in occam 2.

11.4 Consider a system which has 5 processes $(P_1, P_2 .. P_5)$ and 7 resource types $(R_1, R_2 .. R_7)$.

There is one instance of resources 2, 5 and 7 and two instances of resources 1, 3, 4 and 6. Process 1 has been allocated an instance of R_1 and requires an instance of R_7. Process 2 has been allocated an instance of R_1, R_2 and R_3 and requires R_5. Process 3 has been allocated an instance of R_3 and R_4 and requires R_1. Process 4 has been allocated R_4 and R_5 and requires R_2. Process 5 has been allocated R_7.

Is this system in deadlock? Give your reasons.

11.5 A system is in the state described in Table 11.3.

Is this system in a safe or an unsafe state? Give your reasons. A system that is in an unsafe state will not necessarily deadlock. Explain why this is true, give an example of an unsafe state and show how the processes could complete without deadlock occurring.

Table 11.3   The state of a system.

	Current load	Maximum need
Process 1	2	12
Process 2	4	10
Process 3	2	5
Process 4	0	5
Process 5	2	4
Process 6	1	2
Process 7	5	13
Units available = 1		

Chapter 12
Real-time Facilities

In Chapter 1 it was noted that a language for programming embedded systems requires facilities for real-time control. Indeed, the term 'real-time' has been used as a synonym for this class of system. Given the importance of time in many embedded systems it may appear strange that consideration of this topic has been postponed until Chapter 12. Facilities for real-time control are, however, generally built upon the concurrency within the language and, therefore, it is necessary to have covered this area first.

The introduction of the notion of time into a programming language can best be described in terms of four requirements that build upon each other:

(1) Access to a clock, so that the passage of time can be measured.

(2) Delaying a process, so that it is suspended until some future time.

(3) Programming timeouts, so that the non-occurrence of some event (within a specified period of time) can be recognized and dealt with.

(4) Deadline specification and scheduling, so that the necessary time constraints can be specified and met.

Each of these four requirements will now be considered in turn. It must be said at this stage, however, that although deadline scheduling is, in many ways, the essence of the real-time domain it is dealt with very inadequately in most (so-called) real-time languages.

12.1   Access to a clock

If a program is going to interact in any meaningful way with time then it must have access to some method of 'telling the time', or, at least, have some way of measuring the passage of time. This can be done in two distinct ways.

(1)   By including a clock primitive in the language.
(2)   By programming a device driver for a clock device which is attached to the processor.

Clock primitives can range from the very basic to the quite sophisticated. Occam 2 and Ada illustrate these two extremes well.

12.1.1   TIMERs in occam 2

Any occam 2 process can obtain a value of the 'local' clock by reading from a TIMER. To be consistent with the occam 2 model of communication (which is one-to-one) each process must use a distinct TIMER. Reading from a TIMER follows the syntax of a channel read, but the semantics are different in that a TIMER read cannot lead to suspension, that is, the clock is always ready to output.

```
TIMER clock:
INT Time:
SEQ
  clock ? Time    -- read time
```

The value produced by a TIMER is of type INT, but of implementation-dependent meaning: it gives a relative, not absolute, clock value. A single reading of a TIMER is therefore meaningless, but the subtraction of two readings will give a value for the passage of time between the two readings:

```
TIMER clock:
INT old, new, interval:
SEQ
  clock ? old
  -- other computations
  clock ? new
  interval := new MINUS old
```

Table 12.1   Typical values for the granularity
and range of times for a clock.

Granularity	Range (approximately)
1 microsecond	71.6 minutes
100 microseconds	119 hours
1 millisecond	50 days
1 second	136 years

The operator MINUS is used rather than '-' to take account of wrap-around. This occurs because the integer given by a TIMER is incremented by one for each unit of time; eventually the maximum integer is reached, and so for the subsequent 'tick' the integer becomes the most negative one and then continues to be incremented. Users can be unaware of this action as long as they use the appropriate (language-defined) arithmetic operators, which are MINUS, PLUS, MULT and DIVIDE. In effect, each TIMER undertakes a 'PLUS 1' operation for each increment of the clock.

As the above illustrates, the facilities provided by occam 2 are primitive (though arguably, quite adequate). As only one integer is allocated for the clock there is clearly a trade-off between the granularity of the clock (that is, what interval of time each tick of the clock represents) and the range of times that can be accommodated. With a 32-bit integer Table 12.1 gives typical values; the first two values are supported on the transputer implementation of occam 2.

12.1.2   The CALENDAR package in Ada

Access to a clock in Ada is provided by a predefined (compulsory) library package called CALENDAR. This package implements an abstract data type for TIME. It provides a function CLOCK for reading the time and various subprograms for converting between TIME and humanly understandable units such as YEARS, MONTHS, DAYS and SECONDS. The first three of these are given as integer subtypes. SECONDS are, however, defined as a subtype of the primitive type DURATION.

DURATION is a predefined fixed-point real that is provided for time calculations. Both its accuracy and its range are implementation dependent, although its range must be at least 0.0 .. 86400.0 which is the number of seconds in a day. In essence, a value of type DURATION should be interpreted as a value in seconds. At this point it is worth giving the specification of the CALENDAR package (see Program 12.1); note that in addition to the subprograms introduced so far, the package defines arithmetic operators for combinations of DURATION and TIME parameters and comparative operations for TIME values.

Program 12.1

```
package CALENDAR is

  type TIME is private;

  subtype YEAR_NUMBER is INTEGER range 1901 .. 2099;
  subtype MONTH_NUMBER is INTEGER range 1 .. 12;
  subtype DAY_NUMBER is INTEGER range 1 .. 31;
  subtype DAY_DURATION is DURATION range 0.0 .. 86400.0;

  function CLOCK return TIME;

  function YEAR(DATE:TIME) return YEAR_NUMBER;
  function MONTH(DATE:TIME) return MONTH_NUMBER;
  function DAY(DATE:TIME) return DAY_NUMBER;
  function SECONDS(DATE:TIME) return DAY_DURATION;

  procedure SPLIT(DATE : in TIME; YEAR : out YEAR_NUMBER;
                  MONTH : out MONTH_NUMBER; DAY : out DAY_NUMBER;
                  SECONDS : out DAY_DURATION);

  function TIME_OF(YEAR:YEAR_NUMBER; MONTH:MONTH_NUMBER;
                  DAY:DAY_NUMBER; SECONDS:DAY_DURATION := 0.0)
                  return TIME;

  function "+"(LEFT:TIME;RIGHT:DURATION) return TIME;
  function "+"(LEFT:DURATION;RIGHT:TIME) return TIME;
  function "-"(LEFT:TIME;RIGHT:DURATION) return TIME;
  function "-"(LEFT:TIME;RIGHT:TIME) return DURATION;

  function "<"(LEFT,RIGHT:TIME) return BOOLEAN;
  function "<="(LEFT,RIGHT:TIME) return BOOLEAN;
  function ">"(LEFT,RIGHT:TIME) return BOOLEAN;
  function ">="(LEFT,RIGHT:TIME) return BOOLEAN;

  TIME_ERROR : exception;
  -- TIME_ERROR is raised by TIME_OF,"+",and "-"

private
  -- implementation dependent
end CALENDAR;
```

The code required to measure the time taken to perform a computation is apparently quite straightforward.

```
declare
   OLD_TIME, NEW_TIME : TIME;
   INTERVAL : DURATION;
begin
   OLD_TIME := CLOCK;
   -- other computations
   NEW_TIME := CLOCK;
   INTERVAL := NEW_TIME - OLD_TIME;
end;
```

However, this will not produce a meaningful result if the task is descheduled between calls to the clock routine. Similarly, this is true for the occam 2 example.

The Ada facility has a number of advantages over those provided by occam 2. It allows dates and human time to be coordinated with the language clock and it does not restrict the range of times that can be manipulated. However, Ada does not specify a minimum number of digits for the fixed-point DURATION type and so, again, the granularity of the time primitive is implementation dependent.

Because of the nature of clock primitives they often only really provide a coarse measurement of time. If a more accurate clock is required (finer granularity) then it must be programmed directly using a clock device. Indeed, in a number of languages (including Modula-1 and Modula-2) the only way to gain access to a clock is by programming a driver for such a device. This is illustrated in Section 12.1.3 for Modula-1. A similar approach can be used with Modula-2; this is left as an exercise for the reader (Exercise 14.8).

12.1.3   A programmed clock in Modula-1

It is inevitable in a book describing interdependent language features that not all facilities can be described in a logical order. The programming of device drivers, in general, is not considered until Chapter 14. Nevertheless, it is possible to give an overview of a clock module now and leave its implementation to the later chapter.

As already indicated, Modula-1 provides no direct facilities for manipulating time; these have to be provided by the application. First there must be a module to give a data type for time:

```
MODULE timeset;

   DEFINE time, initialize, addtime;

   TYPE time = ...;

   PROCEDURE initialize(VAR T : time; H,M,S,MS : INTEGER);

      ...
```

```
PROCEDURE addtime(VAR T : time; MS : INTEGER);
   ...


   ...
END timeset;
```

The procedure initialize, as its name suggests, sets up a variable of type time when given four integers representing hours, minutes, seconds and milliseconds. Addtime allows a number of milliseconds to be added to objects of type time; other procedures are also necessary; they are not given here as they would be similar in form to those provided in the Ada CALENDAR package.

Next, a device driver for the hardware clock is required;

```
DEVICE MODULE hardwareclock[ .. ];
   DEFINE tick;
   VAR tick : SIGNAL;      (* condition variable *)
   PROCESS handler

      ...
   END handler;
BEGIN
   driver
END hardwareclock;
```

The handler process deals with the interrupts from the clock device. At regular intervals (say, every millisecond) the process also does a send operation on the tick variable (in the terminology of Chapter 8 this would be a signal operation on a condition variable). Given these two modules, it is now possible to construct a clock module:

```
INTERFACE MODULE SystemClock;
   (* defines procedures for getting and setting the time of day *)
   DEFINE GetTime, SetTime;

   (* import the abstract data type time, and the tick signal *)
   USE time, initialize, addtime, tick;

   VAR TimeOfDay, onetick : time;

   PROCEDURE SetTime(t: time);
   BEGIN
      TimeOfDay := t
   END SetTime;

   PROCEDURE GetTime(VAR t: time);
   BEGIN
      t := TimeOfDay
   END GetTime;
```

```
PROCESS clock;
BEGIN
  LOOP
    WAIT(tick);
    addtime(TimeOfDay, onetick)
  END
END clock;
BEGIN
  initialize(TimeOfDay, 0, 0, 0, 0);
  initialize(onetick, 0, 0, 0, 1);
  clock
END SystemClock;
```

A process can measure time by simply making sequential calls on GetTime.

Because these modules are completely under user control they can be altered to give whatever granularity is required. The only limit is the rate of interrupts from the hardware clock device and the overall load on the processor.

12.2   Delaying a process

In addition to having access to a clock, processes must also be able to delay themselves for a period of time. This enables a process to queue on a future event rather than busy wait on calls to the clock. For example, the following Ada code shows how a task can loop while waiting for ten seconds to pass:

```
NOW := CLOCK;
loop
  exit when (CLOCK − NOW) > 10.0;
end loop;
```

To eliminate the need for these busy waits Ada provides a **delay** statement.

```
delay 10.0;
```

The value after **delay** (of type DURATION) is relative (that is, the above statement means 'delay ten seconds from the current time'). It is important to appreciate that delay is an approximate time construct, the inclusion of which in a task indicates that the task will be delayed by at least the amount defined. There is no upper bound specified on the actual delay, and in many situations it may be considerably longer than intended (for example, if a higher-priority process is executing at the time). The important point is that *the delay cannot be less than that given in the delay statement*.

To emphasize the open-ended semantics for delay the corresponding construct in occam 2 actually uses the word AFTER. In contrast to the relative-time construct in Ada, occam 2 uses absolute time. Therefore, to wait for ten seconds to elapse necessitates reading the TIMER clock first, adding ten seconds and then delaying until this time. The value ten seconds is obtained via the constant G which is introduced (here) to give a measure of the granularity of the implementation (G is the number of TIMER updates per second):

```
SEQ
  clock ? now
  clock ? AFTER now PLUS (10 * G)
```

The time over-run associated with both of these constructs is called the **local drift**; it cannot be eliminated using these constructs. It is possible, however, to eliminate the **cumulative drift** that could arise if local drifts were allowed to superimpose. The following code in Ada shows how the computation ACTION is programmed to be executed every seven seconds. This code will compensate for any local drift. For example, if two consecutive calls to ACTION were actually nine seconds apart then the subsequent delay would be for only five seconds (approximately).

```
declare
  NEXT : TIME;
  INTERVAL : constant DURATION := 7.0;
begin
  NEXT := CLOCK + INTERVAL;
  loop
    ACTION;
    delay NEXT − CLOCK;
    NEXT := NEXT + INTERVAL;
  end loop;
end;
```

The occam 2 code would be:

```
INT next, now:
VAL interval IS 7 * G:
SEQ
  clock ? now
  next := now PLUS interval
  WHILE TRUE
    SEQ
      ACTION
      clock ? AFTER next
      next := next PLUS interval
```

As with the discussion, in Section 12.1, of the clocks themselves, these delay primitives should only be considered coarse real-time primitives. More responsive structures must be programmed directly. For example, a delay procedure could easily be added to the SystemClock module given in Section 12.1.3. This is left as an exercise for the reader (Exercise 14.5).

12.3   Programming timeouts

Perhaps the simplest time constraint that an embedded system can have is the requirement to recognize, and act upon, the non-occurrence of some external event. For example, a temperature sensor may be required to log a new reading every second; the failure to give a reading within ten seconds being defined as a fault. In general, a **timeout** is a restriction on the time a process is prepared to wait for a communication.

Real-Time Euclid, (Kligerman and Stoyenko, 1986), which uses semaphores, extends the semantics of wait to include a time bound. The following statement illustrates how a process could suspend itself on the semaphore CALL with a timeout value of 10 seconds:

```
wait CALL noLongerThan 10 : 200
```

If the process is not signalled within ten seconds the exception 200 is raised (exceptions in Real-Time Euclid are numbered). Note, however, that there is no requirement for the process to be actually scheduled and executing within ten seconds.

With synchronous message passing, once a process has committed itself to a communication then it must wait until such an event has occurred. A process with a timeout has the opportunity to do something else if the required communication is not timely. To illustrate the programming of timeouts consider, first, a CONTROLLER task (in Ada) that is called by some other DRIVER task and given a new temperature reading:

```
task CONTROLLER is
  entry CALL(T : TEMPERATURE);
end CONTROLLER;

task body CONTROLLER is
  -- declarations
begin
  loop
    accept CALL(T : TEMPERATURE) do
      NEW_TEMP := T;
    end CALL;
    -- other actions
  end loop;
end CONTROLLER;
```

Now it is required that the controller be modified so that the lack of the entry call is acted upon. This requirement can be provided using the constructs already discussed. A second task is used that delays itself for the timeout period and then calls the controller. If the controller accepts this before the normal call then a timeout has occurred, as shown below:

```
task CONTROLLER is
   entry CALL(T : TEMPERATURE);
   entry TIMEOUT;
end CONTROLLER;

task body CONTROLLER is
   task TIMER is
      entry GO(D : DURATION);
   end TIMER;
   -- other declarations
   task body TIMER is
      DU : DURATION;
   begin
      accept GO(D : DURATION) do
         DU :=D;
      end GO;
      delay DU;
      CONTROLLER.TIMEOUT;
   end TIMER;
begin
   loop
      TIMER.GO(10.0);
      select
         accept CALL(T : TEMPERATURE) do
            NEW_TEMP := T;
         end CALL;
      or
         accept TIMEOUT;
         -- action for timeout
      end select;
      -- other actions
   end loop;
end CONTROLLER;
```

Although the above code will only deal with the first timeout period it can be modified (non-trivially) to deal with continuous performance. Nevertheless, the need for timeouts is so common that a more concise way of expressing it is desirable. This is usually provided in a real-time language as a special form of alternative in a selective wait. The example shown above would, more appropriately, be coded as follows:

```
task CONTROLLER is
   entry CALL(T : TEMPERATURE);
end CONTROLLER:

task body CONTROLLER is
   -- declarations
begin
  loop
    select
      accept CALL(T : TEMPERATURE) do
        NEW_TEMP := T;
      end CALL;
    or
      delay 10.0;
      -- action for timeout
    end select;
    -- other actions
  end loop;
end CONTROLLER;
```

The delay alternative becomes ready when the time delay has expired. If this alternative is chosen (that is, a call is not registered within ten seconds) then the statements after the delay are executed. Within the Ada model it would not make sense to mix an else part, a terminate alternative and delay alternatives. These three structures are, therefore, mutually exclusive; a select statement can have, at most, only one of them. If it is a delay alternative, however, the select can have a number of delays; the one with the shortest duration being the operative one on each occasion.

A timeout facility is common in message-based concurrent programming languages. Occam 2, like Ada, uses the 'delay' primitive as part of a selective 'wait' construct to indicate timeout:

```
WHILE TRUE
  SEQ
    ALT
      call ? new_temp
        -- other actions
      clock ? AFTER (10 * G)
        -- action for timeout
```

where clock is a TIMER.

Both the occam 2 and Ada examples given in this section show how a timeout on a message receive is programmed. Ada actually goes further and allows a timeout on a message send. To illustrate this, consider the

device driver that is feeding temperatures to the CONTROLLER in the Ada
code given at the beginning of this section:

```
loop
   -- get new temperature T
   CONTROLLER.CALL (T);
end loop;
```

As new temperature readings are available continuously (and there
is no point in giving the CONTROLLER an out-of-date value), the device
driver may wish to be suspended while waiting for the controller for only
half a second before withdrawing the call. This is achieved by using a
special form of the select statement which has a single entry call and a
single delay alternative:

```
loop
   -- get new temperature T
   select
      CONTROLLER.CALL(T);
   or
      delay 0.5;
      null;
   end select;
end loop
```

The **null** is not strictly needed but shows again that the delay can
have arbitrary statements following it, that are executed if the delay
expires before the entry call is accepted.

This is a special form of the select statement. It cannot have more than
one entry call and it cannot mix entry calls and accept statements. The action
it invokes is called a **timed entry call**. It must be emphasized that the time
period specified in the call is a timeout value for the call being accepted; *it is
not a timeout on the termination of the associated accept statement.*

When a task only wishes to make an entry call if the called task is
immediately prepared to accept the call, then rather than make a timed
entry call with time zero (which can cause difficulty in distributed systems,
see Chapter 13), a **conditional entry call** can be made:

```
select
   T.E      -- entry E in task T
else
   -- other actions
end select;
```

The 'other actions' are only executed if T is not prepared to accept E
immediately. 'Immediately', means that either T is already suspended on

'accept E' or on a select statement with such an open alternative (and it is chosen).

Timeouts are an important feature of real-time systems; they are, however, far from being the only time constraints of significance. The rest of this chapter deals with the general topic of time deadlines and how to ensure that they are met.

12.4   Deadline specification and scheduling

For many important real-time systems it is not sufficient for the software to be logically correct, the programs must also satisfy timing constraints determined by the underlying physical system. These constraints can go far beyond simple timeouts. Unfortunately, existing practices in the engineering of large real-time systems are, in general, still rather *ad hoc*. Often, a logically-correct system is specified, designed and constructed (perhaps as a prototype) and then tested to see if it meets its timing requirements. If it does not, then various fine tunings and rewrites ensue. The result is a system that may be difficult to understand and expensive to maintain and upgrade. A more systematic treatment of time is required.

Work on a more rigorous approach to this aspect of real-time systems has followed two largely distinct paths (Joseph and Goswami, 1988). One direction of development has concerned the use of formally-defined language semantics and timing requirements, together with notations and logics that enable temporal properties to be represented and analysed. The other path has focused on the performance of real-time systems in terms of the feasibility of scheduling the required work load onto the available resources (processors and so on).

In this book, attention is focused exclusively on the latter work. The reasons for this are threefold. Firstly, the formal techniques are not yet mature enough to reason about large and complex real-time systems. Often, assumptions are made that are not appropriate (for example, maximum parallelism – each process has its own processor). Secondly, there is little reported experience of the use of these techniques in actual real-time systems. Thirdly, to include a full discussion of such methods would involve a substantial amount of material that is outside the scope of this book. This is not meant to imply that the area is not relevant to real-time systems. The understanding of, for example, formal techniques based on CSP, temporal logic, Real-Time Logic (RTL) and specification techniques that incorporate notions of time, is becoming increasingly important. For example, RTL can be used to verify the temporal requirements of a system (Jahanian and Nok, 1986); thereby complementing the use of methods such as VDM and Z for analysing the functional requirements. The interested reader is encouraged to pay particular attention to the further reading section at the end of this chapter.

In the context of scheduling, timing constraints are incorporated into the concurrency model of the language. The timing requirements then become visible characteristics of the software processes. From this it can be observed that two distinctive process types are present in the real-time domain: periodic and aperiodic. Typically, **periodic** processes sample data or execute a control loop and have explicit deadlines that must be met. **Aperiodic**, or *sporadic*, processes arise from asynchronous events outside the embedded computer. These processes have specified response times associated with them. Both periodic and aperiodic processes must, if possible, be analysed to give their *worst-case execution times*. Average execution times may also be obtained.

In general, aperiodic processes are viewed as being activated randomly, following, for example, a Poisson distribution. Such a distribution allows for 'bursty' arrivals of external events but does not preclude any possible concentration of aperiodic activity. It is, therefore, not possible to do worst-case analysis (there is a non-zero probability of any number of aperiodic events occurring). In order to allow worst-case calculations to be made, a minimum period between any two aperiodic events (from the same source) is often defined. If this is the case, the process involved is said to be *sporadic*. In this book the term 'aperiodic' will be used for the general case and 'sporadic' will be reserved for situations where a minimum delay is needed.

To facilitate the specification of the various timing constraints found in real-time applications it is useful to introduce the notion of **temporal scopes**. Such scopes identify the collection of statements with an associated timing constraint (Lee and Gehlot, 1985). The possible attributes of a Temporal Scope (TS) are illustrated in Figure 12.1, and include:

(1)   Deadline – the time by which the execution of a TS must be finished.

(2)   Minimum delay – the minimum amount of time that must elapse before the start of execution of a TS.

(3)   Maximum delay – the maximum amount of time that can elapse before the start of execution of a TS.

(4)   Maximum execution time – of a TS.

(5)   Maximum elapse time – of a TS.

Temporal scopes with combinations of these attributes are also possible. In this chapter the term *deadline* is used to imply any of the above constraints. By associating temporal scopes with processes that embody them, the problem of satisfying timing constraints becomes one of scheduling processes to meet deadlines, or *deadline scheduling*.

Although all computer systems strive to be efficient, and many are described as real-time, further classification is needed in order to deal

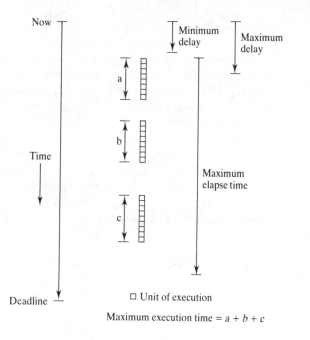

Figure 12.1   Temporal scopes.

adequately with the different levels of importance that time has within applications. A system is said to be *hard* real-time if it has deadlines that cannot be missed for if they are, the system fails. By comparison, a system is *soft* if the application is tolerant of missed deadlines. A system is merely *interactive* if it does not have specified deadlines but strives for 'adequate response times'.

The distinction between hard and soft real-time becomes somewhat blurred in fault-tolerant systems. Nevertheless, it is usually appropriate to use the term **hard** if a specific error recovery (or failsafe) routine is triggered by a missed deadline, and **soft** if the nature of the application is tolerant of the occasional missed deadline or deadlines that are not missed by much. Furthermore, many hard real-time systems will have some deadlines which are soft.

12.4.1   The notion of priority

With interactive operating systems, the notion of priority has been introduced and used to indicate, to the run-time dispatcher, the order in which processes should be executed. Typically, those processes that are dealing with human interaction are given higher priority so that response time is improved. Batch processes are given lower priority and thus are only run when no interactive work is present. Usually, the dispatcher uses a *pre-emptive* scheduler, in that the lower priority process is immediately removed from the processor when a higher-priority process becomes runnable.

To aid in the scheduling of processes, most concurrent programming languages provide a priority model. These facilities can be used for programming interactive applications and are of use in soft real-time systems. In the latter case, priority is useful as it indicates which processes should be run in situations where not all deadlines can be met. To distinguish this use of priority (that is, indicating which processes are most important) the term **preference priority** will be used. In hard real-time systems, or subsystems, all processes are critically important (that is, all deadlines must be met) and the notion of preference priority is less significant.

In Ada, a priority can be associated with a task by use of a **pragma**, for example:

```
task type DEVICE_DRIVER is
    pragma PRIORITY(P);        -- P is a static expression of subtype
                               -- PRIORITY (of type integer)

    entry CALL(...);
    entry RESULT(...);
end DEVICE_DRIVER;
```

This gives a static-priority level to a **task type**. No minimum range of priorities need be supported, but the semantics of PRIORITY require the scheduler to be pre-emptive. The language definition is clear that it cannot be the case that a low-priority task is running in preference to a high priority one if both tasks are runnable and could reasonably use the same processing facility.

The only situation in which a task can have its priority changed is during a rendezvous. Here, the priority of the rendezvous itself is defined to be the maximum of the priorities of the two tasks involved in the rendezvous.

Many criticisms have been made about the poor definition of priority in Ada. For example, Burns *et al.* (1987) note the following.

(1)   All tasks of the same type must have equal priority.

(2)   Tasks without a priority assigned (by the **pragma**) could have a high or a low priority, therefore all tasks must be given a priority if priority is to be used at all.

(3)   A task that is acting as a driver for an external device cannot run permanently at the priority level of the device (see Section 14.3.3 for a discussion of this important problem).

Notwithstanding these difficulties, the priority model allows a programmer to specify preference priorities. Where the model has no influence is in the decision about which partner a task should rendezvous with (if it has a choice). Queues on entries must be handled in a FIFO manner. If the priority of the calling task is to be taken into account then the programmer must make sure that tasks with different priorities call different entries and do so in a consistent manner. Entry families are provided for this purpose. For example, consider a task that provides two entries, one for TAKING a resource and another for RETURNING it:

```
task RESOURCE_CONTROL is
   entry TAKING(...);
   entry RETURNING(...);
end RESOURCE_CONTROL;
```

All clients of this task must call TAKING and will be handled in a FIFO manner. If the client population can be divided into, say, three priority levels then three different TAKING entries are needed so that each priority level has its own FIFO queue. To ease the programming of this structure a family of entries can be used:

```
type PRI is (HIGH, MEDIUM, LOW);


task RESOURCE_CONTROL is
   entry TAKING(PRI)(...);            -- a family definition
   entry RETURNING(...);
end RESOURCE_CONTROL;
```

The body of this kind of task was given in Section 11.3.6 where the problems of giving preference to one entry over another was discussed in a more general context.

In addition to the entry queues being defined to be FIFO, the select statement is considered to work in an arbitrary way. This means that the language does not define which branch of a select should be chosen (if more than one branch has an open guard and a task waiting). Although the term 'arbitrary' does not preclude an implementation from using priority to affect the choice, it does mean that a programmer cannot assume such an interpretation. To use a particular compiler because it has this facility would be contrary to the spirit of Ada.

It was noted in Section 9.5.4 that if the language assumes that the scheduler is working in a non-deterministic way, then it is appropriate for the selective wait construct to be arbitrary. When priority is introduced, the scheduler becomes more constrained; indeed, if a program's tasks all have distinct priorities then the scheduler is totally deterministic. It follows that the selective wait construct should also become deterministic with the priority of the calling tasks being used to control choice.

The occam 2 model is similar to that of Ada's. Static priorities are assigned by the use of a PRI PAR (rather than a PAR):

```
PRI PAR
  P1
  P2
  PAR
    P3
    P4
  P5
```

Relative priorities are used, with the textual order of the processes in the PRI PAR being significant. In the above, P1 has the highest priority; P2 the second highest; P3 and P4 share the next priority level and P5 has the lowest priority. No minimum range of priorities need be supported by an implementation; indeed, the transputer only provides two distinct levels. As with the Ada model, occam 2's ALT does not take account of priority when it is arbitrating between more than one ready alternative.

Both Ada and occam 2 illustrate poor integration between two important language features; namely, the synchronization and priority models. All synchronization primitives give rise to the possibility of a process being suspended. In a real-time programming language these primitives must take account of the priority of the suspended processes. This implies the following.

(1)   If more than one process can be suspended on a single synchronization primitive then the processes must be released in priority order.

(2)   If a language construct can choose between two or more synchronization primitives (in order to release a process) the priority or the processes involved must control the choice.

The first point implies that semaphores, condition variables, monitor access and entry queues must all release processes in priority order. In addition, the second requirement implies that a selective waiting construct (such as the Ada select and occam 2's ALT) must, if there is a choice, release the process with the highest priority.

Unfortunately, these requirements are not sufficient to ensure that a high-priority process is not delayed more than is necessary. Consider, as an example, a system with three tasks; T_1, T_2 and T_3 with priorities P_1, P_2 and P_3 where $P_1 > P_2 > P_3$. If T_1 is suspended while waiting for T_3 to do something (for example, receive a message) then T_2 will be executing in preference to T_3. Therefore, T_1 will be delayed further because T_2 is executing, even though the priority of T_1 is greater than T_2. This phenomenon is known as **priority inversion** (Sha *et al.*, 1987a).

One method of limiting this effect is to use **priority inheritance** (Sha *et al.*, 1987a). With priority inheritance, a process's priority is no longer static; if a process p is suspended while waiting for process q to undertake some computation then the priority of q becomes equal to the priority of p (if it were lower to start with). In the example just given, T_3 will be given the priority of T_1 and will, therefore, run in preference to T_2.

The general case defines the priority of a process to be the maximum of its own default priority and the priorities of all the other processes that are, at that time, dependent upon it.

Note that the Ada model goes some way towards this inheritance by defining the priority of a rendezvous to be the higher of the two priorities of the tasks involved. A full inheritance model would raise the priority of a server task when a call upon it is made, not just when it is accepted.

In general, inheritance of priority would not be restricted to a single step. If task T_1 is waiting for T_3, but T_3 cannot deal with T_1 because it is waiting for T_4 then T_4 as well as T_3 would be given T_1's priority. The implication for the run-time dispatcher is that a process's priorities will often be changing and that it may be better to choose the appropriate process to run (or make runnable) at the time when the action is needed rather than try and manage a queue that is ordered by priority.

In the design of a real-time language, priority inheritance would seem to be of paramount importance. To have the most effective model, however, implies that the concurrency model should have a particular form. With semaphores and condition variables there is no link between the act of becoming suspended and the identity of the process that will reverse this action. Inheritance is, therefore, not possible. With synchronous message passing, indirect naming (for example, use of the channel in occam 2) may also make it difficult to identify the process upon which one is waiting. To maximize the effectiveness of inheritance, direct symmetric naming would be the most appropriate. Although, if such a scheme were adopted then it would become more difficult to program server processes.

Ada uses direct asymmetric naming and a many-to-one relationship between calling and called tasks. If a task calls an entry in another task then its priority can be inherited by the called task. However, if a task executes an accept statement (or a select) upon which there is no immediate call then it cannot give its priority to the potential caller, as it has no way of knowing which task will actually make the call. For example, a typical buffer task in Ada would have at its heart a select with guarded entries to PUT and TAKE:

```
select
    when NOT_FULL ⇒
    accept PUT(...) do
        ...
    end PUT;
```

```
or
  when NOT_EMPTY ⇒
  accept TAKE(...) do
     ...
  end TAKE;
end select;
```

If a high-priority process calls PUT then the server (which would initially have a low priority) will immediately be raised to this high-priority level. But, if the buffer is, at that time, full, it is not possible to pass on the high-priority level to a caller of TAKE and hence, the high-priority task will be delayed until such a call is made.

In terms of priority, the relationship between the run-time dispatcher and the multiprocess program being scheduled should be as follows:

- Within the program the relative importance of the processes is indicated by assigning a *preference priority* to each process.
- The behaviour of synchronization primitives is controlled by the current priority of the tasks involved.

The current priority of a process is dynamic and is, at any one instant, the maximum of:

- its preference priority, and;
- its inherited priority.

To reiterate: neither Ada nor occam 2 provide these facilities.

12.4.2 Specifying deadlines

In both hard and soft real-time systems it is necessary to deal explicitly with deadlines; five types of which were given at the beginning of Section 12.4. Thus, a general scheme for a periodic process is as follows:

```
process periodic_P;
  ...
begin
  loop
    IDLE
    start of temporal scope
      ...
    end of temporal scope
  end;
end;
```

The time constraints take the form of maximum and/or minimum times for IDLE and require that the end of the temporal scope be by some deadline. This deadline can itself be expressed in terms of either

- absolute time, or;
- execution time since the start of the temporal scope, or;
- elapsed time since the start of the temporal scope.

If the process is data sampling, then this would take place at the start of the temporal scope; the accuracy of the IDLE period is thus important. The temporal scope would contain the necessary processing (or simply buffering) of this data and the deadline at the end of the temporal scope is only there to ensure that the process can loop round and be in time to take the next reading.

For a process sending out a regular control signal, the temporal scope incorporates whatever computations are needed in order to calculate the signal's value (this may include taking external readings). The signal itself is sent out at the end of the temporal scope and, hence, deadlines are associated with this event.

Similar deadlines are necessary with aperiodic processes; here the temporal scope is triggered by an external event that will normally take the form of an interrupt:

```
process aperiodic_P;
  ...
begin
  loop
    wait for interrupt
    start of temporal scope
      ...
    end of temporal scope
  end;
end;
```

Clearly, a periodic process has a defined periodicity (that is, how often the process loop is executed); this measure may also be applied to an aperiodic process in which case it means the maximum rate at which this process will cycle (that is, the fastest rate for interrupt arrivals). As stated at the beginning of Section 12.4, such aperiodic processes are known as sporadic.

In some real-time systems, the deadlines may be associated with some data that passes through a number of processes. In order to schedule these processes, it is necessary to partition the available time between the processes that manipulate the data. This partitioning may get quite complicated if the times in each process are dynamic (that is, data dependent) or, even worse, if the path the data takes through the processes is also data dependent. No real-time languages currently address this problem explicitly.

In keeping with many real-time languages (notable exceptions are discussed below), neither Ada nor occam 2 support the explicit specification of deadlines, rather, the delay primitive must be used. The process that executes the delay cannot be continued before the delay is finished. But, unfortunately, as was indicated in Section 12.2, there is no guarantee provided by the definition of either language that the process will be executed immediately the delay has expired. Moreover, as deadlines are not specified, a process may already have missed its deadline by the time the delay is executed (that is, negative delay).

A periodic task, in Ada, must take the following form:

```
task body PERIODIC_T is
begin
  loop
    -- read real-time clock and
    -- calculate the delay necessary
    -- for next deadline (DEL)
    delay DEL;
    -- sample data (for example) or
    -- calculate and send a control signal
  end loop;
end PERIODIC_T;
```

A sporadic (or aperiodic) task that is triggered by an interrupt would contain no explicit time information but would have the following form:

```
task body SPORADIC_T is
begin
  loop
    -- enable the interrupt
    accept INTERRUPT do
      -- execute appropriate actions
    end INTERRUPT;
    -- execute other appropriate actions
  end loop;
end SPORADIC_T;
```

If the interrupt-handling task is not responsive enough then it will not be able to handle one interrupt and return to the accept statement ready for the next.

What the above examples show is that in Ada and occam 2 (and many other so-called real-time languages) the only time constraint that can be guaranteed to be met is the minimum time before the start of a temporal scope. This is achieved with the delay primitive. All other deadline constraints depend on the behaviour of the run-time dispatcher; algorithms for which are now discussed.

The languages that do give support to deadline scheduling have appropriate timing primitives for deadline specification. In Real-Time Euclid (Kligerman and Stoyenko, 1986) processes are static and non-nested. Each process definition must contain activation information that pertains to its real-time behaviour (the term **frame** is used instead of temporal scope). This information takes one of two forms which relate to periodic and sporadic processes:

(1)   periodic *frameInfo* first activation timeOrEvent

(2)   atEvent *conditionId* frameInfo

The clause frameInfo defines the periodicity of the process (including the maximum rate for sporadic processes). The simplest form this can take is an expression in real-time units:

    frame realTimeExpn

the value of these units is set at the beginning of the program.

A periodic process can be activated for the first time in two different ways. It can have a start time defined or it can wait for an interrupt to occur. Additionally, it can wait for either of these conditions. The syntax for timeOrEvent must therefore be one of the following:

(1)   atTime *realTimeExpn*

(2)   atEvent *conditionId*

(3)   atTime *realTimeExpn* or atEvent *conditionId*

conditionId is a condition variable associated with an interrupt. It is also used with sporadic processes.

To give an example of part of a Real-Time Euclid program consider a cyclic temperature controller (Kligerman and Stoyenko, 1986). Its periodicity is 60 units (that is, its periodicity is every minute if the time unit is set to one second) and it is to become active after 600 units (10 minutes) or when a startMonitoring interrupt arrives:

    realTimeUnit := 1.0 % time unit = 1 seconds

    var Reactor: module % Euclid is module based
       var startMonitoring : activation condition atLocation 16 # A10D
          % this defines a condition variable which is mapped onto an interrupt

```
process TempController : periodic frame 60 first activation atTime 600
                                        or atEvent startMonitoring
% import list
%
% execution part
%
end TempController
end Reactor
```

Note that there is no loop within this process. It is the scheduler that controls the required and specified periodic execution.

To illustrate how this code would need to be constructed in Ada the process (task) part is given (a loop is needed here to force the task to cycle round):

```
task body TEMPCONTROLLER is
  -- definitions, including
  T : TIME;
begin
  select
    accept STARTMONITORING;      -- interrupt entry call
  or
    delay 600.0;
  end select;
  loop
    T := CLOCK;                  -- take note of current time
    --
    -- execution part
    --
    delay 60.0 - (CLOCK - T);    -- delay for remainder of
                                 -- 60 seconds
  end loop;
end TEMPCONTROLLER;
```

Not only is this more cumbersome but the scheduler is not aware of the deadline associated with this task. Its correct execution will depend on the process becoming active again almost immediately the delay has expired.

The language Pearl (Werum and Windauer, 1985) also provides explicit timing information concerning the start, frequency and termination of processes. Although the syntax is different, Pearl gives almost the same functionality as that described for Real-Time Euclid. The temperature controller example, however, illustrates one significant difference; a task in Pearl can be activated by a time schedule or an interrupt but *not* both. Therefore, either of the following are admissible in Pearl:

```
AFTER 10 MIN ALL 60 SEC ACTIVATE TempController;

WHEN startMonitoring ALL 60 SEC ACTIVATE TempController;
```

The term ALL 60 SEC means repeat periodically, after the first execution, every 60 seconds.

Whereas Pearl and Real-Time Euclid associate temporal scopes with processes, and therefore necessitate the specification of timing constraints on the process itself, other languages such as DPS (Lee and Gehlot, 1985) provide local timing facilities that apply at the block level.

In general, a temporal scope may need to specify three, distinct, timing requirements (these are similar to the more global requirements provided by Real-Time Euclid):

(1)   delay start by a known amount of time;

(2)   complete execution by a known deadline;

(3)   take no longer than a specified time to undertake a computation.

To illustrate these structures consider the important real-time activity of making and drinking instant coffee:

```
get_cup
put_coffee_in_cup
boil_water
put_water_in_cup
drink_coffee
replace_cup
```

The act of making a cup of coffee should take no more than ten minutes; drinking it is more complicated. A delay of three minutes should ensure that the mouth is not burnt; the cup itself should be emptied within 25 minutes (it would then be cold) or before 17:00 (in other words, 5 o'clock and time to go home). Two temporal scopes are required:

```
start elapse 10 do
  get_cup
  put_coffee_in_cup
  boil_water
  put_water_in_cup
end

start after 3 elapse 25 by 17:00 do
  drink_coffee
  replace_cup
end
```

For a temporal scope that is executed repetitively a time loop construct is useful:

```
from ⟨start⟩ to ⟨end⟩ every ⟨period⟩
```

For example, many software engineers require regular coffee throughout the working day:

```
from 9:00 to 16:15 every 45 do
   make_and_drink_coffee
```

where make_and_drink_coffee could be made up of the two temporal scopes given above (minus the by constraint on the drinking block). Note that if this were done, the maximum elapse time for each iteration of the loop would be 35 minutes; correctly, less than the period for the loop.

Although block-level timing constraints can be specified in this way, they result in processes that experience different schedules during their executions; at times they may even have no deadlines at all. By decomposing processes into subprocesses that have process-based deadlines, it is possible to represent all deadlines as process-level constraints. Thus, the run-time scheduler is easier to implement; for example, in some of the algorithms discussed in Section 12.4.3, a static-priority scheme is sufficient and the scheduler does not need to be explicitly aware of deadlines.

12.4.3 Schedulability

Having derived a collection of processes (by some design activity), all with associated deadlines, the next critically-important activity is to determine whether this set of processes is schedulable. This means that it is possible for all deadlines to be met indefinitely into the future. In general, necessary and sufficient conditions for schedulability are unknown. There are, however, many different algorithms presented in the literature which test for schedulability under certain preconditions and restrictions.

Most approaches assume that there is a fixed set of processes in the system. This is a valid assumption for most hard real-time applications. Each temporal scope is analysed in order to estimate the time that it will take to execute. In order to predict or assess this value (and, more significantly, for this value to be predictable during execution) the use of certain language features must be avoided. These include:

- dynamic allocation of memory
- dynamic creation of processes
- recursion

Other language features are modified; for example, all loops may have upper bounds placed on them. This could take the form of a maximum number of iterations or maximum-time restriction. In Real-Time Euclid (Kligerman and Stoyenko, 1986) a time condition must be placed on all

Table 12.2   A set of processes with 100% utilization.

Process	Period	Execution requirement	Utilization
P_1	80	40	50%
P_2	40	10	25%
P_3	20	5	25%

loops. The compiler converts this condition into a maximum allowable number of iterations. Note that a loop is not terminated in mid iteration; this could lead to the loop invariant being false.

Finally, interprocess communications and external interactions are given timeout values. This allows the execution time for a process to be independent of other processes.

For periodic processes, an examination of the temporal scopes can lead to a measure of **utilization**. This is the fraction of available time for which a processor is dedicated to that process. For example, a process that requires ten milliseconds of execution and has a periodicity of 100 milliseconds furnishes a utilization of 0.1 (or 10%). If the rate of interrupts for an aperiodic process is also known then similar utilizations are calculable. Clearly, the sum of all the utilizations must be less than the number of processors available. But this is not sufficient. For example, it is impossible for two periodic processes on the same processor to start their temporal scopes at the same time, irrespective of the total processor utilization.

One of the simpler equations for schedulability is given by Liu and Layland (1973). They prove that, for a single processor system, a set of n independent, periodic processes with only execution-time deadlines (that is, no constraints on the start of the temporal scope and no elapse-time constraints) is schedulable if the overall processor utilization is less than:

$$n(2^{(1/n)} - 1).$$

For large n this asymptotically approaches 0.693. Therefore, all process sets are schedulable if processor utilization is less than 69%. The above formula is pessimistic in that it assumes the worst possible relationship between the periods of each process (that is, the period lengths are relative primes). If the relationship between the period is more favourable then higher utilization can be tolerated. For example, consider the three processes and their requirements shown in Table 12.2.

The total utilization of the set of processes in Table 12.2 is 100%, nevertheless, they can all be scheduled. (Note that the execution requirement includes the overhead incurred in the scheduling activity.) By comparison with Table 12.2, the three processes in Table 12.3 cannot be scheduled even though their total utilization is only 82%.

Table 12.3   A set of processes with 82% utilization.

Process	Period	Execution requirement	Utilization
P_1	50	12	24%
P_2	40	10	25%
P_3	30	10	33%

Other algorithms use more specific data about each process; for example, the Real-Time Euclid analyser requires (or calculates) the following values for each process (Kligerman and Stoyenko, 1986):

- total Central Processing Unit (CPU) requirement for executing non-interruptible parts;
- total CPU requirement for executing interruptible parts;
- total time spent performing device operations;
- maximum time spent waiting for interprocess communication;
- worst-case time for being blocked by another process;
- worst-case time for being blocked waiting for a device to become available;
- relative size of each process's interruptible parts.

An example of being blocked by another process is, waiting to gain access to a monitor.

In reality, of course, process execution times are stochastic. Rather than a single derived value being used for the execution time of a temporal scope, at least two measures are needed:

(1)   the average execution time, and;
(2)   the worst-case execution time.

For sporadic processes, the average rate of interrupts and the maximum arrival rate are also required. Unfortunately, in many situations the worst-case figure is considerably higher than the average. Interrupts often arrive in bursts and an abnormal sensor reading may lead to significant additional computation. It follows that measuring schedulability with worst-case figures may lead to very low processor utilizations being observed in the actual running system. As a guideline for the minimum requirement, the following two rules should always be complied with:

Rule 1: All processes should be schedulable using average execution times.

Rule 2: All hard real-time processes should be schedulable using worst-case execution times.

A consequent of Rule 1 is that there may be situations in which it is not possible to meet all current deadlines. This condition is known as a **transient overload**; Rule 2, however, ensures that no hard real-time process will miss its deadline. If Rule 2 gives rise to unacceptably low utilizations for 'normal execution' then direct action should be taken to try and reduce the worst-case execution times (or interrupt arrival rates).

12.4.4 Scheduling algorithms

Schedulability is the first step, but it is by no means the only issue. Just because it is feasible to meet all deadlines it does not mean that the run-time dispatcher will work in such a way as to ensure timely behaviour. The development of scheduling algorithms for soft and hard (periodic and aperiodic) real-time systems is an important and very active research area. Pre-emptive and non-pre-emptive algorithms have been advocated and even heuristic approaches have been studied. Not all of these ideas can be considered in the space available in this book. What follows is a discussion of some of the more important algorithms and issues.

The purpose of a scheduling algorithm is to ensure that the run-time scheduler dispatches the runnable processes in an order that will result in all deadlines being met. In effect, it controls the ordering of the dispatch queue. As the position in this queue is a measure of a process's current priority, a scheduling algorithm can be considered as a means of allocating priority. Both static and dynamic priority allocations are possible.

As the scheduler may be required to assign distinct priorities to all processes in the system, it follows that the range of priority must be sufficiently large to accommodate this. It was noted in Section 12.4.1 that this is not guaranteed by either Ada or occam 2.

Pre-emptive preference scheduling

This is the simplest possible algorithm. All processes are given priorities according to their importance to the system (that is, their preference priority). The scheduler always runs the highest-priority process. This guarantees that the highest-priority process will meet its deadline (assuming that the processor is fast enough to run this one process to its deadline). Unfortunately, this is the only assertion that can be made about this algorithm. Consider, for illustration, two processes P_1 and P_2 with periods 50 and 10 units respectively. P_1 requires 10 units of execution to meet its deadline, P_2 needs 2 units of execution. P_1 is given a higher priority than P_2 because it is more important. If both processes start at the same time then the pre-emptive scheduler will run P_1 for 10 units of time and then suspend it for 40 further units (that is, until its deadline is due). Unfortunately, although the processor is now free to run P_2, it is too late for P_2 to meet its first deadline. Cornhill *et al.* (1987) show how a collection of Ada tasks can fail to meet their deadlines even when the processor utilization is less than 60% because of the use of preference priorities.

Scheduling periodic processes

To overcome this difficulty Liu and Layland (1973) proposed the **rate-monotonic** approach for scheduling periodic processes. Rather than assigning a fixed priority to each process according to its importance, this algorithm assigns a fixed priority to each process based on its period: the shorter the period the higher the priority. Pre-emptive scheduling is still employed. It is with this approach that any set of processes can be scheduled if the overall processor utilization is below 69%. Moreover, this algorithm is an optimal static scheme for independent periodic processes. By 'optimal' it is meant that if a process can be scheduled by any fixed priority algorithm then it can also be scheduled by the rate-monotonic scheduling algorithm.

With the example given in the previous section, P_2 would be given the higher priority even though P_1 is the most important process. At the start of execution, P_2 would run for 2 units of time and then P_1 would run for 8 (P_2 has now met its first deadline). P_2 would then run for a further 2 units followed by P_1 executing 2 units. P_2 has met its second deadline and P_1 is ready to meet its first deadline. All subsequent deadlines for both processes are met. A further example of the use of rate-monotonic scheduling is given later in this section.

For soft real-time systems it is necessary to run the most important processes first (if not all deadlines can be met) while running the one with the shortest period first (if all deadlines are attainable). Similarly, in hard systems it is necessary to distinguish between the deadlines that must be met and those (soft) ones that can be missed during a transient overload. A single-priority primitive within a language would appear to be inadequate for this double requirement, although Sha *et al.* (1987b) discuss a transformation that enables the static rate-monotonic algorithm to still be applied. The essence of their approach is to transform the more important processes so that they also have the shorter periods. In the example, the important P_1 process (which has a period of 50 and a processing requirement of 10) could be changed to have a period of 5 and an execution of 1. The rate-monotonic approach would then run it first on all occasions. The new P_1 process (P_1') is different from an ordinary process, with a cycle time of 5, in that it performs different actions in subsequent periods (repeating itself only every 10 periods). P_1' is obtained from P_1 by either:

(1)   adding nine delay requests into the body of the code, or;
(2)   instructing the run-time system to schedule it as ten shorter processes.

In general, it will not be possible to split a process into exactly equal parts. But as long as the largest part is used for calculations of schedulability, the period transformation technique can deal adequately with transient overloads. Moreover, the transformation technique requires only trivial changes to the code, or run-time support.

Periodic and aperiodic systems

The inclusion of aperiodic processes introduces a new kind of event for which the scheduler must cater. If the response time of the aperiodic processes are not critical then they can be run as background tasks. A periodic server task is used to poll the aperiodic processes, the total system can thus be scheduled using a rate-monotonic approach. Unfortunately, in order to cater for bursty sporadic events, it is necessary to assume worst-case behaviour at all times (that is, the maximum arrival rate). As a result, the processor will exhibit poor utilization.

In an attempt to deal more appropriately with aperiodic processes Lehoczky *et al.* (1987) have proposed a number of algorithms. For example, in their 'deferrable server' approach, a sporadic process is allowed to run immediately (and for as long as necessary) provided that the collection of periodic processes is still able to be scheduled. This significantly improves the response time for the sporadic process but it does not guarantee that sporadic deadlines will be met during a transient overload.

Other scheduling algorithms

Two other commonly advocated scheduling algorithms are:

(1)   earliest deadline, and;
(2)   least slack time.

In both of these cases the scheduler must have explicit information about deadlines. With the earliest (or shortest) deadline the scheduler simply runs the process with the closest deadline; once that temporal scope has been completed the next closest deadline is picked and the associated process executed.

To implement least slack time the scheduler needs to know not only all the deadlines but also the amount of execution time required by each process before its deadline. From this, it can calculate which process has the least free time 'on its hands'. This process is picked for execution.

The attractive feature of these algorithms is that they deal well with systems that are mainly comprised of aperiodic processes. Prior calculations of periodicity are not required as the algorithms do the best that they can with the load that is current. When all deadlines can be met, earliest deadline and least slack time are equivalent to the rate-monotonic algorithm; if a system can be scheduled by one then it can be scheduled by them all.

The disadvantage of the earliest deadline and least slack time algorithms is that during a transient overload, deadlines are missed in an unpredictable fashion (Sha *et al.*, 1986). Neither algorithm looks sufficiently into the future to decide if the current load can be scheduled. If they did, they may be able to run only processes with hard-time constraint. However, adjustments that would indicate the relative importance of different 'soft' processes are very difficult to accommodate.

Cyclic executives

In all the approaches to deadlines described so far the software is designed as a collection of processes and the required real-time behaviour is obtained by the use of an appropriate scheduling algorithm. If a sequential language is being used to implement the system then this approach is clearly not possible. A common technique, used before concurrent programming languages became popular, is to construct the software as a cyclic executive. With this technique the program consists of a single control loop within which the code for each logical process is embedded. Unfortunately, if the logical processes have different periods the code for each process cannot be kept together within this control loop. This leads to unstructured programs. To illustrate this approach (and to compare it with the rate-monotonic solution) consider a simple system that consists of three logical processes P, Q and S. Their characteristics are shown in Table 12.4.

For instance, Q cycles round once every 5 units of time and must execute 2 units of processor time each cycle. With a concurrent programming language, the three logical units become actual processes. The rate-monotonic algorithm would assign P the highest priority, then Q and finally S. The observed behaviour of the program is a pattern of process switching that repeats itself every 20 units of time. This pattern is shown in Table 12.5.

Table 12.4 Characteristics of three logical processes.

Process	Period	Duration of temporal scope
P	4	1
Q	5	2
S	10	3

Table 12.5 The pattern of process switching
for three logical processes.

Time	Process	Total execution time for current process
1	P	1
2	Q	1
3	Q	2
4	S	1
5	P	2
6	Q	3
7	Q	4
8	S	2
9	P	3
10	S	3
11	Q	5
12	Q	6
13	P	4
14	S	4
15	S	5
16	Q	7
17	P	5
18	Q	8
19	S	6
20	Idle	–

The reader may like to verify that this sequence corresponds to the given priority values and that all deadlines are met. At the end of the sequence there is a spare unit of time that the scheduler would use up as idle time.

The pattern of execution produced by the rate-monotonic algorithm gives a clear indication of the structure that the cyclic executive must follow. Firstly, the code for Q must be spilt into two equal parts: $Q1$ and $Q2$; (they are equal in the sense that they require the same execution time). S is similarly partitioned into $S1$, $S2$ and $S3$. The cyclic executive's control loop would, therefore, comprise of statement groups taken from the different processes in an order that will ensure that deadlines are met. Not surprisingly, this ordering bears a close resemblance to that produced by the scheduler in Table 12.5:

```
loop
  P; Q1; Q2; S1; P;
  Q1; Q2; S2; P; S3;
  Q1; Q2; P; S1; S2;
  Q1; P; Q2; S3;
  delay 1;
end loop;
```

The advantage of the cyclic executive approach is that there are no overheads associated with a scheduler or with process switching. The disadvantage is that the logic of the design has been lost in the implementation. Within the control loop it is not possible to isolate the code for each process. This results in software that is difficult to read and, hence, to maintain. Moreover, minor changes to the temporal behaviour of the program may lead to substantial alterations to the code, an activity that is bound to be error prone. A further criticism concerns the introduction of error-recovery facilities on a per process basis; the nature of the control loop makes this very difficult and could itself be a cause of error. Finally, during a transient overload it is not possible to distinguish between hard and soft deadlines.

Taking all these criticisms together they far outway the possible advantages. The cyclic executive method is no longer as popular as it once was. As with so many areas of computing, issues of software engineering have gained the ascendancy over matters of mere efficiency.

12.4.5 Scheduling and process synchronization

When processes interact via synchronization primitives, they may become blocked in the middle of their temporal scopes. In order to calculate their worst-case (or average) execution times it is necessary to know the potential length of this blocking time. A static priority scheme is no longer adequate because it gives no bounds on a number of times a process can be blocked (due to priority inversion). Similar problems exist for the earliest deadline and least slack algorithms.

Sha *et al*. (1988) show that with a priority inheritance protocol there is a bound on the number of times a process's temporal scope can be blocked by lower-priority processes. If a process has m critical sections that can lead to it being blocked then the maximum number of times it can be blocked is m. That is, in the worst case, each critical section will be locked by a lower-priority process. (A blocked process is one that is not runnable.)

While the standard inheritance protocol gives an upper bound on the number of blocks a high-priority process can encounter, this bound can lead to unacceptably pessimistic worst-case calculation. This is compounded by the possibility of chains of blocks developing (transient blocking), that is, P_1 being blocked by P_2 which is blocked by P_3 and so on. Moreover, there is nothing that precludes deadlocks in the protocol. All of these difficulties are addressed by the *ceiling protocol* (Sha *et al.*, 1988). When this protocol is used:

- A high-priority process can be blocked once, at most, during its execution by lower-priority processes.
- Deadlocks are prevented.
- Transient blocking is prevented.

The ceiling protocol can best be described in terms of binary semaphores protecting access to critical sections. In essence, the protocol ensures that if a semaphore is locked, by process P_1 say, and could lead to the blocking of a higher-priority process (P_2), then, no other semaphore that could block P_2 is allowed to be locked by any process other that P_1. A process can, therefore, be delayed by not only attempting to lock a previously locked semaphore, but also when the lock could lead to multiple blocking on higher-priority processes.

The protocol takes the following form:

(1)   All processes have a static default priority assigned (perhaps by the rate-monotonic algorithm).

(2)   All semaphores have a ceiling value defined, this is the maximum priority of the processes that use it.

(3)   A process has a dynamic priority that is the maximum of its own static priority and any that it inherits due to it blocking higher-priority processes.

(4)   A process can only lock a semaphore if its dynamic priority is higher than the ceiling of any currently locked semaphore (excluding any that it has already locked itself).

The locking of a first system semaphore is allowed. The effect of the protocol is to ensure that a second semaphore can only be locked if a higher-priority process that uses both semaphores does not exist. Consequently, the maximum amount of time for which a process can be blocked, is equal to the execution time of the longest critical section in any of the lower-priority processes.

The benefit of the ceiling protocol is that a high-priority process can only be blocked once (per activation) by any lower-priority process. The cost of this result is that more processes will experience this block.

It must be emphasized that predictable scheduling in a hard real-time environment with resource allocation is complex and the subject of much research. General-purpose solutions are not possible in polynominal time and therefore are not appropriate for real-time systems. Most approaches impose some constraints on interprocess synchronization. For example, the ceiling protocol considered in this section allows only mutual exclusion and not condition synchronization between processes.

12.5 Fault tolerance

Throughout this book it has been assumed that real-time systems have high reliability requirements. One method of achieving this reliability is to incorporate fault tolerance into the software. The inclusion of timing constraints introduces the possibility of these constraints being broken, for example, timeouts expiring or deadlines not being met.

With soft systems a process may need to know if a deadline has been missed, even though it can accommodate this under normal execution. More importantly, in a hard system (or subsystem), where all deadlines are critical, a missed deadline needs to trigger some error-recovery routine. If the system has been shown to be schedulable under worst-case execution times then it is arguable that deadlines cannot be missed. However, the discussions on reliability in earlier chapters indicated strongly the need for a multifaceted approach to reliability, that is, prove that nothing can go wrong and include routines for adequately dealing with the problems that arise when they do. In this particular situation a deadline could be missed in a 'proven' system if:

- worst-case calculations were inaccurate;
- assumptions made in the schedulability checker were not valid;
- the schedulability checker itself had an error;
- the scheduling algorithm could not cope with a load even though it is theoretically schedulable;
- the system is working outside its design parameters.

In this latter case, for instance, an information overflow manifesting itself as an unacceptable rate of interrupts, the system designers may still wish for failsoft or failsafe behaviour.

All the above are examples of unexpected deadline failures. Some systems may additionally enter anticipated situations in which deadlines are liable to be missed. A good illustration of this is found in systems that experience *mode changes*. This is where some event in the environment occurs which results in certain computations, that have already been initialized, no longer being required. If the system were to complete these computations then other deadlines would be missed; thus it is necessary to prematurely terminate the temporal scopes that contain the computations.

Methods of coping with missed deadlines and mode changes are discussed in the next two sections.

12.5.1 Forward error recovery

If the run-time system is aware of deadlines then it is able to recognize situations in which deadlines have not been met; even better, it may be able to predict these events. To allow the application software to deal with timing errors necessitates a mechanism for informing it that such a 'missed deadline' event has occurred. The natural form for this communication is an exception.

In Real-Time Euclid, for example, where time constraints are associated with processes, numbered exceptions can be defined. Handlers must be provided in each process. For example, consider the following temperature controller process which defines three exceptions.

```
process TempController : periodic frame 60 first activation atTime 600
                                         or atEvent startMonitoring
  % import list
  handler (except_num)
    exceptions (200,201,304)  % for example
    imports (var consul, ...)
    var message : string(80), ...
    case except_num of
      label 200:  % very low temperature
        message := "reactor is shut down"
        consul := message
      label 201:  % very high temperature
        message := "meltdown has begun - evacuate"
        consul := message
        alarm := true   % activate alarm device
      label 304:  % timeout on sensor
                  % reboot sensor device
    end case
  end handler
  %
  % execution part
  %
end TempController
```

With local-time structures it is also appropriate to associate timing errors with exceptions:

```
start (timing constraints) do
  -- statements
exception
  -- handlers
end
```

The handlers in both local and process-based structures should be able to distinguish between:

- overrun deadlines;
- overrun execution times;
- timeouts on communications within the temporal scope;
- other (non-temporal) error conditions.

In addition to the necessary computations required for damage limitation, error recovery and so on, the handler may wish to extend the deadline period and continue execution of the original block. Thus, a *resumption* rather than *termination* model may be more appropriate (see Section 6.2.3).

In a time-dependent system it may also be necessary to give the deadline constraints of the handlers. Usually, the execution time for the handler is taken from the temporal scope itself; for example, in the following, the statement sequence will be prematurely terminated after 19 time units:

```
start elapse 22 do
  -- statements
exception
  when elapse_error within 3 do
    -- handler
end
```

As with all exception models, if the handler itself gives rise to an exception then this can only be deal with at a higher level within the program hierarchy. If a timing error occurs within a handler at the process level then the process must be terminated (or, at least, terminated at the current iteration of the process). Then, there might be some system-level handlers to deal with failed processes or it may be left to the application software to recognize and cope with such events.

If exception handlers are added to the coffee-making example given in Section 12.4.2, then the code would have the form shown in Program 12.2 (exceptions for logic errors such as 'no cups available' are not included). It is assumed that only boil_water and drink_coffee have any significant temporal properties; timing errors are, therefore, due to overrun on these activities.

So far in this section it has been assumed that a missed deadline can be dealt with by the process that actually is responsible for the deadline. This is not always the case. Often, the consequences of a timing error are that other processes must alter their deadlines or even terminate what they are doing. For instance, to complete a critically important computation may require more processor time than is currently available. To obtain the extra time, other less significant processes may need to be 'suspended'.

Program 12.2

```
from 9:00 to 16:15 every 45 do
  start elapse 11 do
    get_cup
    boil_water
    put_coffee_in_cup
    put_water_in_cup
  exception
    when elapse_error within 1 do
      turn_off_kettle            -- for safety
      report_fault
      get_new_cup
      put_orange_in_cup
      put_water_in_cup
    end
  end

  start after 3 elapse 26 do
    drink
  exception
    when elapse_error within 1 do
      empty_cup
    end
  end
  replace_cup
exception
  when any_exception do
    null                         -- go on to next iteration
  end
end
```

With applications that are prone to mode changes, a process (server) may already be undertaking a computation, requested by a client process, when the client decides that the original request is no longer valid; at least not in the form originally given. This is sometimes known as **event-based reconfiguration**. The client now needs to change the flow of control of the server so that the server undertakes one of the following (typically).

(1) Immediately returns the best result that it has obtained so far.

(2) Changes to a quicker (but presumably less accurate) algorithm.

(3) Forgets what it is presently doing and becomes ready to take new instructions – *restart without reload*.

These effects can only be manifest if there is a communication between the processes concerned. Due to the asynchronous nature of this communication, Real-Time Euclid allows a process to raise an exception in another process. Three different kinds of raise statements are supported, except, deactivate and kill; as their names imply, they have increasing severity.

The except statement is essentially the same as the Ada **raise**, the difference is that once the handler has been executed control is returned to where it left off (that is, a resumption model). By comparison, the deactivate statement causes that iteration of the (periodic) process to be terminated. The victim process still executes the exception handler but will then only become reactivated when its next period is due. In order to terminate a process, the kill statement is available; this explicitly removes a process (possibly itself) from the set of active processes. It differs from 'abort' in that the exception handler is executed before termination. This has the advantage that a process may perform some important 'last rites'. It has the disadvantage that an error in the handler could still cause the process to

Program 12.3

```
process TempController : periodic frame 60 first activation atTime 600
                                            or atEvent startMonitoring
  % import list
  handler (except_num)
    exceptions (200,201,304)  % for example
    imports (var consul, ...)
    var message : string(80), ...
    case except_num of
      label 200:  % very low temperature
        message := "reactor is shut down"
        consul := message
      label 201:  % very high temperature
        message := "meltdown has begun - evacuate"
        consul := message
        except alarmProcess : 100   % activate alarm device
      label 304:  % timeout on sensor
                      % reboot sensor device
    end case
  end handler


  wait(temperature_available) noLongerThan 10 : 304
  currentTemperature := ...  % low level i/o
  log := currentTemperature
  if currentTemperature < 100 then
    deactivate TempController : 200
  elseif currentTemperature > 10000 then
    kill TempController : 201
  end if
  %  other computations
end TempController
```

malfunction. A typical example of this would be an infinite loop in the handler.

Program 12.3 illustrates the use of these exceptions, using the temperature control process given at the beginning of this section which has had some detail added to its execution part. Note that, in this Program, exceptions are raised and handled synchronously within the same process, and asynchronously in the alarmProcess. Looking at the Program it can be seen that the process waits on a condition variable; a timeout is specified and an exception number is given. (If this timeout occurs then the numbered exception is raised.) A temperature is then read and logged. Tests on the temperature value could lead to other exceptions being raised. A low value will result in an appropriate message and deactivation until the next period. A high value will result in an even more appropriate, if somewhat futile, message, an exception being raised in an alarm process, and the temperature controller terminating. All available processor time can now be dedicated to the alarm process.

Ada's facilities

It was noted in Section 12.4.2 that Ada provides no direct support for deadlines. There are, therefore, no predefined exceptions that deal with the errors that are associated with missed deadlines. All that an Ada task can do is read the system clock and calculate whether a deadline has been met or not. If it has not, then a user-defined exception could be raised. Moreover, Ada fails to support asynchronous exceptions.

The use of abort for controlling mode changes can be criticized because of the overhead involved in removing a task (and all subtasks) and then reactivating it. There is clearly a need for one task to be able to affect the flow of control of another task. At present, one is forced to use either a rendezvous, thus requiring the affected task to periodically perform a conditional read (or write), or abort. Whether a better solution for Ada is to reintroduce inter-task exceptions is still an issue for debate.

12.5.2 Backward error recovery

As an alternative to using exceptions and forward error recovery, a timing error could invoke backward error recovery. All backward error recovery techniques involve acceptance tests. It is, therefore, possible to include a temporal requirement in these tests. The run-time system can asynchronously fail an acceptance test if the deadline has been overrun. This is illustrated using a timeout facility incorporated within **dialogs** and **colloquys** (Gregory and Knight, 1985) which were discussed in Section

10.3.2. The dialog sequence now becomes:

```
SELECT
    dialog_1
OR
    dialog_2
OR
    dialog_3
TIMEOUT value
    -- sequence of statements
ELSE
    -- sequence of statements
END SELECT;
```

As in Section 10.3.2, on execution, the process first attempts dialog_1, if this succeeds then control is passed to the statement following the SELECT statement. If the dialog fails then dialog_2 is attempted and so on. However, to enable the colloquy concept to handle missed deadlines it is possible to associate a timeout with the SELECT. The timing constraint specifies an interval, during which the process may execute as many dialog attempts as possible. Different processes involved in the dialogs may have different timeout values. If the timeout expires then the currently executing dialog fails, the process's state is restored to what it was on execution of the SELECT statement, and the statements after the TIMEOUT clause are executed. The other processes involved in the dialog also fail, but their actions are determined by the options set in their SELECT statements. They may try another dialog, timeout or fail altogether. As with the ELSE clause, the statements after the TIMEOUT can be considered to be a last attempt to achieve the goal of the process. If it fails then the surrounding colloquy fails.

It is now possible to program a simple deadline mechanism using a dialog sequence consisting of a single dialog attempt and a timeout. For example, consider an Ada-like real-time language which does not explicitly support the specification of deadlines. A task could recover from a deadline error when communicating with many tasks as follows:

```
task body deadline_example is
begin
  loop
    ...
    time := calculated_time_to_deadline;
    slack := calculate_time_for_degraded_algorithm;
    restore := state_restoration_time;
    timeout_value := time - (slack + restore);
    --
    SELECT
      dialog_1;
```

```
        TIMEOUT timeout_value
          -- sequence of statements to recover
          -- from missed deadline
        ELSE
          fail;
        END SELECT;
      end loop;
    end deadline_example;
```

The task first calculates the time delay until the next deadline. It then subtracts from this the time estimated to recover from a missed deadline and the time taken for state restoration. The difference between these values is called the **slack time**. If the dialog has not been completed in this time due to a timing error or a design error then the recovery sequence is initiated.

One means of coping with mode changes is to structure the program, such that the process which is to initiate the change is part of a top-level dialog. This dialog must involve all processes that are to be affected. When a mode change occurs, the initiating process invokes failures, thereby causing all the other processes to be interrupted. They can then restart and accept new instructions.

SUMMARY

The management of time presents a number of difficulties that set embedded systems apart from other computing applications. Current real-time languages are often inadequate in their provisions for this vital area.

The introduction of the notion of time into real-time programming languages has been described in terms of four requirements:

(1)   access to a clock

(2)   delaying

(3)   timeouts

(4)   deadline specification and scheduling

The sophistication of the mechanisms that are provided to measure the passage of time, varies greatly between languages. Occam 2 supports a TIMER facility which merely returns an integer of implementation-defined meaning. Ada goes somewhat further in providing an abstract data type for time and a collection of time-related operators. A different approach is taken in Modula-1 and Modula-2; here, a driver for a clock device must be programmed directly. An application-defined clock primitive must therefore be built.

If a process wishes to pause for a period of time, a delay primitive is needed in order to prevent the process having to busy wait. Such a primitive always guarantees to suspend the process for at least the designated time, but it cannot force the scheduler to run the process immediately that the delay has expired. Therefore, local drift cannot be avoided, although it is possible to limit the cumulative drift that could arise from repeated execution of delays.

For many real-time systems it is not sufficient for the software to be logically correct, the programs must also satisfy timing constraints. Unfortunately, existing practices in the engineering of large real-time systems are, in general, still rather *ad hoc*. To facilitate the specification of timing constraints and requirements it is useful to introduce the notion of a *temporal scope*. Possible attributes of temporal scopes include:

- deadline for completion of execution;
- minimum delay before start of execution;
- maximum delay before start of execution;
- maximum execution time;
- maximum elapse time;

Consideration was given in this chapter as to how temporal scopes can be specified within programming languages.

The degree of importance of timing requirements is a useful way of characterizing real-time systems. Constraints that *must* be met are termed **hard**; those that can be missed occasionally, or by a small amount, are called **soft**.

In order to control the behaviour of a pre-emptive scheduler the notion of *priority* is widely used. Within operating systems, priority gives an indication of the relative importance of each process (preference priority). By comparison, hard real-time systems use priority to guarantee that all deadlines are met (using, for example, the rate-monotonic algorithm for allocating priorities).

Where processes synchronize their executions, a static priority scheme can lead to *priority inversion*. This is where a high-priority process is blocked while waiting for a low-priority process to synchronize, but the low-priority process is not executing as there is a medium-priority process that is runnable. In effect, the high-priority process is being delayed by the medium one, which is an inversion of the designated priorities. One method of limiting the effect of inversion is to use *priority inheritance*; a form of inheritance, called the 'ceiling protocol', defines a maximum blocking time for a high-priority process and is deadlock free.

This chapter is concluded by considering the fault tolerance techniques that can be used to handle missed deadlines.

Further reading

Barringer H. (1985). A Survey of verification techniques for parallel programs. In *Lecture Notes in Computer Science*, **191**. Berlin: Springer-Verlag

Burns A. (1985). *Concurrent Programming in Ada*. Ada Companion Series. Cambridge: Cambridge University Press

Burns A. (1988). *Programming in occam 2*. Wokingham: Addison-Wesley

Galton A., ed. (1987). *Temporal Logics and their Application*. London: Academic Press

Garey M.R. and Johnson D.S. (1979). *Computers and Intractability, A Guide to the Theory of NP-Completeness*. New York: Freeman

Joseph M., ed. (1988). Formal techniques in real-time fault tolerant systems. In *Lecture Notes in Computer Science*, **331**. Berlin: Springer-Verlag

Turski W.M., (1988). Time considered irrelevant for real-time systems. *BIT*, **28**(3), 473–488

EXERCISES

12.1 Some applications need the ability to schedule a task at a particular time. Currently, Ada supports a relative time, but no mechanism is given for delaying until an absolute time. In theory, it should be possible to delay until an absolute time by using the Ada delay statement in conjunction with package CALENDAR, as was shown in Section 12.4.2. In practice, certain difficulties may be encountered. What are these and can they be circumvented?

12.2 Should Ada's timed entry call specify a timeout on the *completion* of the rendezvous, rather than the start of the rendezvous? Give an example of when such an approach might be useful.

12.3 In Section 12.4.1 it was indicated that all Ada tasks of the same type must have the same priority. In order for two identical tasks to have different priorities they must either be defined separately and the code copied, or be created from a generic with the priority as the parameter. Illustrate how the latter can be achieved. Are the two tasks of the same type?

12.4 Consider the following Ada task fragment:

```
task body DYNAMIC_PRIORITY is
begin
    -- execute some code at priority 1
    -- execute some code at priority 2
    -- execute some code at priority 3
end DYNAMIC_PRIORITY;
```

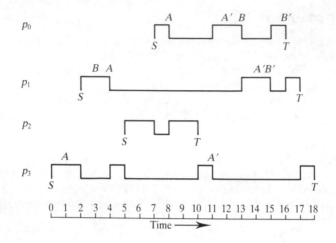

Figure 12.2   Illustration of the behaviour of four periodic processes.

How can this task be programmed in Ada? How efficient is your solution? (Hint: other tasks will be needed.)

12.5   Consider three processes P, Q and S. P has a period of 100 milliseconds in which it requires 30 milliseconds of processing. The corresponding values for Q and S are (5,1) and (25,5) respectively. Assume that P is the most important process in the system, followed by S and then Q.

(a)   Illustrate the behaviour of the scheduler if priority was based on importance.

(b)   What is the processor utilization of P, Q and S?

(c)   How should the processes be scheduled so that all deadlines are met?

12.6   Figure 12.2 illustrates the behaviour of four periodic processes p_0, p_1, p_2 and p_3. These processes have priorities determined by the rate-monotonic scheme, with the result that priority(p_0) > priority(p_1) > priority(p_2) > priority(p_3).

Each process's period starts at time S and terminates at T. The four processes share two resources that are protected by binary semaphores A and B. In Figure 12.2 the tag A (and B) implies 'do a wait operation on the semaphore'; the tag A' (and B') implies 'do a signal operation on the semaphore'. Table 12.6 summarizes the process's requirements.

Figure 12.2 shows the execution histories of the four processes using static priorities. For example, p_1 starts at time 2, executes a

Table 12.6 Summary of the process's requirements.

Process	Priority	Start time	Required processor time	Semaphores used
p_0	10	7	4	A, B
p_1	8	2	5	A, B
p_2	6	5	4	–
p_3	4	0	5	A

successful wait operation on B at time 3 but unsuccessfully waits on A at time 4 (p_3 has already locked A). At time 13 it executes again (that is, it now has lock on A), it releases A at time 14 and B at time 15. It is now pre-empted by p_0, but executes again at time 16. Finally, it terminates at time 17. Redraw this diagram to illustrate the behaviour of these processes if priority inheritance is employed.

Chapter 13
Distributed Systems

Recent advances in hardware and communications technology have made distributed computer systems a viable alternative to uniprocessor and centralized systems in many embedded application areas. The potential advantages of distribution include:

- improved performance through the exploitation of parallelism;
- increased availability and reliability through the exploitation of redundancy;
- dispersion of computing power to the locations where it is used;
- the facility for incremental growth through the addition or enhancement of processors and communications links.

This chapter discusses some of the problems that are introduced when real-time systems are implemented on more than one processor.

13.1 Distributed system definition

For the purposes of this chapter a **distributed computer system** is defined to be:

> a system of multiple autonomous processing elements, cooperating in a common purpose or to achieve a common goal.

This definition is wide enough to satisfy most intuitive notions, without descending to details of physical dispersion, means of communication, and so on. The definition excludes pipeline and array processors, whose elements are not autonomous; it also excludes those computer networks (for example, ARPAnet) whose nodes work to no common

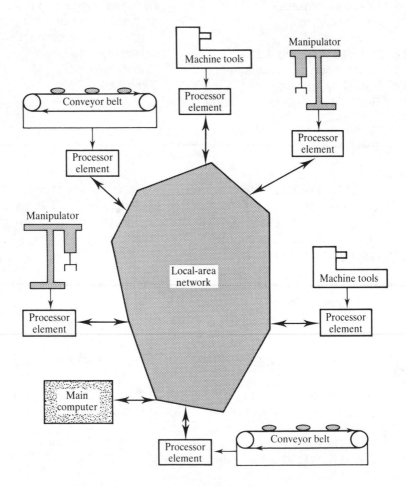

Figure 13.1   A distributed embedded computer system.

purpose. The majority of applications that might sensibly be embedded on multiprocessor architectures – for example, command and control, banking (and other transaction-oriented commercial applications), and data acquisition – fall within the definition. A distributed manufacturing-based system is shown in Figure 13.1.

It is useful to classify distributed systems as either *tightly coupled*, meaning that the processing elements, or nodes, have access to a common memory, and *loosely coupled*, meaning that they do not. The significance of this classification is that synchronization and communication in a tightly-coupled system can be effected through techniques based on the use of common memory, whereas, in a loosely-coupled system some form of message passing is required. It is possible for a loosely-coupled system to contain nodes which are themselves tightly-coupled systems. This chapter will use the term *distributed system* to refer to loosely-coupled architectures. Also, in general, full connectivity will be assumed between processors – issues associated with the routing of messages and so on will not be considered. For a full discussion on these topics see Tanenbaum (1988).

A separate classification can be based on the variety of processors in the system. A **homogeneous** system is one in which all processors are of the same type; a **heterogeneous** system contains processors of different types. Heterogeneous systems pose problems of differing representations of program and data; these problems, while significant, are not considered here. A detailed treatment of data transmission in heterogeneous systems is given by Herlihy and Liskov (1982). This chapter assumes that all processors are homogeneous.

13.2 Overview of issues

So far in this book, the phrase 'concurrent programming' has been used to discuss communication, synchronization and reliability without getting too involved with how processes are implemented. However, some of the issues which arise when distributed applications are considered raise fundamental questions that go beyond mere implementation details. The purpose of this chapter is to consider these issues and their implications for real-time applications. They are:

- *Partitioning and configuration*: At some point during design and implementation, the application must be partitioned and configured for execution on the target system. The point at which partitioning occurs can have bearing on the portability, readability and reliability of the application and the functionality of the real-time programming language.

- *Reliability*: The availability of multiple processors enables the application to become tolerant of processor failure – the application should be able to exploit this redundancy. Although the availability of multiple processors enables the application to become tolerant of processor failure, it also introduces the possibility of more faults occurring in the system which would not occur in a centralized single-processor system. These faults are associated with *partial* system failure and the application program must either be shielded from them, or be able to tolerate them.

- *Distributed control algorithms*: The presence of both true parallelism and physically-distributed processors in an application, plus the possibility that processors and communication links may fail, means that many new algorithms are required for resource control. For example, it may be necessary to access files and data which are stored on other machines; furthermore, machine or network failure must not compromise the availability or consistency of those files or data. Also, as there is no common time reference in a distributed system, each node having its own local notion of time, it is very difficult to obtain a consistent view of the overall system. This can cause problems when trying to provide mutual exclusion in a network environment.

- *Deadline scheduling*: In Chapter 12, the problems of scheduling processes to meet deadlines in a single-processor system was discussed. When the processes are distributed the optimal single-processor algorithms are no longer optimal. New algorithms are needed.

The remainder of this chapter discusses each of these issues in turn.

13.3 Partitioning and configuration

There are many ways in which an application can be partitioned for execution on a distributed system. These may be broadly classified into two basic approaches: *a single program approach* and *a multiprogram approach* (Burns *et al.*, 1987). With the former, the application is written as a single program and then partitioned into fragments which communicate using normal intra-program communication mechanisms. In contrast, in the latter, the application is written as a collection of separate programs, one or more for each machine in the target system. These programs communicate and synchronize their activities using an underlying distributed operating system. The view taken in this book is that distributed applications should, wherever possible, be written as single programs. This enables all interfaces to be checked by the compiler, and it does not restrict process communication to predefined types. For a detailed review of writing a distributed program as a collection of separate Ada programs, the reader is referred to Burns *et al.* (1987); for a case study description of the type of operating system needed see Keeffe *et al.* (1985).

Within the single program approach two general strategies can be identified. These are referred to as (Burns *et al.*, 1987) *post-partitioning* and *pre-partitioning*.

13.3.1 Post-partitioning

As the name implies, this strategy is based on partitioning the program after it has been written. The program is designed without regard to a target architecture: the programmers produce an appropriate solution to the problem at hand and have the full language at their disposal. It is left to other software tools, provided by the programming support environment, to do the following (Burns *et al.*, 1987):

- describe the target configuration (which may be chosen by the designers or forced upon them),
- partition the program into components for distribution,
- allocate (configure) the components to individual nodes.

The argument behind this strategy is threefold. Firstly, if a language contains no facilities for partitioning and configuration management, it is considered inappropriate for a program to contain partitioning or configuration information. Secondly, the strategy promotes portable software – the same program can be mapped onto different target configurations. Thirdly, no restrictions are placed on the way that the language is used. The technology associated with local-area networks is advancing rapidly; it is, therefore, important not to rule out certain forms of communication, say via shared variables, because the cost is currently prohibitive.

The Honeywell Distributed Ada Project (Cornhill, 1983; Jha *et al.*, 1989a) adopts this strategy for using Ada in a distributed environment. An Ada Program Partitioning Language (APPL) (Jha *et al.*, 1989b) is used to express the partitioning and configuration of Ada code onto different processors of the target system. The APPL also allows the partitioner to replicate program fragments in order to enhance reliability and availability. Furthermore, protocols can be specified in cases where run-time synchronization is needed in order to maintain a consistent state for the replicated fragment. To produce the object code for a distributed application, the programmer submits an Ada program and an associated APPL program to the distributed Ada compiler. The compiler checks that the Ada program and the APPL program are legal and mutually consistent, and then produces an input to a linker, along with a distributed run-time support package. The linker then produces an executable object module for each processor in the distributed target.

Some implications of using this technique are:

- it requires a non-trivial partitioning language;
- the run-time cost of replication and partitioning are hidden from the application programmer;
- it cannot utilize compilers from other sources;
- in its full generality, it requires an implementation of remote variable update, remote exception handling, remote task creation, distributed termination, remote procedure call, and remote inter-process communication.

A drawback of this technique is that it is difficult for the programmer to specify what recovery procedures or degraded services are to be used in the event of a processor failure.

Post-partitioning requires the support of appropriate software tools and run-time facilities. By contrast, pre-partioning involves language constructs and design issues. For this reason more attention is given, in this book, to the pre-partitioning approach.

13.3.2   Pre-partitioning

The pre-partitioning strategy is to select a particular module-like construct as the sole unit of partitioning, to be used throughout the design and programming process. The programmer is obliged to accept any constraints that the choice of construct entails. The notion underlying this strategy is that of a **virtual node**, which is an abstraction of a physical node in the distributed system. The characteristics of virtual nodes are as follows:

- They are the units of modularity in a distributed system.
- They are also the units of reuse – wherever possible, programs should be composed of off-the-shelf virtual nodes.
- They provide well-defined interfaces to other virtual nodes in the system.
- They encapsulate local resources. All access to these resources from remote virtual nodes is via the virtual node interface.
- They can consist of one or more processes. These processes may communicate with each other using shared memory. They can also communicate with processes in other virtual nodes via the interfaces provided. This communication is normally via some form of message-passing protocol.

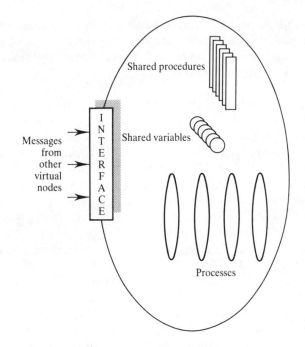

Figure 13.2   The structure of a virtual node.

- More than one virtual node can be mapped onto a single physical node. However, it is worth emphasizing that a virtual node can not be distributed between machines. Decomposing programs into virtual nodes, therefore, defines the granularity of potential distribution of the application, *not* the actual configuration.

- They are the units used for configuration and reconfiguration.

In many ways virtual nodes are analogous to objects in an object-oriented design approach (Atkinson *et al.*, 1988) A virtual node is shown, diagrammatically, in Figure 13.2.

For a language-based construct to be effective as a virtual node it must be supported by the following:

- *Separate compilation*: it should be possible to compile, separately, virtual nodes and place them in libraries.

- *Virtual node types*: it should be possible to create virtual nodes dynamically.

- *Exception handling facilities*: where communication errors or processor failures occur, it should be possible to map these to exceptions so that the application can provide recovery procedures.

- *Dynamic reconfiguration*: in order to allow an application to program recovery procedures and to allow incremental changes to the application, it should be possible to reconfigure dynamically without reinitializing the entire system.

The notion of virtual node is found in most languages which have been designed with the specific intent of supporting distributed programming (for example, the 'group module' in CONIC (Sloman and Kramer, 1987), the 'resource' in SR (Andrews and Olsson, 1986), the 'guardian' of Argus (Liskov and Scheifler, 1983), and the 'processor module' of StarMod (Cook, 1979)). In some languages (for example, Argus) virtual nodes are used to abstract away from the failure properties of physical nodes, and thus, serve not only as a basis for distribution, but also as building blocks for fault-tolerant software (see Section 13.8.6).

Occam 2, although designed for use in a distributed environment, is fairly low-level; it is, therefore, difficult to identify a virtual node precisely. In one sense, all processes are potential virtual nodes as they can only communicate using message passing. In the case of Ada, there is much controversy as to how the language should be used. Modula-2 was designed for a single-processor system; it can be used for programming distributed systems but only by modifying some of the language concepts. The use of these languages will be considered in detail in Sections 13.4–13.6.

The term *virtual node* has been used to cover a variety of distributed programming language constructs. Although these have many detailed differences, they are all based on either processes or modules containing processes. Similarly, although the facilities for synchronization and communication between processes in virtual nodes differ, they are all based on the message-passing primitives identified in Chapter 9. To illustrate the type of facilities available, the languages SR and CONIC are briefly considered. A discussion of Argus is postponed until Section 13.8.6.

Synchronizing resources

Synchronizing Resources SR (Andrews, 1981, 1982; Andrews and Olsson, 1986) is a distributed programming language designed for general-purpose systems implementation. Although it lacks some of the timing facilities of a real-time programming language, it does have many relevant and interesting features.

A virtual node in SR is called a **resource** which is similar in functionality to a module; resources cannot be nested but can be dynamically created. A resource has a specification part, which defines the operations that are provided by the resource, and an implementation part which implements the functionality of the resource. The implementation part of the resource is known as its **body** and, like modules and packages, it has an initialization section as well as declarations, processes, procedures and so on. Unlike a package or a module it also has a finalization section, which is executed just before the resource goes out of scope. This enables the resource to 'clean up' after itself; release other resources, free-up heap space and so on. SR contains statements to create and destroy instances of a resource on particular machines.

Although shared-variable access is allowed between processes in the same resource, operations between resources are parameterized communication channels. SR supports a variety of synchronization models. The client of a resource may request an operation in two ways: via a **call** invocation statement or a **send** invocation statement. A call invocation has the *remote invocation* semantics described in Chapter 9; the issuing process is not resumed until the resource has received the request, serviced it and returned a response. A send invocation is a cross between the asynchronous and the synchronous send, in that the client process is blocked until the message is received by the machine on which the resource resides. The client cannot assume that the message has been received by the resource, only that it has been buffered. With both the call and send invocation statements, client delay can only be avoided by introducing extra buffering processes.

The processes which implement the operations on a resource can do so in two ways. The first is rather like the Ada approach, the **in** statement being similar to the Ada select statement. However, unlike Ada's task entries, processes do not declare the operations as they have already been declared by the resource. Furthermore, guards in the **in** statement may access parameters to operations and, therefore, calls need not necessarily be accepted in a First-In, First-Out (FIFO) order.

The second way an operation can be serviced is via a procedure. When an operation is defined in this way, every time the operation is called, a process is created (transparently) whose body executes the defined procedure. In this respect the operation is treated as a remote procedure call (see Section 9.8).

All possible combinations of client server interactions are possible, although the server can specify restrictions.

CONIC

The CONIC Toolkit provides a language-based approach to the design and production of large, distributed soft real-time embedded systems (Kramer *et al.*, 1987). Fundamental to this approach is the separation of the language for programming the functional requirements of the system (called the CONIC Programming Language (Kramer *et al.*, 1985)) from the language for configuring programs from predefined modules (called the CONIC Configuration Language (Dulay *et al.*, 1985)).

The CONIC Programming Language is based on Pascal, with extensions for modularity and message passing. Both of these are provided by the introduction of a **task module** which replaces the Pascal program unit. A task-module definition specifies a type (possibly with parameters) from which module instances can be created using the configuration language. In general, a program will consist of one or more instances of one or more task modules. Tasks communicate (through ports) using indirect strongly-typed message passing. Each task module declares *entry* and *exit* ports. Messages are received from entry ports and sent to exit ports. CONIC supports both asynchronous and remote invocation message passing depending on the specification of the port. The connection between the entry ports of one module and the exit ports of other modules is performed during system configuration.

In CONIC, the virtual node is called a **logical node** and is defined as a **group module** using the configuration language. This module consists of a set of tasks which execute concurrently within a shared address space. However, the communication between tasks in a group module is the same as the communication between tasks in separate group modules, except that pointers can be passed in the former but not the latter. The interface to a group module is specified in exactly the same manner as the interface to a task module, that is, as entry and exit ports. Configuration of a complex program can, therefore, be done in layers. Firstly, a group module type is defined, along with its entry and exit ports. Secondly, inside the module, instances of task modules are created and the entry and exit ports are linked to each other and to the entry and exit ports of the group. Other group modules can then be defined which instantiate predefined group modules with the appropriate port connections, and so on.

13.4   Virtual nodes and Ada

The *Ada Language Reference Manual* does not dictate how the language is to be used in a distributed environment, and there have been many suggestions that say that Ada does not provide the appropriate abstractions (Wellings, 1987, 1988). Certainly, it is true that when Ada was designed, there was very little experience of language features which support distributed applications. Experiences with languages like CONIC, StarMod, SR, and Argus have indicated that virtual nodes are a useful distribution abstraction, and, consequently, this section will consider how they can be represented in Ada. It should be stressed that this is *not* the only possible approach to using Ada in a distributed environment and that for a full discussion the reader should refer to Burns *et al.* (1987) or Tedd *et al.* (1984). Much of the material in this section is taken from Hutcheon and Wellings (1988) and reports on the experiences of two separate developments: the York Distributed Ada (YDA) project (carried out under the auspices of the ASPECT project (Hutcheon *et al.*, 1989) and the

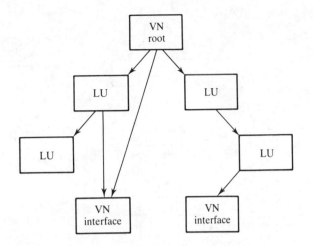

Figure 13.3   One possible structure of a virtual node.

DIADEM project (Atkinson *et al.*, 1988), both of these have investigated the virtual node approach and Ada.

In applying the virtual node idea to Ada, it is necessary to associate some language construct(s) with a virtual node. The most obvious candidates are a task, a package, a procedure or a collection of library units. It is the last that appears to offer the most potential (a task cannot be compiled separately as a library unit, a package is static and a procedure does not providing adequate encapsulation facilities). Furthermore, the library module can be supported easily by tools in the project support environment *without* modification to the compiler.

In order to identify which library units are associated with which virtual nodes, a **root** library unit is specified. The **with** clauses of the root specify all the library units which are components of the virtual note. Note that this includes all the library units which are **with**ed by the library units which are **with**ed by the root library unit, and so on. One or more of these Library Units (LU) provide an interface to the virtual node; the root library unit may also act as an interface library unit. Figure 13.3 shows, diagrammatically, one possible structure of a Virtual Node (VN). The arrows represent the dependencies between library units.

It is possible that two virtual node roots have **with**ed the same library unit; that is, the virtual nodes share a library unit. This presents a problem because when virtual nodes are configured to physical nodes these shared library units have no obvious allocation. Figure 13.4 shows an example where two virtual nodes have two shared library units indicated by 'LU*'. The circles are used to group together all the library units, associated with a virtual node, that can be allocated to a physical node.

In this case, in order that the virtual nodes can be configured to physical nodes, the shared library units must either be the interfaces to

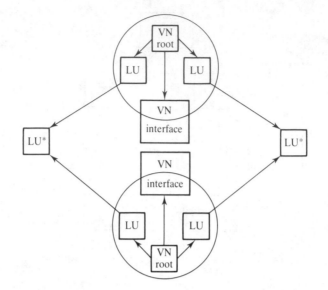

Figure 13.4   Two virtual nodes with shared library units.

other virtual nodes, or must be templates, which means they can be replicated on each virtual node without violating their semantics. Template library units are defined to be without any global state. This means that they are either generics; or packages with only type declarations (including task types) and subprograms which do not access any global memory; or subprograms by themselves.

13.4.1   Virtual nodes in YDA and DIADEM

Although both YDA and DIADEM have adopted the virtual node approach they differ, quite significantly, in detail. The DIADEM project chose a procedure as the root library unit, as it was believed that each virtual node should have a thread of control analogous to a main program in Ada. The interface to a DIADEM virtual node is via one or more packages which contain task specifications. All communication with the virtual node is constrained to be by remote entry call.

In the YDA project, the same library unit is used as both the root of the virtual node and its interface. This is a package which contains procedures and their associated type declarations, compile-time constants, and any embedded packages. The thread of control of the virtual node is the elaboration of the interface package. It is expected that the main processing of the virtual node will be performed by tasks declared locally. Communication between virtual nodes is by remote procedure call.

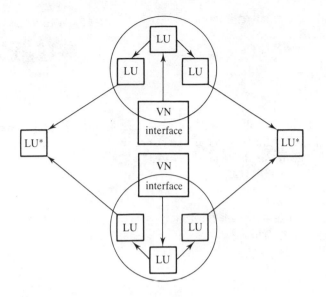

Figure 13.5   Two virtual nodes in YDA with shared library units.

Because YDA chose to have the root and the interface to a virtual node as the same library unit, the overall structure differs from that shown in Figures 13.3 and 13.4, and is given in Figure 13.5.

13.4.2 Configuration

Once a group of library units have been written and grouped together as virtual nodes, it must be possible to configure them for execution on the available processors. The following sections consider a system of five virtual nodes: $V1$, $V2$, $V3$, $V4$ and $V5$.

Configuration for a single processor system

The YDA Ada program takes the form shown overpage (V1_INTERFACE is the root and interface package for $V1$ and so on). When executed, the virtual nodes are elaborated first; note that the *Ada Language Reference Manual* (*ALRM*) allows these to be elaborated in parallel as long as any required partial order is satisfied. Note also that the *ALRM* does not define the relationship between the termination of the main program and the termination of tasks in library units. However, it is expected that revisions to the language will require termination of the main program only when all library tasks can terminate. The YDA approach enforces that the main program will not terminate until *all* the library tasks can terminate.

```
with V1_INTERFACE, V2_INTERFACE, V3_INTERFACE, V4_INTERFACE,
    V5_INTERFACE;
procedure MAIN is
begin
  null;
end;
```

In DIADEM, all virtual nodes have a ROOT procedure which must be called. In order for this to happen concurrently, tasks must be created in the main program, as illustrated below.

```
with V1_ROOT, V2_ROOT, V3_ROOT, V4_ROOT, V5_ROOT;
procedure MAIN is
  task THREAD1; task THREAD2;    -- etc
  task body THREAD1 is
  begin
    V1_ROOT;
  end;
  task body THREAD2 is
  begin
    V2_ROOT;
  end;
  ...
begin
  null;
end;
```

This approach relies on the ROOT procedure not terminating until all virtual nodes are willing to terminate. Consequently, the DIADEM project requires that termination should be programmed as part of the application.

Configuration on five processors

In YDA, the program, when configured for five processors, is syntactically the same as it is for one; that is:

```
with V1_INTERFACE, V2_INTERFACE, V3_INTERFACE, V4_INTERFACE,
    V5_INTERFACE;
procedure MAIN is
begin
  null;
end;
```

This is possible because the virtual nodes can be elaborated in parallel. In practice, five different load modules must be created; however, it should be stressed that the YDA project still views the program as a

Figure 13.6   Intermediate mechanisms for calling client procedures.

single Ada program, although, from the viewpoint of the host development tools (compiler, linkers and so on), it is five Ada programs.

In DIADEM, distribution of five virtual nodes to five processors is achieved by viewing each virtual node as a separate program. The main program of each of the virtual node programs is the root procedure.

In both approaches it is necessary to interface to a package which handles the remote communication. However, once again, the two projects achieve this quite differently, yet both are transparent to the application programmer. To illustrate these differences consider a client procedure library unit which wishes to call the interface to a remote virtual node. In YDA, the procedure would be written as follows:

```
with VN_INTERFACE;
procedure CALL is
begin
    .
    VN_INTERFACE.SERVICE(PARAMETERS);
    .
end;
```

where SERVICE is the name of an interface procedure. As the virtual node will reside on a different machine, the package VN_INTERFACE cannot be called directly. A call from a client procedure in one virtual node to a server procedure in a virtual node located on a different physical processor, is carried out by means of the intermediate mechanisms shown in Figure 13.6.

The Remote Procedure Call (RPC) mechanism is provided by the networked processors and run-time system, while the client and server stubs consist of extra Ada code which is inserted to interface between the original application program and RPC mechanism. These are produced as transformations of the virtual node root (interface) package specification. The client stub replaces the virtual node interface body of a remote virtual node on the client's physical node. When it is called by the client, it packs the call parameters into a record, passes this to the RPC mechanism to carry out the call, then blocks, while waiting for the call to return. When the call returns, the client stub unpacks returned values and passes them to the client (unless an unhandled exception occurred during the call, in which case it reraises the exception in the client).

The server stub, placed on the processor holding the virtual node, is a template for the server task, used as the thread of control to execute the

incoming call. It unpacks the call parameters and uses them to make a call
to the original server subprogram, then packs the results and passes them
to the RPC mechanism to return to the caller. If an unhandled exception
occurs during the call execution, this is caught by the server stub and
passed back to the client stub for propagation.

To summarize, YDA exploits the possibility of having more than
one package body for the same package specification. The client procedure
is simply linked with a client stub body which carries out the communication. There is no change to the source code of the client or the server.

In DIADEM, the client procedure has a similar structure to that of
the YDA procedure:

```
with VN_INTERFACE;
procedure CALL is
begin
    .
    VN_INTERFACE.SERVER.SERVICE(PARAMETERS);
    .
end;
```

where SERVER.SERVICE is a simple entry call (although this could be a
timed or conditional entry call) to the interface task. However, the transformation of this procedure into a separate Ada program, which can be
loaded on the client machine, is very different from YDA's method. The
source of the program is changed by the DIADEM transformation tools to
delete the VN_INTERFACE named in the **with** clause. A procedure stub is
added whose body is compiled separately. This body **with**s a package which
handles the remote communication. The original entry call is changed so
that it calls this new procedure which then performs the remote call. The
transformed client procedure is shown below:

```
procedure CALL is
    procedure REMOTE_ENTRY_SERVICE
        (ORIGINAL_PARAMETER_DECLARATIONS;
        CALL_SUPPORT_PARAMETER_DECLARATIONS) is separate;
begin
    .
    REMOTE_ENTRY_SERVICE(ORIGINAL_PARAMETERS;
        CALL_SUPPORT_PARAMETERS);
    .
end;
```

Although this is done transparently to the programmer, the transformation technique does have implications for the design of virtual nodes.
In particular, because the original interface package specification has been
removed from the client program, any type declarations are also removed.

Consequently, interface packages, in DIADEM, must only contain inter-face tasks specifications; all associated type declarations must be declared in template packages so that they can be **with**ed by both the client and the server programs.

The actual technique of implementing the remote rendezvous is similar to the implementation of the remote procedure call described in this section.

13.4.3   Virtual node types

One of the disadvantages of not having direct language support for virtual nodes is that the notion of a virtual node type becomes difficult to express. YDA has the concept of a generic virtual node; here the interface (root) package must itself be a generic and all other library units associated with the virtual node must be templates (which include generics) or interfaces to other virtual nodes. This allows compile-time creation of instances of the generic virtual node.

DIADEM does allow a limited form of virtual node types, these being virtual nodes consisting only of template units. This prevents virtual node types from having interface packages. Instead, a task type and an associated access type are declared in a template package. This is repli-cated in all virtual nodes which wish to make calls to instances of the virtual node type. When an instance of the virtual node type is created, it creates an instance of the task type (using the allocator) then passes the task access pointer to interested virtual nodes. These access values allow remote entry calls to the task, and are the only access type that DIADEM allows to be passed between virtual nodes.

Instances of virtual nodes cannot be created by other virtual nodes in a system, only by additional code in the main program. The task which calls the root procedure is replaced by a task type in the case of a virtual node type, and creation of a new task from the type creates a new virtual node.

13.4.4   Identifying virtual nodes and their interfaces

In order to support both the YDA and the DIADEM approaches it is necessary to have tools which classify library units according to their virtual node characteristics (root, interface, template). When this has been done it is also necessary to have some mechanism for specifying which library units make up which virtual nodes; how the virtual nodes are to be configured for execution and whether the specified configuration is valid.

In YDA, as virtual nodes have a single interface package which is also the root library unit, all that is required to specify a virtual node is the name of the root library unit. A graphical configuration tool is used to allocate virtual nodes to physical nodes and to check the configuration.

The presence of multiple interfaces makes specifying a virtual node in DIADEM more complex. In particular, when following the **with** clauses of a virtual node root it is necessary to know which virtual node a **with**ed interface package corresponds. An Ada-like specification language is used to describe a virtual node; this includes: the library units defining the parameter types of the interface, the library units which form its callable interface, the external library units which form its calling interface and the virtual node root procedure.

13.4.5   Ada semantic issues

Section 13.4.4 compared the basic approaches of the YDA and the DIADEM projects. Here, language semantic issues are considered to see how closely the two approaches have stayed to the Ada language as described in the *ALRM*.

- *Program elaboration*: One of the problems of executing Ada in a distributed environment is that of the program's elaboration. The *ALRM* states in Section 11.5 that elaboration of a program must conform to a partial ordering in which no unit is elaborated until all units which it names in **with** clauses have been elaborated. This ordering is to try to ensure that no object is used before it has been elaborated.

  One approach would be to elaborate the virtual nodes sequentially in the same order that they would be elaborated in a single processor system. This would ensure that the program has a legal run-time elaboration and enable any elaboration errors to be detected. Unfortunately, such an approach involves a complex mechanism and run-time overhead. Furthermore, it would be a waste of the available processing power. Consequently, both YDA and DIADEM elaborate virtual nodes in parallel. In DIADEM, because a transformed program is viewed as several separate Ada programs, each node elaborates as soon as it is started. If remote calls arrive at a server before the server has been elaborated then an exception is returned to the client. The client must, therefore, be aware that if it tries later the call may succeed. If the client still receives an exception after several calls then it may assume that the elaboration of the distributed programs has failed, and it can initiate some recovery action.

  In YDA, if the system receives an RPC request for a server which has not yet been elaborated, then the call is blocked until the server has finished its elaboration. If the distributed program does have an elaboration order then the program will elaborate without the application software's help. Unfortunately, if the program does not have an elaboration order it will deadlock instead of raising the appropriate exception. For a full discussion on possible elaboration schemes see Hutcheon and Wellings (1989a).

- *Program termination*: Task termination in Ada can be considered in two parts: one is the termination of a task in relation to the states of its children and sibling tasks in the same library unit; the other is the termination of library tasks (those that are directly declared in library packages). As the unit of distribution is based on library packages, the first task termination mechanism is local to each processor – no exchange of messages through a distributed task hierarchy is required. The conditions for the termination of library tasks, and so the entire program, are currently not defined by the *ALRM*. Consequently, DIADEM takes the approach that distributed termination must be performed by the application. As a result, if the programmer gets the wrong termination order for the virtual nodes then a client may call a server node which has terminated. It is not defined what happens in such a situation.

  A distributed YDA program terminates when all tasks have terminated. The implementation depends on tasks which wish to terminate 'pretending' to do so and reactivating if they are called at a later time. The termination of distributed Ada programs is considered in more detail in Chapter 15.

- *Remote task communication*: Implementing remote rendezvous is difficult, as the queue manipulations required for supporting conditional entry calls is complex, and it is difficult to provide a global synchronized clock to support timed calls (Burns *et al.*, 1987; Volz and Mudge, 1987). Because of these problems, the DIADEM project performs the timing of all timed entry calls at the server site. Consequently, it is not possible to take into account any communication delays on the network. They also outlaw problematic issues such as the remote use of the CALLABLE and TERMINATED attributes, and the abortion of remote tasks.

  As the YDA project does not allow tasks to appear in virtual node interfaces the problems of remote timed entry calls, the 'callable' and 'terminated' attributes and task abortion do not occur.

  However, it is clear that any realistic implementation of distributed Ada should provide *both* remote rendezvous and remote procedure calls.

- *Package calendar*: Neither YDA or DIADEM support package CALENDAR. The problem is that it is not a template package and, therefore, cannot be replicated at each site. It does provide a valid YDA virtual node interface and so it could be allocated to a single site but, obviously, the time returned would not be accurate. In DIADEM, CALENDAR would need to be accessed via an interface task.

- *Remote exception propagation*: Both DIADEM and YDA allow exceptions to pass between virtual nodes. In DIADEM, exceptions which are associated with remote requests are declared in template packages, along with the remote data communication types. In YDA, the exceptions are declared in the virtual node interface package.

A problem with both YDA and DIADEM occurs when an exception which has not been declared as part of a virtual node interface is propagated across the interface. In order for exceptions to be passed across the network they must be trapped by the communication layer handling the remote calls, transformed into some global name for transmission, and reraised at the other end. However, the communication layer can only name exceptions which are predefined or defined globally as part of the interface. Consequently, it must trap these unnamed exceptions with 'when others'. Once trapped, their names have disappeared and therefore cannot be passed across the network. Therefore, the approach in both YDA and DIADEM is to pass an exception 'remote_others' across. This exception can only be trapped by the client using 'when others'. On a single-processor system such an exception can also only be handled by a 'when others' clause. Although, in the majority of cases, this is consistent with Ada semantics on a single-processor system, it is possible for an exception to pass out of scope and then back in again as it is propagated. Neither YDA nor DIADEM support this: the name has been lost so it cannot be passed back into scope.

In order for exceptions to be handled in a distributed environment, with the same semantics as in a single-processor environment, it is necessary for the compiler to generate unique identifiers for all exceptions. Furthermore, it must be possible to determine the identity of the currently-handled exception when executing in a 'when others' clause.

13.4.6   Concluding remarks

The YDA and DIADEM projects are of interest to the Ada community because they show that, with a small amount of effort, distributed systems can be built using off the shelf compilers. Both approaches are, in general, compiler-independent but must interface to an Ada run-time support system.

Although both projects try to remain as close as possible to the Ada language definition, both are unable to reproduce, exactly, the required semantics. However, the semantic differences are minor and may be classi-fied into two types: those which are the result of a poor language definition and those which are the result of attempting to be compiler-independent. The former includes: program termination, remote timed entry calls, and package calendar. As for compiler independence, even if a future revision of Ada does clarify these points it is still difficult to see how exceptions can propagate in and out of scope across the network without compiler support for unique exception identifiers.

Whether Ada should, in the long term, support a distribution abstraction, remains an open issue. It is clear that language support is required to get the full benefit of the virtual node approach and this would involve major changes to Ada's definition. Furthermore, the language would be required to define its semantics in the presence of processor and communication failure (see Section 13.7.2). The present lack of distribu-tion support and failure semantics means that it is difficult to provide useful virtual node types and reconfiguration.

13.5   Virtual nodes and Modula-2

Modula-2 was designed primarily for implementation on single-processor computer systems. Its coroutine model of concurrent execution is very flexible and allows many different styles of process and process interaction to be implemented. Unfortunately, the semantics of coroutines are such that only one coroutine can be executing at any one time. It is possible to take a single Modula-2 program and legally execute it on a multiprocessor system, however, *only one processor at a time would be active*. This clearly would give few, if any, advantages over execution on a single processor and is therefore not worthy of further consideration. There are two more useful approaches that can be adopted. The first is to view the distributed applica-tion as more than one Modula-2 program, and the second is to consider the application as a single program and to accept that some changes to the language's definition are inevitable. This section will concentrate on the latter approach, in keeping with the rest of this chapter.

Like Ada, Modula-2 programs can be constructed from library modules. Therefore, it is possible to adopt a similar approach to that used for distributing Ada and to consider a virtual node as a collection of library units (Audsley, 1988). Each node would have a root module from which its composite modules can be identified. This is very similar to the YDA approach for Ada virtual nodes described in Section 13.4. All internode communication is via remote procedure calls, and library modules can be replicated if their semantics are not altered by doing so. Tools can be produced which check for valid distribution configurations and which generate the stub modules and dummy main program modules. Unfor-tunately, this approach raises several problems.

The first problem concerns the SYSTEM module, which defines the coroutine interface. If more than one coroutine is to be active then this module must be replicated on each physical node in the distributed systems. This would clearly alter the semantics of the module and therefore is strictly illegal. Also, any module which implements a higher form of process, such as the PROCESS module described in Chapter 8, must be replicated on each node; again, it is doubtful that this could be done legally. These two modules must, therefore, be treated specially. If this is done and only the higher-level process module is used by the application, then the program can be executed on a single processor or in a distributed environment without modification.

A second problem is to ensure that the procedures made visible in a virtual node interface are actually procedures and not processes. As a process in Modula-2 is declared as a parameterless procedure it is impossible to distinguish between the two. This could cause some very peculiar behaviour, not least the fact that a remote procedure call to a remote process would never return! All the support tools can do in this case is to issue a warning message every time a parameterless procedure is declared in a virtual node interface.

Other problems which involve the elaboration and termination of virtual nodes are similar to those described in Section 13.4 for Ada.

The use of Modula-2 for programming distributed systems will not be considered further in this book.

13.6   Virtual nodes and occam 2

Unlike Ada and Modula-2, occam 2 has been specifically designed so that programs can be executed in a distributed environment, that of a multitransputer network. In general, occam 2's processes do not share memory, so all that is required to support virtual nodes is a mechanism by which several processes may be associated with one node. This is achieved by the PLACED PAR construct. A program constructed as a top-level PAR, such as:

```
PAR
  p1
  p2
  p3
  p4
  p5
```

can be partitioned and configured for distribution, for example, as follows:

```
PLACED PAR
  PROCESSOR 1
    p1
```

```
PROCESSOR 2
  PAR
    p2
    p3
PROCESSOR 3
  PAR
    p4
    p5
```

It is important to notice that the transformation of the program from one that has a simple PAR, to one that uses a PLACED PAR, will not invalidate the program. However, occam 2 does allow variables to be read by more than one process on the same processor. Therefore, a transformation may not be possible if the programmer has used this facility.

For the transputers, it is also necessary to associate each external channel with an appropriate transputer link. This is achieved by using the PLACE AT construct. For example, consider the above example using the integer channels shown in Figure 13.7. The program for execution on a single transputer is:

```
CHAN OF INT c1, c2, c3, c4, c5:
PAR
  p1
  p2
  p3
  p4
  p5
```

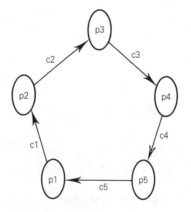

Figure 13.7 Five occam 2 processes connected by five channels.

Program 13.1

```
CHAN OF INT c1, c3, c5:
PLACED PAR
  PROCESSOR 1
    PLACE c1 at 0:
    PLACE c5 at 1:
    p1
  PROCESSOR 2
    PLACE c1 at 2:
    PLACE c3 at 1:
    CHAN OF INT c2:
    PAR
      p2
      p3
  PROCESSOR 3
    PLACE c3 at 0:
    PLACE c5 at 2:
    CHAN OF INT c4:
    PAR
      p4
      p5
```

Program 13.1 shows the occam 2 code for the program if it is configured to three transputers, as illustrated in Figure 13.8.

The ease with which occam 2 programs can be partitioned and
configured for execution on a distributed system is the main advantage that
occam 2 has over Ada and Modula-2.

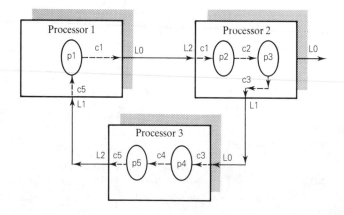

Figure 13.8   Five occam 2 processes configured for three transputers.

13.7   Reliability

It seems almost paradoxical that distribution can provide the means by which systems can be made more reliable yet, at the same time, introduce more potential failures in the system. Although the availability of multiple processors enables the application to become tolerant of processor failure, it also introduces the possibility of faults occurring in the system which would not occur in a centralized single-processor system. In particular, multiple processors introduce the concept of a partial system failure. In a single-processor system, if the processor or memory fails then normally the whole system fails (sometimes the processor may be able to continue and recover from a partial memory failure but, in general, the system will crash). However, in a distributed system it is possible for a single processor to fail while others continue to operate. In addition, the propagation delay through the underlying communications network is unpredictable and messages may take various routes. This, in conjunction with an unreliable transmission medium, may result in messages being lost, corrupted, or delivered in an order different to the order in which they were sent. The increased complexity of the software necessary to tolerate such failures can also threaten the reliability of the system.

13.7.1   Communication protocols

In Chapter 9, and in discussing virtual nodes in this chapter, it has been assumed that interprocess communication can be supported easily and reliably. As has been pointed out, this may not be the case where the communication takes places between heterogeneous processors across an unreliable network, and in practice, complex communication protocols are required. Where the distributed application is viewed as a single program, these protocols would form part of the underlying run-time support system. If the application is viewed as many programs then the communication protocols may have to be accessed directly through library packages. Taking a single program approach eases the difficulty of programming distributed system; in particular (Liskov, 1982):

(1)   Programmers do not have to deal with the underlying form of messages. For example, they do not need to translate data into bit strings suitable for transmission, or to break up the message into packets.

(2)   All messages received by user processes are intact and in good condition. For example, if messages are broken into packets, the run-time system will only deliver them if all the packets arrive at the receiving node and can be properly reassembled. Furthermore, if the bits in a message have been scrambled, either the message is not

delivered or is reconstructed before delivery; clearly, some redundant information is required for error checking.

(3)   Messages received by a process are the kind that the process expects. The process does not need to perform run-time checks.

(4)   Processes are not restricted to communication in terms of a predefined built-in set of types only. Instead, processes can communicate in terms of values of interest to the application. Ideally, if the application is defined using abstract data types, then values of these types can be communicated in messages.

Open systems interconnections

Much effort has been expended on communication protocols for networks and distributed systems. It is beyond the scope of this book to cover this in detail; rather, the reader should refer to Halsall (1988), Tanenbaum (1988) or Sloman and Kramer (1987) for a full discussion of the issues. In general, communication protocols are layered to facilitate their design and implementation. However, many different networks exist, each with its own concept of a 'network architecture' and associated communication protocols. Consequently, without some international standards it is extremely difficult to contemplate interconnecting systems of different origins. Standards have been defined over the last decade by the International Standards Organization (ISO) and involve the concept of Open Systems Interconnections, or OSI. The term *open* is used to indicate that by conforming to these standards a system will be open to all other systems in the world that also obey the same standards. These standards have become known as the OSI Reference Model. It should be stressed that this model is *not* concerned with specific applications of computer communication networks but with the *structuring* of the communication protocols required to provide a reliable, manufacturer-independent communication service.

The OSI Reference Model is a layered model. The layers are shown in Figure 13.9.

The basic idea of layering is that each layer adds to the services provided by the lower layers in order to present a service to higher layers. When viewed from above a particular layer, the ones below it may be considered as a black box which implements a service. The means by which one layer makes use of the service provided by the lower layers is through that layer's *interface*. The interface defines the rules and format for exchanging information across the boundary between adjacent layers. The modules which implement a layer are usually known as *entities*.

In networks and distributed systems each layer may be distributed across more than one machine; in order to provide its service, entities in the same layer on different machines may need to exchange information.

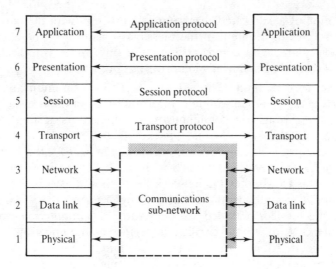

Figure 13.9   The OSI reference model.

Such entities are know as *peer entities*. A *protocol* is the set of rules which governs communication between peer entities.

The OSI model itself does not define protocol standards; by breaking up the network's function into layers, it does suggest where protocol standards should be developed but these standards are outside the model itself. Such standards, however, have been developed.

The functions of each layer are now briefly described.

(1)   **The physical layer**: The physical layer is concerned with transmitting raw data over a communication channel. Its job is to make sure that, in the absence of errors, when one side sends a 1 bit it is received as a 1 bit and not a 0 bit.

(2)   **The data link layer**: The data link layer converts an unreliable transmission channel into a reliable one for use by the network layer. In order for the data link layer to provide a reliable communication channel it must be able to correct errors. There are two basic and familiar techniques used: forward error control and backward error control. Forward error control requires enough redundant information in each message to correct any errors which may occur in its transmission. In general, the amount of redundancy required increases rapidly as the number of information bits increases. Backward error control requires only that the error be detected, once detected, a retransmission scheme can be employed to obtain the correct message (this is the job of the data link layer). Backward error control predominates in the world of networks and distributed systems. Most backward error control techniques incorporate the

notion of a calculated **checksum** which is sent with the message and describes the content of the message. On receipt, the checksum is recalculated and compared with the one sent. Any disagreement indicates that a transmission error has occurred.

(3) **The network layer**: The network layer (or communication subnet layer) is concerned with how information from the transport layer is routed through the communication subnet to its destinations. Messages are broken down into packets which may be routed via different paths; the network layer must reassemble the packets and handle any congestion which may occur. There is no clear agreement as to whether the network layer should attempt to provide a perfect communication channel through the network. Two extremes in the services provided can be identified: *virtual circuits* and *datagrams*. With virtual circuits, a perfect communication channel is provided. All message packets arrive and in sequence. With a datagram service, the network layer attempts to deliver each packet in isolation from the others. Consequently, messages may arrive out of order, or may not arrive at all.

The physical, data link and network layer are network dependent and their detailed operation may vary from one type of network to another.

(4) **The transport layer**: The transport layer (or host-to-host layer) provides reliable host-to-host communication for use by the session layer. It must hide all details of the communication subnet from the session layer in order that one subnet can be replaced by another. In effect, the transport layer shields the customer's portion of the network (layers 5–7) from the carrier's portion (layers 1–3).

(5) **The session layer**: The role of the session layer is to provide a communication path between two application-level processes using the facilities of the transport layer. The connection between users is usually called a **session** and may include a remote login or a file transfer. The operations involved in setting up a session (called binding) include authentication and accounting. Once the session has been initiated the layer must control data exchange, and synchronize data operations between the two processes.

(6) **The presentation layer**: The presentation layer performs transformations on the data that are generally useful, such as text compression or encryption. It also allows an interactive program to converse with any one of a set of incompatible terminals.

(7) **The application layer**: The application layer provides the high-level functions of the network, such as access to databases, mail systems, and so on. The choice of the application may dictate the level of services provided by the lower layers. Consequently, particular application areas may specify a set of protocols throughout all seven

layers which are required to support the intended distributed processing function. For example, an initiative by General Motors has
defined a set of protocols to achieve open interconnection within a
automated manufacturing plant. These are called Manufacturing
Automation Protocols (MAP) (Halsall, 1988).

Lightweight protocols

The OSI model was developed, primarily, for wide-area networks, to
enable open access; wide-area networks are characterized by low bandwidth communication with high error rates. Most distributed embedded
systems will use local-area network technology and will be closed to the
outside world. Local-area networks are characterized by high bandwidth
communication with low error rates. Consequently, although it is possible
to implement language-level interprocess communication using the OSI
approach, in practice, the expense is often prohibitive. Thus, many
designers tailor the communication protocols to the requirements of the
language (the application) and the communication medium. These are
called **lightweight** protocols. A key issue in their design is the degree with
which they tolerate communication failures.

At first glance, it appears that completely reliable communication is
essential if efficient and reliable distributed applications are to be written.
However, this may not always be the case. Consider the types of errors that
can be introduced by a distributed application. If two distributed processes
are communicating and synchronizing their activities to provide a service
then potential errors can occur from:

- Transient errors resulting from interference on the physical communication medium.
- Design errors in the software responsible for masking out transient
  errors in the communication subsystems.
- Design errors in the protocols between the server processes and any
  other servers needed in the provision of the service.
- Design errors in the protocol between the two server processes
  themselves.

To protect against the latter error it is necessary for the server processes to
provide application-level checks (end-to-end checks). The *end-to-end
argument of system design* (Saltzer *et al.*, 1984) states that given the
necessity of such checks for provision of a reliable service, it is not necessary to repeat these checks at lower levels in the protocol hierarchy,
particularly when the communication medium (for example, local-area
networks such as an Ethernet or Cambridge Ring) provides a low-error
rate (but not perfect) transmission facility. In these cases it may be better
to have a fast, less than 100% reliable, communication facility than a

slower 100% reliable facility. Applications which require high reliability can trade in efficiency for reliability at the application level. However, applications which require fast (but not necessarily reliable) service *cannot* trade in reliability for efficiency, if the other approach is taken.

A common language-oriented lightweight protocol is the remote procedure call. This is normally implemented directly on top of a basic communication facility provided by the local-area network. With languages like SR, remote procedure calls, in the absence of machine failures, are considered to be reliable. That is, for each remote procedure call, the procedure is executed once and once only; this is often called *exactly once* RPC semantics. However, in the presence of machine failure this is difficult to achieve because a procedure may be partially or totally executed several times depending on where the crash occurred and where the program is restarted. For a full discussion on the implementation of remote procedure calls see Birrell and Nelson (1984).

13.7.2   Processor failure

In Chapter 5, two general approaches for providing fault-tolerant hardware and software were identified; these were associated with static (masking) and dynamic redundancy. Although hardware fault tolerance does have a major role to play in achieving reliability in the presence of processor and communication failure, an excessive amount of hardware is required to implement triple modular redundancy, and consequently it is expensive (but fast). Therefore, this section concentrates on the provision of fault tolerance through the use of software methods.

Tolerating processor failure through static redundancy

N-version programming was discussed in Chapter 5 in the context of achieving static tolerance to design faults. Clearly, if each of the versions in an N-version program resides on a different processor then this approach will also provide tolerance to processor failure. However, even if no design diversity is employed, it still may be desirable to replicate identical copies of some system components to obtain the required reliability. For the time being it will be assumed that all processors in the system are **failstop**. This means that if a processor malfunctions in any way then it will halt immediately. If processors are not 'failstop' then it is possible that they will send invalid messages to each other. This would introduce an extra level of complexity into the following discussion.

If an application is designed using virtual nodes then it is possible to replicate virtual nodes on different processors. Replicating at the virtual node level enables the system designer to vary the degree of replication according to the importance of a particular virtual node. Cooper (1985) has

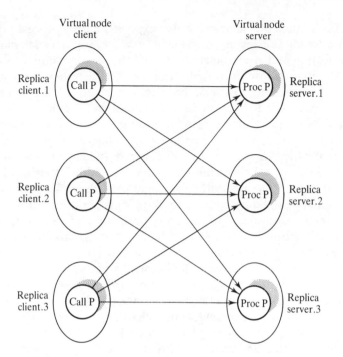

Figure 13.10   Replicated remote procedure calls.

discussed this problem in the context of virtual nodes communicating via remote procedure calls (virtual nodes are called modules by Cooper). For virtual nodes to be replicated transparently to the application programmer they must have deterministic behaviour. This means that for a given sequence of requests to a server virtual node and/or sequence of interrupts, the behaviour of the server is predictable. If this was not the case, the states of each of the replicas in a replicated virtual node (called a **troupe** by Cooper) could end up being different. Consequently, any request made to that troupe could produce a range of results. A troupe must therefore be kept consistent.

If virtual nodes are to be replicated it is also necessary to replicate each internode communication. In the case of remote procedure calls, in order to keep the replicas consistent, it is necessary to have exactly once remote procedure call semantics. As is indicated in Figure 13.10, each client process will potentially execute a one-to-many procedure call and each server procedure will receive a many-to-one request. The run-time system is responsible for coordinating these calls and ensuring the required semantics. This entails periodic probing of server sites with outstanding calls to determine their status; a failure to respond will indicate a processor crash. (See Cooper (1985) for full details.)

An example of a language which explicitly allows process replication is Fault-tolerant Concurrent C (Cmelik *et al.*, 1988). This language has a communication and synchronization model that is very similar to Ada.

Although transparent replication of virtual nodes is an attractive approach to providing tolerance of processor failure, it cannot easily be applied to Ada-based virtual nodes (Hutcheon and Wellings, 1989b). This is because an Ada virtual node can have more than one task, each of which can contain nested tasks. To ensure that replicas do not diverge it is necessary for the run-time agreement protocol (which ensures consistency between replicas) to be executed at every scheduling decision. In a real-time environment the associated overhead of such an approach may well be prohibitive. Providing 'warm' standbys with periodic state-saving may offer a cheaper solution. With such an approach, a virtual node would be replicated on more than one processor. However, unlike full replication, only one copy of the virtual node is active at any one time. The state of this node is periodically saved (typically before and after communication with another virtual node) on the processors with residing replicas. If the primary node fails then a standby can be started from the last checkpoint.

With a post-partitioning approach it is also possible to identify during program configuration parts of the program that need replication. Both full replication and warm standbys are feasible.

Tolerating processor failure through dynamic redundancy

One of the problems of providing fault-tolerance transparently to the application, is that it is impossible for the programmer to specify degraded or safe execution. The alternative to static redundancy and replication is to allow processor(s) failure to be handled dynamically by the application programmer. Clearly, the techniques that have been discussed so far in this book which enable an application to tolerate software design faults (using, for example, atomic actions) will provide some measure of tolerance of hardware faults. In Chapter 5, the four phases of fault tolerance were described: error detection, damage confinement and assessment, error recovery and fault treatment and continued service. In the context of processor failure the following actions must be performed:

(1)   The failure of the processor(s) must be detected and communicated to the remaining processors in the system. Failure detection would normally be done by the underlying distributed run-time support system. However, there must be an appropriate way of communicating to the application software which processors have failed.

(2)   The damage that has occurred because of the failure must be assessed; this requires knowledge of which processes were running on the failed processor(s), which processors and processes remain active (and their state). For this to be achieved, the application

programmer must have control over which virtual nodes are placed on which machines. Furthermore, it must be clear what effect a processor failure has on the processes executing on the failed processor, and their data. Also, the effect of any interaction, either pending or future, with those processes and their data must be defined.

(3)   Using the results of the damage assessment the remaining software must agree on a response to the failure and carry out the necessary actions to effect that response. To achieve maximum tolerance, this part of the recovery procedure must be distributed. If only a single processor performs the recovery operations then failure of that processor will be catastrophic to the application. Recovery will require communication paths between processes being changed so that alternative services can be provided. Also, because the response selected will depend on the overall state of the application, it will be necessary for certain data to be made available on all machines and for this to be held in a consistent state. For example, the actions to be taken following a processor failure in an avionics system will depend on the altitude of the plane. If different processors have different values for this altitude then the chosen recovery procedures may work at cross purposes (Knight and Urquhart, 1987). The algorithm necessary to achieve consistent state between replicated data is considered in Section 13.8.6.

(4)   As soon as is practicable, the failed processor and/or its associated software must be repaired and the system returned to its normal error-free state.

Few of the real-time programming languages considered in this book provide adequate facilities to cope with dynamic reconfiguration after processor failure. The CONIC toolkit does provide an operating system which enables an operator to reconfigure task modules, however this is aimed more at upgrading the system to fix bugs or to introduce new functionality due to changing requirements (Kramer and Magee, 1988). The remainder of this section will consider the problems associated with dynamic reconfiguration using Ada. Reliability and occam 2 will be considered in the next section.

Knight and Urquhart (1987) have performed a comprehensive analysis of the use of Ada in the presence of processor failure. Their discussion considers a more general model of distribution than the virtual node approach adopted in this chapter. Here, the ideas expressed in their work are applied to Ada virtual nodes.

Detecting a processor failure can be achieved either by the use of timeouts on communication or by the specific exchange of 'heartbeat' messages between processors. The latter is preferred as it does not rely on communication between virtual nodes before failure is detected. Once detected, each remaining virtual node must be informed. This can be done in two ways:

(1)   map the failure onto a predefined exception in some or all tasks running in each non-failed virtual node;

(2)   map the failure onto an entry call to some task (or tasks) running in each non-failed virtual node.

The first of these approaches suffers from the asynchronous nature of the raised exception. It cannot be guaranteed that all tasks will be in a position to handle the exception when it is raised, with the result that task failure may propagate onto non-failed processors. Although asynchronous exceptions were allowed in earlier versions of Ada (Ichbiah *et al.*, 1979b) they are not now permitted. However, as was discussed in the previous chapter, there appears to be strong support for their reinstatement.

In the second approach each virtual node has a reconfiguration task. This task has an entry 'failure' with a single parameter of type 'processor identity'. When a processor fails, the 'failure' entry is called in all reconfiguration tasks, with the parameter giving the identity of the failed processor. This, of course, requires a mechanism whereby the reconfiguration task can identify itself to the underlying run-time support system which detects the processor failure. Notionally, the called entries are akin to an interrupt entry, and, therefore, can be identified by a special address clause (see Chapter 14). Alternatively, the reconfiguration task can call a run-time routine to identify itself.

Once these reconfiguration tasks have been notified, they must assess the damage that has been done to the system. This requires knowledge of the actual configuration of virtual nodes to physical processors. In general, this chapter has tried to separate the logical structure of the program (virtual nodes) from its physical implementation. In this case the physical implementation must be known, so it is necessary to provide a mechanism by which the configuration tools can check that the actual configuration conforms to that expected by the program.

The tasks which were executing on a virtual node can be considered to have been aborted. With more general models of distribution, task hierarchies can be distributed. If this is the case then it seems desirable to change the semantics of the abort statement, so that a child task need not be aborted with its parent if it is running on another processor. Thus, for example, if the processor executing the main program fails there need be no obligation to abort all program-defined tasks in the system. With the virtual node approach all tasks are library tasks and hierarchies cannot be constructed across virtual node boundaries, and so the problem does not arise. If tasks in virtual nodes are considered to be aborted then all their data disappears and any attempted communication will result in the exception TASKING_ERROR being raised.

Given that the reconfiguration tasks have assessed the damage and have agreed a response, this will require communication with other tasks within their respective virtual nodes. For real-time systems it is imperative that this communication occurs without delay; unfortunately, there is no way in Ada to force communication on a task if the task is not ready to enter into a rendezvous. To have the tasks poll the reconfiguration task on the off chance that a processor failure has occurred is inelegant, will complicate the structure of those tasks, and will waste processor cycles. The only way Ada allows for this asynchronous interaction is to abort the task and either recreate it or create a replacement task. This is considered by many in the Ada community to be excessive and 'using a sledgehammer to crack a nut'. An asynchronous exception would appear to be the most appropriate mechanism to solve this problem.

Achieving reliable execution of occam 2 programs

Although occam 2 was designed for use in a distributed environment it does not have any failure semantics. Processes which fail due to internal error (for example, array-bound error) are equivalent to the STOP process. A process which is waiting for communication on a channel where the other process is on a failed processor will wait forever, unless it has employed a timeout. However, it is possible to imagine that suitable occam 2 semantics for this event would be to consider both processes as STOPped and to provide a mechanism whereby some other process can be informed.

13.8 Distributed algorithms

Up to now, this chapter has concentrated on the expression of distributed programs in Ada, Modula-2 and occam 2, along with the general problems of tolerating processor and communication failure. This section briefly considers some specific algorithms which are required for controlling and coordinating access to resources in a distributed environment. The purpose of this section is not to give an exhaustive treatment of the various distributed algorithms, but to illustrate the problem areas and to give a flavour of possible solutions. First, however, in order to simplify the discussion of these algorithms, it is useful to establish certain properties that can be relied on in a distributed environment. In particular, it is necessary to show how events can be ordered, how storage can be organized so that its contents survive a processor failure, and how agreement can be reached in the presence of faulty processors.

13.8.1 Ordering events in a distributed environment

In many applications it is necessary to determine the order of events that have occurred in the system. This presents no difficulty for uniprocessor or tightly-coupled systems, which have a common memory and a common clock. For distributed systems, however, there is no common clock and the delay which occurs in sending messages between processors means that these systems have two important properties (Le Lann, 1977).

(1)   For any given sequence of events, it is impossible to prove that two different processes will observe, identically, the same sequence.

(2)   As state changes can be viewed as events, it is impossible to prove that any two processes will have the same global view of a given subset of the system state.

If processes in a distributed application are to coordinate and synchronize their activities in response to events as they occur, it is necessary to place an order on these events. For example, in order to detect deadlock between processes that share resources it is important to know that a process released resource A before requesting resource B (see Section 13.8.5). The algorithm presented here enables events in a distributed system to be ordered and is due to Lamport (1978).

Consider process P which executes the events $p0$, $p1$, $p2$, $p3$, $p4$ ... pn. As this is a sequential process, the event $p0$ must have happened before event $p1$ which must have happened before event $p2$ and so on. This is written as $p0 \rightarrow p1 \rightarrow p2 ... \rightarrow pn$. Similarly, for process Q: $q0 \rightarrow q1 \rightarrow q2$ ... $\rightarrow qn$. If these two processes are distributed and there is no communication between them, it is impossible to say whether $p0$ happened before or after $q0$, $q1$ or, in general, qn. Consider now the case where the event $p1$ is sending a message to Q, and $q3$ is the event which receives the message from P. Figure 13.11 illustrates this interaction.

As the act of receiving a message must occur *after* the message has been sent, then $p1 \rightarrow q3$ and as $q3 \rightarrow q4$, it follows that $p1 \rightarrow q4$. There is still no information as to whether $p0$ or $q0$ happened first. These events are termed *concurrent events*. As neither event can affect the other, it is of no real importance which one is considered to have occurred first. However, it is important that processes which make decisions based on this order all assume the same order.

To order all events totally in a distributed system it is necessary to associate a *time-stamp* with each event. However, this is not a physical time-stamp but, rather, is a logical time-stamp. Each processor in the system keeps a logical clock which is incremented every time an event occurs on that processor. An event $p1$ in process P occurred before $p2$ in the same process if the value of the logical clock at $p1$ is less than the value

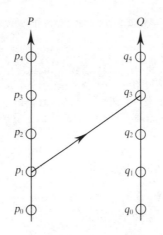

Figure 13.11   Two interacting processes.

of the logical clock at $p2$. Clearly, it is possible using this method for the logical clock associated with each process to get out of synchronization. For example, P's logical clock at $p1$ may be greater than Q's logical clock at $q3$; however, $p1$ must have occurred before $q3$ because a message cannot be received before it has been sent. To resolve this problem it is necessary for every message sent between processes to carry the time-stamp of the event that sent the message. Furthermore, every time a processes receives a message it must set its logical clock to a value which is:

- equal to the time-stamp found in the message plus one – for asynchronous message passing, or:
- equal to the time-stamp – for synchronous message passing

This ensures that no message is received before it is sent.

Using the above algorithm, all events in the system have an associated time-stamp and can be partially ordered accordingly. If two events have the same time-stamp then it is sufficient to use an arbitrary condition, such as the numeric value of process identifiers, to order the events totally.

13.8.2   Implementing stable storage

In many instances, it is necessary to have access to a store whose contents will survive a processor crash; this is called **stable storage**. As the main memory of any processor is volatile it is necessary to use a disk (or any other form of non-volatile storage) as the stable storage device. Unfortunately, write operations to disks are not atomic in that the operation can crash part way through. When this happens it is not possible for a recovery manager to determine whether the operation succeeded or not. To solve this problem each block of data is stored twice on separate areas of the disk. These areas are chosen so that a head crash which occurs while reading one area will not destroy the other; if necessary they can be on physically separate disk drives. It is assumed that the disk unit will indicate if a single write operation completes successfully (using redundancy checks). The approach, in the absence of a processor failure, is to write the block of data to the first area of the disk (this operation may have to be repeated until it succeeds); only when this succeeds is the block written to the second area of the disk.

If a crash occurs while updating stable storage then the following recovery routine can be executed.

```
read_block1;
read_block2;
if both_are_readable and block_1 = block2 then
    -- do nothing, the crash did not affect the stable storage
else
    if one_block_is_unreadable then
        -- copy good block to bad block
    else
        if both_are_readable_but_different then
            -- copy block1 to block2 (or visa versa)
        else
            -- a catastrophic failure has occurred and both
            -- blocks are unreadable
        end
    end;
end;
```

This algorithm will succeed even if there are subsequent crashes during its execution.

13.8.3 Reaching agreement in the presence of faulty processes

In Section 13.7.2 it was assumed that if a processor fails then it 'failstops'; By this, it is meant that the processor stops *all* execution and does not take part in communication with any other processors in the system. Indeed, even the algorithm for stable storage presented in Section 13.8.2 assumes that a processor crash results in the processor immediately stopping its execution. Without this assumption, a malfunctioning processor might perform arbitrary state transitions and send spurious messages to other processors. Thus, even a logically correct program could not be guaranteed to produce the desired result. This would make fault-tolerant systems impossible to achieve. Although much effort can be made to build processors that operate correctly in spite of component failure, it is impossible to guarantee this using a finite amount of hardware. Therefore, this section considers the problem of how a group of processes, executing on different processors, can reach a consensus in the presence of faulty processes within the group. It is assumed that all communication is reliable.

Byzantine generals problem

The problem of agreeing values between processes which may reside on faulty processors is often expressed as the *Byzantine Generals Problem* (Lamport *et al.*, 1982). Several divisions of the Byzantine Army, each commanded by its own general, surround an enemy camp. The generals are able to communicate by messengers and must come to an agreement as to whether to attack the camp. To do this, each observes the enemy camp and communicates his or her observations to the others. Unfortunately, one or more of the generals may be traitors and are liable to convey false information. The problem is for all loyal generals to obtain the same information. In general, $3m + 1$ generals can cope with m traitors. For simplicity, the approach is illustrated with an algorithm for four generals that will cope with one traitor. The reader is referred to the literature for more general solutions (Pease *et al.*, 1980; Lamport *et al.*, 1982).

Consider general Gi and the information that he or she has observed, Oi. Each general maintains a vector V of information that has been received from the other generals. Initially, Gi's vector contains only the value Oi; that is $Vi(j) = $ null (for $i <> j$) and $Vi(i) = Oi$. Each general sends a messenger to every other general indicating his or her observation; loyal generals will always send the correct observation; the traitor general may send a false observation and may send different false observations to different generals. On receiving the observations, each general updates his or her vector and then sends the value of the other three's observations to the other generals. Clearly, the traitor may send observations different from the ones that he or she has received, or nothing at all. In the latter case the generals can choose an arbitrary value.

After this exchange of messages, each loyal general can construct a vector from the majority value of the three values that he or she has received for each general's observation. If no majority exists then they assume no observations.

For example, suppose that the observations of a general lead him or her to one of three conclusions: Attack(A), Retreat(R), or Wait(W). Consider the case where G1 is a traitor, G2 concludes attack, G3: attack and G4: wait. The initial state of each vector is shown in Figure 13.12.

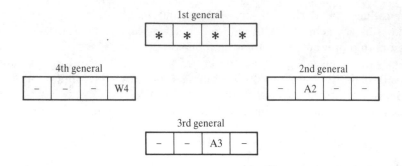

Figure 13.12   Byzantine generals – initial state.

The index into the vector (1..4) gives the number of the general, the contents of the item at that index gives the observation from that general and who reported the observation. Initially, then, the fourth general stores 'wait' in the fourth element of its vector, indicating that the observation came from itself.

After the first exchange of messages the vectors are as shown in Figure 13.13 (assuming that the traitor realizes the camp is vulnerable and sends the retreat and wait messages randomly to all generals).

After the second exchange of messages the information shown in Figure 13.14 is available to each general (again assuming the traitor sends retreat and wait messages randomly).

To illustrate how Figure 13.14 has been derived consider the final row for the fourth general. This has been obtained from the third general (as the 3 indicates) and includes information about the decisions of the first

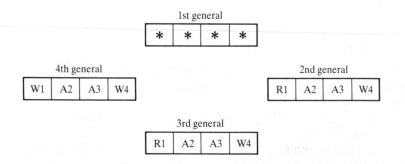

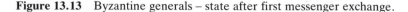

Figure 13.13   Byzantine generals – state after first messenger exchange.

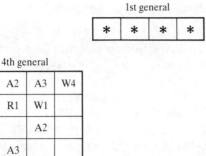

1st general

*	*	*	*

4th general

W1	A2	A3	W4
	R1	W1	
R2		A2	
R3	A3		

2nd general

R1	A2	A3	W4
		R1	R1
R3			W3
W4		A4	

3rd general

R1	A2	A3	W4
	W1		R1
R2			W2
W4	A4		

Figure 13.14 Byzantine generals – state after second messenger exchange.

and the second generals. Hence, R3 in the first column indicates that the third general is of the view that the first general wishes to retreat.

The final (majority) vector is shown in Figure 13.15.

Loyal generals have a consistent view of each others' observations and, therefore, can make the uniform decision.

Using solutions to the Byzantine general problem it is possible to construct a failstop processor by having internally-replicated processors carry out a Byzantine agreement (Schneider, 1984). If the non-faulty processors detect a disagreement they stop execution.

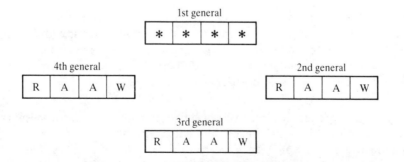

Figure 13.15 Byzantine generals – final state.

13.8.4   Achieving fault-tolerant resource controllers

In Chapter 8, mutual exclusion was studied in the context of shared memory. Synchronization primitives like semaphores and monitors were used to illustrate how processes could obtain mutually-exclusive access to a shared resource. Message-based systems were studied, in Chapter 9, in the context of a client-server paradigm of communication where mutual exclusion is again guaranteed. For reliability considerations, resource controllers should not be centralized, as in the client-server model, because the failure of the server's processor can cause all resources to become unavailable. To avoid this problem either the server itself must be distributed and a distributed mutual exclusion algorithm implemented, or it must be possible to elect a new server in the event of the original server failing. An example algorithm of both these solutions is given in this section.

Distributed mutual exclusion

The algorithm presented here is due to Ricart and Agrawala (1981) and is based on Lamport's algorithm for event ordering which was described in Section 13.8.1. The basic approach is that each process which wishes to enter its critical section, requests permission to do so from all other processes over which it requires mutual exclusion. This request contains the process identifier and the time-stamp of when the request was generated. These time-stamps are coordinated as described in Section 13.8.1.

When a process (P) receives a request from another process (Q) that wishes to enter a critical section it will either give its permission immediately or postpone it, giving it at a later time. This decision is based on the following three factors.

(1)   If P is active in its critical section then it postpones giving its permission to Q.

(2)   If P does not want to enter its critical section, it replies immediately to Q, giving its permission.

(3)   If P wants to enter its section but has not yet been able to do so, it compares the time-stamp associated with Q's request with the time-stamp associated with its own request. It Q's time-stamp is less than P's, Q asked first and so P replies immediately with its permission. If P asked first then P postpones giving its permission.

Only when a process has received permission from all other processes can it enter its critical section. Once it has exited from the section, it must reply to all processes, to which it has postponed replying, indicating that it now gives its permission for them to enter their critical sections.

Although this algorithm is distributed, all processes must be aware of each other's existence. When new processes join or leave the group, communication must take place between the group members so that the list of active processes is kept up to date. This is a disadvantage compared to the simple client-server model which only requires that each client process knows the server. Furthermore, as the algorithm stands it is not robust to processor failure. If a process is lost due to its host's processor failure then the algorithm is deadlocked. Therefore, it requires that all processors be failstop and that processors which have stopped can be detected by the other processes.

Electing a new server

The alternative to distributing control is to have centralized control and to hold an election if the centralized controller fails. In a client-server model this requires all the clients to hold an election amongst themselves to determine who the new server will be. Again, as with the distributed mutual exclusion algorithm, the assumption is that all clients know of each others existence and that processors are failstop. The algorithm presented here is called the 'bully algorithm' and is due to Garcia-Molina (1982). It requires that all processes in the group of clients and server be given a unique priority and that, at any instance, the process with the highest priority is the server process.

When the current server process fails, the first process which notices the fact decides to elect itself as the new server process. To do so it must be the process with the highest priority of the currently available processes. It therefore sends an election message to all processes which have higher priority. If no response is received from these processes within a given time period, it assumes that they all have also failed and elects itself as the new server. It sends a message to all processes which have lower priority, indicating that it is now the server processes.

If, however, a reply is received from a higher-level process, the process abandons its attempt to become server and waits for a message from a higher-priority process, indicating that the higher-priority process is the new server. If no such message is forthcoming the process starts the election procedure again.

When a high-priority process receives an election message from a process of lower priority it responds to it (disparagingly) and starts its own election procedure.

If a process fails and is then restarted, it immediately tries to become the server by holding an election, even if there is an active server. It is for this reason that the algorithm is called the bully algorithm as it tries to bully itself into being server.

13.8.5 Deadlock detection

In Chapter 11, the problem of deadlock was introduced in the context of resource allocation. In that chapter no account was taken of the possible distribution of processes or resources. The topic of deadlock detection and prevention in a distributed environment is complex and has received much attention in the literature, particularly in the context of databases. It is beyond the scope of this book to give a full discussion on this subject, instead, a single algorithm for deadlock detection is presented. This algorithm, from Peterson and Silberschatz (1985) has a centralized algorithm which maintains resource allocation graphs (see Chapter 11). For the purpose of this discussion, it is assumed that if this central site fails then the other processes in the system will elect a new site using an algorithm such as the bully algorithm.

Each site in the system maintains its own local resource allocation graph as in Chapter 11. Periodically, the deadlock-detection controller requests a copy of each of these local graphs and constructs a resource allocation graph for the whole system. Unfortunately, because of the delays in message passing it is probable that the combined sites have an inconsistent view of the total resource allocation state. This may result in the deadlock controller detecting a deadlock which has not occurred.

For example, consider a many-site system where resource R_1 is held on site A, and R_2 on site B. Requests for these resources can come from other sites. The deadlock detection controller resides on site C. Initially, process P_1 (at site B) is waiting for R_1 on site A and has been allocated R_2 on site B. P_2 (at Site D) has been allocated R_1 on site A, and P_3 (at Site A)

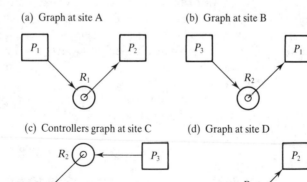

Figure 13.16   A possible resource allocation.

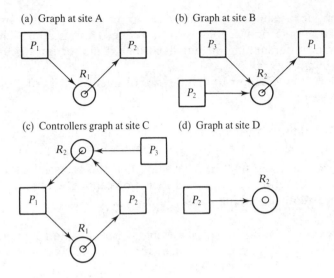

Figure 13.17   A false deadlock.

is waiting for R_2 on site B. The local resource allocation graphs on site A, B and D along with the controller's global graph are shown in Figure 13.16. No cycles exists.

Now consider the case where P_2 releases R_1 and requests R_2. Because there may be delays in these messages arriving at their respective sites, the situation could occur where site B receives the allocation request before site A has received the release request. If the controller decides at this point to check for deadlock then the local and global graphs are those shown in Figure 13.17.

Here, the controller has detected a false deadlock. To resolve this problem every request coming from a remote site carries a unique identifier, for example, a time-stamp. This information is stored in the local resource allocation graphs on both sites. However, when the deadlock controller constructs the global graph it only includes an edge between a resource and a process if the same time-stamped edge appears in more than one local graph. In the example under discussion: as the edge between P_2 and R_1 only appears in one graph with the same time-stamp, it will not be included in the global graph. Requests local to a processor do not carry a time-stamp and, therefore, need only exist once in the system.

13.8.6   Maintaining consistent data – atomic transactions

An important resource in any system is that of long-lived data, be it stored in a file system or in a database. Reliable update of such data, in the presence of processor failure, is important in many embedded computer application, for example, banking and airline reservation systems. In Chapter 10 atomic transactions were introduced as an approach to the fault-tolerant programming of long-lived data. This section discusses the approach in more detail.

Recall from Chapter 10 that the two distinctive properties of atomic transactions are:

(1)   Failure atomicity; meaning that the transaction must either complete successfully or (in the case of failure) have no effect.

(2)   Synchronization atomicity; meaning that the transaction is indivisible in the sense that its partial execution cannot be observed by any concurrently executing transaction.

There are many approaches to achieving synchronization atomicity and these will not be discussed here (see, for example, Ceri and Pelagatti (1985) and Bernstein *et al.* (1987)).

To achieve failure atomicity it is necessary to use stable storage. For a single processor the following two-phased commit protocol (Gray, 1978) can be used to update a file system or database.

(1)   During the first phase, the information to be written at the completion of the transaction is recorded on stable storage in an *intention list*. The last action performed by the phase is said to *commit* the transaction. It should be stressed that no change to the data stored by the file system occurs during this phase.

(2)   During the second phase of the transaction the actual write operation on the data is performed.

If a crash occurs during the transaction, a recovery procedure is performed, either by the restarted crashed processor or by another processor which has detected the crash. This procedure looks on stable storage for an intention list. If the crash occurred before the list was created, the transaction will have had no affect. If the intention list exists and if it has a commit tag then the write operations are performed again using the details from the list. Note that writes can be performed as many times as necessary because the details contain the final value of the data. If, however, no commit tag is found in the intention list, the transaction is aborted and again has no effect.

Using a two-phased commit protocol it is, therefore, possible to obtain failure atomicity because the data is either updated or not; there are no partial updates.

Where data is distributed across a network it is necessary to extend this algorithm so that there is a transaction manager on each site (Gray, 1978). The manager on the site which initiated the transaction is called the *coordinator* and the others are called *participants*. All participants use stable storage and view their role as managing a local transaction with the final decision to commit or abort coming from the coordinator.

The coordinator

During the first phase of the transaction the coordinator performs the following.

- Creates the participants at each of the sites involved and gives them details of the sub-actions that they are to perform.
- Writes the details of the action and the participants to stable storage (the intention list).
- Sends a message to each participant asking if they are ready to commit.
- The participants will either reply: commit or abort. If they all respond 'commit', the coordinator writes commit to stable storage, otherwise it writes abort. If no response is forthcoming then a timeout may be used to infer abort.

During the second phase of the protocol the following actions are performed.

- The coordinator sends a message to all participants requesting that they commit (or abort) their subactions.
- When all participants have responded, the coordinator writes 'done' to stable storage.

Recovery from a coordinator crash

If the coordinator crashes then the recovery procedure is as follows. The intention list is read from stable storage.

- If the transaction has been 'done' then the crash did not affect it.
- If the vote was commit then the transaction must be completed. Messages are sent to the participants requesting that they complete their subactions.
- If there is no vote in the intention list or the vote was to abort the transaction, messages are sent to the participants requesting that they abort their subactions.
- Once the above has been achieved 'done' is written to the intention list.

The participants

The participants once created, and on receiving the 'ready to commit' command from the coordinator, write the details of their subactions to their local intention list. When each receives the commit or abort instruction it completes or aborts its subaction. When this has been achieved it writes 'done' to stable storage.

Recovery from a participant crash

If a participant fails then the following recovery procedure is performed.

- The intention list associated with that participant is read from stable storage to determine the details of the transaction.

- The task waits for communication from the coordinator or the coordinator recovery task.

- If this communication indicates that the first phase of the protocol is in progress then the participant replies abort.

- If this communication indicates the second phase of the protocol is in progress then the participant completes or aborts the local transaction accordingly.

Argus

Argus (Liskov, 1985) is a programming language designed primarily to support applications concerned with the manipulation of long-lived on-line data in a distributed environment. Examples of typical application areas include banking and airline reservation systems. The language supports both the virtual node abstraction (in the form of **guardians**) and the notion of atomic transactions (called atomic actions). An Argus program consists of a collection of guardians. The interface to a guardian is via remote procedure calls (called **handlers**) – a process being created to handle each active RPC. Other processes may be created to run in the background. A guardian's state consists of *stable* and *volatile* objects, the stable objects being periodically written to stable storage. When a guardian crashes, the volatile objects and the active processes are destroyed, but the stable objects survive. During recovery of the guardian's processor, the stable storage of each guardian is examined and the volatile storage is re-created to a consistent state. The guardian can then continue its operation.

Argus supports the notion of an atomic abstract data type. These are like normal abstract data types except that objects of the type possess failure atomicity and synchronization atomicity. Atomic transactions can be written by the Argus programmer, these may start on one guardian and make calls to handlers on other guardians, which in turn may access further remote guardians. Atomic transactions can commit or abort, if they abort then all atomic objects updated during the transaction are restored to their previous state. Transactions interrupted by hardware failure are considered to be aborted.

13.9 Deadline scheduling in a multiprocessor and distributed environment

This chapter has concentrated, throughout, on loosely-coupled distributed systems. It has been assumed that issues concerning multiprocessor systems can be resolved using the shared memory techniques of single-processor systems. This is not the case for scheduling in a multiprocessor environment. This section therefore considers scheduling in *both* multiprocessor and distributed systems.

13.9.1 Multiprocessor systems

The development of appropriate scheduling schemes for multiprocessor systems is problematic. Uniprocessor algorithms are not directly applicable and some of the appropriate methods are counter-intuitive.

Mok and Dertouzos (1978) showed that the algorithms that are optimal for single-processor systems are not optimal for increased numbers of processors. Consider, for example, three periodic processes P_1, P_2 and P_3 that must be executed on two processors. Let P_1 and P_2 have identical deadline requirements, namely a period of 50 time units and an execution requirement (per cycle) of 25 units; let P_3 have requirements of 100 and 80 respectively. If the rate monotonic algorithm (discussed in Chapter 12) is used P_1 and P_2 will have highest priority and will run on the two processors (in parallel) for their required 25 units. This will leave P_3 with 80 units of execution to accomplish in the 75 units that are available. The fact that P_3 has two processors available is irrelevant (one will remain idle). As a result of applying the rate-monotonic algorithm, P_3 will miss its deadline even though average processor utilization is only 65%. However, an allocation that maps P_1 and P_2 to one processor and P_3 to the other easily meets all deadlines.

Other examples can show that earliest deadline or least slack time formulations are similarly non-optimal. This difficulty with the optimal uniprocessor algorithms is not surprising as it is known that optimal scheduling for multiprocessor systems is NP-complete (that is, the computational time rising exponentially with the number of processes) (Graham et al., 1979). It is, therefore, necessary to look for ways of simplifying the problem, and algorithms that give adequate sub-optimal results.

Allocation of periodic processes

The previous illustration showed that judicious allocation of processes can significantly affect schedulability. Consider another example; this time let four processes be executing on the two processors, and let their cycle times be 10, 10, 14 and 14. If the two 10s are statically allocated to the same processor (and by implication the two 14s to the other) then 100% processor utilization can be achieved. The system is schedulable even if execution times for the four processes are, say, 5, 5, 10 and 4. However, if a 10 and a 14 were placed together on the same processor (as a result of dynamic allocation) then maximum utilization drops to 83%.

What this example appears to show is that it is better to allocate periodic processes statically rather than let them migrate and, as a consequence, potentially downgrade the system's performance. Even on a tightly-coupled system running a single run-time dispatcher it is better to keep processes on the same processor rather than try and utilize an idle processor (and risk unbalancing the allocation).

If static deployment is used, then the rate-monotonic algorithm (or other optimal uniprocessor schemes) can test for schedulability on each processor. In performing the allocation, processes that are harmonically related should be deployed together (that is, to the same processor) as this will help increase utilization.

Allocation of aperiodic processes

As it appears expedient to allocate periodic processes statically then a similar approach to aperiodic processes would seem to be a useful model to investigate. If all processes are statically mapped then the algorithms discussed in Section 12.4.4 can be used on each processor (that is, each processor, in effect, runs its own scheduler/dispatcher).

To calculate execution times (worst case or average) requires knowledge of potential blocking. Blocking within the local processor can be bounded by inheritance or ceiling protocols. However, in a multiprocessor system there is another form of blocking; this is when a processes is delayed by a process on another processor. This is called remote blocking and is discussed in the next section.

One of the drawbacks of a purely static allocation policy is that no benefits can be gained from spare capacity in one processor when another is experiencing a transient overload. For hard real-time systems each processor would need to be able to deal with worst-case execution times for its periodic processes, and maximum arrival times and execution times for its sporadic load. To improve on this situation Stankovic *et al.* (1985) and Ramamritham and Stankovic (1984) have proposed more flexible task-scheduling algorithms.

In their approach, which is described in terms of a distributed system, all periodic processes are statically allocated but aperiodic processes can migrate. The following protocol is used:

(1)   Each aperiodic process arrives at some node in the network (this could be a processor in a multiprocessor system running its own scheduler).

(2)   The node at which the aperiodic process arrives then checks to see if this new process can be scheduled, together with the existing load. If it can, the process is said to be *guaranteed* by this node.

(3)   If the node cannot guarantee the new processes it looks for alternative nodes that may be able to guarantee it. It does this using knowledge of the state of the whole network and by *bidding* for spare capacity in other nodes.

(4)   The process is thus moved to a new node where there is a high probability that it will be scheduled. However, because of race conditions the new node may not be able to schedule it once it has arrived. Hence, the guarantee test is undertaken locally; if the process fails the test then it must move again.

(5)   In this way, an aperiodic process is either scheduled (guaranteed) or it fails to meet its deadline.

The usefulness of their approach is enhanced by the use of a linear heuristic algorithm for determining where a non-guaranteed process should move. This heuristic is not computationally expensive (unlike the optimum NP-hard algorithm) but does give a high degree of success; that is, there is a high probability that the use of the heuristic will lead to an aperiodic process being scheduled (if it is schedulable at all).

The cost of executing the heuristic algorithm and moving the aperiodic processes is taken into account by the guarantee routine. Nevertheless, the scheme is only workable if aperiodic processes can be moved, and that this movement is efficient. Some aperiodic processes may be tightly coupled to hardware unique to one node and will have at least one component that must execute locally.

Remote blocking

If consideration is now given to process interaction in a multiprocessor system then the complexity of the scheduling is further increased (Garey and Johnson, 1975; Lenstra *et al.*, 1977 and Ullman, 1976) (that is, at least NP-complete). Here, the discussion is restricted to the interactions that take the form of mutual exclusive synchronization for controlling resource usage.

In the flexible system, described in the previous section, in which aperiodic processes are moved in order to find a node that will guarantee them, heuristics have been developed that take into account resource usage (Zhao, 1986; Zhao *et al.*, 1987a and Zhao *et al.*, 1987b). Again, these heuristics give good results (in simulation) but cannot guarantee all processes in all situations.

For static allocation of periodic and aperiodic processes, schedulability is a function of execution time which is a function of blocking time. It was noted in the previous section that multiprocessor systems give rise to a new form of blocking – remote blocking. In order to minimize remote blocking the following two properties are desirable:

(1)   Wherever possible a process should not use remote resources (and thereby be subject to remote blocking).

(2)   Remote blocking should only result from executing remote critical sections, not remote pre-emption.

The first property, which also reduces interprocessor communication, can be achieved, to a certain degree, by judicious allocation of the processes; so that all processes that use a particular critical section (together with the critical section itself) reside on the same processor. This is a further argument for static allocation, and it suggests that migration of aperiodic processes could be counter-productive.

Reducing remote access represents a second criteria for allocation; the two now being:

(1)   group the processes according to their periods (that is, harmonic periods together), or;

(2)   group the processes according to their resource usage.

These criteria are independent and, therefore, not simultaneously achievable on all applications. A compromise allocation would need to be made, based on the particular characteristics of the application.

Although remote blocking can be minimized by appropriate process deployment, it cannot, in general, be eliminated. Therefore, the second property must be considered.

In a uniprocessor system it is correct for a high-priority process to pre-empt a lower priority one. But, in a multiprocessor system, this is not necessarily desirable. If the two processes are on different processors then it would be expected that they would execute in parallel. However, consider the following example of three processes; H, M and L, with descending priority levels. Processes H and L run on one processor; M runs on the another but 'shares' a critical section that resides with, and is used by, L. If L is executing in the critical section when M wishes to use some data protected by it, then M must be delayed. But, if H now starts to execute it will pre-empt L and thus further delay M. Even if L was given M's priority (that is, remote inheritance) H would still execute.

To minimize this remote pre-emption, the critical section can be made non-pre-emptable (or at least only pre-emptable by other critical sections). An alternative formulation is to define the priority of the critical section to be higher than all processes in the system. Non-pre-emption is the protocol used by Mok (1983). As critical sections are often short when compared to non-critical sections of code, this non-pre-emption is an acceptable rule.

Rajkumar *et al.* (1988) have proved that with non-pre-emption, remote blocking can only take place when a required resource is already being used; that is, when an external critical section is locked. They go on to define a form of ceiling protocol appropriate for multiprocessor systems.

Transient overloads

It has already been noted that with static allocation schemes, spare capacity in one processor cannot be used to alleviate a transient overload in another processor. Each processor must deal with the overload as best it can (that is, by making sure that missed deadlines correspond to less important processes). If a flexible scheme is used to allocate aperiodic processes then some migration can be catered for. Unfortunately, the schemes discussed so far in this section have the following properties (during transient overload):

(1)   Aperiodic deadlines are missed, rather than periodic ones.

(2)   Aperiodic deadlines are not missed in an order that reflects importance.

Point (1) may, or may not, correspond to an applications requirement; point (2) is, however, always significant if the application has any hard deadlines attached to sporadic activity.

A compromise situation is possible (between the static and flexible approaches) if a static allocation is used for normal (non-overload) operation, with controlled migration being employed for tolerance of transient overloads. With this approach, each processor attempts to schedule all aperiodic and periodic processes assigned to it. If a transient overload is experienced (or better still predicted) then a set of processes that will miss their deadlines is isolated. This set will correspond to the least important collection of active processes (this could be achieved using rate-monotonic scheduling and period transformation).

An attempt is then made to move these processes which are destined to miss their deadlines. Note that this set could contain aperiodic and/or periodic processes. The movement of a periodic process will be for one complete cycle of its execution. After the execution of this cycle it will 'return' to its original processor. At the receiver processor all incoming processes will arrive as aperiodic, and unexpected, events.

In the new processor the new processes will be scheduled according to their priorities (deadlines). This may even cause local processes to miss their deadlines (potentially) if their importance is less than the new arrivals. A chain of migrations could then ensue. It must, however, be emphasized that migration is not a normal action; rather, it is a form of error recovery after transient overload. A well-specified system may never experience such events.

The advantage of this approach to transient overloads is that there is an increased chance that deadlines will be missed in the less important (soft) processes. It also deals adequately with systems in which aperiodic deadlines are more crucial than the periodic ones. Of course, an optimal scheme would miss the least important deadlines in the entire system (rather than just locally) but the computations necessary to obtain this optimum are too intensive for real-time applications.

13.9.2   Distributed systems

When moving from consideration of shared-memory systems to distributed architectures it is usual to encounter increased complexity. However, in the case of scheduling, the differences are not significant. This is because the analysis of shared-memory systems has lead to a model of parallelism that is, essentially, loosely coupled. For example, static allocation is a method usually considered more appropriate for distributed real-time systems. Also, the need to minimize remote action (remote blocking) is commensurate with good distributed design.

Only when processes migrate from one node to another could the temporal characteristics of the distributed system be significant. It has been seen that process migration can be used to give flexibility or to counter transient overloads. One method of reducing the time-penalty associated with moving a complete process from one node to another is to anticipate the migration and to have a copy of the code at the receiver node.

For instance, a two-processor system could have statically-allocated jobs and be structured to meet all hard deadlines locally, even during worst-case computation times. At each node there are also soft processes that may miss their deadlines during extreme conditions. Copies of these soft processes could be held on each node so that a potential overload could be tolerated by moving some form of process-control block (containing state information) between nodes.

This is a general approach; whether it is appropriate for any particular application would depend on the characteristics of the application and the hardware on which it is implemented. It would be necessary to make sure that a deadline would not be missed by an even greater margin as a result of migration. This behaviour, which is part of the phenomenon known as 'bottleneck migration', can dictate the use of a strategy that precludes migration. After all, transient overloads are indeed 'transient' and so, some form of local recovery may be more desirable.

Remote procedure calls

The above analysis implies that a program is configured between processors (or nodes) using the partitioning (although they may be contained in virtual nodes). Access to remote resources is via shared memory, under the control of a remote critical section. It has been shown that execution of such critical sections must be undertaken at a high priority if remote blocking is to be minimized. An application may, however, choose to distribute a process between more than one processor. If this is done then the process can be said to reside on one processor, but its 'thread of control' may pass to another processor. In general, this will be accomplished by remote procedure calls.

The use of a remote procedure introduces yet another form of remote blocking. As with critical sections, remote pre-emption can only be minimized if the procedure is given top priority. The invocation of a remote procedure is undertaken by a surrogate process that is aperiodic in nature. The local scheduler must execute this aperiodic process immediately if remote pre-emption is not to take place. If more than one 'remote' procedure needs to be executed at the same time then some pre-emption is inevitable.

Giving surrogate processes high priorities could lead to transient overload. Therefore, the local scheduler needs to know how important the external process is, in order to decide which deadlines to forfeit.

Remote rendezvous

In most of the discussion so far it has been assumed that critical sections are protected by some low-level primitive. Remote access can, therefore, be accommodated by using a remote procedure that contains the necessary calls to the local primitives. With high-level languages the critical section will be embedded in a server process. Usage of the critical section is undertaken by this server on behalf of client processes. Requests take the form of interprocess communications (for example, rendezvous). To access a remote server process requires some sort of remote call. This could take the form of a procedure activation but could also be a remote rendezvous.

Where critical sections are embodied in processes then remote preemption is minimized, but only if these server processes are given higher priorities than other processes.

Scheduling access to communications networks

Communication between processes on different machines in a distributed system requires messages to be transmitted and received on the underlying communication subsystem. In general, these messages will have to compete with each other in order to gain access to the network medium (for example, a bus or ring). In order for hard real-time processes to meet their deadlines it will be necessary to schedule access to the communication subsystem in a manner which is consistent with the scheduling of processes on each processor. If this is not the case then priority inversion may occur when a high-priority process tries to access the communications network. Standard protocols such as those associated with an Ethernet or token ring do not support real-time hard deadline traffic as they tend to queue messages in a FIFO order (Sha and Lehoczky, 1986).

Although the communication channel is just another resource, there are at least four issues which distinguish the channel-scheduling problem from processor scheduling (Stankovic, 1988, Sha and Lehoczky, 1986).

(1)   Unlike a processor, which has a single point of access, a communications channel has many points of access – one for each attached physical node. Therefore, a distributed protocol is required.

(2)   While pre-emptive algorithms are appropriate for scheduling processes on a single processor, pre-emption during message transmission will mean that the entire message will need retransmitting.

(3)   In addition to the deadlines imposed by the application processes, deadlines may also be imposed by buffer availability – the contents of a buffer must be transmitted before new data can be placed in it.

(4)   In processor scheduling it is common to use the concept of priority to distinguish hard real-time processes from soft ones. Furthermore, it is usually assumed that the scheduler can support a sufficient range of priority levels, say to support rate-monotonic scheduling. For some communications networks (for example, buses) only a limited number of distinct priority levels are allowed to resolve bus contention.

Currently, little work has been carried out on the use of communication networks in a hard real-time environment. Typically, *ad hoc* approaches are taken; a notable exception is the work by Sha and Lehoczky (1986) who have investigated the behaviour of the rate-monotonic scheduling algorithm in the context of bus scheduling.

SUMMARY

This chapter defined a distributed computer system to be a collection of autonomous processing elements, cooperating in a common purpose or to achieve a common goal. Some of the issues which arise when considering distributed applications raise fundamental questions that go beyond simple aspects of implementation. They are: partitioning and configuration, reliability, distributed control algorithms and deadline scheduling.

Partitioning and configuration

At some point during design and implementation, the application must be partitioned and configured for execution on the target system. Two basic approaches were identified: a single program approach and a multi-program approach. With the former, the application is written as a single program and then partitioned into fragments which communicate using normal intra-program communication mechanisms. In the latter, the application is written as a collection of separate programs, one for each machine in the target system. These programs communicate and synchronize their activities using an underlying distributed operating system.

Within the single program approach two general strategies were identified: post-partitioning (partitioning the program after it has been written) and pre-partitioning (selecting particular language constructs as the sole units of partitioning, to be used throughout the design and programming process).

The notion underlying pre-partitioning is that of a virtual node, which is an abstraction of a physical node in the distributed system. Virtual node-type constructs can be found in most languages which have been designed with the specific intent of supporting distributed programming (for example, the 'group module' in CONIC, and the 'resource' in SR). Occam 2, although designed for use in a distributed environment, is fairly low level; it is, therefore, difficult to identify a virtual node precisely. In one sense, all top-level processes are potential virtual nodes as they can only communicate using message passing. In the case of Ada, there is much controversy as to how the language should be used; two approaches were compared. Modula-2 was designed for a single-processor system; it can be used for programming distributed systems but only by modifying some of the language concepts.

Reliability

Although the availability of multiple processors enables the application to become tolerant of processor failure, it also introduces the possibility of new types of faults occurring which would not be present in a centralized single-processor system. In particular, multiple processors introduce the concept of a partial system failure. Furthermore, the communication media may lose, corrupt, or change the order of, messages.

Communication between processes across machine boundaries requires layers of protocols so that transient error conditions can be tolerated. Standards have been defined over the last decade by the International Standards Organization and involve the concept of Open Systems Interconnections (OSI). The OSI Reference Model is a layered model consisting of the application, presentation, session transport, network, data link and physical layers. It was developed, primarily, for wide-area networks, to enable open access; wide-area networks are characterized by low-bandwidth communication with high error rates. Most distributed embedded systems will, however, use local-area network technology and will be closed to the outside world. Local-area networks are characterized by high-bandwidth communication with low error rates. Consequently, although it is possible to implement language-level inter-process communication using the OSI approach, in practice, the expense is often prohibitive. Consequently, many designers tailor the communication protocols to the requirements of the language (the application) and the communication medium. These are called lightweight protocols.

Processor failure can be tolerated through static or dynamic redundancy. If an application is designed using virtual nodes then it is possible to replicate virtual nodes statically on different processors. Replicating at the virtual-node level enables the system designer to vary the degree of replication according to the importance of a particular virtual node. One of the problems of providing fault-tolerance transparently to the application is that it is impossible for the programmer to specify degraded or safe execution. The alternative to static redundancy and replicating virtual nodes is to allow processor failure to be handled dynamically by the application programmer. This requires: the failure of the processor to be detected and communicated to the remaining processors in the system; the damage that has occurred must then be assessed; using these results the remaining software must agree on a response and carry out the necessary actions to effect that response; and, as soon as is practicable, the failed processor and/or its associated software must be repaired and the system returned to its normal error-free state. Few of the real-time programming languages provide adequate facilities to cope with dynamic reconfiguration after processor failure.

Distributed control algorithms

The presence of true parallelism in an application, together with physically distributed processors and the possibility that processors and communication links may fail, require many new algorithms for resource control. The following algorithms were considered: event ordering, stable storage implementation, Byzantine agreement protocols, distributed mutual exclusion, distributed deadlock detection and distributed two-phase commit protocols. Many distributed algorithms assume that processors are 'failstop', this means either they work correctly, or they halt immediately when a fault occurs.

Deadline scheduling

Unfortunately, the general problem of dynamically allocating processes to processors (so that system-wide deadlines are met) is computationally expensive. It is, therefore, necessary to implement a less flexible allocation scheme. One rigid approach is to deploy all processes statically or to allow only the non-critical ones to migrate.

In order to prohibit a local process from being unduly blocked by remote activity, a number of techniques were discussed. These methods all attempt to give an upper bound on the time a process can be delayed by remote blocking.

Further reading

Atkinson C., Moreton T. and Natali A. (1988). *Ada for Distributed Systems*. Ada Companion Series. Cambridge: Cambridge University Press

Bernstein P.A., Hadzilacos V. and Goodman N. (1987). *Concurrency Control and Recovery in Database Systems*. Reading MA: Addison-Wesley

Ceri S. and Pelagatti G. (1985). *Distributed Databases Principles and Systems*. Singapore: McGraw-Hill

Chambers F.B., Duce D.A. and Jones G.P., eds. (1984). *Distributed Computing*. APIC Studies in Data Processing No. 20. London: Academic Press

Coulouris G.F. and Dollimore F. (1988). *Distributed Systems, Concepts and Design*. Wokingham: Addison-Wesley

Duce D.A., ed. (1984). *Distributed Computing Systems Programme*. IEE Digital Electronic and Computing Series. London: Peter Peregrinus

Halsall F. (1988). *Data Communications, Computer Networks and OSI* 2nd edn. Wokingham: Addison-Wesley

Keeffe D., Tomlinson G.M., Wand I.C. and Wellings A.J. (1985). *PULSE: An Ada-based Distributed Operating System*. APIC Studies in Data Processing Series. London: Academic Press

Lampson B.W., Paul M., and Siegert H.J., eds. (1981). *Distributed Systems Architecture and Implementation*. Berlin: Springer-Verlag

Mok A.K. (1983). Fundamental design problems of distributed systems for hard real-time environments. *PhD Thesis*, Laboratory for Computer Science, MIT/LCS/TR-297

Needham R.M. and Herbert A.J. (1982). *The Cambridge Distributed Computing System*. London: Addison-Wesley

Northcutt J.D. (1987). *Mechanisms for Reliable Distributed Real-Time Operating Systems: The Alpha Kernel*. Orlando FL: Academic Press

Perrott R.H. (1987). *Parallel Programming*. Wokingham: Addison-Wesley

Popek G.J. and Walker B.J. (1985). *The LOCUS Distributed System Architecture*. Cambridge MA: The MIT Press

Raynal M. (1988). *Distributed Algorithms and Protocols*. Chichester: John Wiley

Sloman M. and Kramer J. (1987). *Distributed Systems and Computer Networks*. Hemel Hempstead: Prentice-Hall

Tanenbaum A.S. (1988). *Computer Networks*. Hemel Hempstead: Prentice-Hall

Tanenbaum A.S., and van Renesse R. (1985). Distributed operating systems. *ACM Computing Surveys*, **17**(4), 419–70

Zedan H.S.M., ed. (1989). *Distributed Systems Theory and Practice*. London: Butterworth Scientific

EXERCISES

13.1   Discuss some of the *disadvantages* of distributed systems.

13.2   Discuss the extent to which a single Ada program can be distributed across a network using the virtual node approach without compiler support.

13.3   From a data abstraction viewpoint discuss why variables should not be visible in a virtual node interface.

13.4   To what extent can Ada virtual node types be simulated with a task type declared in a template package, and with the ability to pass task access pointers across the network? Can the same approach be applied to Modula-2 (given the appropriate language modifications discussed in this chapter).

13.5   Discuss the meaning of Ada's timed and conditional entry calls in a distributed environment. (Hint: see Volz and Mudge (1987)).

13.6   The following occam 2 process has five input channels and three output channels. All integers received down the input channels are output to all output channels:

```
INT I,J,temp:
WHILE TRUE
  ALT I = 1 FOR 5
    in[I] ? temp
      PAR J = 1 FOR 3
        out[J] ! temp
```

Because this process has an eight-channel interface it cannot be implemented on a single transputer unless its client processes are on the same transputer. Transform the code so that it can be implemented on three transputers. (Note, a transputer has only four links.)

13.7 Sketch the layers of communication that are involved when the French delegate at the United Nations Security Council wishes to talk to the Russian delegate. Assume that there are interpreters who translate into a common language (say, English) and then pass on the message to telephone operators. Does this layered communication follow the ISO OSI model?

13.8 Why do the semantics of remote procedure calls differ from the semantics of ordinary procedure calls?

13.9 You are asked to implement a remote procedure call facility using the OSI network layer. Would you prefer a datagram service or a virtual circuit?

13.10 What would be the implications if the Ada language was to define that tasks which were executing on failed processors are deemed to be aborted? (Hint: consider tasks hierarchies which are distributed across a network.)

13.11 Compare and contrast the stable storage and replicated data approaches for achieving reliable system data which will survive a processor failure.

13.12 Redo the Byzantine generals problem given in Section 13.8.3 with G1 as the traitor, G2 concluding retreat, G3 concluding wait and G4 concluding attack.

13.13 You are given the choice between an Ethernet and a token ring as the communication subsystem for a real-time distributed system. Which would you use if you were concerned with deterministic access under heavy loads?

Chapter 14
Low-level Programming

One of the main characteristics of an embedded system is the requirement that it interacts with special-purpose input and output devices. Unfortunately, there are many different types of device interfaces and control mechanisms. This is mainly because: different computers provide different methods of interfacing with devices; different devices have separate requirements for their control; and identical devices from different manufacturers have different interfaces and control requirements.

In order to provide a rationale for the high-level language facilities needed to program low-level devices, it is necessary to understand the basic hardware input/output functions. Therefore, this chapter considers these mechanisms first, then deals with language features in general, and, finally, gives details of particular languages.

14.1   Hardware input/output mechanisms

In this section, an overview of hardware input and output facilities is given. The analysis is based on that given by Perry (1978).

As far as input and output devices are concerned there are two general classes of computer architecture: one with a logically separate bus for memory and input/output (I/O) and the other with memory and I/O devices on the same logical bus. These are represented, diagrammatically, in Figures 14.1 and 14.2.

The interface to a device is normally through a set of registers. With logically separate buses for memory and I/O devices, the computer must have two sets of assembly instructions: one for accessing memory and one for accessing device registers. The latter normally takes the form of:

    IN   AC, PORT
    OUT   AC, PORT

Where IN reads the contents of the device register identified by PORT into the accumulator AC, and OUT writes the contents of the accumulator to the device register. (The term PORT is used here to indicate an address on the I/O device bus.) There may also be other instructions for reading a device's status. The Zilog Z80 is an example of such an architecture, although it uses the same physical bus.

With devices on the same logical bus, certain addresses will access a memory location and others will access a device. This approach is called **memory mapped I/O**. The LSI-11 and the Motorola M68000 computers have memory mapped I/O.

It is necessary to interface with a device in order to: control the device's operations (for example, initializing the device, and preparing the device for the transfer of data) and to control the data transfer (for example, initiating or performing the data transfer). It is possible to describe two general mechanisms for performing and controlling input/output. These are: status-driven control mechanisms and interrupt-driven control mechanisms.

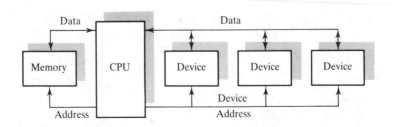

Figure 14.1 Architecture with separate buses.

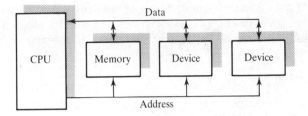

Figure 14.2   Memory-mapped architecture.

14.1.1   Status driven

With this type of input/output control mechanism, a program performs explicit tests in order to determine the status of a given device. Once the status of the device has been determined the program is able to carry out the appropriate actions. Typically, there are three kinds of hardware instructions that support this type of mechanism. These are:

(1)   test operations that enable the program to determine the status of the given device;

(2)   control operations that direct the device to perform non-transfer device-dependent actions such as positioning read heads;

(3)   I/O operations that perform the actual transfer of data between the device and the CPU.

Although devices with status-driven I/O were common a few years ago, as they were inexpensive, nowadays, because of the continuing decrease in hardware cost, most devices are interrupt driven. However, interrupts can, of course, be turned off and polling of device status used instead.

14.1.2   Interrupt driven

Even with this input/output mechanism, there are many possible variations depending on how the transfers need to be initiated and controlled. Three of these variations are: interrupt-driven program-controlled, interrupt-driven program-initiated, and interrupt-driven channel-program controlled.

Interrupt-driven program-controlled

Here, a device requests an interrupt as a result of encountering certain events, for example, the arrival of data. When the request is acknowledged, the processor suspends the executing process and invokes a designated interrupt-handling process which performs appropriate actions in response to the interrupt. When the interrupt-handling process has performed its function, the state of the processor is restored to its state prior to the interrupt, and control of the processor is returned to the suspended process.

Interrupt-driven program-initiated

This type of input-output mechanism is often referred to as **Direct Memory Access** (DMA). A DMA device is positioned between the input/output device and main memory. The DMA device takes the place of the processor in the transferral of data between the I/O device and memory. Although the I/O is initiated by the program, the actual transfers of data are controlled by the DMA device (one block at a time). For each piece of data to be transferred a request is made by the DMA device for a memory cycle and the transfer is made when the request is granted. When the transfer of the entire block is completed, a *transfer complete* interrupt is generated by the device. This is handled by the interrupt-driven program-controlled mechanism.

Interrupt-driven channel-program controlled

Channel-program controlled input/output extends the concept of program initiated input/output by eliminating, as much as possible, the involvement of the central processor in the handling of I/O devices. The mechanism consists of three major components: the hardware channel and connected devices, the channel program, and the input/output instructions.

The hardware channel's operations include those of the DMA devices given above. In addition, the channel directs device-control operations as instructed by the channel program. The execution of channel programs is initiated from within the application. Once a channel has been instructed to execute a channel program, the selected channel and device proceed independently of the central processor, until the specified channel program has been completed or some exceptional condition has occurred. Channel programs normally consist of one or more channel control words which are decoded and executed one at a time by the channel.

14.1.3   Elements required for interrupt-driven devices

As can be seen from the foregoing section the role of interrupts in controlling input/output is an important one. They allow input/output to be performed asynchronously and so avoid the 'busy waiting' or constant status-checking that is necessary if a purely status-controlled mechanism is used.

In order to support interrupt-driven input and output, the following mechanisms are required.

Context-switching mechanisms

When an interrupt occurs, the current processor state must be preserved and the appropriate service routine activated. Once the interrupt has been serviced, the original process is resumed and execution continues. Alternatively, a new process may be selected by the scheduler as a consequence of the interrupt. This whole process is known as *context switching* and its actions can be summarized as follows.

- Preserving the state of the processor immediately prior to the occurrence of the interrupt.
- Placing the processor in the required state for processing the interrupt.
- Restoring the suspended process state after the interrupt processing has been completed.

The state of the process executing on a processor consists of:

- The memory address of the current (or next) instruction in the execution sequence.
- The program status information (this may contain information concerning the mode of processing, current priority, memory protection, allowed interrupts, and so on).
- The contents of the programmable registers.

The type of context switching provided can be characterized by the extent of the process-state preservation, and restoration that is performed by the hardware. Three levels of context switching can be distinguished:

(1)   basic – just the program counter is saved;

(2)   partial – the program counter and the program status word are saved;

(3)   complete – full context of the process is saved.

Depending on the degree of processor-state preservation required it may be necessary to supplement the actions of the hardware by explicit software support.

Interrupting device identification

Devices differ in the way they must be controlled; consequently, they will require different interrupt-handling routines. In order to invoke the appropriate handler, some means of identifying the interrupting device must exist. Four interrupting device identification mechanisms can be distinguished: vectored, status, polling and high-level language primitive.

A **vectored** mechanism for identifying the interrupting device consists of a set of dedicated (and usually contiguous) memory locations called an interrupt vector and a hardware mapping of device addresses onto the interrupt vector.

An interrupt vector may be used by one particular device or may be shared by several devices. The programmer must associate a particular interrupt vector location explicitly with an interrupt service routine. This may be done either by setting the vector location to the address of the service routine, or by setting it to an instruction that causes a branch to occur to the required routine. In this way the service routine is directly tied to an interrupt vector location, which, in turn, is indirectly tied to a device or set of devices. Therefore, when a particular service routine is invoked and executed, the interrupting device has been implicitly identified.

A **status** mechanism for identifying an interrupting device is used for machine configurations on which several devices are connected to a device controller and they do not have unique interrupt vectors. It is also used in the case where a generalized service routine will initially handle all interrupts. With this mechanism, each interrupt has an associated status word which specifies the device causing the interrupt and the reason for the interrupt (among other things). The status information may be provided automatically by the hardware in a dedicated memory location for a given interrupt or class of interrupts, or it may need to be retrieved by means of some appropriate instruction.

The **polling** device identification mechanism is the simplest of all. When an interrupt occurs, a general interrupt service routine is invoked to handle the interrupt. The status of each device is interrogated in order to determine which device has requested the interrupt. When the interrupting device has been identified the interrupt is serviced in the appropriate manner.

With some modern computer architectures, interrupt handling is directly associated with a **high-level language primitive**. With these systems an interrupt is often viewed as a synchronization message down an associated channel. In this case, the device is identified by the channel which becomes active.

Interrupt identification

Once the device has been identified, the appropriate interrupt-handling routine must determine why it generated the interrupt. In general, this can be supplied by either, status information provided by the device, or by having different interrupts from the same device occurring through different vectored locations or channels.

Interrupt control

Once a device is switched on and has been initialized, although it may be able to produce interrupts, they will be ignored unless the device has had its interrupts enabled. This control (enabling/disabling) of interrupts may be performed by means of the following interrupt-control mechanisms.

Status interrupt control mechanisms provide flags, in either an interrupt state table or via device and program status words, to enable and disable the interrupts. The flags are accessible (and may be modified) by normal bit-oriented instructions or special bit-testing instructions.

Mask interrupt control mechanisms associate device interrupts with particular locations in an interrupt mask word. The interrupt mask word may be addressable by normal bit-oriented (or word-oriented) instructions or may be accessible only through special interrupt masking instructions.

Level interrupt control mechanisms have devices associated with certain levels. The current level of the processor determines which devices may or may not interrupt. Only those devices with a higher logical level may interrupt. When the highest logical level is active, only those interrupts which cannot be disabled (for example, power fail) are allowed. This does not explicitly disable interrupts and, so, interrupts at a lower logical level than the current processor level will still be generated, and will not need to be re-enabled when the processor level falls appropriately.

Priority control

Some devices have higher urgency than others and, therefore, a priority facility is often associated with interrupts. This mechanism may be static or dynamic and is usually related to the device-interrupt control facility and the priority levels of the processor.

14.1.4 A simple example of an input/output system

In order to illustrate the various components of an I/O system, a simple machine is described. It is loosely based on the LSI-11 and Motorola 68000 series of computers.

Each device which is supported on the machine has as many different types of registers as are necessary for its operation. These 16-bit registers are memory mapped. The most common types used are: **Control and Status Registers** (CSRs) which contain all the information on a device's status, and allow the device's interrupts to be enabled and disabled. **Data Buffer Registers** (DBRs) act as buffer registers for temporarily storing data which is to be transferred into or out of the machine via the device.

A typical control and status register for the machine has the following structure:

```
bits
15 - 12 : Errors            -- set when device errors occur
11      : Busy              -- set when the device is busy
10 - 8  : Unit select       -- where more than one device is being
                            -- controlled
7       : Done/ready        -- I/O completed or device ready
6       : Interrupt enable  -- when set enables interrupts
5 - 3   : reserved          -- reserved for future use
2 - 1   : Device function   -- set to indicate required function
0       : Device enable     -- set to enable the device
```

The typical structure of a data buffer register used for a character-orientated device is:

```
bits
15 - 8 : Unused
 7 - 0 : Data
```

A device may have more than one of each of these registers, the exact number being dependent on the nature of the device.

Interrupts allow devices to notify the processor when they require service; they are vectored. When an interrupt occurs, the processor stores the current Program Counter (PC) and the current Program Status Word (PSW) on the system stack. The PSW will contain, among other things, the processor priority. Its actual layout is given below:

```
bits
15 - 11 : Mode information
10 -  8 : Unused
 7 -  5 : Priority
 4 -  0 : Condition codes
```

The condition codes contain information on the result of the last processor operation.

The new PC and PSW are loaded from two pre-assigned consecutive memory locations (the interrupt vector). The first word contains the address of the interrupt service routine and the second contains the PSW including the priority at which the interrupt is to be handled. A low-priority interrupt handler can be interrupted by a higher-priority interrupt.

This example I/O system will be returned to in Section 14.3.3.

14.2 Language requirements

As noted in the previous section, one of the main characteristics of an embedded system is the need to interact with input and output devices, all of which have their particular characteristics. The programming of such devices has traditionally been the stronghold of the assembly-language programmer, but languages like Ada, Modula-1, Modula-2 and occam 2 have now attempted to provide high-level mechanisms for these low-level functions. This makes device driving and interrupt-handling routines easier to read, write and maintain. A major difficulty, however, lies in deciding what features are required in a high-level language in order to program usable device handlers conveniently. Although the subject is still not well understood we can identify *encapsulation facilities* and an *abstract model* of device handling as being particular requirements (Young, 1982).

14.2.1 Modularity and encapsulation facilities

Low-level device interfacing is necessarily machine dependent and, therefore, not portable. In any software system it is important to separate the non-portable sections of code from the portable ones. Wherever possible, it is advisable to encapsulate all the machine-dependent code into units which are clearly identifiable. In Modula-1 and Modula-2 the unit of encapsulation is the *module*. However, as will be shown in Section 14.3.2, the Modula-2 approach to interrupt handling is somewhat inelegant. With Modula-1, the code associated with devices must be encapsulated into a *device module*. In Ada the package is used. In occam 2 the only facility is the PROC.

14.2.2 An abstract model of device handling

A device can be considered to be a processor performing a fixed task. A computer system can, therefore, be modelled as several parallel processes which need to communicate and synchronize. Synchronization is provided by the interrupt. Chapters 7, 8 and 9 showed how communication and synchronization between processes can be achieved either by shared memory or by message passing. Both of these models may be applied to device handling.

14.3 The shared-memory model of device handling

In this model, processes communicate using shared device registers with the interrupt providing the synchronization. Its implementation requires the following.

(1)   *Facilities for addressing and manipulating device registers*; This requires the ability to associate a variable in the program with a physical location in memory, normally the I/O register itself. Where registers have an internal structure it should be possible to represent this as a user-defined record structure. If the device registers are accessed using special instructions, the read and write operations on the program defined variables must be translated to the appropriate I/O instructions.

(2)   *A suitable representation of interrupts*; An interrupt is normally mapped onto the condition synchronization primitive provided by the concurrent programming language.

14.3.1 Modula-1

Modula-1 was one of the first high-level programming languages which had facilities for programming device drivers. Although Modula-2 has succeeded Modula-1, its model of device driving is not as elegant. Modula-2 will be considered in Section 14.3.2, here, attention is focused on Modula-1.

In Modula-1 the unit of modularity and encapsulation is the module. A special type of module, called an *interface module*, which has the properties of a monitor, is used to control access to shared resources. Process interact via signals (condition variable) using the operators WAIT, SEND and AWAITED (see Chapter 8). A third type of module, called a *device module* is a special type of interface module used to encapsulate the interaction with a device. It is only from within a device module that the facilities for handling interrupts and manipulating device registers can be used.

Addressing and manipulating device registers

Associating a variable with a register is fairly straightforward. In Modula-1 this is expressed by an octal address following the name in a declaration. For example, a data buffer register for the simple I/O architecture described in Section 14.1.4 would be defined as:

```
VAR rdbr[177562B] CHAR;
```

where 177562B denotes an octal address which is the location of the register in memory.

The mapping of a character into a character buffer register is also a straightforward activity, since the type has no internal structure. A control and status register is more interesting. In Modula-1, only scalar data types can be mapped onto a device register; consequently, registers which have internal structures are considered to be of the predefined type BITS whose definition is:

```
TYPE bits = ARRAY 0 : no_of_bits_in_word OF BOOLEAN;
```

Variables of this type are packed into a single word. A control and status register at octal address 177560 can therefore be defined by the following Modula-1 code:

```
VAR rcsr[177560B] : BITS;
```

To access the various fields in the register an index into the array is supplied by the programmer. For example, the following code will enable the device:

```
rcsr[0] := TRUE;
```

and the following turns off interrupts:

```
rcsr[6] :=FALSE;
```

In general, these facilities are not powerful enough to handle all types of register conveniently. The general structure of the control and status register was given in Section 14.1.4:

```
bits
  15 - 12  : Errors
  11       : Busy
  10 - 8   : Unit select
  7        : Done/ready
  6        : Interrupt enable
  5 - 3    : reserved
  2 - 1    : Device function
  0        : Device enable
```

To set the selected unit (bits 8–10) using Boolean values is very clumsy. For example, the following statements set the device unit to the value 5.

```
rcsr[10] := TRUE;
rcsr[9] := FALSE;
rcsr[8] := TRUE;
```

It is worth noting that, on many machines, more than one device register can be mapped to the same physical address. Consequently, several variables may be mapped to the same location in memory. Furthermore, these registers are often read-or write-only. Therefore, care must be taken when manipulating device registers. In the above example, if the control and status register was a pair of registers mapped to the same location, the code presented will probably not have the desired affect. This is because, to set a particular bit may require code to be generated which reads the current value into the machine accumulator. As the control register is write-only, this would produce the value of the status register. It is advisable, therefore, to have other variables in a program which represent device registers. These can be manipulated in the normal way. When the required register format has been constructed it may then be assigned to the actual device register. Such variables are often called *shadow device registers*.

Interrupt handling

The facilities for handling interrupts in Modula-1 are based around the concept of an ideal hardware device. This device has the following properties (Wirth, 1977a).

- Each device operation is known to produce, either no interrupt or at least one.
- After an interrupt has occurred, the device status indicates whether or not another interrupt will occur.
- No interrupt arrives unexpectedly.
- Each device has a unique interrupt location.

The facilities provided by Modula-1 may be summarized by the following points.

- Each device has an associated *device module*.
- Each device module has a *hardware priority* specified in its header following the module name.
- *All code within the module executes at the specified hardware priority*.
- Each interrupt to be handled within a device module requires a process called a device process.
- When the device process is executing it has sole access to the module (that is, it holds the monitor lock).
- A *device process* is not allowed to call any non-local procedures and cannot send signals to other device processes. This is to ensure that device processes will not be blocked inadvertently.
- When a device process sends a signal, the semantics of the SEND operation are different from those for ordinary processes; in this case, the receiving process is not resumed but the signalling process continues. Again, this is to ensure that the process is not blocked.

- WAIT statements within device processes may only be of rank one (highest level).

- An interrupt is considered to be a form of signal, the device process, however, instead of issuing a WAIT request issues a DOIO request.

- The address of the vector through which the device interrupts is specified in the header of the process.

- *Only device processes can contain DOIO statements*.

- DOIO and WAIT calls lower the processor priority and, therefore, release the monitor lock.

- Only one instance of a device process may be activated.

For example, consider a device module which handles a real-time clock for the simple machine architecture outlined in Section 14.1.4. On receipt of an interrupt, the handler sends a signal to a process which is waiting for the clock to tick.

```
DEVICE MODULE rtc[6];            (* hardware priority 6 *)

  DEFINE tick;
  VAR tick : SIGNAL;

  PROCESS clock[100B];
    VAR csr[177546B] : BITS;
  BEGIN
    csr[6] := TRUE;              (* enable interrupts *)
    LOOP
      DOIO;
      WHILE AWAITED(tick) DO
        SEND(tick);
      END
    END
  END;
BEGIN
  clock;                         (* create one instance of the clock process *)
END rtc;
```

The heading of the device module specifies an interrupt priority of 6, at which, all code within the module will be executed. The value 100B on the process header indicates that the device will interrupt through the vector at address (octal) 100. After enabling interrupts, the device process enters a simple loop of waiting for an interrupt (the DOIO) and then sending sufficient signals (that is, one per waiting process). Note that the device process does not give up its mutually exclusive access to the module when it sends a signal, but continues until it executes the DOIO statement.

The following illustrates how Modula-1 deals with the general characteristics of an interrupt-driven device which were outlined in Sections 14.1.2 and 14.1.3.

- *Device control*: I/O registers are represented by variables.
- *Context switching*: The interrupt causes an immediate context switch to the interrupt handling process, which waits using the DOIO.
- *Interrupt device identification*: The address of the interrupt vector is given with the device process's header.
- *Interrupt identification*: In the above example only one interrupt was possible. In general, however, the device status register should be checked to identify the cause of the interrupt.
- *Interrupt control*: The interrupt control is status driven and provided by a flag in the device register.
- *Priority control*: The priority of the device is given in the device module header. *All* code in the module runs at this priority.

An example of a terminal driver

To illustrate further the Modula-1 approach to device driving, a simple terminal device module is presented in Program 14.1. The terminal has two components: a display and a keyboard. Each component has an associated control and status register, a buffer register and an interrupt.

Two procedures are provided in order to allow other processes in the program to read and write characters. These procedures access a bounded buffer to allow characters to be typed ahead for input, and buffered for output. These buffers must be included in the device module

Program 14.1

```
DEVICE MODULE terminal[4];

DEFINE readch, writech;

CONST n = 64;                         (* buffer size *)

VAR KBS[177560B]: BITS;               (* keyboard status *)
    KBB[177562B]: CHAR;               (* keyboard buffer *)
    DPS[177564B]: BITS;               (* display status *)
    DPB[177566B]: CHAR;               (* display buffer *)
    in1, in2, out1, out2 : INTEGER;
    n1, n2 : INTEGER;
    nonfull1, nonfull2,
    nonempty1, nonempty2 : SIGNAL;
    buf1, buf2 : ARRAY 1:n OF CHAR;
```

```
PROCEDURE readch(VAR ch : CHAR);
  BEGIN
    IF n1 = 0 THEN WAIT(nonempty1) END;
    ch := buf1[out1];
    out1 := (out1 MOD n) + 1;
    DEC(n1);
    SEND(nonfull1)
END readch;


PROCEDURE writech(ch : CHAR);
BEGIN
    IF n2 = n THEN WAIT(nonfull2) END;
    buf2[in2] := ch;
    in2 := (in2 MOD n) + 1;
    INC(n2);
    SEND(nonempty2)
END writech;


PROCESS keyboarddriver[60B];
BEGIN
  LOOP
    IF n1 = n THEN WAIT(nonfull1) END;
    KBS[6] := TRUE;
    DOIO;
    KBS[6] := FALSE;
    buf1[in1] := KBB;
    in1 := (in1 MOD n)+1;
    INC(n1);
    SEND(nonempty1)
  END
END keyboarddriver;


PROCESS displaydriver[64B];
BEGIN
  LOOP
    IF n2 = 0 THEN WAIT(nonempty2) END;
    DPB := buf2[out2];
    out2 := (out2 MOD n) + 1;
    DPS[6] := TRUE;
    DOIO;
    DPS[6] := FALSE;
    DEC(n2);
    SEND(nonfull2)
  END
END displaydriver;
```

Program 14.1   (cont.)

```
BEGIN
   in1 := 1; in2 := 1;
   out1 := 1; out2 := 1;
   n1 := 0; n2 := 0;
   keyboarddriver;
   displaydriver
END terminal.
```

because device processes *cannot* call non-local procedures. Although separate modules for the display and keyboard could have been used, they
have been combined to illustrate that a device module can handle more
than one interrupt.

Timing facilities

As mentioned in Chapter 12, Modula-1 provides no direct facilities for
manipulating time; these have to be provided by the application. In that
chapter an interface module was given, SystemClock, which maintained the
time of day. This required a device module which handles the clock
interrupt and then issues a signal every second. This module is now
presented; it is a modified version of the one previously defined in Section
12.1.3. The hardware clock is assumed to tick every fiftieth of a second.

```
DEVICE MODULE hardwareclock[6];
   DEFINE tick;
   VAR tick : SIGNAL;
   PROCESS handler[100B];
      VAR count : INTEGER;
         statusreg[177546B] : BITS;
   BEGIN
     count := 0;
     statusreg[6] := TRUE;
     LOOP
       DOIO;
       count := (count + 1) MOD 50;
       IF count = 0 THEN
         WHILE AWAITED(tick) DO
           SEND(tick)
         END
       END
     END
   END handler;
BEGIN
   driver
END hardwareclock;
```

Program 14.2

```
INTERFACE MODULE SystemClock;
(* defined procedures for getting and setting the time of day *)
DEFINE GetTime, SetTime;

(* import the abstract data type time, and the tick signal *)
USE time, initialize, add, tick;

VAR TimeOfDay, onesec : time;

PROCEDURE SetTime(t : time);
BEGIN
  TimeOfDay := t;
END SetTime;

PROCEDURE GetTime(VAR t : time);
BEGIN
  t := TimeOfDay
END GetTime;

PROCESS clock;
BEGIN
  LOOP
    WAIT(tick);
    addtime(systemtime, onesec)
  END
END clock;
BEGIN
  inittime(systemtime, 0, 0, 0);
  inittime(onesec, 0, 0, 1);
  clock;
END SystemClock;
```

The interface module which maintains the time of day (from Chapter 12) is given in Program 14.2.

Note that the clock process is logically redundant. The device process could increment systemtime directly, thereby saving a context switch. However, it is not allowed in Modula-1 for a device process to call a non-local procedure.

Delaying a process

In real-time systems it is often necessary to delay a process for a period (see Chapter 12). Although Modula-1 has no direct facilities for achieving this, they can be programmed. This is left as an exercise for the reader (see Exercise 14.5).

Problems with the Modula-1 approach to device driving

Modula-1 was designed to attack the stronghold of assembly language programming – that of interfacing to devices. In general, it has been considered a success, however, there are a few criticisms that have been levelled at its facilities:

(1)   Modula-1 does not allow a device process to call a non-local procedure, because device processes must be kept as small as possible and must run at the hardware priority of the device. To call procedures defined in other modules whose implementation is hidden from the process might lead to unacceptable delays. Furthermore, it would require these procedures to execute at the device's priority.

Unfortunately, as a result of this restriction, programmers either have to incorporate extra functionality into a device module which is *not* directly associated with driving the device (as in the terminal driver example, where a bounded buffer was included in the device module), or they have to introduce extra processes to wait for a signal sent by a device process. In the former case this can lead to very large device modules and in the latter, unnecessary inefficiency.

(2)   Modula-1 only allows a single instance of a device process because the process header contains the information necessary to associate the process with the interrupt. This makes the sharing of code between similar devices difficult; the problem is compounded by not being able to call non-local procedures.

(3)   Modula-1 was design for memory-mapped machines and, consequently, it is difficult to use its facilities for programming devices which are controlled by special instructions. However, it is easy to imagine a simple extension to solve this problem. Young (1982) suggests the possibility of using the following notation:

```
VAR x AT PORT 46B : INTEGER;
```

The compiler is then able to recognize when a port is being addressed and can generate the correct instruction.

(4)   It has already been pointed out that many device registers are read- or write-only. It is not possible to define variables that are read- or write-only in Modula-1.

14.3.2 Modula-2

The Modula-2 low-level facilities for programming devices are, as with Modula-1, based on the concepts of an ideal device and memory-mapped I/O.

Addressing and manipulating device registers

As in Modula-1, variables can be associated with memory locations by placing an address in the declaration. Modula-2's equivalent to Modula-1's type BIT is the type BITSET. This is a set of integers between 0 and $N-1$ where N is the number of bits in a word on the machine on which the language is implemented. Objects of this type are packed into a single word and the elements in the set represent the bit position in the word. The normal set operations are allowed, thereby giving bit manipulation facilities. In particular, two standard generic procedures are offered:

```
INCL(s, x)    (* include element x in set s *)
EXCL(s, x)    (* exclude element x from set s *)
```

These can be used to turn bits on and off. For example, the following fragment of code declares a control and status register for a device and turns on interrupts.

```
VAR csr[177546B]: BITSET;

BEGIN
  ...
  INCL(csr, 6);
  ...
END
```

Interrupt handling and device encapsulation

Modula-2 does not have the concept of a process represented in the language, instead, it supports the notion of coroutines and provides a primitive for transferring control between them. It was shown in Chapter 8 how the process concept could be implemented, with semaphores provided for synchronization. Note that when coroutines share data, mutual exclusion is not required as coroutines explicitly transfer control, and therefore, a process in a critical section will never be disturbed.

Unfortunately, as soon as interrupt handling is introduced into the system, the coroutine's automatic provision of mutual exclusion breaks down. If the interrupt-handling routine is itself a coroutine then it may be resumed without an explicit transfer from another coroutine. This means that all other coroutines can no longer assume undisturbed execution. To allow mutual exclusion to be programmed in the presence of interrupts, Modula-2 provides a monitor. This monitor, however, is simply a module with an associated hardware priority; rather like a device module in Modula-1. As all code in the module executes at the hardware priority it can not be interrupted by a device of the same priority. It is this monitor that provides the modularity and encapsulation facility for device programming. Unlike a Modula-1 device module, a monitor can call an external procedure if the procedure is declared in a monitor whose priority is greater than the priority of the caller. A monitor procedure can also call an external procedure if the module in which the procedure is declared has no priority (that is, it is not resident in another monitor). The effect of this on the priority of the processor is as follows:

- If the called procedure is not resident in a monitor, the process's priority is maintained during the execution of the called procedure.

- If the called procedure is resident in a monitor whose priority is higher than the caller's priority, the priority is raised to the higher level for the duration of the call. On exit from the called procedure the process's priority returns to the original priority of the caller.

- If the called procedure is resident in a monitor whose priority is lower than the caller's priority, the call is deemed illegal. The result of such a call is implementation-dependent.

An interrupt is equated to a coroutine switch to the interrupt-handling routine. To be in a position to accept the interrupt, the routine must have executed the Modula-1 equivalent of DOIO. In Modula-2 this is represented by a special coroutine transfer called IOTRANSFER. This has three parameters: the name of the interrupt-handling coroutine, the coroutine to be resumed and the address of the interrupt vector that is associated with the interrupt to be handled. When an interrupt occurs, the currently executing coroutine is assumed to request a transfer to the interrupt-handling coroutine.

To give an example of interrupt handling in Modula-2, recall from Chapter 8 the definition of a module which provides the process abstraction. This module is now modified to provide a process abstraction for interrupt handling. The procedure doio which takes a single parameter, that of the interrupt vector address (the type ADDRESS being imported from the SYSTEM module), is added. Note that this module must now be a monitor as the routines which manipulate semaphores may be called by interrupt handlers. The priority of the module should be the highest priority that is supported by the implementation.

```
DEFINITION MODULE Processes[HighestPriority];

(* This module provides a semaphore based synchronization *)
(* scheme. It also provides a process abstraction. *)

FROM SYSTEM IMPORT ADDRESS;

EXPORT QUALIFIED semaphore, initialize, wait, signal, terminate, idle, startprocess, doio;

TYPE semaphore;
```

```
PROCEDURE initialize (VAR S : semaphore; C : CARDINAL);

PROCEDURE wait (VAR S : semaphore);

PROCEDURE signal (VAR S : semaphore);

PROCEDURE terminate;

PROCEDURE idle;

PROCEDURE startprocess (P : PROC);

PROCEDURE doio(V : ADDRESS);

END Processes.
```

As part of the implementation of this module the procedure doio is needed. When called, the procedure finds the next process to run and then transfers to it using the IOTRANSFER mechanism. The procedure is resumed on an interrupt. The interrupted process is placed into the dispatch queue and the routine returns to handle the interrupt.

```
PROCEDURE doio(V : ADDRESS) ;
(* this procedure choses the next coroutine to *)
(* execute and then issues an I/O transfer *)
VAR
   lastprocess : processid;
BEGIN
   lastprocess := currentprocess;      (* lastprocess is handler *)
   remove(dispatchqueue, currentprocess)     (* get new process *)

   (* run new process and prepare for interrupt *)
   IOTRANSFER(lastprocess ↑ , currentprocess ↑ ,V);
   (* interrupt has occurred *)

   insert(dispatchqueue, currentprocess);
   currentprocess = lastprocess;
END doio;
```

The interrupt handler itself is encapsulated in a monitor. The interface with the handler and the rest of the program can be provided as procedures defined by the monitor. As the monitor executes at the priority of the device, these procedures will not be interrupted. Program 14.3 shows an interrupt handler for a terminal keyboard.

Program 14.3

```
MODULE Keyboard[4]; (* 4 < HighestPriority *)

    FROM Processes IMPORT doio, wait, startprocess, semaphore, signal, initialize;
    EXPORT QUALIFIED take;
    MODULE BUFFER;

      (* must be inside the monitor for mutual exclusion *)

      IMPORT wait, signal, initialize, semaphore;

      EXPORT append, take;

      CONST size = 32;
      TYPE rng = { 0 .. size − 1 }
      VAR
         BUF : ARRAY[0 .. size − 1] OF CHAR;
         top, base : rng;
         SpaceAvailable, ItemAvailable: semaphore;
      PROCEDURE append(I : INTEGER);
      BEGIN
         wait(SpaceAvailable);
         BUF[top] := I;
         top := (top + 1) MOD size;
         signal(ItemAvailable)
      END append;

      PROCEDURE take(VAR I : INTEGER);
      BEGIN
         wait(ItemAvailable);
         I := BUF[base];
         base := (base + 1) MOD size;
         signal(SpaceAvailable)
      END take;

    BEGIN (* BUFFER *)
      top := 0;
      base := 0;
      initialize(SpaceAvailable, size);
      initialize(ItemAvailable, 0)
    END BUFFER;

    VAR
      csr[177560B]: BITSET;      (* control status register *)
      dbr[177562B] : CHAR;       (* data buffer register *)
```

```
PROCEDURE handler;
BEGIN
  LOOP
    INCL(csr, 6);          (* turn interrupts on *);
    doio(60B);
    EXCL(csr, 6);          (* turn interrupts off *)
    append(dbr)            (* store data in buffer *);
  END
END
BEGIN                      (* keyboard *)
  startprocess( handler )
END.
```

This style of handler makes several assumptions:

- If the handler is blocked on the wait call on the semaphore then the hardware priority of the process is lowered. Although the device cannot interrupt, other devices of the same priority can.
- The signal call does not cause a context switch.

Final comments on Modula-2 interrupt-handling facilities

Coroutines are a low-level facility that enable concurrent processes to be implemented on a single-processor system. However, in spite of their great flexibility they have severe limitations when used in a parallel environment. The parallelism introduced by interrupts makes it impossible to provide mutual exclusion between coroutines, particularly if pre-emptive priority-driven scheduling is employed. For these reasons, it is necessary to introduce the monitor into Modula-2. Unfortunately, Modula-2 equates mutual exclusion with processor priority. While this provides adequate support for single-processor systems, it was shown in Chapter 13 that the model cannot be easily applied in a distributed environment.

14.3.3   Ada

Although the Ada rendezvous has been considered to be message-based, tasks can communicate using shared variables. It is this model which is used for interfacing with devices.

Addressing and manipulating device registers

Ada presents the programmer with a comprehensive set of facilities for specifying the implementation of data types. These are collectively known as *representation clauses*; and they indicate how the types of the language are to be mapped onto the underlying hardware. A type can only have a single representation. The representation is specified separately from the logical structure of the type. Of course, the specification of the representation of a type is optional and can be left to the compiler.

A representation clause can be either an *address clause* or a *type representation clause*.

An address clause specifies the required address in memory of a variable, constant, subprogram, task or entry. If I/O registers are memory mapped they can be associated with variables; for example:

```
RDBR : CHARACTER;
for RDBR use at 8#177560#;
```

declares a character data buffer at octal location 177560. Notice the separation of the object's definition from its address.

One of the limitations of the facilities provided by Modula-1 and Modula-2 is the inability to define the representation of user-defined record structures. This is required so that they can be mapped on to device registers, thereby allowing individual components of the register to be accessed by fields in the record. Ada provides such a facility through its type representation clauses. There are three classes: enumeration representation clauses, record representation clauses, and length clauses.

In order to illustrate the use of these mechanisms consider the following type declarations which represent a typical control and status register of the simple machine defined in Section 14.1.4.

```
type ERROR_T is (READ_ERROR, WRITE_ERROR, POWER_FAIL,
                 OTHER);
type FUNCTION_T is (READ, WRITE, SEEK);
type UNIT_T is new INTEGER range 0 .. 7;

type CSR_T is record
   ERRORS  : ERROR_T;
   BUSY    : BOOLEAN;
   UNIT    : UNIT_T;
   DONE    : BOOLEAN;
   IENABLE : BOOLEAN;
   DFUN    : FUNCTION_T;
   DENABLE : BOOLEAN;
end record;
```

An enumeration clause specifies the internal codes for the literals of the enumeration type. For example, the internal binary codes for the function required by the device above may be:

```
01 – READ
10 – WRITE
11 – SEEK
```

In Ada this is specified by:

```
type FUNCTION_T is (READ, WRITE, SEEK);
for FUNCTION_T use (READ ⇒1, WRITE ⇒2, SEEK ⇒3);
```

A record representation clause specifies the storage representation of records; that is, the order, position and size of its components. The bits in the record are numbered from 0; the range in the component clause specifies the number of bits to be allocated. There is also an alignment clause which forces each record of the given type to be on a boundary address.

For example, the control status register is given by:

```
WORD:constant :=2;              -- no. of bytes in a word
for CSR_T use
   record at mod WORD;          -- put on word boundary
      ERRORS  at 0 range 15 .. 12;
      BUSY    at 0 range 11 .. 11;
      UNIT    at 0 range 10 .. 8;
      DONE    at 0 range 7 .. 7;
      IENABLE at 0 range 6 .. 6;
      DFUN    at 0 range 2 .. 1;
      DENABLE at 0 range 0 .. 0;
end record;
```

A length clause specifies the amount of storage that is to be associated with a type. In this example the register is a single 16-bit word; in Ada this can be defined as follows:

```
ONE_WORD : constant := 16;
for CSR_T'SIZE use ONE_WORD;
```

The control and status register can therefore be fully specified by:

```
WORD : constant :=2;            -- bytes in a word
ONE_WORD : constant := 16;      -- bits in a word


type ERROR_T is (READ_ERROR, WRITE_ERROR, POWER_FAIL,
                 OTHER);
type FUNCTION_T is (READ, WRITE, SEEK);
type UNIT_T is new INTEGER range 0 .. 7;
```

```
type CSR_T is record
   ERRORS    : ERROR_T;
   BUSY      : BOOLEAN;
   UNIT      : UNIT_T;
   DONE      : BOOLEAN;
   IENABLE   : BOOLEAN;
   DFUN      : FUNCTION_T;
   DENABLE   : BOOLEAN;
end record;

for ERROR_T use (READ_ERROR ⇒ 1, WRITE_ERROR ⇒ 2,
                 POWER_FAIL ⇒ 3, OTHER ⇒ 4);
for FUNCTION_T use (READ ⇒ 1, WRITE ⇒ 2, SEEK ⇒ 3);

for CSR_T use
   record at mod WORD;              ––put on word boundary
      ERRORS  at 0 range 15 .. 12;
      BUSY    at 0 range 11 .. 11;
      UNIT    at 0 range 10 .. 8;
      DONE    at 0 range 7 .. 7;
      IENABLE at 0 range 6 .. 6;
      DFUN    at 0 range 2 .. 1;
      DENABLE at 0 range 0 .. 0;
end record;

for CSR_T'SIZE use ONE_WORD;
TCSR : CSR_T;
for TCSR use at 8#177566#;
```

Note that bits 3,4 and 5 (which were reserved for future use) have not been specified.

Interrupt handling

In Ada, an interrupt is identified through its association with a particular entry. The association is effected by means of an *address clause* attached to the entry specification; the address clause, whose format is necessarily machine dependent, defines a specific interrupt from a particular source.

When an interrupt occurs, a call is made to the associated entry. When the call is accepted, the rendezvous is executed at a priority higher than that of any user-defined task, thus ensuring that interrupt handling takes precedence over 'normal' processing. The entry call may be viewed as ordinary entry call, a conditional entry call or a timed entry call, depending on the kind of interrupt and on the implementation. Control information associated with the interrupt may be passed to the handling task by the 'in' parameters of the entry. The interrupt handler may enable and disable the interrupt mechanism by modifying the appropriate control registers.

The treatment of interrupt priorities is not well defined. Firstly, the language does not discriminate between the hardware priorities of different interrupts. Such discrimination can be achieved only through implementation-dependent interpretation of information supplied in the address clauses of interrupt entries. Secondly, there is no association between the software priority pragma (and hence, the priority of interrupt handlers) and the hardware priority of the interrupts themselves. Consider, for example, the simple interrupt handler below:

```
task HIGH_PRIORITY_HANDLER is
  entry INTERRUPT;
  for INTERRUPT use at ...;              -- address clause
  pragma PRIORITY(HIGH);                 -- high task priority
end;


task body HIGH_PRIORITY_HANDLER is
begin
  loop
  accept INTERRUPT do
    -- this code is executed at
    -- hardware (highest) priority
  end;
    -- this code is executed at task priority,
    -- allowing low priority devices to interrupt!
  end loop;
end;
```

The handler deals with high-priority interrupts, and is, therefore, allocated a high task priority. However, it can be interrupted outside the rendezvous by a low-priority interrupt, and cannot guarantee to return to the accept statement in time to catch the next high-priority interrupt. Even if there is no code after the rendezvous, the handler is interruptible while returning to the start of the loop. Conversely, if the task is a low-priority handler then once it is handling the interrupt in the accept statement, a higher-priority interrupt could not get through (unless address clause information had been used in the way suggested above).

One solution to this problem is to provide an implementation-defined pragma which relates the priority of the handler to that of the interrupt. The implementation must ensure that the handler always runs at the given hardware priority. Such a solution contravenes the language reference manual (*Ada Language Reference Manual* 13.5.1.2). Alternatively, if the interrupt handler has a sufficiently simple structure it is possible for an optimization to remove the task context and have the accept statement executed directly by the hardware. Consequently, there will be no code remaining to run at the lower priority.

A further problem with interrupt handling in Ada concerns the passing of data from the handler to other consumer tasks. The normal means of communication is the rendezvous, but consider the simple keyboard handler below.

```
task KEYBOARD_HANDLER is
  entry GET(CH : out CHARACTER);
  entry INTERRUPT;
  for INTERRUPT use at KEYBOARD_INTVECT;
  pragma HARDWARE_PRIORITY(4);      -- not strict Ada
end KEYBOARD_HANDLER;

task body KEYBOARD_HANDLER is
  LOCAL_CHAR : CHARACTER;
begin
  loop
    accept INTERRUPT do
      -- take character from input register
      -- and put it in local_char
    end INTERRUPT;
    accept GET(CH : out CHARACTER) do
      CH := LOCAL_CHAR;
    end GET;
  end loop;
end KEYBOARD_HANDLER;
```

The basic defect of this approach is that the interrupt handler may be blocked while waiting for a call to the GET entry. This could be avoided by giving the GET entry an **else** or a **delay** alternative, so that the handler does not wait indefinitely if no call to GET is made. This style of interrupt handler is adequate only if the consumers are known to consume each character faster than the device produces the next one.

Another attempt to solve the problem is given in Program 14.4.

In the solution given in Program 14.4 the interrupt handler maintains a local buffer. When the buffer is full the interrupt is disabled, and when the buffer is empty the get entry is closed. The major defect of the solution is that the interrupt entry may not be accepted if the get entry is also open. The semantics of the select statement do not require the interrupt alternative to be given priority over others. (However, an implementation is free to choose always to accept the interrupt first.) A further defect of the solution in Program 14.4 (and of the previous one) is that it implies a context switch between tasks each time a character is passed from the handler to a consumer. This may result in an unacceptable time penalty. Furthermore, because the interrupt-handling task contains a local environment it is not possible for the run-time support system to optimize the context switch. This again increases the overhead of the approach.

Program 14.4

```
task KEYBOARD_HANDLER is
  entry GET(CH : out CHARACTER);
  entry INTERRUPT;
  for INTERRUPT use at KEYBOARD_INTVECT;
  pragma HARDWARE_PRIORITY(4);     -- not strict Ada
end KEYBOARD_HANDLER;


task body KEYBOARD_HANDLER is
  BUFFSIZE : constant INTEGER := ...;
  type BUFF_T is array (1 .. BUFFSIZE) of CHARACTER;
  BUFFER : BUFF_T;
  COUNT : INTEGER range 0 .. BUFFSIZE := 0;
begin
  loop
    select
      accept INTERRUPT do
        -- take character from input register and put it in buffer
        COUNT := COUNT + 1;
      end INTERRUPT;
    or
      when COUNT > 0 =>
        accept GET(CH : out CHARACTER) do
          -- remove character from buffer and assign it to ch
          COUNT := COUNT - 1;
        end GET;
    end select;
    If COUNT = BUFFSIZE then
      --disable interrupts
    else
      -- enable interrupts
    end if;
  end loop;
end KEYBOARD_HANDLER;
```

A standard solution to the problem in Modula-1 is to encapsulate the handler and the buffer in a package (called a device module). Interrupts are disabled when the buffer is full and signals are used to block consumers when the buffer is empty. The consumer's interface to the package is a procedure which delivers a character. The semantics of device modules in Modula-1 guarantees mutual exclusion between the interrupt handler and the consumers executing the GET procedure. A similar solution in Ada would require definition of further pragmas to define signalling entries, and to specify that the device package should behave like a monitor. As an alternative to the latter pragma, the routines could turn off the device's interrupts when entering a critical section, although this introduces a potentially pathological race condition.

The final solution presented in this section adopts this approach. It also restricts the code in the interrupt-handling task so that a fast-context switch can occur. This solution is based on the one proposed by the Ada Run Time Environment Working Group (1986) and is shown in Program 14.5.

Program 14.5

```
package KEYBOARD_HANDLER is
  function GET_CHAR return CHARACTER;
end KEYBOARD_HANDLER;


package body KEYBOARD_HANDLER is

  -- bounded buffer declaration, device registers declaration and so on

  task CONTROLLER is
    pragma PRIORITY(HIGH);
    entry GET ( CH : out CHARACTER);
    entry I_SIGNAL;
    pragma SIGNAL_ENTRY(I_SIGNAL);
  end CONTROLLER;


  task INTERRUPT_HANDLER is
    pragma INTERRUPT_TASK;
    entry DONE;
    for DONE use at 16#VECTOR ADDRESS#;
  end INTERRUPT_HANDLER;


  task body CONTROLLER is
  begin
    loop
      select
        when not BUFFER_EMPTY =>
          accept GET ( CH : out CHARACTER) do
            -- turn off device interrupts, take character out of buffer
            -- if empty set buffer_empty to TRUE, turn on device interrupts
          end GET;
      or
        when BUFFER_EMPTY =>
          accept I_SIGNAL;
      end select;
    end loop;
  end CONTROLLER;
```

```
task body INTERRUPT_HANDLER is
begin
  loop
    accept DONE do
      -- place data in the buffer, if buffer full throw data away
      BUFFER_EMPTY := FALSE;
      select
        CONTROLLER.I_SIGNAL;
      else
        null;
      end;
    end DONE;
  end loop;
end INTERRUPT_HANDLER;


function GET_CHAR return CHARACTER is
  TMP : CHARACTER;
begin
  CONTROLLER.GET(TMP);
  return TMP;
end GET_CHAR;


begin
  -- initialize buffer, enable device, turn on interrupts
end KEYBOARD_HANDLER;
```

The new pragmas in the solution in Program 14.5 have the following meaning:

- SIGNAL_ENTRY – this specifies that the entry has no body associated with its accept. This means that if an interrupt-handling task calls the entry then no context switch is required. The rendezvous can be terminated immediately and the interrupt-handling task can continue without blocking.

- INTERRUPT_TASK – this indicates that the interrupt-handling task only accesses variables which are global to a library package. The task, therefore, has no local variables. Moreover, the structure of the task is a loop (with no control variable) and a simple accept statement. The code in the accept statement will never block. These restrictions enable the compiler to place the address of the handling code in the interrupt vector. The code in the accept statement, if necessary, can be augmented to save whatever state is required. Only one entry is allowed in the task and this entry must not be called by a software task.

These restrictions should cut down the overhead associated with switching to the interrupt-handling routine, to a level comparable with assembly-code interrupt handling.

It should, perhaps, be noted that although these pragmas allow interrupt handling in Ada to be carried out in an efficient manner, they are nevertheless implementation-dependent.

The hope is that Ada implementors will support these pragmas (or agree to support a different set). However, it may be too much to hope that a compiler will be able to enforce these restrictions.

Accessing input/output devices through special instructions

Ada provides a standard package called LOW_LEVEL_IO which can be used to generate privileged instructions.

```
package LOW_LEVEL_IO is
  -- declarations of possible types
  -- for device and data
  -- declaration of overloaded
  -- procedures for these types

  procedure SEND_CONTROL(DEVICE : DEVICE_TYPES;
          DATA : in out DATA_TYPES);
  procedure RECEIVE_CONTROL(DEVICE : DEVICE_TYPES;
          DATA : in out DATA_TYPES);

end LOW_LEVEL_IO;
```

Of course, there is nothing to stop device drivers using this package for memory-mapped architectures. Indeed, some books on Ada recommend this approach as it concentrates the interface to the device registers in a few procedures (Hibbard *et al.*, 1981). The approach adopted in this book is to localize the code within a single device-handling package. The effect is the same. In both cases interrupts are viewed as entry calls.

Machine code inserts

If special instructions are required then assembler code may have to integrate with Ada code. Assembler or machine code inserts are obviously at variance with the abstract constructs of the rest of the language, and should only be used when absolutely necessary.

The machine code insertion mechanism enables programmers to write Ada code which contains visible non-Ada objects. This is achieved in a controlled way by only allowing machine code instructions to operate within the context of a subprogram body. Moreover, if a subprogram contains code statements then it can contain only code statements and 'use' clauses (comments and pragmas being allowed as usual).

As would be expected, the details and characteristics of using code inserts are largely implementation-dependent; implementation-specific pragmas and attributes may be used to impose particular restrictions and calling conventions on the use of objects that define code instructions. A CODE statement has the following structure:

```
CODE_STATEMENT ::= TYPE_MARK'RECORD_AGGREGATE;
```

The base type of the TYPE_MARK must be declared within a predefined library package called MACHINE_CODE. It is this package that provides record declarations (in standard Ada) to represent the instructions of the target machine. The following example is from the *Ada Language Reference Manual* (*ALRM* 13.8.7):

```
M : MASK;
procedure SET_MASK; pragma INLINE(SET_MASK);

procedure SET_MASK is
  use MACHINE_CODE;
begin
  SI_FORMAT'(CODE ⇒ SSM,B ⇒ M'BASE_REG,D ⇒ M'DISP);
  —— M'BASE_REG and M'DISP are implementation-specific
  —— predefined attributes
end;
```

The pragma INLINE instructs the compiler to include inline code, rather than a procedure call, whenever the subprogram is used.

Even though this code insertion method is defined in Ada, the language makes it quite clear (*ALRM* 13.8.4) that an implementation need not provide a MACHINE_CODE package. If it does not, the use of machine code inserts is prohibited.

Pragma INTERFACE

This facility allows a procedure or function specification to be used as an interface between Ada and subprograms written in other languages. The pragma names the language (and thereby the calling convention) and the subprogram (see *ALRM* 13.9). For example:

```
package FORT_LIB is
  function SQRT(X : FLOAT) return FLOAT;
  function EXP(X : FLOAT) return FLOAT;
private
  pragma INTERFACE(FORTRAN,SQRT);
  pragma INTERFACE(FORTRAN,EXP);
end FORT_LIB;
```

Ada bodies for the subprograms are not given in the Ada program, which is in contrast to the use of machine code inserts.

Again, there is no requirement on any implementation to support any particular language INTERFACE. However, if an interface to the assembler of the target machine is provided then it is clearly possible to write input/output routines in assembler and use them as ordinary subprograms within an Ada program.

14.4   The message-based model of device handling

Section 14.3 showed how a shared-memory model of communication and synchronization could be mapped onto machines with memory-mapped I/O. However, the model did not handle machines with special instructions elegantly, and resorted to either special procedures or variables of a special type which were recognized by the compiler. In this section the occam 2 language is examined as an example of a message-based concurrent programming language which uses messages to control devices.

14.4.1   Occam 2

Although occam 2 was designed for the transputer, in the following discussion it is considered as a machine-independent language. The model is presented first and then consideration is given to its implementation on memory-mapped and special instruction machines. As with shared-memory device driving the three issues of device encapsulation, register manipulation and interrupt handling must be considered.

Modularity and encapsulation facility

The only encapsulation facility provided by occam 2 is the procedure and, therefore, it is this that must be used to encapsulate device drivers.

Addressing and manipulating device registers

Device registers are mapped on to PORTs which are conceptually similar to occam 2 channels. For instance, if a 16-bit register is at address X then a port P is defined by:

```
PORT OF INT16 P:
PLACE P AT X:
```

Note that this address can be interpreted as either a memory address or a device address, depending on the implementation. Interaction with the device register is obtained by reading or writing to this port:

```
P ! A -- write value of A to the port

P ? B -- read value of port into B
```

A port cannot be defined as read- or write-only. The distinction between ports and channels in occam 2, which is a significant one, is that there is no synchronization associated with the port interaction. Neither reads nor writes can lead to the executing process being suspended; a value is always written to the address specified and, similarly, a value is always read. A port is thus a channel in which the partner is always ready to communicate.

Occam 2 provides facilities for manipulating device registers using shift operations and bitwise logical expressions. There is, however, no equivalent to Modula-1's bit type or Ada representation specifications.

Interrupt handling

An interrupt is handled in occam 2 as a rendezvous with the hardware process. Associated with the interrupt there must be an implementation-dependent address (ADDR) which, in the simple input/output system described in this chapter, is the address of the interrupt vector; a channel is then mapped onto this address:

```
CHAN OF ANY Interrupt:
PLACE Interrupt AT ADDR:
```

Note that this is a channel and not a port. This is because there is synchronization associated with an interrupt where there is none associated with access to a device register.

The data protocol for this channel will also be implementation-dependent.

The interrupt handler can wait for an input from the designated channel thus:

```
INT Any: -- define Any to be of the protocol type
SEQ
  -- using ports enable interrupt
  Interrupt ? Any
  -- actions necessary when interrupt has occurred.
```

The run-time support system must, therefore, synchronize with the designated channel when an external interrupt occurs. To obtain responsiveness, the process handling the interrupt will usually be given a high priority. Therefore, not only will it be made executable by the interrupt event but it will, within a short period of time, actually be executing (assuming that no other high-priority process is running).

To cater for interrupts which are lost if not handled within a specified period, it is necessary to view the hardware as issuing a timeout on the communication. Due to the asymmetry of the occam 2 ALT construct the handler must execute:

```
Interrupt ! Any
```

Implementation on memory-mapped and special instruction machines

To map the occam 2 model of device driving to memory-mapped machines simply requires that input and output requests on ports be mapped to read and write operations on the device registers.

To map the model to special instruction machines requires the following:

- an occam 2 PORT to be associated with an I/O port using the PLACE statement;
- the data which is sent to an occam 2 PORT to be placed in an appropriate accumulator for use with the output machine instruction;
- the data which is received from an occam 2 PORT to become available, via an appropriate accumulator, after the execution of the input instruction.

An example device driver

To illustrate the use of the low-level input/output facilities that occam 2 provides, a process will be developed that controls an Analogue to Digital Converter (ADC) for a memory-mapped machine. The converter samples some environmental factors such as temperature, then translates the measurements it receives and provides scaled integer values on a register. One such converter has a 16-bit control register, the structure of which is shown in Table 14.1.

In order to read a particular analogue input, a channel address (not to be confused with an occam 2 channel) is given in bits 8 to 10 and then bit 0 is set to start the converter. When a value has been loaded into the results register the device will interrupt the processor. The error flag will then be checked before the results register is read. During this interaction it may be desirable to disable the interrupt.

The device driver will loop around receiving requests and providing results; it is programmed as a PROC with a two-channel interface. When an

Table 14.1 Structure of a 16-bit control register.

Bit	Name	Meaning
0	Analogue/digital start	Set to 1 to start a conversion.
6	Interrupt enable/disable	Set to 1 to enable interrupts.
7	Done	Set to 1 when conversion is complete.
8–10	Channel	The converter has 8 analogue inputs, the particular one required is indicated by the value of the channel.
15	Error	Set to 1 by the converter if device malfunctions.

address (for one of the 8 analogue input channels) is passed down 'input' a 16-bit result will be returned via channel 'output'.

```
CHAN OF INT16 request:
CHAN OF INT16 return:
PROC ADC(CHAN OF INT16 input, output)
  -- body of PROC, see below
PRI PAR
  ADC(request, return)
  PAR
    -- rest of program
```

A PRI PAR is desirable as the ADC must handle an interrupt each time it is used.

Within the body of the PROC the interrupt channel and the two PORTs must first be declared:

```
PORT OF INT16 Control.Register:
PLACE Control.Register AT #AA12#:
PORT OF INT16 Buffer.Register:
PLACE Buffer.Register AT #AA14#:
CHAN OF ANY Interrupt:
PLACE Interrupt AT #40#:
INT16 Control.R:   -- variable representing control register
```

Where #AA12# and #AA14# are the defined hexidecimal addresses for the two registers, and #40# is the interrupt vector address.

To instruct the hardware to undertake an operation requires bits 0 and 6 to be set on the control register; at the same time, all other bits apart from those between 8 and 10 (inclusive) must be set to zero. This is achieved by using the following constants;

```
VAL INT16 zero IS 0:
VAL INT16 Go IS 65:
```

Program 14.6

```
INT16 Address:
SEQ
  input ? Address
  IF
    (Address < 0) OR (Address > 63)
      output ! MOSTNEG INT16   -- error condition
    TRUE
      SEQ
        Control.R := zero
        Control.R := Address << 8
        Control.R := Control.R BITOR Go
        Control.Register ! Control.R
```

Having received an address from channel 'input' its value must be assigned to bits 8 through 10 in the control register. This is accomplished by using a shift operation. The actions that must be taken in order to start a conversion are shown in Program 14.6.

Once an interrupt has arrived, the control register is read and the error flag and Done are checked. To do this, the control register must be masked against appropriate constants:

```
VAL INT16 Done IS 128:
VAL INT16 Error IS MOSTNEG INT16:
```

MOSTNEG has the representation 1 000 000 000 000 000. The checks are thus:

```
SEQ
  Control.Register ? Control.R
  IF
    ((Done BITAND Control.R) = 0) OR ((Error BITAND Control.R) <> zero)
      -- error
    TRUE
      -- appropriate value is in buffer register
```

The device driver is structured so that three attempts are made to get a correct reading.

Although the device driver will be run at a high priority, the client process, in general, will not and hence, the driver would be delayed if it attempted to call the client directly and the client was not ready. With input devices that generate data asynchronously this delay could lead to the driver missing an interrupt. To overcome this, the input data must be

Program 14.7

```
PROC buffer(CHAN OF INT put, get)
  CHAN OF INT Request, Reply:
  PAR
    VAL INT Buf.Size IS 32:
    INT top, base, contents:
    [Buf.Size]buffer:
    SEQ
      contents := 0
      top := 0
      base := 0
      INT Any:
      WHILE TRUE
        ALT
          contents < Buf.Size & put ? buffer [top]
            SEQ
              contents := contents + 1
              top := (top + 1) REM Buf.Size
          contents > 0 & Request ? Any
            SEQ
              Reply ! buffer[base]
              contents := contents - 1
              base := (base + 1) REM Buf.Size
    INT Temp: -- single buffer process
    VAL INT Any IS 0: -- dummy value
    WHILE TRUE
      SEQ
        Request ! Any
        Reply ? Temp
        get ! Temp
  :
```

buffered. A suitable circular buffer is given in Program 14.7. Note that because the client wishes to read from the buffer and, because the ALT in the buffer cannot have output guards, another single buffer item is needed. To ensure that the device driver is not delayed by the scheduling algorithm, the two buffer processes (as well as the driver) must execute at high priority.

The full code for the PROC is given in Program 14.8.

Program 14.8

```
PROC ADC(CHAN OF INT16 input, output)
  PORT OF INT16 Control.Register:
  PLACE Control.Register AT #AA12#:
  PORT OF INT16 Buffer.Register:
  PLACE Buffer.Register AT #AA14#:
```

Program 14.8 (cont.)

```
CHAN OF ANY Interrupt:
PLACE Interrupt AT #40#:
TIMER CLOCK:
        Contol.R:   rest
INT16 Control.R:  -- variable representing control buffer
INT16 Buffer.R:   -- variable representing results buffer
INT Time:

VAL INT16 zero IS 0:
VAL INT16 Go IS 65:
VAL INT16 Done IS 128:
VAL INT16 Error IS MOSTNEG INT16:
VAL INT Timeout IS 600000:   -- or some other appropriate value
INT Any:
INT16 Address, i:
BOOL Found, Error:
CHAN OF INT16 Buff.In:

PAR
  buffer(Buff.In, output)
  WHILE TRUE
    SEQ
      input ? Address
      IF
        (Address < 0) OR (Address > 63)
          Buff.In ! MOSTNEG INT16 -- error condition
        TRUE
          SEQ
            i := 1
            Error := FALSE
            Found := FALSE
            WHILE (i < 3) AND ((NOT Found) AND (NOT Error))
              -- Three attempts are made to get a reading from
              -- the ADC. This reading may be either correct or
              -- is flagged as being an error.
              SEQ
                Control.R := zero
                Control.R := Address << 8
                Control.R := Control.R BITOR Go
                Control.Register ! Control.R
                CLOCK ? Time
                ALT
                  Interrupt ? Any
                    SEQ
                      Control.Register ? Control.R
                      IF
                        ((Done BITAND Control.R) = 0) OR
                              ((Error BITAND Control.R) <> zero)
```

```
                    SEQ
                      Error := TRUE
                      Buff.In ! MOSTNEG INT16 -- error condition
                  TRUE
                    SEQ
                      Found := TRUE
                      Buffer.Register ? Buffer.R
                      Buff.In ! Buffer.R
              CLOCK ? AFTER Time PLUS Timeout
                -- The device is not responding
                i := i + 1
        IF
          (NOT Found) AND (NOT Error)
            Buff.In ! MOSTNEG INT16
          TRUE
            SKIP
  :
```

Device driving in occam 2

The above example illustrates some of the difficulties in writing device drivers and interrupt handlers in occam 2. In particular, there is no direct relationship between the hardware priority of the device and the priority assigned to the driver process. To ensure that high-priority devices are given preference, it is necessary to order all the device drivers appropriately at the outer level of the program in a PRI PAR construct. Note, however, that the transputer currently only supports two priority levels.

The other main difficulty stems from the lack of data structures for representing device registers. This results in the programmer having to use low-level bit-manipulation techniques which can be error prone.

14.5 Older real-time languages

The first generation of real-time programming languages (RTL/2, Coral 66 and so on) provide no real support for concurrent programming or for the programming of devices. Interrupts are typically viewed as procedure calls, and very often, the only facility available for accessing device registers is to allow assembly language code to be embedded in the program. For example, RTL/2 (Barnes, 1976) has a code statement as follows:

```
code code_size, stack_size
    mov  R3,@variable
    ...
    ...
@rtl
```

One disadvantage of this approach is that in order to access RTL/2 variables, knowledge of the structure of the code generated from the compiler is needed.

Another common feature with early real-time languages is that they tend to be weakly typed. Therefore, variables can be treated as fixed-length bit strings. This allows the individual bits and fields of registers to be manipulated using low-level operators, such as logical shift and rotate instructions. However, the disadvantages of having weak typing by far outweigh the benefits of this flexibility.

SUMMARY

One of the main characteristics of an embedded system is the requirement that it interacts with special purpose input and output devices. To program device drivers in high-level languages requires:

- the ability to pass data and control information to and from the device;
- the ability to handle interrupts.

Normally, control and data information is passed to devices through device registers. These registers are either accessed by special addresses in a memory-mapped I/O architecture, or via special machine instructions. Interrupt handling requires context switching, device and interrupt identification, interrupt control, and device prioritization.

The programming of devices has traditionally been the stronghold of the assembly-language programmer, but languages like Ada, Modula-1, Modula-2 and occam 2 have now attempted to provide high-level mechanisms for these low-level functions. This makes device-driving and interrupt-handling routines easier to read, write and maintain. The main requirement of a high-level language is that it provides an abstract model of device handling. Encapsulation facilities are also required, so that the non-portable code of the program can be separated from the portable part.

The model of device handling is built on top of the language's model of concurrency. A device can be considered to be a processor performing a fixed process. A computer system can, therefore, be modelled as several parallel processes which need to communicate and synchronize. Synchronization is provided by the interrupt. Both the shared-memory and message-based models of communication can be used by the device driver.

In the shared-memory model the driver and the device communicate using the shared device registers, and the interrupt provides the
synchronization. Its implementation requires the following:

(1)   Facilities for addressing and manipulating device registers.

(2)   A suitable representation of interrupts. An interrupt is normally
       mapped onto the condition synchronization primitive provided by
       the concurrent programming language.

Modula-1, Modula-2 and Ada all present the programmer with a shared
memory-model of device handling. In Modula-1, driver processes are
encapsulated in device modules which have the functionality of monitors.
Device registers are accessed as scalar objects or arrays of bits, and an
interrupt is viewed as a signal on a condition variable. In Modula-2,
device drivers are considered to be coroutines; registers are treated as
scalars or bit sets, and interrupts as coroutine switches. A form of monitor
is also used to guarantee mutually exclusive access to critical regions in
the presence of an interrupt. In Ada, device registers can be defined as
scalars and user-defined record types, with a comprehensive set of
facilities for mapping types onto the underlying hardware. Ada device
drivers contain tasks, and interrupts are viewed as hardware-generated
entry calls to the handling task.
        Only occam 2 presents a message-based view of device driving to
the programmer. Device registers are accessed as special channels,
called ports, and interrupts are treated as content-free messages down
channels.

Further reading

Allworth S.T. and Zobel R.N. (1987). *Introduction to Real-time System Design*.
       London: Macmillan
Foster C.C. (1981). *Real Time Programming – Neglected Topics*. Reading MA:
       Addison-Wesley
Holden J. and Wand I.C. (1980). An assessment of Modula. *Software Practice and
       Experience*. **10**(11), 593–621
Tanenbaum A.S. (1987). *Operating Systems Design and Implementation*.
       Englewood Cliffs NJ: Prentice-Hall
Whiddett D. (1987). *Concurrent Programming for Software Engineers*. Chichester:
       Ellis Horwood
Young S.J. (1982). *Real Time Languages: Design and Development*. Chichester:
       Ellis Horwood

EXERCISES

14.1 The control field of an X25 datalink packet is 8 bits long (numbered
left to right as bits 0 to 7). If bit 0 is 0, the control field is an
information frame; if bit 0 is 1 and bit 1 is 0, the control field is a
supervisory frame; if bit 0 and bit 1 are both 1, the control field is an
unnumbered frame. Control fields for an information frame have
the following format:

```
bit 0   : 0
bits 1-3 : the sequence number of the packet
bit 4    : a boolean (the poll/final bit no = 0,
                                       yes = 1)
bits 5-7 : the next sequence number expected
```

For supervisory frames the control field has the following
format:

```
bit 0    : 1
bit 1    : 0
bits 2-3 : a type field (0 = receive ready,
           1 = reject, 2 = receive not
           ready, 3 = selective reject )
bit 4    : the poll/final bit
bits 5-7 : the next sequence number expected
```

For unnumbered frames the control field has the following
format:

```
bit 0   : 1
bit 1   : 1
bits 2-3 : a type field (0 = SABM, 1 = DISC,
           2 = UA, 3 = CMDR)
bit 4    : the poll/final bit
bits 5-7 : a modifier (assume an integer)
```

Define, in Ada, the formats of each of the fields as if they
were unrelated.

Ada provides a variant record facility, the structure of the
control field can be expressed by the following skeleton Ada code:

```
type CNTRL_FIELD is
   (INFORMATION, SUPERVISORY, UNNUMBERED);
```

```
type
   CONTROL_FIELD(CLASS:CNTRL_FIELD) is
   record
      -- common fields
      case CLASS is
         when INFORMATION ⇒
            -- information fields
         when SUPERVISORY ⇒
            -- supervisory fields
         when UNNUMBERED ⇒
            -- unnumbered fields
      end case;
   end record;
```

Consider how you would define the supervisory and unnumbered frames as a single variant record. How easy is it to add the information frame? (Note that you have to define the position and size of the discriminant).

14.2 Consider a computer which is embedded in a patient-monitoring system (assume the simple I/O system given in this chapter). The system is arranged so that an interrupt is generated at the highest hardware priority, through vector location 100 octal, every time the patient's heart beats. In addition, a mild electric shock can be administered via a device-control register, the address of which is 177760 octal. The register is set up so that every time an integer value 'x' is assigned to it the patient receives 'x' volts over a small period of time.

If no heartbeat is recorded within a five second period then the patient's life is in danger. Two actions should be taken when the patient's heart fails: the first is that a 'supervisor' task should be notified so that it may sound the hospital alarm, the second is that a single electric shock of five volts should be administered. If the patient fails to respond then the voltage should be increased by one volt for every further five seconds.

Write an interrupt-handling task, in Ada, which monitors the patient's heart and initiates the actions described above. You may assume that the supervisor task is given by the following specification.

```
task SUPERVISOR is
   entry SOUND_ALARM;
end SUPERVISOR;
```

14.3 Rewrite your answer to Question 14.2 in occam 2 and Modula-2.

14.4   Consider a simple robot arm, connected to a computer with a simple I/O system, which can only be moved along the horizontal axis. The device is controlled by two registers: a data register at octal location 177234 and a control register at octal location 177326. When the device is enabled (by setting bit 6 in the control register) and a coordinate is placed in the data register, the robot arm moves to that coordinate, and an interrupt is generated (through location octal 56 and at a hardware priority of 4) when the arm is in the new position.

   Define a Modula-1 device module so that a Modula-1 process may move the arm to a particular position by calling the routine MOVETOPOSITON, defined by the device module, with a parameter indicating the required position. The procedure should return when the arm is located at the new position. You may assume that only one process at a time will call MOVETOPOSITION.

14.5   Design a Modula-1 device module which enables a calling process to be delayed for a number of clock ticks. Calling processes should interact with the device module by a procedure called DELAY which takes an integer parameter indicating the duration of the delay in ticks. The procedure returns when the delay time has expired. You may assume that the priority of the clock device is six; its interrupt vector location is at octal location 100 and its control and status register is at address octal 177546 and is 16 bits long. Bit 6 of this register, when set, enables interrupts.

14.6   Rewrite the keyboard device driver, given in Section 14.3.3, in occam 2.

14.7   Rewrite the analogue to digital converter, given in Section 14.4.1 in Ada and in Modula-2.

14.8   Rewrite the clock device driver, given in Section 14.3.1 in Modula-2.

14.9   Some applications are required to handle interrupts from many identical devices. Is it possible to instantiate each handler from a single Ada task type? Why not? Do similar problems occur in Modula-2 and occam 2?

14.10   How would you write several Ada interrupt handlers for identical tasks and still share code?

Chapter 15
Efficiency of Implementation

The efficiency of the code generated by a language compiler is often considered to be of primary importance. This is, however, in many ways a poor metric for assessing an implementation. In real-time systems what is actually important is the meeting of deadlines or the attainment of adequate response times. An efficient implementation plays a significant role in delivering schedulability, but it should not be considered the overriding factor in deciding which language to use or design method to follow. Having said this, a grossly inefficient compiler would clearly be an inappropriate tool to employ; such inefficiencies being an indication of a poorly-engineered product. This chapter discusses some of the issues associated with the efficient implementation of high-level real-time programming languages.

15.1 Motivation

One of the clear benefits of using a high-level language is that programs are constructed using primitives that are abstracted away from considerations of implementation and representation. In using these high-level constructs the programmer, particularly in the real-time domain, must have confidence that the language has been designed in such a way that not only are useful abstractions available to the user, but that these abstractions lead to

477

a sensible and relatively efficient implementation on the designated hardware. Not only should the programmer have this confidence but it must be based on knowledge, not faith.

With imperative programming languages and standard von Neumann processors there is still a strong resemblance between the structures of the source program and the executing code. Code generation is, therefore, reasonably straightforward and now well understood (at least, for sequential programs). Other language paradigms such as functional programming, do not lead to efficient implementation on the currently-available hardware, although they present the user with, arguably, better abstractions. They cannot, therefore, be used for real-time work yet.

But, even with imperative languages, there are some features that seem difficult to implement and others that could be considered inherently inefficient. Ada tasking, for example, has been the subject of much criticism in this area (see Section 15.2.1). In this chapter areas of language design are examined that give rise to potential inefficiencies; methods of improvement are then discussed.

An unfortunate consequence of using a language that has features perceived as being inherently inefficient is that the expressive power of the language is reduced to, in effect, an 'efficient' subset. For example, if process creation is considered to be expensive, a programmer may choose to construct a pool of reusable agent processes. The result is a program that is not easily seen as a transformation of its design; it is more difficult to understand and hence more error prone and costly to maintain. This situation becomes even worse if a later version of the compiler shows that the suspect feature was indeed not inherently inefficient (merely transiently so). The contrived program is now the inefficient one.

There is an argument that says that the design and construction of programs should only concentrate on the logical behaviour of the required system (this being sufficiently difficult to achieve in its own right). Issues of schedulability or acceptable levels of efficiency should only be examined at the testing stage. If a system fails such a test then more processing power is introduced; either in the form of a quicker processor or by increasing the number of processors. After all, processing power is very cheap; especially when compared to the overall cost of most applications.

Clearly, this argument has merit and will be appropriate in some areas. There are however two considerations that mitigate against it;

(1)   The movement from a single processor to a multiprocessor (or from a closely-coupled to a distributed system) may require fundamental changes to the design of the software; this will be very costly at this late stage.

(2)   Weight or space restrictions may prohibit increased hardware (for example, airborne embedded systems).

There will also be mass-produced systems where the cost of an extra, say, 32-bit processor per product will be financially significant.

15.2   Problem areas

The three major areas of language design considered in this book are concurrency, error recovery and distribution. Each of these is now examined to ascertain whether the features that have been found to be important for the production of reliable real-time programs give rise to inefficient implementations. These high overheads may be due to inherent properties of these features or to the difficulty in finding a strategy for implementation that is acceptable.

As indicated in the previous section, the production of efficient code from a sequential program section should not present the implementor with any major difficulty. Although, at one time, procedure calls were considered an extravagance that could not be afforded in real-time programs, implementations now deal with them quite adequately. And there is always the possibility of generating inline expansion rather than an actual call. It is important to keep this example in mind when considering the following 'problem area'.

15.2.1   Concurrency

The use of a concurrent programming language inevitably incurs an implementational overhead. Processes require a run-time support system that keeps track of process states and dispatches runnable processes to the available processors. These activities take up time that would otherwise be of use to the application program. One measure of the efficiency of a run-time system is the **context switch**, that is, the time it takes to switch from executing one process to starting to execute another. Clearly, if the architecture of the processor results in processes sharing many registers, and the semantics of the language imply that a context switch could happen at any time, then each process will have a large volatile environment and switching will take more time. The **volatile environment** is the totality of data that must be stored when a process is removed from the processor and subsequently reinstated when the process next executes.

Synchronization primitives also generate an implementational overhead as they involve queues and require such actions as interrupt disabling (and enabling). Higher-order primitives such as message passing may result in greater time loss, as shared memory is not exploited as efficiently as it might be.

One common difficulty with the current generation of concurrent programming languages is that the necessary run-time support environment often comes as a fixed, inflexible utility. A specific program may not use all the language features but it cannot tailor the support system for more optimal performance. Interestingly, older languages did give more control in this area. Also, complete flexibility comes with Modula-2 where the user must construct the run-time utility to support the chosen process abstraction. This obviously enables an effective kernel to be built.

Of the other two major languages considered in this book, occam 2 has been designed and implemented (on the transputer) with efficiency considerations paramount; a number of the techniques used are discussed in Section 15.3. Ada's tasking model has, by comparison, been the subject of much criticism. For example, a simple rendezvous took, on most early implementations, approximately one millisecond. Therefore, if an application had a response time in the order of a few milliseconds then the execution of a rendezvous was a luxury it could not afford. Task creation and termination were also both very slow in early run-time support systems. Because of these metrics for Ada, a number of large embedded systems projects chose not to use tasking (even though they were committed to using Ada). It was felt that they were forced, by efficiency considerations, to program without the help of concurrency.

If context switches are expensive, then message-based languages have the added problem that they require more processes to be present in the program than would be the case with a language incorporating, say, monitors. To use a monitor does not involve a context switch (although it will invoke some low-level synchronization primitive); a similar request of a resource-controlling process will need at least two switches. A transaction that requires two rendezvous will consume four such changes. Thus, process proliferation is a problem, which is made more acute by many design methods that naturally lead to the use of large numbers of activities and buffers, both of which must be realized as processes.

15.2.2 Reliability

This book has discussed a wide range of facilities which enable both the designer and the programmer of embedded systems to increase the reliability of their software. These range from the provision of recovery blocks and exception handling, to nested atomic transaction, and duplication of entire systems and subsystems. In all cases, reliability is achieved by adding redundancy to the system. Inevitably, this is going to add overheads to the execution of programs.

An important consideration in the design of real-time programming language facilities is that they should not consume overheads if they are not being used by the program. For example, a program which does not use exception handlers should not be penalized because the language and its support system offer this facility.

Where forward or backward error recovery is used, there is, inevitably, a run-time cost when an exception is raised or an acceptance test fails. It was noted in Chapter 6 that it is arguable whether the error-free behaviour of a program should incur an overhead. Ideally, it should not, however, if a small overhead for normal execution results in a much reduced cost when an error occurs, this may be a desirable compromise.

15.2.3 Distribution

One of the main motivations for considering distributed systems is to improve the cost/performance ratio of the underlying hardware. Unfortunately, the added complexity introduced by remote communication and distributed control algorithms often means that this promise is not fulfilled. In particular, many layers of communication protocol handlers can sometimes swallow up any increase in raw processing power.

An important consideration in the design of distributed real-time applications is where to put the error-checking code. The temptation, when providing layers of software, is to place error-checking code at each layer in order to achieve a highly reliable service. As Chapter 13 showed this can be extremely costly and is often not what is required anyway. The *end-to-end argument* of system design (Saltzer *et al.*, 1984) shows that it is sometimes better to provide a less than reliable service at lower layers, because higher-level protocols must carry out their own error checking anyway. This checking will catch errors in lower-level software as a side effect.

If distributed transactions are to be supported then there is a cost associated with the two-phase commit protocol. In particular, the use of stable storage (which may itself be replicated) is expensive.

15.3 Improving efficiency

In this section, a number of techniques are reviewed that are aimed at improving the efficiency of real-time programs. These techniques range from special-purpose hardware to program transformation tools, and include issues of language (and program design), effective implementation algorithms and compiler optimizations. Taken together they represent a powerful arsenal with which to attack the argument that real-time efficiency can only result from assembler or machine code programming.

In some situations, activities in the development stage of a program can ensure that the software, produced is to a very high standard, thus cutting down on the need for redundancy at run time to cope with design errors. Examples of these include, using proven design methodologies, using programming languages which perform exhaustive compile-time checks, and comprehensive testing. Mathematical techniques for proving program correctness are becoming increasingly important, however, the sheer size and complexity of real-time systems is such that these techniques cannot yet be applied to systems in their entirety.

15.3.1 Language issues

One of the motivations for using a high-level language is that more checks can be incorporated into the compiler, rather than be left as run-time tests (with their associated overheads). The type model forms the basis of these compile-time checks, and its extension to include separately compiled modules is a significant improvement over the mere linking of program units. Although these checks may, irritatingly, increase the time it takes to compile a program; this is not really an important factor or insurmountable problem, especially if the benefit of slow compilation is fast execution.

It was noted at the beginning of this chapter that efficiency considerations should not be the criteria by which language features are assessed. Models of abstraction, expressive power and ease of use are far more significant factors. No useful purpose would, therefore, be met by listing the various concurrency models that have been discussed in this book, in some kind of efficiency (or inefficiency) league table. Perhaps the only two general points worth noting are that message-based communication is not as well suited to shared-memory implementation as shared variables; but that the opposite is true for distributed-memory implementation.

Nevertheless, it is reasonable to examine language details (actual or proposed) to see if certain features or primitives introduce inefficiencies that outweigh their possible advantages. With Ada, the designers have allowed certain restrictions in order to make life easier for the implementors; for example, nested accept statements cannot refer to the same entry. Although this rule goes against considerations of orthogonality in language design, it does make the implementation more efficient. Another 'feature' not allowed in Ada or occam 2 is for the selective 'wait' construct to receive and send messages. Even though this symmetric form is allowed within the CSP formalism, its implementation on distributed hardware requires a low-level protocol that is quite extensive and time consuming. The languages have, therefore, disallowed this form. This is less of an inconvenience for Ada as data can be passed in the opposite direction to the message (by using **out** parameters).

Chapters 10, 11 and 12 of this book have discussed the need to modify the real-time facilities of Ada and occam 2. For example, the following have been advocated:

(1)   Using priority to influence the choice made by the selective wait construct.

(2)   In Ada, having the entry queue ordered by priority.

(3)   Allowing priority to be inherited.

(4)   Allowing guards to have access to the parameters of incoming messages.

All of these alternative designs will lead to increased overhead. They do, however, have the benefits that they either increase the power of the priority primitive, or reduce the number of rendezvous needed for an important class of transaction.

Of the features that Ada supports there are two rules that lead to an inefficient context switch. The first is, again, to do with priority and is the insistence that a pre-emptive scheduler is used in the run-time system. As soon as a higher-priority task is runnable it must take over from a lower priority one. Although this need for a timely context switch is implied by the use and meaning of 'priority', the insistence on an immediate pre-emptive switch removes from the run-time system some of its man-oeuvrability. In occam 2 no such definition of priority is enshrined in the language semantics. This gives rise to a much more effective implementation algorithm (see Section 15.3.6).

The second language feature concerns functions. Ada allows a function to contain arbitrary computations. It is, therefore, quite acceptable for a function to declare new tasks. These tasks must be activated before the function can continue, with the result that a complicated expression (containing a call to such a function) will need to be suspended during its evaluation. This will, typically, be at a time when a significant number of shared registers are being employed. Again, it can be seen that occam 2 has a better thought out design; its functions are not allowed to have internal processes. Nor can they contain any channel actions or non-local assignments.

15.3.2   Effective programs

Effective programs result from the use of appropriate data structures and efficient algorithms. Luckly, there is ample literature in this area. The collective termination of a group of processes, for example, is a problem for which a number of algorithms (of varying degrees of efficiency) have been proposed. The provision of a terminate alternative on the selective wait statement simplifies (considerably) these algorithms for the Ada language.

When choosing data structures and algorithms the programmer must always strike a balance between elegance and run-time overhead. At issue here is not so much the efficiency of implementation, but the predictability of the associated real-time cost. For instance, recursive techniques may not be suitable unless an upper bound on the depth of recursion is definable and effective stack management is provided.

Other factors that influence the effectiveness of software are those concerning how well a program fits onto the actual hardware on which it must run. The lifespan of a computer language by far outlasts that of computer hardware. Indeed, with the continuing use of FORTRAN and Cobol it is, perhaps, arguable that computer languages never die (they do, however, occasionally mutate). It follows that any general-purpose language is going to be used with a host of different hardware architectures. This is particularly true in the real-time world where many different processors are commonly targeted; sometimes, even from the same compiler. As a consequence of this variation, on every distinct processor there are going to be language features that are implemented very efficiently, and there are going to be other features that are not.

An abstract approach implies, under normal circumstances, that the programmer should not be aware (and should certainly not take into account) issues of parochial efficiency. The real-time programmer may, however, need, at some stage, to consider in detail the form his or her program is going to take on the actual designated hardware. There may be a need to 'speed up the programs by $X\%$' (where X could be anywhere between 2 and 200). In such circumstances, extreme care must be taken if errors are not to be introduced by these last minute refinements. Indeed, in many cases these changes would not be needed if more care had been taken earlier. For example, in Ada, it is easy to give initial values to variables upon declaration; but the tendency to initialize a whole array, 'because the first part had to be initialized anyway', could lead to significant overheads on some processors. Another common source of inefficiencies is redundant code in loops, although some compiler optimizations may remove these inefficiencies.

Other speed ups can be derived from tailoring the target code; for example, optimizing where variables are stored. A language that allows these attributes to be added without changes to the logic of the program is clearly beneficial. Ada, Modula-2 and occam 2 all support this distinction between operation and implementation.

A different approach to producing effective programs is to cater for new implementations at the initial programming stage. Specifically, if efficiency difficulties are to be alleviated by the addition of processors, then a program that is already built up as a collection of communicating processes is going to be far easier to redistribute. This is one of the major attractions of the very low-level concurrency that occam 2 encourages. For an appropriately-designed program only very minor changes are needed to move it from one processor to a collection (even hundreds) of processors.

15.3.3   Program transformations

The previous section discussed how more efficient programs can be obtained by changing the software so that it becomes more effective on the chosen target hardware. It was, however, also noted that such changes are error prone and must be undertaken with extreme care. A more systematic approach to such program editing is to restrict changes to those that can be shown to be transformations.

Informally, a **transformation** can be said to change the structure of a program without changing its meaning. This does not imply that the behaviour of the transformed and the original programs will be identical; in particular, the speeds at which they execute will differ (this being one of the objectives in performing the transformation). To form a single complex transformation to a sizeable program, in a way that guarantees that the program will not become invalid, is far from a trivial undertaking. Rather, it is better to apply a series of simple transformations, each of which clearly leaves the program essentially the same as before. These simple transformations can be considered to be the *laws* of the language.

One of the attractive features of occam 2 is that it is amenable to the construction of such laws, and hence to the application of transformations. Laws for occam 2 can be derived because the semantics of the language have been formally specified; the laws themselves are quite simple because occam 2 prohibits the two language 'features' that would significantly complicate their form; namely:

(1)   functions that have side effects;
(2)   communication via shared variables.

Without these constructs it is possible to analyse a fragment of code in isolation from the rest of the program. The motivations for deriving laws and applying transformations are:

- To change a clear but inefficient program into an efficient but, perhaps, obscure one.
- To change a sequential program into a concurrent one, to exploit parallel hardware.
- To change a concurrent program into a sequential one for more efficient execution on a single processor.
- To change a physically infeasible program (that is, one that cannot be implemented on the available hardware) into one that is physically feasible.

A comprehensive set of transformation laws for occam 1 has been provided by Roscoe and Hoare (1986). A discussion of these laws as they apply to occam 2 is given by Burns (1988).

Not only is there a comprehensive set of laws defined for occam, but software tools exist that will (under user guidance) perform the specified transformations automatically. If these tools are, themselves, reliable, then the user can be confident that the transformed program is as viable as the original. Unfortunately, no laws or tools are currently available for Ada or Modula-2.

15.3.4   Effective implementation strategies

Language semantics do not dictate the form that an implementation must take. To do so would, clearly, be inappropriate. It follows that the efficiency of a real-time program is heavily dependent upon the strategies used by compiler implementors.

In this section, four areas are examined in order to illustrate that efficient algorithms do exist for the language features that have been expounded in this book. These areas concern the implementation of channels, interrupt handling, process termination and exception propagation. The aim here is not to provide an exhaustive treatment of how to implement all the controversial features of high-level real-time languages, but rather, to illustrate that given time, implementors will tend to improve on the algorithms that originally appear in support of any new language feature.

Channels

A naive implementation of message-based communication would, on a shared-memory system, copy the message into a buffer and then copy the contents of this buffer into the memory of the receiver process. For large messages this would represent a quite expensive operation. A much more efficient algorithm involves the direct transfer of the message from one process to another, with a flag being used to indicate which process arrived at the rendezvous first.

To give more detail on this, consider a channel-based synchronized message-passing model. When a channel is declared, a word of memory is allocated (regardless of the size of the message) together with a FREE/BUSY flag. When a process wishes to operate on that channel (input or output) it first checks the flag to see if the channel is FREE. If it is, it then places the 'start of message' address in the channel word; it sets the channel flag to BUSY and suspends itself. Eventually (for a correct program) another process will apply the inverse operation to this channel. The channel flag is now found to be BUSY and so a rendezvous can immediately take place. The message is transferred using the address in the channel word, and in the direction dictated by the program. As a final action, the original suspended process is made runnable again and the channel flag is set FREE. The Modula-2 process abstraction presented in the Appendix uses this strategy.

The above algorithm uses a word of memory and a flag for each channel declared. This can be further simplified by incorporating the flag into the channel word. For example, if 0 (zero) is an invalid address, then FREE could be represented by that value; a channel word value other than zero is taken to mean BUSY, with its actual value being the required address for communication.

With this effective implementation strategy for channels, it should be noted that, when a process suspends itself on a channel, it does not know the state of the process with which it is trying to communicate. In Ada, an exception is raised if the partner task has already terminated. This useful reaction could only be incorporated into the channel model if a more inefficient implementation were used.

Interrupts

Because interrupts occur asynchronously, their handling can result in significant overheads. With concurrent programming languages it is usual to associate each interrupt handler with a process; it is also usual to assign these processes higher priorities than other program processes. An immediate context switch, therefore, invariably follows the arrival of an interrupt. As, in general, context switches are expensive, the meaning of the term 'immediate' becomes significant.

If the language explicitly prescribes priority-based pre-emptive scheduling (as does Ada) then an implementation is forced to do the switch at the first possible occasion. However, a more relaxed language definition does allow the implementation to delay the process change for a small period of time. This delay cannot be too long or the basic responsiveness of the system will be compromised. Nevertheless, the following algorithm is feasible (it has two parts):

(1)   The compiler ensures that the code generated from any program is periodically context free

(2)   Process switching (in particular to an interrupt handler) takes place only when the currently executing process is context free

A process is said to be **context free** if, at that instance, it is making use of only the minimum number of shared registers (program counter and perhaps one or two others).

The effect of this algorithm is that the size of the context (the volatile environment of the process) is kept very small. Its swapping in and out can thus be done quickly.

To keep the postponement acceptable, the time between successive context free states must be upper-bounded and small. This will result in the generated machine code having wasteful copy-out instructions inserted.

The overall effect upon efficiency will not be universally beneficial, but can be quite substantial on certain architectures.

Occam 2's implementation on the transputer uses this algorithm. The maximum latency before running a high-priority process (assuming a low priority one was actually executing when the high-priority process became runnable) is some 60 processor cycles (including 15 cycles for the context switch itself). On a 50 nanosecond per cycle transputer this is a latency (maximum) of 3 microseconds, which compares very favourably with language systems that switch immediately to the high-priority process but take 500 microseconds (half a rendezvous) to do so.

Finally, if the above approach is not possible because of a strict pre-emptive model of scheduling, then it may be necessary to enforce certain restrictions on the code of interrupt handlers so that context switch time can be kept to a minimum (see Section 14.3.3 for an example of such a restriction with Ada).

Termination

It was noted in Section 9.5.2 that programming efficient termination phases is non-trivial. Ada removes this difficulty by the provision of a terminate alternative on the select, but there remains the problem of making sure that the implementation is, itself, efficient. On a single-processor unit this is quite straightforward, but on a distributed system it is necessary to use a more complex algorithm. With a post-partioning approach to distributed Ada, it is possible for task hierarchies to be distributed between processors. If a task wishes to leave a block then all tasks created in that block must have already terminated, or be waiting on a select with an open terminate alternative. The following algorithm, which is given by Raymond (1987) is developed from one designed for an extended version of CSP (Francez and Rodeh, 1982) and involves the sending out of waves of messages.

The task that wishes to leave a block sends out a wave of WANT_TO_ DIE messages to its immediate children (in the dependency tree). It then waits for replies that are either YES or NO. If all children answer YES then it may terminate the block by sending DIE messages to all children. If, however, any child answers NO a new wave is sent out.

From the child's point of view it takes one of the following actions:

(1)   If it has already terminated it answers YES.
(2)   If it is busy it refuses to accept the WANT_TO_DIE message.
(3)   If it is waiting on a select with an open terminates alternative and it has its own dependent children, then it passes on the WANT_TO_DIE message and replies YES only if it gets the message YES from all its children.
(4)   If it is waiting on a select with an open terminate alternative, and it has no children, it answers YES.

The only exception to this rule is when a 'busy' task calls another task that has already answered YES. In this case, the calling task must take responsibility for an incorrect YES being propagated, by itself replying NO. The attractive feature of this algorithm is that tasks (that is, the processors on which they run) need only respond to the WANT_TO_DIE message if they are currently idle. Moreover, a new wave is only started when a YES needs to be countermanded. The only point of detail missing from this description is that the wave generator must ensure that a complete set of YES replies are in answer to the current wave.

It is clear that support for termination of a program in a distributed environment will inevitably, entail an overhead at run time. However, by using a distribution model which does not allow tasks hierarchies to be constructed across machine boundaries (for example, by the use of virtual nodes), this overhead can be kept to a minimum. Full details of possible approaches to virtual node termination are given by Hutcheon and Wellings (1989b).

Exceptions

This book has suggested that exception handling can be used as a framework from within which many fault-tolerance techniques can be implemented. It is, therefore, critical that exception and exception handling be implemented efficiently. Baker and Riccardi (1986) discuss the problems of implementing Ada exceptions with the goal of minimizing time and storage resources. As they point out:

> Exceptions and exception handling are woven intricately into the fabric of Ada, so that it is difficult to separate their implementation from that of several other language features. In particular, an exception involves exiting a context. Code propagating an exception must, therefore, perform any processing required on exit from a contextual unit. This involves aspects of tasking, storage management, and local-nonlocal referencing environments.

A major overhead associated with exceptions and tasking concerns the propagation of an exception outside an accept statement. This requires the raising of the exception in the calling task, ensuring that the normal end of rendezvous code has been executed and reraising the exception in the called task. Further code must be executed when a task, as a result of an exception, wishes to leave a context within which it has dependent tasks. This, of course, cannot be allowed until the dependent tasks have terminated. If a task does terminate as a result of an exception, then code must be executed to test to see if a master context can be left or if a master task can be terminated.

Even when there are no dependent tasks, the propagation of an exception from a contextual unit still entails overheads. This is because some action must be taken to restore the environment of the contextual unit in which the exception will be handled. Typically, this involves removing activation records from the run-time stack, restoring the current activation base address and stack top, deallocating heap storage, and restoring the nonlocal referencing environment (Baker and Riccardi, 1986).

Although, inevitably, there is some overhead associated with supporting exception handling in a language, this can be isolated so that the program does not incur excessive overheads on its normal error-free execution. Baker and Riccardi (1986) give the following guidelines to achieve this:

- Separate the checks for whether an exception has been raised and not handled within an accept statement, from the normal processing for the end of rendezvous.

- Use static mapping to keep track of the context for recovery from an exception.

- Use separate exit codes or interpreted tables, for propagating exceptions.

- Place code for generating exceptions where it need not be jumped around during normal execution.

In Chapter 6, various models of exception handling were discussed. Although most of the languages which support exception handling provide the termination model, there is no clear indication as to whether exception propagation (that is, the dynamic association between the occurrence of an exception and an appropriate handler) is necessarily the most efficient strategy to use. It is possible that some of the overheads mentioned above could be reduced by adopting a model which does not require exception propagation (for example, the model used by CHILL).

The other issues associated with exception handling, which may affect the efficiency of the generated code, is the effect that the presence of exceptions and exception handlers has on optimization techniques. It is known that certain well-defined optimizations cannot be easily achieved in Ada because of exceptions. For a full discussion on this important topic see Kirchgassner et al. (1983).

15.3.5 Compiler optimizations

Having chosen an appropriate strategy for implementation, further optimizations can be applied when an actual program is presented to the compiler. There are a number of standard optimizations that a compiler can perform on sequential code, but this section looks beyond these techniques to optimizations that are applicable to concurrency features.

The first improvement that can be made is for the run-time system to be simplified to support just those language features that the program actually needs. Any program in, for example, Ada may omit reference to, say, timed entry calls, delay statements, aborts, or terminate alternatives. A 'tailor made' run-time support system should perform somewhat better than the generally inflexible 'all-in' system. Another approach to improving the run-time support system is to allow the programmer to specify certain characteristics required by the application. The compiler (or equivalent software tool) must then be able to respond to these specifications.

A different type of compiler optimization is *process removal*. This is aimed at reducing the number of context switches by, in effect, reducing the number of processes that are actually executing in the final target code.

Habermann and Nassi (1980) have suggested that one way of performing process removal, in Ada, is to move, whenever possible, to a monitor-like representation of shared objects. Consider, for example, a shared object on which all operations must be mutually exclusive. The normal representation of this object would include the following synchronizing task:

```
task SYNCHRONIZER is
  entry OP1(...);
  entry OP2(...);
  ...
end SYNCHRONIZER;

task body SYNCHRONIZER is
begin
  loop
    select
      accept OP1 (...) do
        ...
      end OP1;
    or
      accept OP2 (...) do
        ...
      end OP2;
    or
      ...
    end select;
  end loop;
end SYNCHRONIZER;
```

Mutually-exclusive behaviour of these operators is guaranteed by the serial execution of accept statements by the single synchronizing task.

As noted above, each operation on the object requires two context switches.

A fully optimized representation of the object removes the synchronizing task altogether. Each accept statement is replaced by a procedure, and the clients' entry calls are replaced by ordinary procedure calls. Mutual exclusion is effected through semaphore operations (or their equivalent) provided in the run-time system; these operations are inserted before and after each procedure call, or at the start and finish of each procedure body. The effect of this transformation is to remove the context switches at the cost of performing primitive operations on a semaphore.

The transformation illustrated above is generalized by Schauer (1982) as follows:

(1)   Move all statements that are outside a rendezvous into the preceding rendezvous.

(2)   Restructure each accept statement as a procedure.

(3)   Encapsulate in a 'start procedure' all statements that precede the first accept statement.

(4)   Replace each guard by a test, such that a closed guard results in suspension on a semaphore (or similar entity).

(5)   Replace each entry call by the corresponding procedure call.

(6)   Replace the task initialization by a call to the start procedure.

One might hope that a compiler could recognize when this kind of optimization is possible, and generate code accordingly. Failing that, it is reasonable to expect a compiler to support a pragma that allows the programmer to request that the associated task be 'optimized away'. Such a pragma would be analogous to a pragma for removing procedure calls. Note that removal of a task not only reduces the number of context switches required, but also reduces the general overhead of task management (Schauer, 1982).

Habermann and Nassi (1980) have described a transformation applicable to tasks with more complex structures than that shown above. Their transformation allows for nested accept statements, aborts, exceptions raised during a rendezvous, and the existence of more than one accept body for an entry. The resulting optimization is weaker than that described earlier (the task is not completely removed), but reduces the number of context switches by one in most circumstances.

15.3.6 Purpose-built hardware

Given that many millions of dollars have been spent on the development of the Ada language, it is perhaps, appropriate to counter accusations of inefficiency by noting that a much smaller investment in hardware could produce an efficient 'Ada machine'. The feasibility of such a machine is a good (inverse) measure of the 'inherent' inefficiency of the language design.

Those architecture projects that have already attempted to build specialized hardware for Ada have provided some very encouraging results. For example, Ericsson (1986) has reported that their purpose-built multiprocessor system (the SDS80/A) can accomplish a simple rendezvous in 60 microseconds. This result comes from having both tasks on the same processor; for a remote rendezvous the figure is only raised to 70 microseconds. They have also produced similarly impressive measurements for task creation, activation and termination.

Ada machines are beginning to appear. The real benefits of purpose-built hardware can however best be illustrated by considering an occam 2 machine – the transputer. A standard transputer contains, on a single chip, a 32-bit 50ns processor, a 64-bit floating point co-processor, internal memory and four communication links for direct connection to other transputers. An address bus joins external memory to the internal provision by means of a continuous address space. Typically, a transputer will have 4K bytes of internal memory; this acts as, in effect, a large collection of non-sharable registers for the executing processes.

The four links are connected to the main processor via four link interfaces. These interfaces can, independently, manage the communications of the link (including direct access to memory). As a result, a transputer can simultaneously communicate on all four links (in both directions), execute an internal process and undertake a floating-point operation.

The transputer has a reduced instruction set but with an operations stack of only three registers. Each instruction has been designed to be of use in the code-generation phase of the occam 2 compiler; direct programming in assembler, although allowed, has not been taken into account in the design of the instruction set. Being a reduced instruction machine, not all instructions are immediately available; those that are directly accessible are precisely those that are commonly generated from real occam 2 programs.

Unfortunately, the transputer can only support a two-level priority model. But by this restriction a run-time support system, that is, essentially, cast in silicon can be provided. The result of this architecture (plus the axiom that context switches only take place when the operations stack is empty) is a context switch of only 0.75 microseconds.

Although the operational characteristics of a single transputer are impressive it is only when they are grouped together that their full potential is realized. Transputers use point-to-point communication, which has the disadvantage that a message may have to be forwarded to its destination via intermediates if no direct link is available. Nevertheless, a link transfer rate of 20 megabits per second and a transmission failure rate that has been designed to be less than 0.1 FIT (less than one failure in ten thousand million operating hours) gives a real-time engine of considerable power and reliability.

SUMMARY

Although efficiency is an important metric by which implementations are judged, it is not considered here to be one of the primary requirements of real-time systems. For all but the trivially small application, this chapter has argued against those who advocate (on the grounds of resultant efficiency) low-level programming. The overriding requirements for correctness and reliability necessitate a more abstract level of programming then can be achieved with machine code or assembler.

Nevertheless, concurrency primitives and exception handling do significantly complicate the implementation of a language, and it is possible for the resulting overheads to be too high for real-time applications. In this chapter, some of the techniques that enable effective implementations of high-level language constructs to be made have been described. These were:

(1)   program transformations,

(2)   effective implementation strategies,

(3)   compiler optimizations,

(4)   purpose-built hardware.

Taken together, these techniques represent a strategy for implementation (and programming) that will enable most real-time systems to be constructed using the language features described in this book. Unfortunately, those who commission real-time systems have a habit of stating requirements that are (almost by definition) at the very edge of what is possible. In these circumstances, software engineers have a responsibility to make absolutely clear the bounds of feasibility and, more importantly, where increased efficiency will cause reliability and safety to be compromised.

Further reading

Baker T.P. and Riccardi G.A. (1985). Ada tasking: from semantics to efficient implementation. *IEEE Software* 2(2), 34–46

Burns A. (1988). Programming in occam 2. Wokingham: Addison-Wesley

Burns A., Lister A.M. and Wellings A.J. (1987). A Review of Ada Tasking. *Lecture Notes in Computer Science*, **262**. Berlin: Springer-Verlag

Eventoff W., Harvey D. and Price R. (1980). The rendezvous and monitor concept: is there an efficiency difference?. In *Proceedings of the ACM-SIGPLAN Symposium on the Ada Programming Language*, SIGPLAN **15**(11), 156–65

Hoppe J. (1980). A simple nucleus written in Modula-2: a case study. *Software Practice and Experience*, **10**(9), 697–706

EXERCISES

15.1 Should the real-time system's programmer be aware of the implementation cost of all the implementation language's features?

15.2 Compare the ease of use of a process abstraction written in Modula-2 with the equivalent abstraction directly supported by a language.

15.3 Sketch the implementation of a fully symmetrical ALT construct for a single-processor system.

15.4 Discuss the problems of implementing Ada's timed and conditional entry calls in a distributed environment. In particular, consider the effect on the protocol of both communication and processor failure. (Hint: see Volz and Mudge (1987)).

Chapter 16
A Case Study in Ada

In this chapter, a case study is presented which includes
many of the facilities described in this book. Ideally, the study
should be given in Ada, Modula-2 and occam 2. Unfortunately,
space is limited so the study is restricted to Ada only. Ada has
been chosen because it is in more widespread use (in the real-
time domain) than the other two languages.

16.1 Mine drainage

The example that has been chosen is based on one which commonly
appears in the literature (it possesses many of the characteristics which
typify embedded real-time systems). It concerns the software necessary to
manage a simplified pump control system in a mining environment
(Kramer *et al.*, 1983). The system is used to pump mine water, which
collects in a sump at the bottom of the shaft, to the surface. A simple
schematic diagram illustrating the system is given in Figure 16.1.

The system consists of two stations: one which controls the pump
itself and one which monitors the environment in which the pump operates. The pump control station monitors the water levels in the sump.
When the water reaches a high level the pump is turned on and the sump is
drained until the water reaches the low level. A flow of water in the pipes

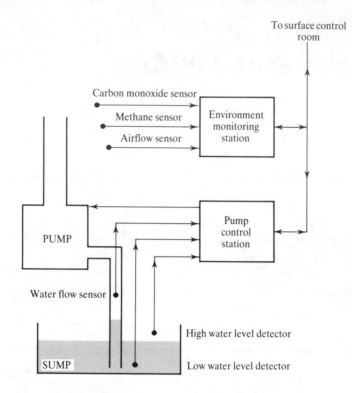

Figure 16.1   A mine drainage control system.

can be detected if required. The environment monitor detects the level of methane (CH_4) in the air; there is a level beyond which it is not safe to operate the pump. The monitor also measures the level of carbon monoxide (CO) in the mine and detects whether or not there is an adequate flow of air.

The system is controlled from the surface via an operator's console. Typically, there would also be a real-time database management system which would log the system events and allow them to be retrieved and displayed upon request.

16.2   The PAMELA method

In order to represent the software design diagrammatically, a precise and structured pictorial notation is required. Rather than use a general-purpose notation, such as that employed in JSD (see Chapter 2), it has been decided to use an Ada-specific methodology. The diagrams presented in this chapter follow closely (though not completely) those proposed in the PAMELA (Process Abstraction Method for Embedded Large

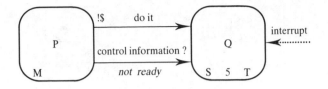

Figure 16.2   A PAMELA-like part diagram.

Applications) method. PAMELA is a scheme devised by Cherry (1986). It supports hierarchical decomposition and an object-oriented design process.

The basic building block in PAMELA is the process. Figure 16.2 illustrates part of a PAMELA-like diagram.

P is the name of a multi-thread process (that is, a package containing one or more tasks, this is indicated by the M) whereas Q is a single task with priority 5 and description T. In Chapter 9 it was noted that tasks can be considered to follow 13 basic idioms; T gives an indication of the appropriate idiom.

Processes are linked by arrows which represent the direction of data-flows. The '!' indicates that P instigates the call of 'do it'; whereas Q calls P to get the control information passed (that is, '?' at Q's end of the data-flow). The '$' with the '!' indicates a timed entry call. If an exception could be raised during process interaction then the name of the exception is given in italics. To distinguish an interrupt entry from a normal dataflow a broken arrow is used.

16.3   Top-level description

The relationship between the control system and the external devices is shown in Figure 16.3. Note that only the high and low water sensors communicate via interrupts; all the other devices are either polled or directly controlled.

The polled devices (which will be controlled by periodic processes) have the defined periods (in seconds) that are shown in Table 16.1.

Table 16.1   Cycle times for periodic processes.

Polled device	Period
CH_4 sensor	10.0
CO sensor	25.0
Water flow sensor	30.0
Air flow sensor	60.0

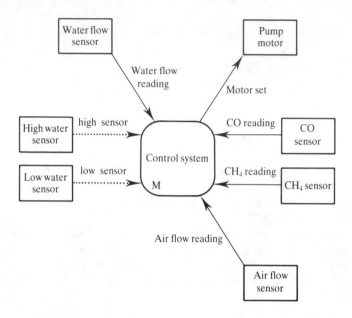

Figure 16.3 Master graph showing external objects.

Each external device is controlled by one or two registers: a Control and Status Register (CSR) and a Data Buffer Register (DBR). Table 16.2 indicates the hardware address of the interrupt location (if used) and the registers, of each device.

Each register is 16 bits long. The control and status registers have the format shown in Figure 16.4. For the CH_4 and CO ADC devices the 'device operation' bit is used to start the conversion (only one input channel is assumed).

Table 16.2 Hardware device registers.

Device	Interrupt address	CSR	DBR
High water sensor	16#40#	16#AA10#	–
Low water sensor	16#44#	16#AA12#	–
Water flow sensor	–	16#AA14#	–
Pump motor	–	16#AA16#	–
CH_4 sensor	–	16#AA18#	16#AA1A#
CO sensor	–	16#AA1C#	16#AA1E#
Air flow sensor	–	16#AA20#	–

15		10		7	6		0	Bit
Device error		Device operation		Done	Interrupt enable		Device enable	

Figure 16.4 Control and status register bits.

The two data buffer registers return a scaled integer value which represents the level of gas in the surrounding atmosphere. The ADC provides a 10-bit reading which is mapped on to the least significant bits of the register. A reading between 0 and 1023 is, therefore, possible. For the methane, a value of 400 (on this scale) is considered too high. The associated value for carbon monoxide is 600.

16.4 First-level decomposition

The control system is naturally decomposed into four main subsystems: Pump Controller (PC), Environment Monitor (EM), Operator Console Interface(OCI) and Data Logging and Retrieval (DLR). Figure 16.5 illustrates this decomposition.

The relationship between these four subsystems is shown in Figure 16.6.

There are, in all, 14 different dataflows between the four subsystems (note that some arrows are used to represent more than one dataflow). Six of these interactions are merely data logging actions and are shown as timed entry calls on the DLR (timed entry calls are used so that critical control functions are not adversely delayed by a tardy DLR).

The environmental monitor calls 'alarm' in the OCI if any of its readings are too high. In addition, it also calls the pump controller if it

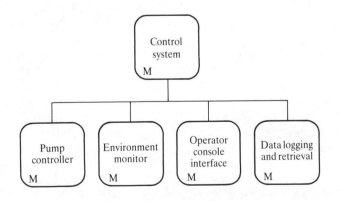

Figure 16.5 Hierarchical decomposition of the control system.

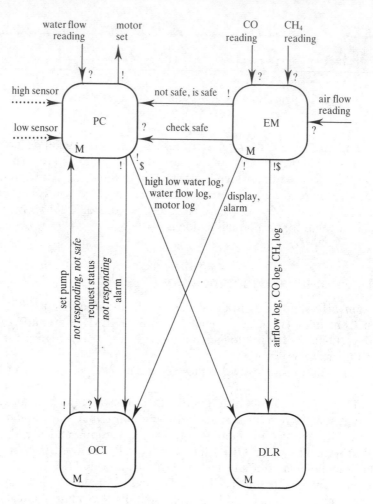

Figure 16.6   First-level description of control system.

finds that the methane level is dangerous (it will subsequently reverse this effect by calling 'is safe' when the methane level falls).

As an additional reliability feature, the PC will always check that the methane level is low before starting the pump. If PC finds that the pump cannot be started (or that the water does not appear to be flowing when the pump is notionally on) then it also calls 'alarm' in the OCI.

The OCI itself has a multi-level interface. As well as receiving the alarm calls, it can request the status of the pump and attempt to override the high and low water sensors by directly operating the pump. However, in the latter case the methane check is still made, with an exception being used to inform the operator that the pump cannot be turned on. An exception is also used to inform the OCI that the pump control software is not responding.

16.4.1   Package specifications for the control subsystems

Each of the subsystems is represented in Figure 16.6 as a multi-threaded process. It is assumed that each subsystem can potentially be implemented on a separate processor – in the terminology of Chapter 12 they are virtual nodes. Where possible, a procedural interface is used between virtual nodes. This model is employed here, apart from within the DLR. In order for the other components to make timed entry calls on the logger it must have a task visible within its interface.

It is now possible to give the Ada code for the packages represented in Figure 16.6. Firstly, a set of global type declarations are grouped together into an appropriate library unit. The meaning of each type declaration within this package should be clear.

Global type declarations

```
package SYSTEM_TYPES is

    type PUMP_STATUS is (ON, OFF, DISABLED);

    type METHANE_STATUS is (MOTOR_SAFE, MOTOR_UNSAFE);

    type WATER_MARK is (HIGH, LOW);

    type CH4_READING is new INTEGER range 0 .. 1023;
    type CO_READING is new INTEGER range 0 .. 1023;

    type MOTOR_STATE_CHANGES is (MOTOR_STARTED,
        MOTOR_STOPPED, MOTOR_SAFE, MOTOR_UNSAFE);

    type ALARM_REASON is (HIGH_METHANE, HIGH_CO, PUMP_DEAD,
                          DATA_LOGGER_DEAD, NO_AIR_FLOW,
                          CH4_DEVICE_ERROR, CO_DEVICE_ERROR,
                          UNKNOWN_ERROR);

    WATER_FLOW_SENSOR_PERIOD : constant DURATION := 30.0;
    AIR_FLOW_SENSOR_PERIOD : constant DURATION := 60.0;
    CH4_SENSOR_PERIOD : constant DURATION := 10.0;
    CO_SENSOR_PERIOD : constant DURATION := 25.0;

    CO_HIGH : constant CO_READING := 600;
    CH4_HIGH : constant CH4_READING := 400;

end SYSTEM_TYPES;
```

Package specifications for each of the four subsystems can now be given.

The pump controller

```
with SYSTEM_TYPES; use SYSTEM_TYPES;
package PUMP_CONTROLLER is

   NOT_SAFE : exception;
   -- raised by operator_console_interface.set_pump
   NOT_RESPONDING : exception;
   -- raised by operator_console.set_pump and
   -- environment_monitor.stop_pump

   package ENVIRONMENT_MONITOR_INTERFACE is
      procedure NOT_SAFE;
      procedure IS_SAFE;
   end ENVIRONMENT_MONITOR_INTERFACE;

   package OPERATOR_CONSOLE_INTERFACE is
      function REQUEST_STATUS return PUMP_STATUS;
      procedure SET_PUMP(TO : PUMP_STATUS);
   end OPERATOR_CONSOLE_INTERFACE;

   -- calls function check_safe in
   -- environment_monitor.pump_controller_interface

   -- calls entries waterflow_log and high_low_water_log and motor_log in
   -- data_logging_retrieval.pump_controller_interface

   -- calls procedure pump_alarm in
   -- operator_console.pump_controller_interface

end PUMP_CONTROLLER;
```

Environment monitoring

```
with SYSTEM_TYPES; use SYSTEM_TYPES;
package ENVIRONMENT_MONITOR is

   package PUMP_CONTROL_INTERFACE is
      function CHECK_SAFE return METHANE_STATUS;
   end PUMP_CONTROL_INTERFACE;

   -- calls procedures is_safe and not_safe in
   -- pump_controller.environment_monitor_interface
   -- calls procedure alarm in
   -- operator_console_interface.environment_monitor_interface
```

```
                -- calls entries airflow_log, CO_log, CH4_log
                -- in data_logging_retrieval.environ_mon_interface

            end ENVIRONMENT_MONITOR;
```

Data logging and retrieval

```
            with SYSTEM_TYPES; use SYSTEM_TYPES;
            package DATA_LOGGING_RETRIEVAL is

                task ENVIRONMENT_MONITOR_INTERFACE is
                    entry CO_LOG(READING : CO_READING);
                    entry CH4_LOG(READING : CH4_READING);
                    entry AIRFLOW_LOG(READING : BOOLEAN);
                    pragma PRIORITY(0);
                end ENVIRONMENT_MONITOR_INTERFACE;

                task PUMP_CONTROLLER_INTERFACE is
                    entry HIGH_LOW_WATER_LOG(MARK : WATER_MARK);
                    entry WATER_FLOW_LOG(READING : BOOLEAN);
                    entry MOTOR_LOG(STATE : MOTOR_STATE_CHANGES);
                    pragma PRIORITY(0);
                end PUMP_CONTROLLER_INTERFACE;

                -- there would also be an interface for the
                -- operator console

            end DATA_LOGGING_RETRIEVAL;
```

Operator console interface

```
            with SYSTEM_TYPES; use SYSTEM_TYPES;
            package OPERATOR_CONSOLE is

                package ENVIRONMENT_MONITOR_INTERFACE is
                    procedure ALARM(REASON: ALARM_REASON);
                end ENVIRONMENT_MONITOR_INTERFACE;

                package PUMP_CONTROLLER_INTERFACE is
                    procedure ALARM(REASON: ALARM_REASON)
                        renames ENVIRONMENT_MONITOR_INTERFACE.ALARM;
                end PUMP_CONTROLLER_INTERFACE;

                -- calls request_status in pump_controller.operator_console_interface
                -- calls set_pump in pump_controller.operator_console_interface

            end OPERATOR_CONSOLE;
```

Consideration will now be restricted to the pump controller and environmental monitor.

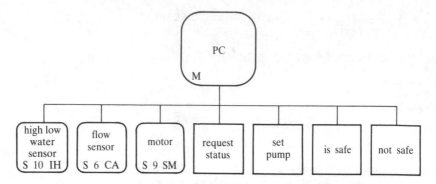

Figure 16.7   Hierarchical decomposition of the pump controller.

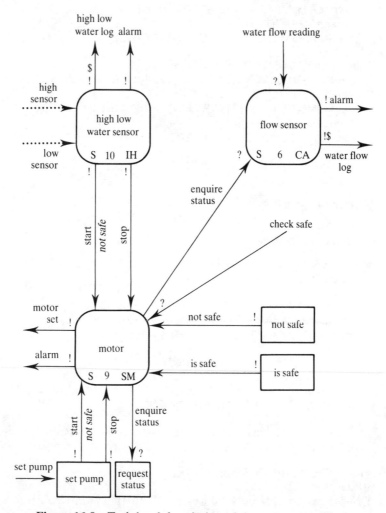

Figure 16.8   Task-level description of the pump controller.

16.5   Pump controller

The decomposition appropriate to the pump controller is shown in Figure 16.7. In this figure, the square boxes represent the subprograms that form the interface to the pump controller. The other components are tasks; with three task idioms being used:

- IH – Interrupt Handler
- CA – Cyclic Activity (that is, periodic task)
- SM – State Machine

Each task has also been assigned a priority (this is discussed in Section 16.7).

Figure 16.8 illustrates the interactions between the seven components of the pump controller. The procedures are straightforward and many of the data flows were introduced earlier in Figure 16.6 (for example, the 'alarm' signals). Internal to the pump controller there are seven new dataflows; they all concern the motor. This task accepts calls to stop, start, enquire status, not safe and is safe.

It is now possible to give the code for the body of the pump controller package.

16.5.1   Pump controller package body

```ada
with SYSTEM; use SYSTEM;
package body PUMP_CONTROLLER is

  task HIGH_LOW_WATER_SENSOR is
    entry HIGH_SENSOR;
    entry LOW_SENSOR;

    for HIGH_SENSOR use at 16#40#;        -- interrupt address
    for LOW_SENSOR use at 16#44#;         -- interrupt address

    pragma PRIORITY(10);

  end HIGH_LOW_WATER_SENSOR;

  task FLOW_SENSOR is
    pragma PRIORITY(6);
  end FLOW_SENSOR;
```

```
task MOTOR is
  entry START;       -- can raise NOT_SAFE_TO_START
  entry STOP;
  entry IS_SAFE;
  entry NOT_SAFE;
  entry ENQUIRE_STATUS(CURRENT_PUMP_STATUS:
      out PUMP_STATUS);
  pragma PRIORITY(9);
end MOTOR;

task body HIGH_LOW_WATER_SENSOR is separate;
task body FLOW_SENSOR is separate;
task body MOTOR is separate;

package body OPERATOR_CONSOLE_INTERFACE is separate;
package body ENVIRONMENT_MONITOR_INTERFACE is separate;

end PUMP_CONTROLLER;
```

The code for the interface packages follows directly:

Operator console interface package body

```
separate(PUMP_CONTROLLER)

package body OPERATOR_CONSOLE_INTERFACE is

  function REQUEST_STATUS return PUMP_STATUS is
    CURRENT_PUMP_STATUS : PUMP_STATUS;
  begin
    MOTOR.ENQUIRE_STATUS(CURRENT_PUMP_STATUS);
    return CURRENT_PUMP_STATUS;
  end;

  procedure SET_PUMP(TO : PUMP_STATUS) is
  begin
    if TO = OFF then
      MOTOR.STOP;
    elsif TO = ON then
      MOTOR.START;       -- any exception propagates to caller
    else
      MOTOR.NOT_SAFE;
    end if;
  exception
    when TASKING_ERROR =>
      raise NOT_RESPONDING;
  end SET_PUMP;

end OPERATOR_CONSOLE_INTERFACE;
```

Environment monitoring interface package body

```
with OPERATOR_CONSOLE;
separate(PUMP_CONTROLLER)

package body ENVIRONMENT_MONITOR_INTERFACE is

  procedure NOT_SAFE is
  begin
    MOTOR.NOT_SAFE;
    OPERATOR_CONSOLE.PUMP_CONTROLLER_
        INTERFACE.ALARM(HIGH_METHANE);
  exception
    when TASKING_ERROR ⇒
      OPERATOR_CONSOLE.PUMP_CONTROLLER_
          INTERFACE.ALARM(PUMP_DEAD);
      raise NOT_RESPONDING;

  end NOT_SAFE;

  procedure IS_SAFE is
  begin
    MOTOR.IS_SAFE;
  exception
    when TASKING_ERROR ⇒
      OPERATOR_CONSOLE.PUMP_CONTROLLER_
          INTERFACE.ALARM(PUMP_DEAD);
      raise NOT_RESPONDING;

  end IS_SAFE;

end ENVIRONMENT_MONITOR_INTERFACE;
```

Before giving the code for each of the tasks within the pump controller it is necessary to consider the programming of the device registers. In this system all the control/status registers are of the same type. It is, therefore, appropriate to define a single package that can be used for all the device driver tasks. This package is called DEVICE_REGISTER.

Device register definition

```
package DEVICE_REGISTER is

  WORD : constant := 2;        -- two bytes in a word
  ONE_WORD : constant := 16;   -- 16 bits in a word
  -- register field types
  type DEVICE_ERROR is (CLEAR, SET);
  type DEVICE_OPERATION is (CLEAR, SET);
  type INTERRUPT_STATUS is (I_DISABLED, I_ENABLED);
  type DEVICE_STATUS is (D_DISABLED, D_ENABLED);
```

```
      -- register type itself
      type CSR is
        record
          ERROR_BIT    : DEVICE_ERROR;
          OPERATION    : DEVICE_OPERATION;
          DONE         : BOOLEAN;
          INTERRUPT    : INTERRUPT_STATUS;
          DEVICE       : DEVICE_STATUS;
        end record;

      -- bit representation of the register field
      for DEVICE_ERROR use (CLEAR ⇒ 0, SET ⇒ 1);
      for DEVICE_OPERATION use (CLEAR ⇒ 0, SET ⇒ 1);
      for INTERRUPT_STATUS use (I_DISABLED ⇒ 0, I_ENABLED ⇒ 1);
      for DEVICE_STATUS use (D_DISABLED ⇒ 0, D_ENABLED ⇒ 1);
      for CSR use
        record at mod WORD;
          ERROR_BIT    at 0 range 15 .. 15;
          OPERATION    at 0 range 10 .. 10;
          DONE         at 0 range 7 .. 7;
          INTERRUPT    at 0 range 6 .. 6;
          DEVICE       at 0 range 0 .. 0;
        end record;
      for CSR'SIZE use ONE_WORD;
    end DEVICE_REGISTER;
```

The code for the three tasks can now be given, in Programs 16.1 to 16.3.

Program 16.1   High and low water sensor interrupt-handling task body

```
      with DATA_LOGGING_RETRIEVAL;
      with OPERATOR_CONSOLE;
      with DEVICE_REGISTER; use DEVICE_REGISTER;
      separate(PUMP_CONTROLLER)

      task body HIGH_LOW_WATER_SENSOR is

        -- sporadic task

        -- define control and status registers
        -- for the high and low water switches
        HWCSR : DEVICE_REGISTER.CSR;
        for HWCSR use at 16#AA10#;
        LWCSR : DEVICE_REGISTER.CSR;
        for LWCSR use at 16#AA12#;
        WATER : WATER_MARK;
```

```
begin
  -- enable devices
  HWCSR.DEVICE := D_ENABLED;
  LWCSR.DEVICE := D_ENABLED;

  loop
    begin
      -- enable interrupts
      HWCSR.INTERRUPT := I_ENABLED;
      LWCSR.INTERRUPT := I_ENABLED;
      begin
        select
          accept HIGH_SENSOR;
          MOTOR.START;
          WATER := HIGH;
        or
          accept LOW_SENSOR;
          MOTOR.STOP;
          WATER := LOW;
        end select;
      exception
        when TASKING_ERROR ⇒
          OPERATOR_CONSOLE.PUMP_CONTROLLER_
              INTERFACE.ALARM(PUMP_DEAD);
      end;

      select
        DATA_LOGGING_RETRIEVAL.PUMP_CONTROLLER_
            INTERFACE.HIGH_LOW_WATER_LOG(WATER);
      or
        delay 10.0;
      end select;

    exception

      when NOT_SAFE ⇒
        OPERATOR_CONSOLE.PUMP_CONTROLLER_
            INTERFACE.ALARM(HIGH_METHANE);
      when TASKING_ERROR ⇒
        OPERATOR_CONSOLE.PUMP_CONTROLLER_
            INTERFACE.ALARM(DATA_LOGGER_DEAD);
      when others ⇒
        OPERATOR_CONSOLE.PUMP_CONTROLLER_
            INTERFACE.ALARM(UNKNOWN_ERROR);
    end;
  end loop;
end HIGH_LOW_WATER_SENSOR;
```

HIGH_LOW_WATER_SENSOR is a straightforward interrupt handler task. It accepts interrupts from both the high and low water sensors. Once such an interrupt has arrived it calls the appropriate entry in the motor. After receiving a call (and notifying the motor) the event is logged at the DLR. This logging takes the form of a timed entry call. The task is prepared to wait ten seconds for a response before looping round and becoming ready for the next interrupt. If any exception is raised during this task interaction with other components in the system, then 'alarm' is called in the OCI. Note that if the OCI component has failed then the system is deemed to be beyond repair and the device controller also terminates.

Program 16.2   Water flow sensor handling task body.

```
with DATA_LOGGING_RETRIEVAL;
with OPERATOR_CONSOLE;
with CALENDAR; use CALENDAR;
with DEVICE_REGISTER; use DEVICE_REGISTER;
separate(PUMP_CONTROLLER)

task body FLOW_SENSOR is

  -- periodic task

  START_TIME : CALENDAR.TIME;
  WATER_FLOW : BOOLEAN := FALSE;
  CURRENT_PUMP_STATUS: PUMP_STATUS;

  -- define control and status register
  -- for the flow switch
  WFCSR : DEVICE_REGISTER.CSR;
  for WFCSR use at 16#AA14#;

begin
  -- enable device
  WFCSR.DEVICE := D_ENABLED;
  loop
    begin
      START_TIME := CALENDAR.CLOCK;
      MOTOR.ENQUIRE_STATUS(CURRENT_PUMP_STATUS);

      -- read device register
      WATER_FLOW:= (WFCSR.OPERATION = SET);
      if CURRENT_PUMP_STATUS = ON and not WATER_FLOW then
        -- give time for pump to cause a flow
        delay 10.0;
        -- read device register again
        WATER_FLOW:= (WFCSR.OPERATION = SET);
        if CURRENT_PUMP_STATUS = ON and not WATER_FLOW then
          OPERATOR_CONSOLE.PUMP_CONTROLLER_INTERFACE.
            ALARM(PUMP_DEAD);
        end if;
      end if;
```

```
     select
         DATA_LOGGING_RETRIEVAL.PUMP_CONTROLLER_INTERFACE.
             WATER_FLOW_LOG(WATER_FLOW);
     or      -- delay until next period
         delay(CALENDAR.CLOCK - (START_TIME
                                 + WATER_FLOW_SENSOR_PERIOD));
     end select;
     -- may be 0.0
     delay(CALENDAR.CLOCK - (START_TIME
                             + WATER_FLOW_SENSOR_PERIOD));
   exception
     when TASKING_ERROR ⇒
         OPERATOR_CONSOLE.PUMP_CONTROLLER_INTERFACE.
             ALARM(DATA_LOGGER_DEAD);
     when others ⇒
         OPERATOR_CONSOLE.PUMP_CONTROLLER_INTERFACE.
             ALARM(UNKNOWN_ERROR);
   end;
 end loop;

end FLOW_SENSOR;
```

FLOW_SENSOR task is a standard example of a periodic process. During each period it checks to see if the motor is running and the water flowing. As the water sensor is some distance from the pump, it is possible for the pump to have just started running but that no water has reached the sensor. To cater for this event a delay is used before a second reading of the water flow is made. 'Alarm' is called only if there is no flow when the second reading is taken. At the end of this action, it calculates the time delay before its next period. It will then be prepared to wait this time for the DLR to respond to its data logging request. Once this has occurred the task executes a delay until the start of its next period.

Program 16.3   Pump motor task body.

```
   with DATA_LOGGING_RETRIEVAL;
   with ENVIRONMENT_MONITOR;
   with DEVICE_REGISTER; use DEVICE_REGISTER;
   with OPERATOR_CONSOLE;
   separate(PUMP_CONTROLLER)

   task body MOTOR is
       MOTOR : PUMP_STATUS := OFF;
       RETURN_CONDITION: PUMP_STATUS := OFF;
   -- define control and status register for the motor
       PCSR : DEVICE_REGISTER.CSR;
       for PCSR use at 16#AA14#;
```

Program 16.3   (cont.)

```
            package LOG renames DATA_LOGGING_RETRIEVAL;
            package ENVIRONMENT renames ENVIRONMENT_MONITOR.
                  PUMP_CONTROL_INTERFACE;
begin
      -- enable device
      PCSR.DEVICE := D_ENABLED;
      PCSR.OPERATION := CLEAR;      -- motor off
      loop
        begin
          select
            accept START do
              if MOTOR = OFF or MOTOR = DISABLED then
                if ENVIRONMENT.CHECK_SAFE = MOTOR_SAFE then
                  MOTOR := ON;
                  PCSR.OPERATION := SET;      -- turn on motor
                  select
                    LOG.PUMP_CONTROLLER_INTERFACE.
                        MOTOR_LOG(MOTOR_STARTED);
                  or
                    delay 10.0;
                  end select;
                elsif MOTOR = DISABLED then
                  raise PUMP_CONTROLLER.NOT_SAFE;
                end if;
              end if;
            end START;
          or
            accept STOP;
            if MOTOR = ON then
              PCSR.OPERATION := CLEAR;      -- turn off motor
              MOTOR:= OFF;
              select
                LOG.PUMP_CONTROLLER_INTERFACE.
                    MOTOR_LOG(MOTOR_STOPPED);
              or
                delay 10.0;
              end select;
            end if;
          or
            accept NOT_SAFE;
            if MOTOR /= DISABLED then
              RETURN_CONDITION := MOTOR;
              MOTOR := DISABLED;
              PCSR.OPERATION := CLEAR;      -- turn off motor
              select
                LOG.PUMP_CONTROLLER_INTERFACE.
                    MOTOR_LOG(MOTOR_UNSAFE);
```

```
            or
                delay 10.0;
            end select;
        end if;
    or
        accept IS_SAFE do
            select
                LOG.PUMP_CONTROLLER_INTERFACE.
                    MOTOR_LOG(MOTOR_SAFE);
            or
                delay 10.0;
            end select;
            if RETURN_CONDITION = ON then
                PCSR.OPERATION := SET;      -- start motor
                select
                    LOG.PUMP_CONTROLLER_INTERFACE.
                        MOTOR_LOG(MOTOR_STARTED);
                or
                    delay 10.0;
                end select;
            end if;
            MOTOR := RETURN_CONDITION;
        end IS_SAFE;
    or
        accept ENQUIRE_STATUS(CURRENT_PUMP_STATUS:
                out PUMP_STATUS) do
            CURRENT_PUMP_STATUS := MOTOR;
        end ENQUIRE_STATUS;
    end select;
    exception
        when PUMP_CONTROLLER.NOT_SAFE ⇒
            OPERATOR_CONSOLE.PUMP_CONTROLLER_INTERFACE.
                ALARM(HIGH_METHANE);
        when TASKING_ERROR ⇒
            OPERATOR_CONSOLE.PUMP_CONTROLLER_INTERFACE.
                ALARM(DATA_LOGGER_DEAD);
        when others ⇒
            OPERATOR_CONSOLE.PUMP_CONTROLLER_INTERFACE.
                ALARM(UNKNOWN_ERROR);
    end;
end loop;


exception
    when others ⇒
        MOTOR := DISABLED;
        PCSR.OPERATION := CLEAR;      -- turn off motor

end MOTOR;
```

Although this MOTOR task is the most complicated in the system its behaviour is quite simple. It responds to its entries and changes the state of the pump as a consequence. If the request is for the motor to be turned on (and it is not currently working) then a check is made of the environmental monitor's reading of the methane level. Only if this value is acceptable is the physical motor started.

The environmental monitor will call the motor task when the air becomes unsafe. If the motor is currently running it is immediately turned off. At a later time if 'is safe' is called then the pump will be returned to its original state. If it was previously running then it will be turned on again; if not then its state will change to 'off'. As with the other tasks, error conditions are passed on as alarms and data logging activities are programmed with timeouts. If an alarm call fails (due to the OCI malfunctioning) then the motor task will terminate. As a final act, however, it will make sure that the motor is off.

16.6 Environmental monitor

The other main subsystem is now considered. An appropriate decomposition is shown in Figure 16.9.

Note that the 'check safe' component is a subprogram. This will allow the pump controller to observe the current state of the methane level without blocking. All other components are single-threaded periodic tasks.

The task-level view of these components is shown in Figure 16.10.

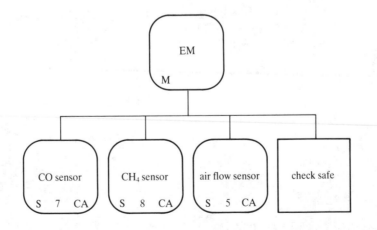

Figure 16.9 Hierarchical decomposition of the environment monitor.

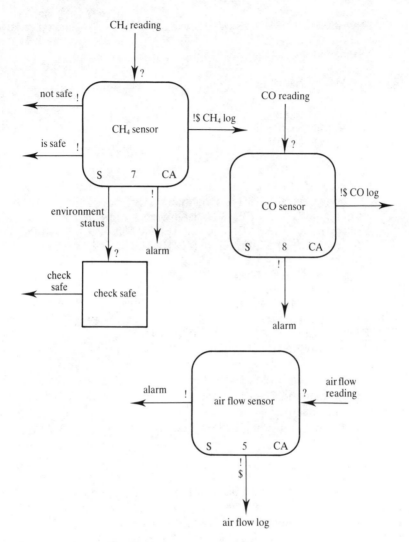

Figure 16.10 Task-level description of the environment monitor.

16.6.1 Environment monitoring package body

The code for the package body follows directly from Figure 16.10.

```
with SYSTEM; use SYSTEM;
package body ENVIRONMENT_MONITOR is
```

```
ENVIRONMENT_STATUS : METHANE_STATUS;      -- shared variable
task CO_SENSOR is
   pragma PRIORITY(7);
end;
task CH4_SENSOR is
   pragma PRIORITY(8);
end;
task AIR_FLOW_SENSOR is
   pragma PRIORITY(5);
end;

task body CO_SENSOR is separate;
task body CH4_SENSOR is separate;
task body AIR_FLOW_SENSOR is separate;
package body PUMP_CONTROL_INTERFACE is
   function CHECK_SAFE return METHANE_STATUS is
   begin
      return ENVIRONMENT_STATUS;
   end CHECK_SAFE;
end PUMP_CONTROL_INTERFACE;
begin
   ENVIRONMENT_STATUS := MOTOR_UNSAFE;
end ENVIRONMENT_MONITOR;
```

Note that the variable ENVIRONMENT_STATUS is a shared variable, accessed via the function CHECK_SAFE. It is updated by the device controller for the methane sensor.

All that now remains is for the three task bodies to be coded.

CH$_4$ sensor handling task body

Analogue to digital converters work in many different ways and have a range of operational characteristics. The code presented in Program 16.4 is for a simple converter. Having been asked for a reading (by setting CH4CSR.OPERATION) the device will perform the conversion, place the scaled integer on the data buffer register and then set the done bit on the control/status register. The driver task loops around waiting for the done bit to be set. Other types of converter are interrupt-driven or give a continuous reading in the data buffer. To protect the software from a faulty device (that is, one that never sets the done bit) the task delays for 0.5 seconds and then checks the flag. The device's operational characteristics dictate that the reading should be available well within the time range. If the done bit is not set then an error condition is reported to the operator console.

Once a reading has been obtained it is compared with the HIGH value and, if necessary, the appropriate call in the pump controller is made. Alternatively, if the reading is below the HIGH level, and the motor is disabled (unsafe), then a call to re-enable the motor is undertaken. To

Program 16.4

```ada
with DATA_LOGGING_RETRIEVAL;
with PUMP_CONTROLLER; use PUMP_CONTROLLER;
with OPERATOR_CONSOLE;
with CALENDAR; use CALENDAR;
with DEVICE_REGISTER; use DEVICE_REGISTER;
separate(ENVIRONMENT_MONITOR)

task body CH4_SENSOR is

   -- periodic task

   START_TIME : CALENDAR.TIME;
   CH4_PRESENT : CH4_READING;
   -- define control and status register
   -- for the CH4 ADC
   CH4CSR : DEVICE_REGISTER.CSR;
   for CH4CSR use at 16#AA18#;
   -- define the data register
   CH4DBR : CH4_READING;
   for CH4DBR use at 16#AA1A#;
   for CH4DBR'SIZE use ONE_WORD;
   JITTER_RANGE : constant CH4_READING := 40;
begin
   CH4CSR.DEVICE := D_ENABLED;
   loop
      begin
         START_TIME := CALENDAR.CLOCK;
         CH4CSR.OPERATION := SET;      -- start conversion
         delay 0.5;                    -- wait for conversion
         if not CH4CSR.DONE then
            OPERATOR_CONSOLE.ENVIRONMENT_MONITOR_INTERFACE.
               ALARM(CH4_DEVICE_ERROR);
         else
            -- read device register for sensor value
            CH4_PRESENT := CH4DBR;
            begin
               if CH4_PRESENT > CH4_HIGH then
                  if ENVIRONMENT_STATUS = MOTOR_SAFE then
                     PUMP_CONTROLLER.ENVIRONMENT_MONITOR_INTERFACE.
                        NOT_SAFE;
                     ENVIRONMENT_STATUS := MOTOR_UNSAFE;
                  end if;
               elsif (CH4_PRESENT < (CH4_HIGH - JITTER_RANGE)) and
                     (ENVIRONMENT_STATUS = MOTOR_UNSAFE) then
                  PUMP_CONTROLLER.ENVIRONMENT_MONITOR_INTERFACE.
                     IS_SAFE;
                  ENVIRONMENT_STATUS := MOTOR_SAFE;
               end if;
```

Program 16.4   (cont.)

```
            exception
              when TASKING_ERROR ⇒
                OPERATOR_CONSOLE.ENVIRONMENT_MONITOR_INTERFACE.
                    ALARM(PUMP_DEAD);
            end;


            select
              DATA_LOGGING_RETRIEVAL.
                  ENVIRONMENT_MONITOR_INTERFACE.
                  CH4_LOG(CH4_PRESENT);
            or
                delay(CALENDAR.CLOCK − (START_TIME
                                            + CH4_SENSOR_PERIOD));
              end select;
            end if;
            delay(CALENDAR.CLOCK − (START_TIME              −− could be 0.0
                                        + CH4_SENSOR_PERIOD));
          exception
            when TASKING_ERROR ⇒
              OPERATOR_CONSOLE.ENVIRONMENT_MONITOR_INTERFACE.
                  ALARM(DATA_LOGGER_DEAD);
              delay(CALENDAR.CLOCK − (START_TIME            −− could be 0.0
                                        + CH4_SENSOR_PERIOD));
            when others ⇒
              OPERATOR_CONSOLE.PUMP_CONTROLLER_INTERFACE.
                  ALARM(UNKNOWN_ERROR);
              PUMP_CONTROLLER.ENVIRONMENT_MONITOR_INTERFACE.
                  NOT_SAFE;
              ENVIRONMENT_STATUS := MOTOR_UNSAFE;
              delay(CALENDAR.CLOCK − (START_TIME            −− could be 0.0
                                        + CH4_SENSOR_PERIOD));
          end;
        end loop;
    exception
      when others ⇒
          −− One possible exception that would be caught is CONSTRAINT_ERROR
          −− which could theoretically be generated by the sensor reading going out of
          −− range. However, as this is a 10 bit device register which is mapped to the
          −− least significant end of a 16 bit memory location the error should not
          −− occur, and is therefore not caught explicitly.
          OPERATOR_CONSOLE.PUMP_CONTROLLER_INTERFACE.
              ALARM(UNKNOWN_ERROR);
          PUMP_CONTROLLER.ENVIRONMENT_MONITOR_INTERFACE.NOT_SAFE;
          −− try and turn motor off before terminating
          ENVIRONMENT_STATUS := MOTOR_UNSAFE;
    end CH4_SENSOR;
```

prevent the motor being continually switched on and off when the methane level is hovering around the HIGH level a JITTER_RANGE is incorporated into the test for MOTOR_SAFE.

The above algorithm uses a simple tactic to decide if the methane level is acceptable. Other strategies might involve monitoring the change in methane level so that predictions could be made about the likelihood of a HIGH reading in the future.

Having taken a reading (and undertaken whatever communications with the pump controller are appropriate) the task uses up the rest of its period attempting to log its reading in the DLR. It then delays for whatever time is needed to complete its temporal scope.

CO sensor handling task body

The CO controller is a simplified version of the CH_4 task. On finding a high level its only role is to inform the operator, this is shown in Program 16.5.

Program 16.5

```
with DATA_LOGGING_RETRIEVAL;
with CALENDAR; use CALENDAR;
with DEVICE_REGISTER; use DEVICE_REGISTER;
with SYSTEM; use SYSTEM;
with OPERATOR_CONSOLE;
separate(ENVIRONMENT_MONITOR)


task body CO_SENSOR is


    -- periodic task


    CO_PRESENT : CO_READING;
    START_TIME : CALENDAR.TIME;
    -- define control and status register
    -- for the CO ADC
    COCSR : DEVICE_REGISTER.CSR;
    for COCSR use at 16#AA1C#;
    -- define the data register
    CODBR : CO_READING;
    for CODBR use at 16#AA1E#;
    for CODBR'SIZE use ONE_WORD;
begin
    COCSR.DEVICE := D_ENABLED;
```

Program 16.5   (cont.)

```
loop
  begin
    START_TIME := CALENDAR.CLOCK;
    COCSR.OPERATION := SET;        -- start conversion
    delay 0.5;                     -- wait for conversion
    if not COCSR.DONE then
      OPERATOR_CONSOLE.ENVIRONMENT_MONITOR_INTERFACE.
          ALARM(CO_DEVICE_ERROR);
    else
      -- read device register for sensor value
      CO_PRESENT := CODBR;
      if CO_PRESENT > CO_HIGH then
        OPERATOR_CONSOLE.ENVIRONMENT_MONITOR_INTERFACE.
            ALARM(HIGH_CO);
      end if;
      select
        DATA_LOGGING_RETRIEVAL.
            ENVIRONMENT_MONITOR_INTERFACE.
            CO_LOG(CO_PRESENT);
      or
        delay(CALENDAR.CLOCK - (START_TIME
                              + CO_SENSOR_PERIOD));
      end select;
    end if;
    -- could be 0.0
    delay(CALENDAR.CLOCK - (START_TIME + CO_SENSOR_PERIOD));
  exception
    when TASKING_ERROR =>
      OPERATOR_CONSOLE.ENVIRONMENT_MONITOR_INTERFACE.
          ALARM(DATA_LOGGER_DEAD);
      -- could be 0.0
      delay(CALENDAR.CLOCK - (START_TIME + CO_SENSOR_PERIOD));
    when others =>
      -- One possible exception that would be caught is
      -- CONSTRAINT_ERROR which could theoretically be generated
      -- by the sensor reading going out of range. However, as this is a
      -- 10 bit device register which is mapped to the least significant
      -- end of a 16 bit memory location the error should not occur, and
      -- is therefore not caught explicitly.
      OPERATOR_CONSOLE.PUMP_CONTROLLER_INTERFACE.
          ALARM(UNKNOWN_ERROR);
      -- could be 0.0
      delay(CALENDAR.CLOCK - (START_TIME + CO_SENSOR_PERIOD));
  end;
  end loop;
end CO_SENSOR;
```

Air flow sensor handling task body

The air flow sensor is also very simple, as shown in Program 16.6, it needs a long sample time and only signals a lack of air flow if no current has been detected over this period. It signals the lack of air flow via the set bit in the control/status buffer. The controller task merely checks this value and calls alarm if no flow is observed.

Program 16.6

```
with DATA_LOGGING_RETRIEVAL;
with CALENDAR; use CALENDAR;
with DEVICE_REGISTER; use DEVICE_REGISTER;
with SYSTEM; use SYSTEM;
with OPERATOR_CONSOLE;
separate(ENVIRONMENT_MONITOR)


task body AIR_FLOW_SENSOR is

  -- periodic task
  START_TIME : CALENDAR.TIME;
  AIR_FLOW : BOOLEAN;


  -- define control and status register
  -- for the flow switch
  AFCSR : DEVICE_REGISTER.CSR;
  for AFCSR use at 16#AA20#;
begin
  -- enables device
  AFCSR.DEVICE := D_ENABLED;
  loop
    begin
      START_TIME := CALENDAR.CLOCK;
      -- read device register for flow indication (operation bit set to 1);
      AIR_FLOW := AFCSR.OPERATION = SET;
      if not AIR_FLOW then
        OPERATOR_CONSOLE.ENVIRONMENT_MONITOR_INTERFACE.
            ALARM(NO_AIR_FLOW);
      end if;
      select
        DATA_LOGGING_RETRIEVAL.
            ENVIRONMENT_MONITOR_INTERFACE.
            AIRFLOW_LOG(AIR_FLOW);
      or
        delay(CALENDAR.CLOCK - (START_TIME
                              + AIR_FLOW_SENSOR_PERIOD));
      end select;
```

Program 16.6   (cont.)

```
        -- could be 0
        delay(CALENDAR.CLOCK - (START_TIME
                            + AIR_FLOW_SENSOR_PERIOD));
    exception
      when TASKING_ERROR ⇒
        OPERATOR_CONSOLE.
            ENVIRONMENT_MONITOR_INTERFACE.
            ALARM(DATA_LOGGER_DEAD);
      when others ⇒
        OPERATOR_CONSOLE.
            PUMP_CONTROLLER_INTERFACE.ALARM(UNKNOWN_ERROR);
    end;
  end loop;
end AIR_FLOW_SENSOR;
```

16.7   Real-time control

The Ada program units given in the previous section constitute an implementation of part of a mine control system. Neither the body of the OCI
nor the DRL have been given. Clearly, it is a real-time system as all the
external events have well-defined time constraints imposed upon them.
Failure to meet any of these constraints could endanger the people working
in the mine. Indeed, the system can be defined to be hard real-time as it is
possible to define the maximum arrival rate of the interrupts from the high
and low water sensor. A check on schedulability would require an estimate
of worst-case execution times, which itself requires information about the
implementation hardware. It is not appropriate to give this information
here but such analysis would need to be carried out in a real system.
Fortunately, the amount of computation in the application is low and the
time constraints although hard, are not difficult ones to meet. It should,
therefore, be possible to schedule the complete system onto a single
processor.

    In Chapter 12, it was noted that the only facilities Ada provides for
controlling scheduling is a static priority scheme. Assume, therefore, that
there exists a type PRIORITY which has a range of at least $0 .. 10$. Those
elements of the OCI and DRL which are not critical are allocated priority 0
(the lowest). The periodic processes can be assigned a priority using the
rate-monotonic scheme. There remains, therefore, the high/low water
sensor, the motor and the OCI alarm handler (which was not given in the
earlier code). In order for the interrupt handler to be responsive it is given
the highest software priority. The motor task (and the OCI alarm handler)
are state machines that only execute when called from other tasks. They
must, therefore, have a high priority so that they do not block tasks such as

Table 16.3 Allocation of priorities.

Task	Priority
HIGH_LOW_WATER_SENSOR	10
MOTOR	9
ALARM_HANDLER	9
CH_4_SENSOR	8
CO_SENSOR	7
FLOW_SENSOR	6
AIR_FLOW_SENSOR	5
ENVIRONMENTAL_MONITOR _INTERFACE	0
PUMP_CONTROLLER_INTERFACE	0
Others	0

the methane sensor (remember that Ada does not allow priority inheritance to be used). It follows that priorities should be allocated according to Table 16.3. The values in the table were used in the implementation given so far.

16.8 Fault tolerance and distribution

Chapter 5 identified four sources of faults which can result in an embedded system software failure.

(1)   Inadequate specification.

(2)   Faults introduced from design errors in software components.

(3)   Faults introduced by failure of one or more processor components of the embedded systems.

(4)   Faults introduced by transient or permanent interference in the supporting communication subsystem.

It is these last three on which this book has concentrated. They are now discussed in turn in relation to the case study. Ada's approach to software fault tolerance is to use exception handling as a framework from within which error recovery can be built.

Design errors

As this case study is necessarily simplified the scope for fault tolerance of software design errors is small. In the example, the PAMELA design methodology, in conjunction with the Ada data abstraction facilities, has been used in an attempt to prevent faults from entering the system during the design and implementation phases. In a real application this would then be followed by a comprehensive testing phase to remove any faults which had nevertheless been introduced. Simulations may also be used.

Any residual design faults in the program will cause unanticipated errors to occur. Although backward error recovery or N-version programming is ideal for recovering from these types of errors, there is little scope in the example for design diversity; furthermore, Ada does not support recovery blocks. The example assumes that all unanticipated errors will result in exceptions being raised, which, if not handled by the invoking task, will cause that task to be terminated. Consequently, it is assumed that communication between tasks may produce the exception TASKING_ERROR. If this does occur then the operator is immediately informed of the situation to allow manual intervention. Although mine flooding is serious, the application's requirements dictate that fire is more dangerous, therefore, error handling always attempts to ensure that the pump is turned off (failsafe).

Timing errors may be tolerated by the use of timed entry calls on communication with the DLR tasks.

Although Ada does not contain the notion of an atomic action, it should be noted that all task interactions only involve the transfer of data between two tasks. Therefore, the Ada rendezvous will, in effect, be an atomic action.

Processor failure

In general, if the mine control system was implemented on a single-processor computer and any part of the processor failed, then the whole system would be in jeopardy. Consequently, either some form of hardware redundancy must be applied or distribution is required. Control systems of the kind found in mines are naturally distributed. The top-level decomposition illustrated in Figure 16.5 shows four components that could clearly execute on distinct processes. Indeed, the structure of these components follows the design requirements of virtual nodes.

It was noted in Chapter 13 that Ada does not define failure semantics for partially failed programs. But, if a processor failure is viewed as an abort on all tasks executing on that processor, then the use of the exception TASKING_ERROR will enable most processor failures to be dealt with. Where communication between virtual nodes is via remote procedure calls, (for example, where the motor task calls the function 'check safe' in the environmental monitor, in order to check whether or not it is safe to start the motor) then the underlying virtual node implementation will raise an appropriate exception to indicate a processor failure.

Communication failures

As has already been mentioned in Section 13.7.2, there are no failure semantics associated with Ada. Consequently, it is difficult to express the actions to be performed in the event of communication failure. It has been assumed that all transient communication failures will be masked out by the underlying distributed systems implementation. If a more permanent failure occurs then an appropriate exception should be raised by the implementation, which the application can then handle.

Other hardware failures

So far in this section it has been assumed that only the processor and the communications subsystem can fail. Clearly, it is equally likely that the sensors may fail, either through deterioration or through damage. In the example presented in this chapter, no attempt has been made to increase the reliability of the sensors, as this book has only touched upon hardware redundancy techniques. One approach would be to replicate each sensor and have each replica controlled by a different task. The tasks would then have to communicate in order to compare results. These results would inevitably be slightly different and, therefore, some form of matching algorithm would be required.

SUMMARY

This case study has been included to illustrate some of the issues discussed in this book. Unfortunately, a single, relatively small, application cannot exercise all the important concepts that have been covered. In particular, issues of size and complexity are clearly not addressable within this context.

Nevertheless, it is hoped that the case study has helped to consolidate the reader's understanding of a number of topics, for example:

- top-down design and decomposition;
- concurrency and Ada's model of message-based communication;
- forward error recovery techniques and fault-tolerant design;
- periodic and sporadic processes;
- priority and scheduling;
- distribution using virtual nodes.

Further reading

The case study given in this chapter is discussed in the following:

Nielson K. and Shumate K. (1988). *Designing Large Real-Time Systems with Ada.* New York: McGraw-Hill

Shrivastava S.K., Mancini L. and Randell B. (1987). On the duality of fault-tolerant structures. *Lecture Notes in Computer Science*, **309**, 19–37. Springer-Verlag

Sloman M. and Kramer J. (1987). *Distributed Systems and Computer Networks.* London: Prentice-Hall

EXERCISES

16.1   If water is seeping into the mine at approximately the same rate as the pump is taking water out, the high water interrupt could be generated many times. Will this effect the behaviour of the software?

16.2   If the data logger accepts a call, but does not complete it, will it effect the rest of the system?

16.3   All of the periodic tasks given in this chapter have a similar structure. Can they be represented as instantiations of a single generic task (encapsulated in a package)?

16.4   Given the overall design description of the mine drainage system, write the Modula-2 and occam 2 versions of the Ada code presented in this chapter.

16.5   Software fault tree analysis (Leveson and Harvey, 1983) is a technique used to analyse the safety of a software design; it can be applied to programs written in Ada (Leveson and Stolzy, 1983). Analyse the program given in this chapter using this technique.

Chapter 17
Conclusions

The distinguishing characteristic of real-time systems is that correctness is not just a function of the logical results of program execution, but of the time at which these results are produced. This one characteristic makes the study of real-time systems quite separate from other areas of computing. The importance of many real-time systems also places unique responsibilities on the practitioner. As more and more computers are being embedded in engineering applications, the greater is the risk of human, ecological or economic catastrophe. These risks arise from the problem of not being able to prove (or at least convincingly demonstrate) that all temporal and functional constraints will be met in all situations.

Real-time systems can be classified in a number of ways. The first is the degree to which the application can tolerate tardiness in the system's responses. Those which have some flexibility are termed *soft* real-time systems; those with temporal rigidity are called *hard*. A deadline of three hours may be hard but easily attainable; one of three microseconds (hard or soft) presents the developer with considerable difficulty. Where deadlines, or response times, are very short then the system is often called *real* real-time.

A non-real time system can wait almost indefinitely for processors and other system resources. As long as such a system possesses *liveness* then it will execute appropriately. This is not the case with a real-time system. Because time is bounded and processors are not infinitely fast, a real-time program must be seen to be executing on a system with limited resources. It becomes necessary, therefore, to schedule the use of these resources between competing requests from different parts of the same program; a far from trivial endeavour.

Other characteristics of a typical modern real-time system are:

- they are often geographically distributed;
- they may contain a very large and complex software component;
- they must interact with concurrent real-world entities;
- they may contain processing elements which are subject to cost, size or weight constraints.

529

It follows from the very nature of most real-time applications that there is a stringent requirement for high reliability. This can also be formulated as a need for dependability and safety. Often, there is an almost symbiotic relationship between the computer system and its immediate environment. One cannot function without the other; as in a fly-by-wire aircraft. To give high levels of reliability requires fault tolerant hardware and software. There is a need for tolerance of loss of functionality and missed deadlines (even for hard real-time systems).

The combination of temporal requirements, limited resources, concurrent environmental entities and high reliability requirements (together with distributed processing), presents the systems engineer with unique problems. Real-time systems is now recognized as a distinct discipline. It has its own body of knowledge and theoretical foundation. From an understanding of the science of large real-time systems the following will emerge:

- Specification techniques that can capture temporal and fault tolerance requirements.

- Design methods that have, at their heart, temporal requirements, and that can deal with methods of providing fault tolerance and distribution.

- Programming languages and run-time support systems that can be used to implement these designs.

This book has been concerned with the characteristics and requirements of real-time systems, fault tolerance techniques, models of concurrency, time-related language features, resource control, distribution and low-level programming techniques. Throughout, attention has been given to the facilities provided by current real-time languages, in particular Ada, Modula-2 and occam 2.

Although the Ada programming language was designed to address many of the real-time issues within a single-language framework, it is now widely accepted that it has not totally succeeded in achieving its stated design goals. Ada, with an appropriate project support environment, has successfully addressed many of the software engineering issues associated with the production of large soft real-time software. It has failed, however, to cope adequately with most of the hard (and real) real-time problems. Its model of concurrency has come under much criticism for its lack of flexibility and its potential inefficiency. Because of this, the take-up of Ada has been much slower than was originally expected; Ada was to be the dominant language of the 80s! Unfortunately, as the end of the century approaches, there is still much distrust of the language in the embedded computer systems industry.

Modula-2 is a much more modest language without the pretensions of Ada, consequently, it has received less criticism. However, the language

Table 17.1 Summary of the facilities provided by Ada, Modula-2 and occam 2.

Facility	Ada	Modula-2	occam 2
Support for programming in the large	Yes	Yes	No
Support for concurrent programming	Yes	Yes	Yes
Support for execution in a distributed environment	With help of tools	No	Yes
Facilities for fault-tolerant programming	Exceptions	May be defined by some implementations	None
Real-time facilities	Clock and task delay	Programmer supplies own	Clock and delay
Model of device handling	Shared memory	Shared memory	Message passing
Efficient implementations	Yet to be proved	Yes	Yes

is limited by its coroutine model of concurrency, which makes program execution in a distributed system impossible without changing the semantics of the language. Furthermore, its lack of structured exception handling facilities causes difficulties in the programming of reliable systems.

Occam 2 is the newest of the three languages that have been considered in detail. The overriding constraints on its design have been the requirement for the language to operate in a distributed environment, and for it to have formal semantics and efficient implementation. This has resulted in a very simple language which, it can be argued, lacks the necessary abstractions for programming large systems. In general, however, occam 2 has been warmly received by the real-time community. Nevertheless, for occam 2 to become more established it must become available on processors other than the transputer.

Table 17.1 summarizes the facilities provided by Ada, Modula-2 and occam 2.

To give an actual example of a real-time system a case study has been described. Due to necessity this was a relatively small system. Many of the challenges facing real-time computing are, however, manifest only in the large complex application. In order to give an impression of the kind of system that will be contemplated in the near future consider one proposed project: the international space station *Freedom*.

The space station is due for commission in 1996, at which point it should consist of one station, two free-flying platforms and one orbital transfer vehicle. Also, there is, of course, ground control. When first occupied, the space station will probably support six people and will have a computer architecture based on a fibre optic local area network with, perhaps, 11 clusters of processors. A cluster will contain, typically, three processors; the network itself will be fault tolerant and replicated. The number of clusters may rise to over 20 as the station becomes fully operational. Each different flying structure, and ground control, will be linked via a wide area network. As well as the NASA components, the European Space Agency and the Space Authority in Japan will have structures integrated into the NASA station.

The primary function of the computer system is mission and life support. Other activities include flight control (particularly of the orbital transfer vehicle), external monitoring, the control and coordination of experiments, and the management of the mission database. A particularly important aspect of the on-board software is the interface it presents to the flight personnel.

It has already been decided that the application language for the space station will be Ada. It has also been estimated that over ten million lines of application code will be needed for the on-board systems. Much more code will be required for system software, ground control, simulators and the host development environment itself.

The on-board execution environment for the space station has the following pertinent characteristics:

(1)   It is large and complex (that is, there is a large variety of activities to be computerized).

(2)   It must have non-stop execution.

(3)   It will have a long operational life (perhaps over 30 years).

(4)   It will experience evolutionary software changes (without stopping).

(5)   It must have highly-dependable execution.

(6)   It will have components with hard and soft real-time deadlines (response times).

(7)   The distributed system may contain heterogeneous processors.

To meet the challenges of this kind of application the science of real-time systems must itself develop. There are still many research themes to explore. Even the current state of understanding, which has been the focus of attention in this book, is rarely put into practice. In a search for the 'next generation' of real-time systems, Stankovic (1988) identifies the following research issues.

- Specification and verification techniques that can handle the needs of real-time systems with a large number of interacting components.
- Design methodologies that consider timing properties from the very beginning of the design process.
- Programming languages with explicit constructs to express time-related behaviour.
- Scheduling algorithms that can handle complex process structures and resource constraints, and timing requirements of varying granularity.
- Run-time support, or operating system functions, designed to deal with fault-tolerant resource usage.
- Tool support for predicting the worst case and average execution times for software.
- Communication architectures and protocols for efficiently dealing with messages that require timely delivery.
- Architecture support for fault tolerance.
- Integration support for artificial intelligence (expert system) components.

To this list can be added:

- Programming languages with explicit support for atomic actions, recovery blocks or conversations.
- Programming languages with explicit support for distribution (including failure semantics).
- Programming languages with explicit support for dynamic change management (that is, the ability to do software upgrades to non-stop systems).
- Concurrency models that adequately deal with synchronous and asynchronous events.

It is to be hoped that some readers of this book will be able to contribute to these research themes.

Appendix A
A Modula-2 Implementation of a Real-Time Process Abstraction

A.1 Definition

Wirth (1984) showed how a synchronization primitive, similar to the channel construct available in occam 2 could be implemented in Modula-2. More recently, Collado *et al.* (1987) have presented a Modula-2 process abstraction that fully implements the CSP communication model that is the basis of both Ada and occam 2. In particular, they present an implementation of the selective wait construct, whereby a process can wait on the arrival of one of a number of messages (each associated with a distinct channel).

The process model given by Burns *et al.* (1988) and presented here, has a different interface to that presented by Collado *et al.* (1987). It also has an implementation that follows, more closely, the efficient scheme used by an occam 2 program when running on a single transputer. However, the motivation behind this new process abstraction is not merely to copy the semantics of CSP, but to provide an effective interface for real-time programming in Modula-2. This interface is based on the synchronization model of occam 2 (that is, one-to-one channels) but is significantly different in the area of selective waiting.

Program A.1 gives the definition module for the proposed process abstraction. It provides a priority mechanism, a naming utility, time facilities, a means of starting and terminating processes, a channel abstraction and a comprehensive suite of selective wait constructs. These facilities will be discussed in turn.

Program A.1 A process abstraction.

```
DEFINITION MODULE processes;
    (* This module provides a process abstraction with a message *)
    (* based synchronization scheme. It also provides time primitives. *)
    FROM timemod IMPORT time;
    FROM SYSTEM IMPORT WORD;
```

Program A.1   (cont.)

```
TYPE channel;
  guardedchannel = RECORD
    chan : channel;
    guard : BOOLEAN
  END;
  selectalgorithm = (static,dynamic,FIFO);
  priority = CARDINAL;
  identity = CARDINAL;


PROCEDURE clock() : time;
PROCEDURE delay(T : time);


PROCEDURE send(VAR C : channel; M : ARRAY OF WORD);
PROCEDURE receive(VAR C : channel; VAR M : ARRAY OF WORD);


PROCEDURE select(VAR gdchans : ARRAY OF guardedchannel; VAR M : ARRAY OF
    WORD; VAR alt : CARDINAL; selectal : selectalgorithm);
PROCEDURE selectordelay(VAR gdchans : ARRAY OF guardedchannel; del : time;
    VAR M : ARRAY OF WORD; VAR alt : CARDINAL; VAR timedout: BOOLEAN;
    selectal : selectalgorithm);
PROCEDURE selectorterminate(VAR gdchans : ARRAY OF guardedchannel;
    VAR M : ARRAY OF WORD; VAR alt : CARDINAL; selectal : selectalgorithm);
PROCEDURE selectelsecontinue(VAR gdchans : ARRAY OF guardedchannel;
    VAR M : ARRAY OF WORD; VAR alt : CARDINAL; VAR continued : BOOLEAN;
    selectal : selectalgorithm);


PROCEDURE initialize(VAR C : channel);
  (* from main block *)
PROCEDURE sendreg(VAR C : channel);
  (* form user process *)
PROCEDURE receivereg(VAR C : channel);
  (* from user process *)


PROCEDURE currentpriority() : priority;
PROCEDURE newpriority(PR : priority);


PROCEDURE ownid() : identity;


PROCEDURE terminate;
  (* a process itself *)
PROCEDURE idle;
  (* called by main block after starting processes *)


  PROCEDURE startprocess (P : PROC; id : identity; initialpriority : priority);
END processes.
```

Priority

Priority is used within real-time programs to indicate the relative importance of processes. Although some language implementations restrict the allowable range of priority (to only two levels in some cases) many scheduling algorithms need a wide range. For example, the rate-monotonic approach (Liu and Layland, 1973) requires all processes to be given distinct priorities that are generated from the frequency of process execution; the shorter the period the higher the priority. Priority, in this abstraction, is entirely under user control; the run-time scheduler implements a pre-emptive algorithm using these user specified priorities. Two procedures are defined for viewing and changing priority:

```
PROCEDURE currentpriority() : priority;
PROCEDURE newpriority(PR : priority);
```

Note that, here, the term priority means the factor used to order the dispatch queue in the run-time scheduler. It has nothing to do with the Modula-2 priority provision, which can be used to provide a low-level mutual exclusion facility (see Chapter 14).

Process identity

One of the criticisms of Ada's tasking model is that tasks are not named (Burns *et al.*, 1987). Within the implementation of this process module, a process id is used that is constructed in the following way (some minor details have been omitted for clarity):

```
TYPE condition = (Runnable,SusInput,SusOutput,SusDelay,SusSelect,SusSelDelay);
    chanptr = POINTER TO channode;
    channode = RECORD
                ch : channel;
                next : chanptr
            END;
    processid = POINTER TO RECORD
                pro : PROCESS;
                ident : identity;
                crntpri : priority;
                CASE cd : condition OF
                Runnable: |
                SusInput,SusOutput: chan : channel | (* channel suspended on *)
                SusSelect,SusSelDelay : chanset : chanptr (* channels suspended on *)
                END
            END
```

This structure is necessarily hidden from the module user. However, some form of identity is useful. Again, the full range of CARDINAL is made available. In the current implementation no check is made for uniqueness of identity although this could be added. A process can find out its own identity by calling the function:

```
PROCEDURE ownid() : identity;
```

A short example that illustrates the benefits of having process identities is given in Section A.3.

Process initialization and termination

Any parameterless procedure can be instantiated as a process in the main body of the program by a call of startprocess:

```
PROCEDURE startprocess (P : PROC; id : identity; initialpriority : priority);
```

Note that an identity and an initial priority must be provided. The effect of this call is to create a new process and to associate it with the PROC parameter. The new process is added to the dispatchqueue which holds the list of runnable processes (in priority order). No explicit cobegin/coend structure is supported in this abstraction. However, the main body will continue to execute until a call is made of the procedure idle. The main body will then be blocked until all processes have terminated; it then continues.

Processes themselves can terminate in two ways: first by calling the procedure terminate, or alternatively by calling selectorterminate (see page 540). The implementation of startprocess, idle and terminate follow closely the algorithm described in Chapter 8.

Time constructs

Following the facilities provided in Ada, an abstract data type for time is constructed in the module timemod. It is assumed that any application wishing to use time will have a hardware clock available and an appropriate driver written in Modula-2. This driver will update a data structure through a 'clock' function. It will also support a queue of suspended processes (suspended on delay). The actions of the driver are as follows:

(1) when an interrupt arrives the current running process is placed in the dispatchqueue;

(2) 'clock' is updated;

(3) any delayed process whose delay has now expired is also added to the dispatchqueue;

(4) a process is removed from the dispatchqueue (this will have the highest priority), and;

(5) IOTRANSFER is called (again).

These semantics ensure that a delayed process will be added to the dispatchqueue at the earliest possible time (commensurate with the delay); whether this process is actually executed immediately will depend upon its priority relative to the other processes in the dispatchqueue.

Channel abstraction

The type channel is provided in the processes module as an abstract data type. Before any declared channel can be used it must be initialized in the main program and registered for send and receive operations in the two processes (PROCs) that will use it:

```
PROCEDURE initialize(VAR C : channel);

PROCEDURE sendreg(VAR C : channel);
PROCEDURE receivereg(VAR C : channel);
```

The semantics of channel usage allow only a single reader and a single writer process. A run-time error is produced if a channel is misused (an error is also produced if a channel is reregistered).

A channel can be used to communicate objects of any type and size; communication is synchronous.

```
PROCEDURE send(VAR C : channel; M : ARRAY OF WORD);
PROCEDURE receive(VAR C : channel; VAR M : ARRAY OF WORD);
```

A run-time check is made to ensure that the size of object in the send and receive are identical. No other checks can be made with the low-level generic facilities of Modula-2.

Selective waiting

Rather than the structural select given by Collado *et al.* (1987) a procedural interface is given here. Again, following Ada, four different selective wait forms are given:

```
PROCEDURE select(VAR gdchans : ARRAY OF guardedchannel; VAR M : ARRAY OF
    WORD; VAR alt : CARDINAL; selectal : selectalgorithm);

PROCEDURE selectordelay(VAR gdchans : ARRAY OF guardedchannel; del : time;
    VAR M : ARRAY OF WORD; VAR alt : CARDINAL; VAR timedout: BOOLEAN;
    selectal : selectalgorithm);

PROCEDURE selectorterminate(VAR gdchans : ARRAY OF guardedchannel;
    VAR M : ARRAY OF WORD; VAR alt : CARDINAL; selectal : selectalgorithm);

PROCEDURE selectelsecontinue(VAR gdchans : ARRAY OF guardedchannel;
    VAR M : ARRAY OF WORD; VAR alt : CARDINAL; VAR continued : BOOLEAN;
    selectal : selectalgorithm);
```

as the parameters to the different forms are not identical an interface of distinct procedures was preferred. The ordinary select works on an array of guardedchannels:

```
guardedchannel = RECORD
   chan : channel;
   guard : BOOLEAN
END;
```

and returns not only the message read but also a flag to show which channel was used. Note that, in the form given here, all channels used in a select must pass data of the same type. This restriction could, however, be removed by returning a variant record. A call of select will delay the process until one channel (which is open, that is, channel.guard = TRUE) has a process ready to perform a send operation.

A process can select between a number of otherwise distinct channels by assigning these channels into a local array of guardedchannels. The sending process is unaware of whether a select or a receive is to be used for communication with the send.

If, when a select is executed, none of the guards are TRUE then a run-time error occurs. The other forms of select allow a process to either;

(1)   wait for a period of real-time for a call; then continue if none have arrived (that is, timeout);

(2)   terminate if all other processes have already terminated, or are similarly waiting on selectorterminate;

(3)   continue execution immediately if there are no outstanding calls on the select.

The provision of a terminate alternative, which is not available in occam 2, significantly simplifies the programming of program termination.

Select algorithm

While Ada and occam 2 define the action of selective waiting to be arbitrary, in the sense that if there is more than one outstanding call on the select, then the one chosen for communication is not defined; however, this is not adequate for real-time applications. Here, a more deterministic selective wait is required (see Chapter 12 for a discussion of this important issue). Unfortunately, there is no single algorithm for selective waiting that will cater for all situations that could arise. Indeed, three distinct choice mechanisms can be argued for:

(1) static priority – this is analogous to occam's PRI ALT. The channel, that is ready when searching from the beginning of the array, is chosen.

(2) dynamic priority – here, the priority of the client (caller) processes determines the choice.

(3) FIFO priority – the process that has been waiting the longest is used to identify the channel that must be selected.

Static priority is used to give preference to one operation over another (for example, writes over reads).

In the process abstraction presented here all three algorithms are available and each select must identify which one is required. For applications where only one algorithm is needed then the implementation module can be simplified for efficiency.

A.2 Implementation

The full details of the implementation module is given in Program A.2.

Program A.2

```
IMPLEMENTATION MODULE processes;

FROM SYSTEM IMPORT ADDRESS,PROCESS,TSIZE,NEWPROCESS,TRANSFER,
                   WORD,SIZE,ADR,MAXCARD;
FROM Storage IMPORT ALLOCATE,DEALLOCATE;
FROM queuemod IMPORT queue,create,empty,insert,remove;
FROM InOut IMPORT WriteString,WriteLn;
FROM PID IMPORT processid,chanptr,channode,condition;
FROM timemod IMPORT time,add,before;

CONST ProcessSize = 5120;

TYPE
    error = (deadlock,senderror,receiveerror,regerror, sizerror,openguarderror);
    chanstates = (free,busy);
    channel = POINTER TO chan;
    chan = RECORD
              writeid : processid;
              readid : processid;
              state : chanstates;
              ptr : ADDRESS;
              size : CARDINAL;
              timestamp : time
           END;
```

Program A.2   (cont.)

```
MODULE clockhandler;
  IMPORT time, processid;
  EXPORT QUALIFIED now, timedelay, cancel;
  VAR present : time;
  PROCEDURE now() : time;
  BEGIN
    INC(present);
    RETURN present
  END now;
  PROCEDURE timedelay(P : processid; del : time);
  (* calls SwitchProcess *)
  BEGIN
  END timedelay;
  PROCEDURE cancel(P : processid);
  BEGIN
  END cancel;
BEGIN
  present := time(0)
END clockhandler;


VAR
  dispatchqueue : queue;
  NumberActiveProcesses, NumberSelectTerminate: CARDINAL;
  currentprocess : processid;
  mainwaiting : BOOLEAN;
  idleprocess : processid;


PROCEDURE errorprint(E : error);
BEGIN
  WriteLn;
  CASE E OF
    deadlock : WriteString('System in Deadlock') |
    senderror : WriteString('Channel send process ');
        WriteString('does not match registration') |
    receiveerror : WriteString('Channel receive process ');
        WriteString('does not match registration') |
    regerror : WriteString('Attempt to reregister channel') |
    openguarderror : WriteString('No Open Guards') |
    sizerror : WriteString('Message sizes incompatible')
  END;
  WriteLn;
  WriteString('Program is Aborted');
  WriteLn;
  HALT
END errorprint;
```

```
PROCEDURE clock() : time;
BEGIN
   RETURN clockhandler.now()
END clock;

PROCEDURE delay(T : time);
BEGIN
   clockhandler.timedelay(currentprocess,T)
END delay;

PROCEDURE SwitchProcess;
(* This procedure will switch from executing currentprocess *)
(* to the one that is at the head of the dispatchqueue. *)
(* It is assumed that a test for a non-empty queue has already *)
(* been made *)
VAR
   lastprocess : processid;
BEGIN
   lastprocess := currentprocess;
   remove(dispatchqueue,currentprocess);                    (* get new process *)
   TRANSFER(lastprocess ↑ .pro,currentprocess ↑ .pro)      (* run new process *)
END SwitchProcess;

PROCEDURE initialize (VAR C : channel);
BEGIN
   NEW(C);
   C ↑ .writeid := NIL;
   C ↑ .readid := NIL;
   C ↑ .state := free;
END initialize;

PROCEDURE sendreg(VAR C : channel);
BEGIN
   IF C ↑ .writeid = NIL THEN
      C ↑ .writeid := currentprocess
   ELSE
      errorprint(regerror)
   END
END sendreg;

PROCEDURE receivereg(VAR C : channel);
BEGIN
   IF C ↑ .readid = NIL THEN
      C ↑ .readid := currentprocess
   ELSE
      errorprint(regerror)
   END
END receivereg;
```

Program A.2   (cont.)

```
PROCEDURE releasechans(VAR ptr :chanptr; VAR alt : CARDINAL; chan :
channel);
(* Called by send when released process was suspended on a select; *)
(* alt returns the alternative associated with the channel actually chosen *)
(* This procedure is also called by selectbody after a timeout. *)
(* In this case the result returned in alt and the channel variable are *)
(* redundant *)
VAR tempcpr : chanptr;
BEGIN
  WHILE ptr <> NIL DO
    tempcpr := ptr;
    IF ptr ↑ .ch = chan THEN
      alt := ptr ↑ .alternative
    END;
    ptr ↑ .ch ↑ .state := free;
    ptr := ptr ↑ .next;
    DISPOSE(tempcpr)
  END
END releasechans;


PROCEDURE send(VAR C : channel; M : ARRAY OF WORD);
VAR reladdress : CARDINAL;
    lastprocess : processid;
    chanid : CARDINAL;
BEGIN
  IF currentprocess <> C ↑ .writeid THEN
    errorprint(senderror)
  END;
  IF C ↑ .state = free THEN
    C ↑ .state := busy;
    C ↑ .timestamp := clockhandler.now();
    currentprocess ↑ .cd := SusInput;
    currentprocess ↑ .chan := C;
    C ↑ .ptr := ADR(M);
    C ↑ .size := SIZE(M);
    IF empty(dispatchqueue) THEN
      errorprint(deadlock)
    ELSE
      SwitchProcess
    END
  ELSE
    IF C ↑ .size <> SIZE(M) THEN
      errorprint(sizerror)
    END;
    FOR reladdress := 0 TO HIGH(M) DO
      C ↑ .ptr := C ↑ .ptr + reladdress;
      C ↑ .ptr ↑ := M[reladdress]
```

```
    END;
    IF (C↑.readid↑.cd = SusSelect) OR (C↑.readid↑.cd = SusSelDelay) THEN
        releasechans(C↑.readid↑.chanset,chanid,C);
        C↑.readid↑.chosenchannel := chanid;
        IF C↑.readid↑.cd = SusSelDelay THEN
            clockhandler.cancel(C↑.readid)
        END
    ELSE
        C↑.state := free
    END;
    C↑.readid↑.cd := Runnable;
    IF C↑.readid↑.crntpri > currentprocess↑.crntpri THEN
        insert(dispatchqueue,currentprocess);
        lastprocess := currentprocess;
        currentprocess := C↑.readid;
        TRANSFER(lastprocess↑.pro,currentprocess↑.pro)
    ELSE
        insert(dispatchqueue, C↑.readid)
    END
  END
END send;



PROCEDURE receive(VAR C : channel; VAR M : ARRAY OF WORD);
VAR reladdress : CARDINAL;
    lastprocess : processid;
BEGIN
    IF currentprocess <> C↑.readid THEN
        errorprint(receiveerror)
    END;
    IF C↑.state = free THEN
        C↑.state := busy;
        currentprocess↑.cd := SusOutput;
        currentprocess↑.chan := C;
        C↑.ptr := ADR(M);
        C↑.size := SIZE(M);
        IF empty(dispatchqueue) THEN
            errorprint(deadlock)
        ELSE
            SwitchProcess
        END
    ELSE
        IF C↑.size <> SIZE(M) THEN
            errorprint(sizerror)
        END;
        FOR reladdress := 0 TO HIGH(M) DO
            C↑.ptr := C↑.ptr + reladdress;
            M[reladdress] := C↑.ptr↑
        END;
```

Program A.2   (cont.)

```
            C ↑ .state := free;
            C ↑ .writeid ↑ .cd := Runnable;
            IF C ↑ .writeid ↑ .crntpri > currentprocess ↑ .crntpri THEN
               insert(dispatchqueue,currentprocess);
               lastprocess := currentprocess;
               currentprocess := C ↑ .writeid;
               TRANSFER(lastprocess ↑ .pro,currentprocess ↑ .pro)
            ELSE
               insert(dispatchqueue, C ↑ .writeid)
            END
         END
      END receive;

      PROCEDURE insertchan(C : channel; alt : CARDINAL);
      (* Used by select to add channels to the list of open send *)
      (* channels that the parent process is waiting for *)
         VAR newnode : chanptr;
      BEGIN
         NEW(newnode);
         newnode ↑ .ch := C;
         newnode ↑ .alternative := alt;
         newnode ↑ .next := currentprocess ↑ .chanset;
         currentprocess ↑ .chanset := newnode
      END insertchan;

      PROCEDURE selectbody(VAR gdchans : ARRAY OF guardedchannel;
            VAR M : ARRAY OF WORD; VAR alt : CARDINAL; VAR cont : BOOLEAN;
            term : BOOLEAN; VAR delayed : BOOLEAN; delayamount : time;
            al : selectalgorithm);
      (* Called by select, selectorterminate selectordelay and selectelsecontinue *)
      VAR max, reladdress, I : CARDINAL;
         lastprocess : processid;
         guardfound : BOOLEAN;
         highP : INTEGER;
         oldest : time;
         timealt, iteration, tempvalue : CARDINAL;
         tempchannel : channel;
      BEGIN
         max := HIGH(gdchans);
         guardfound := FALSE;
         highP := −1;      (* arbitrary low value *)
         oldest := clockhandler.now();      (* arbitrary value of present *)
         iteration := 0;
         WHILE iteration <= max DO
            IF currentprocess <> gdchans[iteration].chan ↑ .readid THEN
               errorprint(receiveerror)
            END;
```

```
  IF gdchans[iteration].guard THEN
    guardfound := TRUE;
    IF gdchans[iteration].chan ↑ .state = busy THEN
      IF highP < INTEGER(gdchans[iteration].chan ↑ .writeid ↑ .crntpri) THEN
        highP := gdchans[iteration].chan ↑ .writeid ↑ .crntpri;
        alt := iteration
      END;
      IF before(gdchans[iteration].chan ↑ .timestamp,oldest) THEN
        oldest := gdchans[iteration].chan ↑ .timestamp;
        timealt := iteration
      END;
      IF al = static THEN
        iteration := max      (* forced exit *)
      END
    END
  END;
  iteration := iteration + 1
END;
IF highP >= 0 THEN      (* ready alternative found *)
  IF al = FIFO THEN
    alt := timealt
  END;
  IF gdchans[alt].chan ↑ .size <> SIZE(M) THEN
    errorprint(sizerror)
  END;
  FOR reladdress := 0 TO HIGH(M) DO
    gdchans[alt].chan ↑ .ptr := gdchans[alt].chan ↑ .ptr + reladdress;
    M[reladdress] := gdchans[alt].chan ↑ .ptr ↑
  END;
  gdchans[alt].chan ↑ .state := free;
  gdchans[alt].chan ↑ .writeid ↑ .cd := Runnable;
  IF gdchans[alt].chan ↑ .writeid ↑ .crntpri > currentprocess ↑ .crntpri THEN
    insert(dispatchqueue,currentprocess);
    lastprocess := currentprocess;
    currentprocess := gdchans[alt].chan ↑ .writeid;
    TRANSFER(lastprocess ↑ .pro,currentprocess ↑ .pro)
  ELSE
    insert(dispatchqueue, gdchans[alt].chan ↑ .writeid);
  END;
  cont := FALSE;
  delayed := FALSE
ELSE (* no ready alternatives *)
  IF cont THEN RETURN END;
  IF term AND (NumberActiveProcesses − NumberSelectTerminate = 1)
            AND empty(dispatchqueue) THEN
    terminate
    (* all other processes are waiting on terminate alternatives *)
  END;
```

Program A.2 (cont.)

```
            IF NOT guardfound THEN
               errorprint(openguarderror)
            END;
            IF delayed THEN
               currentprocess ↑ .cd := SusSelDelay        (* no channels ready and timeout *)
            ELSE
               currentprocess ↑ .cd := SusSelect;         (* no channels ready *)
            END;
            currentprocess ↑ .chanset := NIL;
            FOR I := 0 TO max DO
               IF gdchans[I].guard THEN
                  gdchans[I].chan ↑ .state := busy;
                  insertchan(gdchans[I].chan,I);
                  gdchans[I].chan ↑ .ptr := ADR(M);
                  gdchans[I].chan ↑ .size := SIZE(M);
               END;
            END;
            IF term THEN
               NumberSelectTerminate := NumberSelectTerminate + 1
            END;
            IF delayed THEN
               clockhandler.timedelay(currentprocess,delayamount);
               IF currentprocess ↑ .cd = SusSelDelay THEN       (* timeout *)
                  releasechans(currentprocess ↑ .chanset,tempvalue,tempchannel);
                  currentprocess ↑ .cd := Runnable;
               ELSE      (* currentprocess ↑ .cd = Runnable *)
                  delayed := FALSE;
                  alt := currentprocess ↑ .chosenchannel
               END;
               RETURN
            END;
            IF empty(dispatchqueue) THEN
               errorprint(deadlock)
            ELSE
               SwitchProcess
            END;
            alt := currentprocess ↑ .chosenchannel;
            IF term THEN
               NumberSelectTerminate := NumberSelectTerminate − 1
            END
         END
      END selectbody;


      PROCEDURE select(VAR gdchans : ARRAY OF guardedchannel; VAR M : ARRAY
                        OF WORD; VAR alt : CARDINAL; selectal : selectalgorithm);
      VAR contortimeout : BOOLEAN;
         zerotime : time;
```

```
BEGIN
  contortimeout := FALSE;
  zerotime := time(0);
  selectbody(gdchans,M,alt,contortimeout,FALSE,contortimeout,zerotime,selectal)
END select;

PROCEDURE selectorterminate(VAR gdchans : ARRAY OF guardedchannel;
  VAR M : ARRAY OF WORD; VAR alt : CARDINAL; selectal : selectalgorithm);
VAR contortimeout : BOOLEAN;
  zerotime : time;
BEGIN
  contortimeout := FALSE;
  zerotime := time(0);
  selectbody(gdchans,M,alt,contortimeout,TRUE,contortimeout,zerotime,selectal)
END selectorterminate;

PROCEDURE selectelsecontinue(VAR gdchans : ARRAY OF guardedchannel;
    VAR M : ARRAY OF WORD; VAR alt : CARDINAL; VAR continued :
    BOOLEAN;
    selectal : selectalgorithm);
VAR timeout : BOOLEAN;
  zerotime : time;
BEGIN
  timeout := FALSE;
  zerotime := time(0);
  continued := TRUE;
  selectbody(gdchans,M,alt,continued,FALSE,timeout,zerotime,selectal)
END selectelsecontinue;

PROCEDURE selectordelay(VAR gdchans : ARRAY OF guardedchannel; del : time;
      VAR M : ARRAY OF WORD; VAR alt : CARDINAL; VAR timedout:
      BOOLEAN;
      selectal : selectalgorithm);
VAR continue : BOOLEAN;
BEGIN
  continue := FALSE;
  timedout := TRUE;
  selectbody(gdchans,M,alt,continue,FALSE,timedout,del,selectal)
END selectordelay;

PROCEDURE newpriority(PR : priority);
BEGIN
  currentprocess ↑ .crntpri:= PR
END newpriority;

PROCEDURE currentpriority() : priority;
BEGIN
  RETURN currentprocess ↑ .crntpri
END currentpriority;
```

Program A.2   (cont.)

```
            PROCEDURE ownid() : identity;
            BEGIN
              RETURN currentprocess ↑ .ident
            END ownid;

            PROCEDURE terminate;
            VAR
              lastprocess : processid;
            BEGIN
              NumberActiveProcesses := NumberActiveProcesses − 1;
              IF NOT empty(dispatchqueue) THEN
                SwitchProcess
              ELSIF (NumberActiveProcesses = NumberSelectTerminate) AND mainwaiting
              THEN
                lastprocess := currentprocess;
                currentprocess := idleprocess;
                TRANSFER(lastprocess ↑ .pro,currentprocess ↑ .pro)
              ELSE
                errorprint(deadlock)
              END
            END terminate;

            PROCEDURE idle;
            BEGIN
              IF NumberActiveProcesses > 0 THEN
                IF empty(dispatchqueue) THEN
                  errorprint(deadlock)
                ELSE
                  mainwaiting := TRUE;
                  idleprocess := currentprocess;
                  SwitchProcess
                END
              END
            END idle;

            PROCEDURE startprocess (P : PROC; id : identity; initialpriority : priority);
            VAR
              newprocess : processid;
              workspace : ADDRESS;
            BEGIN
              NumberActiveProcesses := NumberActiveProcesses + 1;
              ALLOCATE(workspace,ProcessSize);
              NEW(newprocess);
              newprocess ↑ .ident := id;
              newprocess ↑ .crntpri := initialpriority;
              NEWPROCESS(P,workspace,ProcessSize,newprocess ↑ .pro);
              newprocess ↑ .cd := Runnable;
              insert(dispatchqueue,newprocess)
            END startprocess;
```

```
       BEGIN (* module initialization *)
         create(dispatchqueue);
         NumberActiveProcesses := 0;
         NumberSelectTerminate := 0;
         mainwaiting := FALSE;
         idleprocess := NIL;
         NEW(currentprocess);
         currentprocess ↑ .ident := MAXCARD;
         currentprocess ↑ .crntpri := MAXCARD;
         currentprocess ↑ .cd := Runnable
       END processes.
```

A.3   A short example

To illustrate how a pipeline of continuously executing processes can be generated from the same PROC (but with different identities) a simple structure is coded:

```
       MODULE pipelineprogram;

       FROM processes IMPORT ...

       CONST max = 64;      (* say *)
       VAR pipeline : ARRAY[0 .. max + 1] OF channel;
          i : CARDINAL;

       PROCEDURE element;
         VAR name : identity;
            left,right : channel;
            tempvariable : (* some type *)
       BEGIN
         name := ownid();
         left := pipeline[name];
         right := pipeline[name + 1];
         receivereg(left);
         sendreg(right);
         LOOP
            receive(left,tempvariable);
              (* uses and updates tempvariable *)
            send(right,tempvariable)
         END
       END element;     (* followed by declaration of other processes *)
```

```
BEGIN
  FOR i := 0 TO max + 1 DO
    initialize(pipeline[i])
  END;
  FOR i := 0 TO max DO
    startprocess(element,i,0)
  END;
  (* start other processes *)
  idle
END pipelineprogram.
```

Bibliography

Ada Run Time Environment Working Group (1986). *A Catalog of Interface Features and Options for the Ada Run Time Environment*. ACM

Allworth S.T. and Zobel R.N. (1987). *Introduction to Real-time Software Design*. London: Macmillan

Ammann P.E. and Knight J.C. (1988). Data diversity: an approach to software fault tolerance. *IEEE Transactions on Computers*. **C-37**(4), 418–25

Anderson T. and Lee P.A. (1981). *Fault Tolerance Principles and Practice*. Englewood Cliffs NJ: Prentice-Hall International

Andrews G.R. (1981). Synchronising resources. *ACM Transactions on Programming Languages and Systems*, **3**(4), 405–31

Andrews G.R. (1982). The distributed programming language SR – mechanisms, design and implementation. *Software Practice and Experience*, **12**(8), 719–54

Andrews G.R. and Schneider F. (1983). Concepts and notations for concurrent programming. *ACM Computing Surveys*, **15**(1), 3–44

Andrews G.R. and Olsson R.A. (1986). The evolution of the SR language. *Distributed Computing*, **1**(3), 133–49

Atkinson C., Moreton T. and Natali A. (1988). Ada for Distributed Systems. Ada Companion Series. Cambridge: Cambridge University Press

Audsley N. (1988). Distributing programs written in Modula-2. *Student Project*. Department of Computer Science, University of York, UK.

Avizienis A. and Ball D.E. (1987). On the achievement of a highly dependable and fault-tolerant air traffic control system. *Computer*, **20**(2), 84–90

Avizienis A., Lyu M. and Schutz W. (1988). *Multi-Version Software Development: A UCLA/Honeywell Joint Project for Fault-Tolerant Flight Control Systems*. CSD-880034, Department of Computer Science, University of California, Los Angeles

Back M.J. (1986). *The Design of the UNIX Operating System*. Englewood Cliffs NJ: Prentice-Hall

Baker T.P. and Riccardi G.A. (1986). Implementing Ada exceptions. *IEEE Software*, **3**(5), 43–51

Barnes J.G.P. (1976). *RTL/2 Design and Philosophy*. London: Heyden International Topics in Science

Barnes J.G.P. (1984). *Programming in Ada* 2nd edn. Wokingham: Addison-Wesley

Barringer H. and Kuiper R. (1983). Towards the hierarchical, temporal logic, specification of concurrent systems. In *Proceedings of the STL/SERC Workshop on the Analysis of Concurrent Systems*. Berlin: Springer-Verlag

Ben-Ari M. (1982). *Principles of Concurrent Programming*. Englewood Cliffs NJ: Prentice-Hall

Bernstein P.A., Hadzilacos V. and Goodman N. (1987). *Concurrency Control and Recovery in Database Systems*. Reading MA: Addison-Wesley

Birrell A.D. and Nelson B.J. (1984). Implementing remote procedure calls. *ACM Transactions on Computer Systems*, **2**(1), 39–59

Birtwistle G. *et al.* (1973). *Simula Begin*. NJ: Averbach Pennsauken

Black A.P. (1982). *Exception Handling: The Case Against*. 81–01–02, University of Washington Seattle, Dept. of Computer Science

Bloom T. (1979). Evaluating synchronisation mechanisms. In *Proceedings of the Seventh ACM Symposium on Operating System Principles*. Pacific Grove California: ACM, 24–32

Booch G. (1986). *Software Engineering with Ada* 2nd edn. Menlo Park CA: The Benjamin/Cummings Publishing Company Inc

Brauer W., ed. (1980). Net theory and applications. In *Lecture Notes in Computer Science*, **84**. Berlin: Springer-Verlag

Brilliant S.S. Knight J.C. and Leveson N.G., (1987). The consistent comparison problem in N-version software. *ACM Software Engineering Notes*, **12**(1), 29–34

Brinch-Hansen P. (1970). The nucleus of a multiprogramming system. *CACM*, **13**(4), 238–50

Brinch-Hansen P., (1973). *Operating System Principles*. Englewood Cliffs NJ: Prentice-Hall

Brinch-Hansen P. (1975). The programming language concurrent Pascal. *IEEE Transactions on Software Engineering*, **SE-1**(2), 199–206

Brinch-Hansen P. (1981a). The design of Edison. *Software Practice and Experience*, **11**, 363–96

Brinch-Hansen P. (1981b). Edison: a multiprocessor language. *Software Practice and Experience*, **11**(4), 325–61

Brown A.W. (1988). An introduction to integrated project support environments. *Journal of Information Technology*, **3**(3), 194–203

Brown Boverie and Cie (1985). *Modula-2/RXS Reference Manual*

Buhr R.J.A. (1984). *System Design with Ada*. Englewood Cliffs NJ: Prentice-Hall International

Bull G. and Lewis A. (1983). Real-time BASIC. *SOFTWARE – Practice and Experience*, **13**(11), 1075–92

Bull G. and Mitchell R. (1983). Exception handling considered harmful. *IFAC-IFIP Workshop on Real-Time Programming*, Hatfield, UK 93–6

Burns A. (1983). Enhanced input/output in Pascal. *SIGPLAN Notices*, **18**(11)

Burns A. (1985a). Efficient initialisation routines for multi-processor systems programmed in Ada. *Ada Letters*, **5**(1), 55–60

Burns A. (1985b). *Concurrent Programming in Ada*. Ada Companion Series. Cambridge: Cambridge University Press

Burns A. (1988). *Programming in occam 2*. Wokingham: Addison-Wesley

Burns A. and Robinson J. (1986). ADDS – a dialogue development system for the Ada programming language. *International Journal of Man–Machine Studies*, **24**, 153–70

Burns A., Lister A.M. and Wellings A.J. (1987). A review of Ada tasking. In *Lecture Notes in Computer Science*. Berlin: Springer-Verlag

Burns A., Davies G.L. and Wellings A.J. (1988). A Modula-2 implementation of a real-time process abstraction. *SIGPLAN Notices*, **23**(10), 49–58

Campbell R.H. and Randell B. (1983). *Error Recovery in Asynchronous Systems*. Technical Report 186, Computing Laboratory, University of Newcastle-upon-Tyne, UK

Cardelli L. *et al.* (1988). *Modula-3 Report*. OCR-1, Olivetti Research Centre

CCITT (1980). *CCITT High Level Language (CHILL) Recommendation Z.200*. Geneva: CCITT

Ceri S. and Pelagatti G. (1985). *Distributed Databases Principles and Systems*. Singapore: McGraw-Hill

Chen L. and Avizienis A. (1978). N-version programming: a fault-tolerance approach to reliability of software operation. In *Digest of Papers, The Eigth Annual International Conference on Fault-Tolerant Computing*, Toulouse, France

Cheriton D.R. (1984). The V. Kernel: a software base for distributed systems. *IEEE Software*, **1**(2), 19–43

Cheriton, D., Malcolm M.A., Melen L.S. and Sager G.R. (1979). Thoth, a portable real-time operating system. *CACM*, **22**(2), 105–115

Cherry G.W. (1986). *Pamela Designers Handbook*. Reston VA: Thought Tools Incorporated

Cmelik R.F., Gehani N.H. and Roome W.D. (1988). Fault tolerant concurrent C: a tool for writing fault tolerant distributed programs. In *The Eighteenth Annual International Symposium on Fault-Tolerant Computing Digest of Papers*

Collado M., Morales R. and Moreno J.J. (1987). A Modula-2 implementation of CSP. *ACM SIGPLAN Notices*, **22**(6), 25–38

Conway M.E. (1963). Design of a separable transition-diagram compiler. *Communications of the ACM*, **6**(7), 396

Cook R.P. (1979). MOD – a language for distributed programming. In *Proceedings of the 1st International Conference on Distributed Computing Systems*, Huntsville, Alabama, pp. 233–41

Cooper E.C. (1985). *Replicated Distributed Programs*. UCB/CSD 85/231, Computer Science Division, University of California, Berkeley, California

Cornhill D. (1983). A survivable distributed computing system for embedded application programs written in Ada. *Ada Letters*, **3**(3), 79–86

Cornhill D., Sha L., Lehoczky J.P, Rajkumar R. and Tokuda H. (1987). Limitations of Ada for real-time scheduling. In *Proceedings of the International Workshop on Real Time Ada Issues, ACM Ada Letters*. **7**(6), 33–9

Deitel H.M. (1984). *An Introduction to Operating Systems* (Revised First Edition). Reading MA: Addison-Wesley

Dijkstra E.W. (1965). Solution of a problem in concurrent program control. *Communications of the ACM*, **8**(9), 569

Dijkstra E.W. (1968a). Cooperating sequential processes. In *Programming Languages* (Genuys F., ed.). London: Academic Press

Dijkstra E.W. (1968b). The structure of THE multiprogramming system. *Communications of the ACM*, **11**(5), 341

Dijkstra E.W. (1975). Guarded commands, nondeterminacy, and formal derivation of programs. *CACM*, **18**(8), 453–7

Dix A.J., Harrison M.D. and Runciman C. (1987). Interactive models and the principled design of interactive systems. In *Proceedings ESEC '87*. Berlin: Springer-Verlag

Dulay N., Kramer J., Magee J., Solman M. and Twidle K. (1985). *The CONIC Configuration Language Version 1.3*. DOC 84/20, Department of Computing, Imperial College of Science & Technology, UK

Elrad T. and Maymir-Ducharme F. (1986). Introducing the preference control primitive: experiences with controlling nondeterminism in Ada. In *Proc. Washington Ada Symposium*

Ericsson (1986). *SDS80/A Standardised Computing System for Ada*. Document Number L/BD 5553

Feldman J.A. (1979). High level programming for distributed computing. *CACM*, **22**(1), 353–68

Ford G.A. and Wiener R.S. (1985). *Modula-2 A Software Development Approach*. Chichester: John Wiley & Son

Francez N. and Rodeh M. (1982). Achieving distributed termination without freezing. *IEEE Transactions on Software Engineering*, **SE-8**(3), 287–92

Garcia-Molina H. (1982). Elections in distributed systems. *IEEE Transactions on Computers*, **C-31**(1), 48–59

Garey M.R. and Johnson D.S. (1975). Complexity results for multiprocessor scheduling under resource constraint. *SIAM J. Comput.* **4**, 397–411

Garman J.R. (1981). The bug heard round the world. *Software Engineering Notes*, **6**(3), 3–10

Gentleman W.M. (1981). Message passing between sequential processes: the reply primitive and the administrator concept. *Software Practice and Experience*, **11**(5), 435–66

Goel A.L. and Bastini F.B. (1985). Software reliability. *IEEE Transactions on Software Engineering*, **SE-11** (12), 1409–10

Goldberg A. and Robson D. (1983). *Smalltalk-80: The Language and its Implementation*. Reading MA: Addison-Wesley

Graham R.L. *et al.* (1979). Optimization and approximation in deterministic sequencing and scheduling: a survey. *Ann. Discrete Math*, **5**, 287–326

Gray J.N. (1978). Notes on data base operating systems. In *Operating Systems An Advanced Course, Lecture Notes in Computer Science*. No. 60, 339–481. Berlin: Springer-Verlag

Gregory S.T. and Knight J.C. (1985). A new linguistic approach to backward error recovery. In *Fifteenth Annual International Symposium on Fault-Tolerant Computing Digest of Papers*, pp. 404–9

Habermann A.N. and Nassi I. (1980). *Efficient Implementation of Ada Tasks*. CMU-CS-80-103, Department of Computer Science, Carnegie-Mellon University Pittsburgh PA

Hall J.A. (1987). Integrated project support environments. *Computer Standards and Interfaces*, **6**(1), 89–96

Halsall F. (1988). *Data Communications, Computer Networks and OSI* 2nd edn. Wokingham: Addison-Wesley

Hecht H. and Hecht M. (1986a). Software reliability in the systems context. *IEEE Transactions on Software Engineering*, **SE-12**(1), 51–8

Hecht H. and Hecht M. (1986b). Fault-tolerant software. In *Fault-Tolerant Computing Theory and Techniques* Volume II (Pradhan D.K., ed.), pp. 659–85. Englewood Cliffs NJ: Prentice-Hall

Herlihy M. and Liskov B. (1982). A value transmission method for abstract data types. *ACM TOPLAS*, **4**(4), 527–51

Hibbard P., Hisgen A., Rosemberg J. and Sheiman M. (1981). Programming in Ada: examples. In *Studies in Ada Style*. New York: Springer-Verlag

Hoare C.A.R. (1974). Monitors – an operating system structuring concept. *CACM*, **17**(10), 549–57

Hoare C.A.R. (1978). Communicating sequential processes. *CACM*, **21**(8), 666–7

Hutcheon A.D. and Wellings A.J. (1988). The virtual node approach to designing distributed Ada programs. *Ada User*, **9**(Supplement), 35–42

Hutcheon A.D. and Wellings A.J. (1989a). Elaboration and termination of distributed Ada programs. In *Ada: The Design Choice, Proceedings Ada-Europe Conference, Madric*. Cambridge: Cambridge University Press

Hutcheon A.D. and Wellings A.J. (1989b). Tolerating processor failure using the virtual node approach to the distributed execution of Ada programs. In *The Virtual Node Approach to Programming Distributed Embedded Systems in Ada*. Department of Computer Science, University of York, UK

Hutcheon A.D., Snowden D.S. and Wellings A.J. (1989). Programming and debugging distributed target systems. In *ASPECT: An Interated Project Support Environment* (Hitchcock P., ed.). Cambridge MA: MIT Press

Ichbiah *et al.* (1979a). *Rationale For The Design Of The Green Programming Language*. Honeywell, Inc. and Cii Honeywell Bull

Ichbiah J.D. *et al.* (1979b). *Reference Manual For The Green Programming Language*. Honeywell, Inc. and Cii Honeywell Bull

Iverson K.E. (1962). *A Programming Language*. New York: Wiley

Jackson K. (1986). Mascot 3 and Ada. *Software Engineering Journal*, **1**(3), 121–35

Jackson M.A. (1975). *Principle of Program Design*. London: Academic Press Inc

Jahanian F. and Mok A.K. (1986). Safety analysis of timing properties in real-time systems. *IEEE Transactions on Software Engineering*, **SE-12**(9)

Jalote P. (1985). *Atomic Actions in Concurrent Systems*. UIUCDCS-R-85-1223, Department of Computer Science, University of Illinois

Jha, R., Eisenhauer G., Kamrad II J.M. and Cornhill D. (1989a). An implementation supporting distributed execution of partitioned Ada programs. *Ada Letters*, **9**(1), 147–60

Jha, R., Kamrad II J.M. and Cornhill D. (1989b). Ada program partitioning language: a Notation for distributing Ada programs. *IEEE Transactions on Software Engineering*, **15**(3), 271–80

Jones C.B. (1986). *Systemic Software Development Using VDM*. London: Prentice-Hall

Joseph M. and Goswami A. (1985). *Formal Description of Real-time Systems: A Review*. RR129, Department of Computer Science, University of Warwick UK

Keeffe D., Tomlinson G.M., Wand I.C. and Wellings A.J. (1985). *PULSE: An Ada-based Distributed Operating System*. APIC Studies in Data Processing Series. London: Academic Press

Kemeny J. *et al.* (1979). *Report of the President's Commission on the Accident at Three Mile Island*. Washington: Government Printing Office

Kirchgassner W., Uhl J., Persch G., Dausmann M., Drossopoulou S., Jansohn H.S. and Landwehr R. (1983). Optimization in Ada. *Ada Letters*, **3**(3), 45–57

Kligerman E. and Stoyenko A.D. (1986). Real-time Euclid: a language for reliable real-time systems. *IEEE Transactions on Software Engineering*, **SE-12**(9), 941–9

Knight J.C., Leveson N.G. and St.Jean L.D. (1985). A large scale experiement in N-version programming. In *Digest of Papers, The Fifteenth Annual International Symposium on Fault-Tolerant Computing*, pp. 135–9, Michigan, USA

Knight J.C. and Urquhart J.I.A. (1987). On the implementation and use of Ada on fault-tolerant distributed systems. *IEEE Transactions of Software Engineering*, **SE-13**(5), 553–63

Kramer J., Magee J., Sloman M.S. and Lister A.M. (1983). CONIC: an integrated approach to distributed computer control systems. *IEEE Proceedings (Part E)*, **180**(1), 1–10

Kramer J., Magee J., Sloman M., Twidle K. and Dulay N. (1985). *The CONIC Programming Language*. DOC 84/19, Department of Computing, Imperial College of Science and Technology, UK

Lamport L. (1978). Time, clocks, and the ordering of events in a distributed system. *CACM*, **21**(7), 558–65

Lamport L. (1983). Specifying concurrent program modules. *Transactions on Programming Languages and Systems*, **5**(2), 190–222, ACM

Lamport L. (1986). The mutual exclusion problem. *Journal of ACM*, **33**(2), 313–26

Lamport L., Shostak R. and Pease M. (1982). The Byzantine Generals problem. *Transactions on Programming Languages and Systems*, **4**(3), 382–401 ACM

Lampson B.W. and Redell D. (1980). Experience with processes and monitors in Mesa. *CACM*, **23**(2), 105–17

Le Lann G. (1977). Distributed systems – towards a formal approach. In *Proceedings of the IFIP Congress*, pp. 155–60, North Holland Publishing Company

Laprie J.C. (1985). Dependable computing and fault tolerance: concepts and terminology. In *Digest of Papers, The Fifteenth Annual International Symposium on Fault-Tolerant Computing*, pp. 2–11, Michigan, USA

Lauer H. and Needham R. (1978). On the duality of operating system structure. In *Proceedings of the Second International Symposium on Operating System Principles*, pp. 3–19 IRIA

Lawton J.R. and France N. (1988). The transformation of JSD specification into Ada. *Ada User*, **8**(1), 29–44

Lee I. and Gehlot V. (1985). Language constructs for distributed real-time programming. In *Proceedings of the Real-time Systems Symposium, IEEE Computer Society Press*. pp. 57–56

Lee P.A., Ghani N. and Heron K. (1980). A recovery cache for the PDP-11. *IEEE Transactions on Computers*, **C-29**(6), 546–9

Lehman M.M. and Belady L.A. (1985). The characteristic of large systems. In *Program Evolution – Process of Software Change, APIC Studies in Data procesing* No. 27, pp. 289–329

Lehoczky J.P., Sha L. and Stronsnider J.K. (1987). *Aperiodic Scheduling in a Hard Real-Time Environment*. Technical Report, Carnegie-Mellon University Pittsburgh PA

Lenstra J.K., Rinnooy A.H.G. and Brucker P. (1977). Complexity of machine scheduling problems. *Ann. Discrete Math*, **1**

Leveson N.G. (1986). Software safety: why, what and how. *ACM Computing Surveys*, **18**(2), 125–63

Leveson N.G. and Harvey P.R. (1983). Analyzing software safety. *IEEE Transactions on Software Engineering*, **SE-9**(5), 569–79

Leveson N.G. and Stolzy J.L. (1983). Safety analysis of Ada programs using fault trees. *IEEE Transactions on Reliability*, **R-32**(5), 569–79

Liskov B. (1982). On linguistic support for distributed programs. *IEEE Transactions on Software Engineering*, **SE-8**(3), 203–10

Liskov B. (1985). The Argus language and system. In *Distributed Systems Methods and Tools for Specification, An Advanced Course* (Paul M. and Siegert H.J., eds.). Springer-Verlag: Berling

Liskov B. and Scheifler R. (1983). Guardians and actions: linguistic support for robust, distirbuted programs. *ACM Transactions on Programming Languages and Systems*, **5**(3), 381–404

Liskov B. and Snyder A. (1979). Exception handling in CLU. *IEEE Transactions on Software Engineering*, **SE-5**(6), 546-58

Liskov B., Snyder A., Atkinson R. and Schaffert C. (1977). Abstract mechanisms in CLU. *CACM*, **20**(8), 564–76

Liskov B., Herlihy M and Gilbert L. (1986). Limitations of remote procedure call and static process structure for distributed computing. In *Proceedings of Thirteenth Annual ACM Symposium on Principles of Programming Languages*. St. Petersburg Beach, Florida, pp. 150–9

Lister A.M. (1977). The problem of nested monitor calls. In *ACM, Operating Systems Review*, **11**(3), 5–7

Lister A.M. (1984). *Fundamentals of Operating Systems* 3rd edn. London: Macmillan Computer Science Series

Liu C.L. and Layland J.W. (1973). Scheduling algorithms for multiprogramming in a hard real-time environment. *JACM*, **20**(1), 46–61

Lomet D.B. (1977). Process structuring, synchronisation and recovery using atomic actions. *SIGPLAN*, **12**(3), 128–37

Maibaum T.S.E., Khosla S. and Jeremaes P. (1986). A modal (action) logic for requirements specification. In *Software Engineering 86*. (Brown P.J. and Barnes D.J., eds.). London: Peter Peregrinus

Martin D.J. (1982). Dissimilar software in high integrity applications in flight controls. *AGARD Symposium on Software for Avionics* 36-1 to 36-13

May D. and Shepherd R. (1984). Occam and the transputer. In *Proc. IFIP Workshop on Hardware Supported Implementation of Concurrent Languages in Distributed Systems*, University of Bristol, UK

McDermid J.A. (1989). Assurance in high integrity software. In *High Integrity Software* (Sennett C.T., ed.). London: Pitman

Meyer B. (1987). Eiffel: programming for usability and extendibility. In *ACM SIGPLAN Notices*, **22**(2), 85–90

Mok A.K. (1983). Fundamental design problems of distributed systems for hard real time environments. *PhD Thesis*, Laboratory for Computer Science, MIT/LCS/TR-297

Mok A.K. and Dertouzos M.L. (1978). Multiprocessor scheduling in a hard real-time environment. In *Proc. 7th Texas Conf. Comput. Syst.*

Moon D.A. (1986). Object-oriented programming with flavors. In *ACM SIGPLAN Notices*, **21**(11), 1–8

Mullery G.P. (1979). CORE – a method for controlled requirement specification. In *Proc. 4th International Conference on Software Engineering*, IEEE Computer Society Press

Northcutt J.D. (1987). *Mechanisms for Reliable Distributed Real-Time Operating Systems: The Alpha Kernel*. Orlando FL: Academic Press

Owicki S.S and Lamport L. (1982). Proving liveness properties of concurrent programs. *TOPLAS*, **4**(4), 455–95

Pease M., Shostak R. and Lamport L. (1980). Reaching agreement in the presence of faults. *Journal of the ACM*, **27**(2), 228–34

Perry D.E. (1978). High level language features for handling I/O devices in real-time systems. *D.Phil Thesis*, Faculty of the Stevens Institute of Technology, New Jersey

Peterson J.L. and Silberschatz A. (1985). *Operating System Concepts* 2nd edn. Reading MA: Addison-Wesley

Pyle I.C. (1985). *The Ada Programming Language* 2nd edn. London: Prentice-Hall International

Rajkumar R., Sha L. and Lehoczky J.P. (1988). *Real-Time Synchronization Protocols for Multiprocessors.* Department of Computer Science, Carnegie-Mellon University Pittsburgh PA

Ramamritham K. and Stankovic J.A. (1984). Dynamic task scheduling in hard real-time distributed systems. *IEEE Software*, 1(3), 65–75

Randell B. (1975). System structure for software fault tolerance. *IEEE Transactions on Software Engineering*, SE-1(2), 220–32

Randell B. (1978). Reliable computer systems. In *Operating Systems, An Advanced Course* (Bayer R., Graham R.M. and Seegmuller G., eds.) pp. 282–391. Berlin: Springer-Verlag

Randell B., Lee P.A. and Treleaven P.C. (1978). Reliability issues in computing system design. *ACM Computing Surveys*, 10(2), 123–65

Rashid R.F. and Robertson G.G. (1981). Accent: a communication oriented network operating system kernel. In *Proceedings of the Eight ACM Symposium on Operating Systems Principles*, pp. 64–75, Pacific Grove, California

Raymond K.A. (1987). Streams: a model of message passing. *PhD Thesis*, Dept. of Computer Science, University of Queensland

Reason J. (1979). Actions not as planned: the price of automation. In *Aspects of Consciousness* (Underwood G. and Stevens R., eds.). London: Academic Press

Ricart G. and Agrawala A.K. (1981). An optimal algorithm for mutual exclusion in computer networks. *Communications of the ACM*, 24(1), 9–17

Robinson J. and Burns A. (1985). A dialogue control system for the design and implementation of user interfaces in Ada. *Computer Journal*, 28(1), 22–8

Roscoe A.W. (1985). Denotational semantics for occam. In *Lecture Notes in Computer Science*. Berlin: Springer-Verlag

Roscoe A.W. and Hoare C.A.R. (1986). *The Laws of Occam Programming.* Oxford University Programming Research Group, PRG-53

Rouse W.B. (1981). Human-computer interaction in the control of dynamic systems. *Computer Surveys*, 13(1), 71–89

Rovner P. (1986). Extending Modula-2 to build large, integrated systems, *IEEE Software*, 3(6), 46–57

Saltzer J.H., Reed D.P. and Clark D.D. (1984). End-to-end arguments in system design. *ACM Transactions on Computer Systems*, 2(4), 277–88

Schauer J. (1982). Vereinfachung von prozess – Systemen durch seqentialisievung, 30/82, Institut fur Informatik, Bericht

Schneider F.B. (1984). Byzantine Generals in action: implementing fail-stop processors. *Transactions on Computer Systems*, 2(2), 145–54, ACM

Sha L. and Lehoczky J.P. (1986). Performance of real-time bus scheduling algorithms. *ACM Performance Evaluation Review, Special Issue*, 14(1), 44–55

Sha L., Lehoczky J.P. and Rajkumar R. (1986). Solutions for some practical problems in prioritizing preemptive scheduling. In *Proceedings IEEE Real-Time Systems Symposium*

Sha L., Rajkumar R. and Lehoczky J.P. (1987a). *The Priority Inheritance Protocol: An Approach to Real-Time Synchronization*. Department of Computer Science, Carnegie-Mellon University Pittsburgh PA

Sha L., Lehoczky J.P. and Rajkumar R. (1987b). Task scheduling in distributed real-time systems. In *Proceedings of IEEE Industrial Electronics Conference*

Sha L., Rajkumar R. and Lehoczky J.P. (1988). *Priority Inheritance Protocols: An Approach to Real-Time Synchronization*. Department of Computer Science, Carnegie-Mellon University Pittsburgh PA

Shrivastava S.K. (1978). Sequential Pascal with recovery blocks. *SOFTWARE – Practice and Experience*, **8**(2), 177–86

Shrivastava S.K. (1979a). Concurrent Pascal with backward error recovery: language features and examples. *SOFTWARE – Practice and Experience*, **9**(12), 1001–20

Shrivastava S.K. (1979b). Concurrent Pascal with backward error recovery: implementation. *SOFTWARE – Practice and Experience*, **9**(12), 1021–34

Shrivastava S.K. and Banatre J. (1978). Reliable resource allocation between unreliable processes. *IEEE Transactions on Software Engineering*, **SE-4**(3), 230–40

Sloman M. and Kramer J. (1987). *Distributed Systems and Computer Networks*. Englewood Cliffs NJ: Prentice-Hall

Smedema C.H., Medema P. and Boasson M. (1983). *The Programming Languages Pascal, Modula, CHILL, Ada*. Englewood Cliffs NJ: Prentice-Hall

Spivey M. (1987). *The Z Notation A Reference Manual*. JMS-87-12b, Oxford University Computing Laboratory, PRG

Stankovic J.A. (1988). *Real-Time Computing Systems: The Next Generation*. COINS Technical Report 88-06, Department of Computer and Information Science, University of Massachusetts, Amherst MA

Stankovic J.A., Ramamritham K. and Cheng S. (1985). Evaluation of a flexible task scheduling algorithm for distributed hard real-time systems. *IEEE Trans. Computers*, **34**(12), 1130–43

Stroustrup B. (1986). *The C++ Programming Language*. Reading MA: Addison-Wesley

Stroustrup B. (1988). *What is object-oriented programming? IEEE Software*, **5**(3), 10–20

Tanenbaum A.S. (1988). *Computer Networks*. Englewood Cliffs NJ: Prentice-Hall

Tedd M., Crespi-Reghizzi S. and Natali A. (1984). *Ada for Multi-microprocessors*. The Ada Companion Series. Cambridge: Cambridge University Press

Teichrow D. and Hershey E.A. (1977). PSL/LSA: a computer-aided technique for structured documentation and analysis of imformation processing systems. *IEEE Transactions on Software Engineering*, **SE-3**(1), 41–8

Tesler L. (1986). Object Pascal report. *Structured Language World*, **9**(3)

Ullman J.D. (1976). Complexity of sequence problems. In *Computers and Job/Shop Scheduling Theory* (Coffman E.G., ed.). Chichester: Wiley

US Department of Defense (1978). *STEELMAN Requirements for High Order Computer Programming Languages*. US Department of Defense

Department of Defense (1980). *Requirements for Ada Programming Support Environment – Stoneman*. US Department of Defense

Department of Defense (1983). *Reference Manual for the Ada Programming Language*. ANSI/MIL-STD 1815. US Department of Defense

Volz R.A. and Mudge T.N. (1987). Timing issues in the distributed execution of Ada programs. *IEEE Transactions on Computers*, **C-36**(4), 449–59

Wegner P. (1987). Dimensions of object-based language design. In *Object-Oriented Programming Languages and Application Systems Conference '87*, Orlando, Florida, USA, *ACM SIGPLAN Notices*, **22**(12), pp. 168–182

Wellings A.J. (1987). Issues in distributed processing – session summary. *Proceedings of the 1st International Workshop on Real Time Ada Issues, ACM Ada Letters*, **7**(6), 57–60

Wellings A.J. (1988). Distributed exedution: units of partitioning – session summary. In *Proceedings of the 2nd International Workshop on Real Time Ada Issues, ACM Ada Letters, Ada Letters*, **8**(7), 85–8

Wellings A.J., Keeffe D. and Tomlinson G.M. (1984). A problem with Ada and resource allocation. *Ada Letters*, **3**(4), 112–23

Welsh J. and Lister A.M. (1981). A comparative study of task communication in Ada. *Software Practice and Experience*, **11**(3), 257–90

Werum W. and Windauer H. (1985). *Introduction to PEARL Process and Experiment Automation Realtime Language*. Friedr. Vieweg & Sohn

Whitaker W.A. (1978). The US Department of Defense common high order language effort. *ACM SIGPLAN Notices*, **13**(2), 19–29

Wirth N. (1977a). Design and implementation of Modula. *Software Practice and Experience*, **7**, 67–84

Wirth N. (1977b). Modula: a language for modular multiprogramming. *Software Practice and Experience* **7**(1), 3–35

Wirth N. (1983). *Programming in Modula-2*, 2nd edn. Berlin: Springer-Verlag

Wirth N. (1984). *Schemes for Multiprogramming and their Implementation in Modula-2*. ETH Institut fur Informatik Report 59a

Wirth N. (1988a). Type extensions. *Transactions on Programming Languages and Systems*, **10**(7), 671–90

Wirth N. (1988b). The programming language Oberon. *SOFTWARE – Practice and Experience*, **18**(7), 671–90

Wirth N. (1988c). From Modula to Oberon. *SOFTWARE – Practice and Experience*, **18**(7), 661–70

Xerox Corporation (1985). *Mesa Language Manual Version 5.0* Xerox Corporation

Yemini S. (1982). On the suitability of Ada multitasking for expressing parallel algorithms. In *Proceedings of the Ada TEC Conference on Ada*, Arlington, pp. 91–97

Young S.J. (1982). *Real Time Languages: Design and Development*. Chichester: Ellis Horwood

Zhao W. (1986). A heuristic approach to scheduling hard real-time tasks with resource requirements in distributed systems. *PhD Thesis*, Laboratory for Computer Science, MIT, Boston MA

Zhao W., Ramamritham K. and Stankovic J.A. (1987a). Preemptive scheduling under time and resource constraints. *IEEE Transactions on Computers*, **36**(8), 949–60

Zhao W, Ramamritham K and Stankovic J.A. (1987b). Scheduling tasks with resource requirements in hard real-time systems. *IEEE Transactions Software Engineering*, **SE-13**(5), 564-77

Index